Curriculum Development:
Program Improvement

Curriculum Development:
Program Improvement

Francis P. Hunkins
University of Washington

CHARLES E. MERRILL PUBLISHING COMPANY
A Bell & Howell Company
Columbus Toronto London Sydney

Published by
CHARLES E. MERRILL PUBLISHING CO.
A Bell & Howell Company
Columbus, Ohio

This book was set in Times Roman and Helvetica.
Production Coordination: Judith Rose Sacks
Cover Design Coordination: Will Chenoweth
Cover Photo: Larry Hamill

Library of Congress Catalog Card Number: 79-90226
International Standard Book Number: 0-675-08177-7
Printed in the United States of America
1 2 3 4 5 6 7 8 9 10—85 84 83 82 81 80

To

My mother,
Marguerite F. Hunkins

My father,
Franklin P. Hunkins

My brother,
Paul J. Hunkins

Contents

Preface

Curriculum Development: Program Improvement provides readers involved in curricular activities with an understanding of curriculum and of how to generate programs systematically.

The chapter-by-chapter elaboration of a curriculum development model is a feature — and strength — of this book. The reader is familiarized with a procedure by which one can participate in program development — from conception through final maintenance. In following the model, the reader systematically examines curricular phenomena and can apply particular procedures to the task of program development.

Throughout the discussion of this development model, the emphasis is on being systematic. We obtain a *systems view* by (a) noting common characteristics of phenomena, (b) identifying relationships among phenomena and among principles, and (c) organizing phenomena into conceptual schemes that can be displayed as systems models. A systems view enables us to employ the approach to curricular action commonly called *system analysis*.

A systems approach to curriculum is a way of thinking. It is not a narrow vehicle for dehumanizing education, nor is it a means of making all students uniform in learning or behavior. Rather, it is a way of planning curricula so that we can optimize students' learning, increase their humanity, and foster their diversity.

The curriculum development model presented in this book, while drawing on the systems orientation, does not demand that one must be locked into a rigid procedure of program development. It is hoped that the reader will realize that by approaching program development systematically, one can successfully confront and effectively manage current and future challenges regarding the curriculum.

Primary audiences for this book are persons in public schools, institutions of higher learning, and educational training components of various businesses and community agencies. Teachers at all levels of education comprise a major audience, for they are the implementers and the maintainers of the programs created. Secondary audiences include all individuals interested in educational programs and their creation.

At this time, I want to express my appreciation to Kenneth T. Henson of Texas A & M University and William L. Walker of Indiana State University, who were reviewers for this manuscript. Also, my thanks to Gil Imholz of Charles E. Merrill, who provided direction throughout the development and final production of the book, and to Judy Sacks for her editorial assistance. I wish to thank Fred Kinne, who was involved in the beginning deliberations regarding this book. I also would like to thank my colleagues in the Area of Curriculum and Instruction at the College of Education, University of Washington, with whom I have had valuable discussions about curriculum. Additionally, I would like to express my appreciation to my friend and colleague, O. L. Davis, Jr., College of Education, University of Texas at Austin, who introduced me, many years ago, to the field of curriculum.

I express my gratitude to my wife, who typed the manuscript and continually provided useful critiques. I thank my children for their understanding in allowing me the time to work extensive hours on this project.

F. P. H.

PART ONE

The Field of Curriculum

The Nature of Curriculum and Curriculum Planning

The tasks of education are profoundly complex and the demands being advanced by numerous interest groups present educators with what at times certainly seem like impossible tasks. In recent years, the concern for and commitment to education has been evidenced in governmental financial support, both federal and local; in extensive legislation as to what the schools should be doing; and in increased dialogue among many groups, both professional and lay, affected by and interested in educational decisions. Underlying such dialogue is the belief that education serves as the most dynamic vehicle for improving the quality of life for all citizens of the United States.

Assuring the quality of life—enabling individuals to improve their social and physical environments—is probably the most fundamental and crucial issue confronting humanity. This concern manifests itself worldwide. However, for individuals to improve their social and physical environments, they as citizens must apprehend how they relate to their fellow human beings. Attention to this concern relates to the search for excellence in education.

Many persons, school advocates and critics alike, are questioning the quality of the schools and articulating demands that the schools be responsive to public requests and to students' needs. These requests and criticisms are

3

difficult for educators to process, for great diversity of views exists. Each person's perception of the quality of life varies with his or her own philosophical viewpoint of life itself. Likewise, individuals adhere to a multiplicity of ideas as to what is excellence. These ideas differ in relation to one's standards, aspirations, creativity, and sense of wonder regarding the world of ideas and reality.

Certainly, the school's paramount goal is excellence in education, but realistic educators understand that the search is complex and ongoing.

Schools attempting to respond to legions of diverse groups often open themselves up to criticism of being ineffectual. Some critics fault the schools for omitting what they, the critics, deem essential content or instructional process. Others demand attention to and correction of programs and practices they consider as flagrant abuses within the schools.

Many persons charged with managing the schools, and more specifically with managing and creating curricula, welcome such criticism for it forces them to contemplate most carefully their actions and to delineate the justifications for curricular offerings. Responsible critics and other concerned citizens can provide views or plans useful to educators. However, many critics repeatedly voice oughts and ought nots regarding the school's functioning, but neglect to provide suggestions aimed at correcting educational deficiencies. Frequently, critics both within and outside the educational system deal in what Metcalf and Hunt (1974) call irrelevant utopias—utopias presented without any indication as to how one can attain the vision presented.

Even if curriculum specialists and generalists in the schools are provided with precise suggestions as to ways to address public concerns, the jobs of creating, implementing, maintaining and evaluating programs are vast. Part of the complexity of responding rests with the unprecedented range of demands. Currently, the educational community is bombarded with requests that it respond to needs relating to international tensions, citizens' rights, automation, the knowledge explosion, the shrinking earth, energy crises, population crises, and new moralities and life styles (Neagley & Evans, 1967). Additionally, the school is being asked to deal dynamically with students' earlier maturity, cultural diversity, and differing cognitive styles of learning. Concurrently, a growing number of citizens is demanding a return to the basics of education as defined by reading, writing, and arithmetic, while others are requesting that schools provide novel experiences and content to enable students to advance to the future.

Another factor contributing to the difficulty of responding is that many persons perceive education, its curriculum and instructional methods, rather simplistically. An overview of educational history reveals successive waves of polarization of positions regarding the role of the schools and the purpose of the curriculum. Presently, many persons view teaching as telling and believe that the curriculum can cater to all students' needs if educators will just state precisely their objectives and devise appropriate testing instruments. At the other extreme are individuals urging that schools merely provide students with opportunities to explore their existence within the world of knowledge. To these people the precise stating of objectives is anathema to quality education.

Throughout our educational history and presently, those making particular requests upon the school and its curricula have often evidenced an "either-or" type of thinking; either stress this curriculum or this method, or emphasize that curriculum or that method. It is either back to the basics or education for the future, either precise objectives or no objectives. Such thinking stresses single principles, frequently behaviorist learning principles. Sometimes concerned individuals advance the needs of society as the paramount guiding principle for educational activity. Still others argue that the nature of the disciplines or subject matter must be the primary guiding principle for constructing educational programs. A major task of curriculum experts is convincing such persons of the multidimensional nature of educational purposes, approaches and outcomes.

To convince varied publics of education's purposes and also to deal with the multitude of inputs requires precision in curricular functioning. However, Unruh (1975) notes that "curriculum development activities in the past show a seeming lack of rigorous, systematic thinking about curriculum development . . . " (p. 3). The lack of precision in planning contributes to educators having difficulty in handling current public demands in America.

Initiating precise planning will not diminish, nor should it, the diversity of our nation or the complexities and dissimilarities of numerous public requests. But, precise planning should allow us to educate the public as to the school's nature and purposes as well as to generate programs meaningful to students. Planning is a political as well as educational process. It involves issues and controversies within a time and social perspective.

In our recent past, the public seemed to have been oriented to nonparticipation. Presently, a large percentage of people believe the current and emerging demands on the educational system are such that meaningful responses will not be forthcoming unless more citizens, including students, are involved in the planning and decision-making process. Such involvement requires coordination, not only of the stages of decision-making relating to creating curricula but relating to organizing and coordinating groups of individuals. Responsive curricularists discover and activate effective ways of channeling the concerns and efforts of parties interested in and affected by the educational process. Of course, "good plans may not guarantee good programs, but programs are rarely if ever good by accident" (Saylor & Alexander, 1974, p. 3). In addition to accepting the need for precision planning, curriculum persons must also be as exact in conceptualizing the program or programs (curricula) that should result from such activity.

PHILOSOPHICAL ORIENTATIONS

Curriculum is for the good of individuals and society and because of this major thrust, it is permeated with philosophical views.[1] Some persons stress the mate-

---

[1]See Marler (1970) for a good overview of metaphysics, epistemology, and axiology as they relate to education.

rial dimension of reality rather than the spiritual dimension; others emphasize the soundness of ideas over the data of reality. Still others believe that all knowledge is derived from reality—from nature. Some persons differentiate their approach to life and to the curriculum primarily from the methods and means of processing data from reality. Finally others define reality in terms of the individual's own existence.

To a very real degree, philosophy and curriculum address the same problem, What shall a person become? What can a person become? Positing curriculum questions about what should be taught is an aspect of educational philosophy.

Since philosophy is so central to initial curriculum deliberation, curricularists must define their own philosophical orientations. To achieve such understanding, the curriculum specialist will need to study the past and present philosophical orientations that have affected and are affecting the school's total functioning. The process of self-discovery can be aided in part if the curriculum person will utilize some of the methodologies of the various philosophical camps.

However, a curriculum does not result from a simple linear deduction from philosophical stance to actual school practice and curriculum. Such a deduction is far too simple. True, the philosophical orientation one brings to the educational tasks influences to varying degrees the type of curriculum design advanced, the stated purpose for the curriculum, and the nature of the students' experiences planned in the curriculum. But factors relating to society, the nature of students, competence of staff, adequacy of facilities, adequacy of financing, input of legislation, among other things, also influence the nature and direction of curricula.

Idealism

Scholars and educators in the idealist camp consider the elements of the mind as primary. Reality exists only as it is experienced and conceptualized. Truth to the idealist is an idea. Blanshard (1939) discussed the free idea. "A free idea is an explicit thought which is independent of what is given at the time in sense" (p. 258). Education emphasizing idealism is principally an enterprise in getting students to grasp things mentally and to utilize ideas and concepts, for it is in ideas and concepts that one will find truth.

To the idealist, learning is allowing individuals to achieve the realization of goodness and truth. Since these factors are unchanging, the curriculum will of necessity be fixed. Accepted traditional materials of instruction are appropriate for this curriculum. The subject matter of literature and history and any other subject matter that is essentially symbolic in character would be included in the curriculum.

Realism

Realists view reality as essentially materialistic. For them, the focus of the curriculum is the empirically observable world. The curriculum is developed from knowledge of observable phenomena. Since all real knowledge comes from our perceptions, we must reject any ideas not based in perception. The perception of the real world will yield true ideas by virtue of their correspondence with facts observed. One investigates things in order to uncover the truth, not to invent it. Thus, physical science and mathematics are considered most important. It is through mathematics that the material world is comprehended. To realists, the curriculum is knowledge organized for delivery to the student's mind. The student's mind is considered as a receptacle into which information is stored. Usually, the lecture and textbooks are the major vehicles for delivering information to students (Morris, 1961).

Perennialism

Comprising a subgroup under realism, perennialists posit that the curriculum should consist primarily of a core of subject matter that would remain unchanged over time. Grammar, reading, rhetoric and logic, and mathematics would comprise the basic curriculum for both the elementary and secondary levels of schooling. The "Great Books of the Western World," introduced into the curriculum at the secondary school level, would be a basic building block of the curriculum (Tanner & Tanner, 1975).

To perennialists the major question is What is man? Their response is that man is a rational animal focusing his energies primarily on rational aspects of life, on uncovering truth. Knowledge is essentially unchanging; therefore, education needs to achieve constancy in its curriculum. Hutchins (1953) claimed:

> Every man has a function as a man. The function of a citizen or a subject may vary from society to society, and the systems of training, or adaptation, or instruction, or meeting immediate needs may vary with it. But the function of a man as man is the same in every age and in every society, since it results from his nature as a man. The aim of an educational system is the same in every age and in every society where such a system can exist; it is to improve a man as man. (p. 68)

Essentialism

Essentialism is quite similar to perennialism. Both views consider the curriculum as knowledge organized for a specific purpose, primarily that of catering to the rational dimensions of individuals. Essentialists argue that the curriculum must center on the intellectual training of individuals and only particular organizations of knowledge can facilitate such intellectual development. But, they do realize that the curriculum must allow for modern laboratory science and cater to students' needs to study in the areas of social sciences, vocational education, physical education, art and music and other "nonacademic" areas. However, these other curricular areas must not infringe on the essential core of the curriculum.

Pragmatism

Pragmatism as a philosophical orientation was initially developed by Charles Sanders Peirce. For Peirce, pragmatism was essentially a method employed for clarifying ideas and concepts by clearing away the confusions extant in existing metaphysical views. But it was William James who brought pragmatism into the central area of philosophical discussion. He indicated that there was really nothing new in the pragmatic method. It really presented a somewhat radical but less objectionable rethinking of a familiar attitude in philosophy—the empiricists' attitude. James (1907) noted:

> A pragmatist turns his back resolutely and once and for all upon a lot of inveterate habits dear to professional philosophers. He turns away from abstraction and insufficiency, from verbal solutions, from bad "a priori" reasons, from fixed principles, closed systems, pretended absolutes and origins. He turns toward concreteness and adequacy, toward facts, toward action and towards power.   (p. 13)

Dewey was very instrumental in extending the pragmatic view to the general society and specifically to education. To Dewey, the term pragmatic meant only submitting all thinking, all reflective consideration and its consequences to a final meaning and test. Dewey developed the term "instrumentalism" which focused on the key point that language is an instrument which transforms raw experience in accordance with the aims of humans (Kurtz, 1966).

The idea of a situation is central to Dewey's philosophy and to his theory of inquiry. Inquiry was triggered by conflicts arising within an immediate experience (primary experience). These conflicts were processed by reflective thinking (secondary experience) until a solution was reached. Much of the current stress on process learning draws its support from pragmatic foundations.

Naturalism, Experimentalism, Progressivism

Dewey's work was responsible in large measure for the development of naturalism. Naturalism, interpreted broadly, meant considering and interpreting phenomena in terms of natural causes and principles. Nagel in 1957 advanced the central tenets of his naturalism: "naturalism embraces a generalized account of the cosmic scheme and of man's place in it, as well as a logic of inquiry" (p. 6).

Many in education currently use naturalism interchangeably with experimentalism. As either naturalism or experimentalism, it exists as one of the most influential philosophies in the United States today. Educators can take special note of it, for educational progressivism has emanated from the experimentalist camp.

Experimentalism emphasizes observing the reality of human experience. To the experimentalist reality is just as individuals experience it. In a very real sense, persons construct reality to serve particular purposes. One does not measure the truthfulness of reality, but rather its usefulness. For instance, geography as an organizer for the curriculum cannot be judged as to its truthfulness. In reality, there are mountains, rivers, cities, and people living in or in relation to such phenomena. But, such phenomena constitute geography only because scholars interested in studying such phenomena say that they comprise geography. It is a useful invented classification of the world in which we live rather than a truthful classification.

Experimentalism employs the scientific method to observe reality. This method controls and systematizes observed experiences into limited, analyzable units to enable one to comprehend particular phenomena and apply such information when necessary. For the curricularist this approach to curriculum suggests not only the content but the manner (processes) in which one experiences and even creates it.

Progressivism is the educational version of experimentalism. The progressivists' central thesis is that all learning originates with self needs, curiosities, interests and problems. This basic premise stands regardless of the age of the students (Morris, 1961). The scientific method is utilized to learn about this reality, but the focus eschews the security of settled truth. To the progressivists truth is relative; it is created. Truth is contextual and curriculum content is considered true in light of certain contexts or certain times based on what we currently know. The student in such a curriculum develops a questioning posture that facilitates analyzing and synthesizing his or her world.

Buchler (1955), an advocate of humanistic naturalism, an extension of pragmatism, developed the concept of query. For Buchler, query is the interrogative stance of the individual perceiving his or her reality.

> Query is that form of human experience which originates partly in a compound of imagination and wonder. It is exemplified by philosophy, by the inquiry of pure science, by art, by what remains of religion liberated from the proprietary conception of belief, and by a number of informal but not undisciplined human processes which express themselves in some purposive pattern of utterance. (p. 114)

Query is more than mere method; it is an orientation to life; it is the ability to generate questions of significance to channel one's realities and to process such questions so that conclusions are achieved and judged. Here one can see a melding of the content and method (content and process) that became so evident in the curricular efforts of the late '60s. This fusion is still with us.

Existentialism and Phenomenology

Presently, the philosophical realm is in a state of flux. Wild (1955) noted, "Modern philosophy has paid too much attention to the tools of logic and analysis and the building of vast constructive systems, and far too little to the ranges of immediate data that lie beyond the province of the restricted sciences" (pp. 15–16). Wild noted that in metaphysics there is a flight from that concern because immediate experiences of persons have been ignored and dismissed as meaningless verbalism. Many curricularists now note that we should concern ourselves with those inner experiences of individuals that cannot be quantified. The intentionality of thought, which is difficult if not currently impossible to measure precisely, has caused those concerned with epistemology and logic to repudiate the ontological views of the other philosophical stances. Into the void has arisen subjectivism or phenomenalism or skepticism. Wild felt that existentialism offered new inspiration and hope for reviving and reconceptualizing philosophy. [2]

The thrust of existentialism is upon phenomenological investigations of human experiences that are usually neglected—awareness and its structure, moods of feeling such as guilt and care, and upon choice and its condition. From analyzing the totality of people's experiences the existentialist develops the ontology, the reality of humankind. Its method rests heavily upon choice and decision—upon human freedom. Freedom is the central concept regarding existence; it is a way of being-in-the-world (Reck, 1968). To the existentialist, the major questions are What is Man? Who is God? and What is the Cosmic Purpose?

Existentialism has been and continues to be widely discussed among both philosophers and educators. Much of the humanism movement is rooted in existentialism. But the impact of existentialism has not been as great on academic philosophy in the United States or upon American education as one might have thought. Many American philosophers and educators reject some of the major premises of the existential thrust. Kierkegaard's view that "truth is subjectivity" has caused many to discount existential thought. The emphasis on human existence to the neglect of other levels and manifestations of being has also been considered a weakness of this orientation to life.

Many educators have rejected this view because of the difficulty, if not impossibility, of measuring precisely the world of the existentialist. Furthermore, educational existentialists have not been precise in spelling out what an existential curriculum would look like. Most likely an existential curriculum would stress the humanities. Subjects emphasized would be those that enable students to make private choices and to engage in personal decision-making. Subjects fostering in students a hope in existence, creativity in learning, and awe for their participation in reality would comprise the central core. For curricularists, existentialism may not present precise answers as to how the curriculum might look, but it can provide one with general directions in which to aim the total curriculum. The realistic curriculum person realizes that this philosophical orientation, as is true with the other philosophical views, will need to be considered in light of the social, political, economic, cultural contexts in which schools exist. Additionally, a blending of several philosophical orientations will most likely be more appropriate than developing a curriculum reflecting only one philosophical orientation.

Phenomenology is another philosophy that is gaining prominence in Europe and in some curriculum circles in the United States. Husserl is the person most responsible for this view of reality. Created to refute "psychologism" which reduces subject matter of logic and mathematics to psychological generalizations, the phenomenological approach centers on dealing abstractly and in-

---

[2] The reader is encouraged to read Blackham (1967). This book has the writings of Kierkegaard, Nietzsche, Jaspers, Marcel, Heidegger, and Sartre, major existentialists.

tuitively with experiences in which certain kinds of objects are perceived. The aim is to analyze directed or "intentional" experiences and to discern their relationships to their objects and to other experiences. Attention also is given to the examination of the different kinds of objects that we deal with mentally. But, the phenomenologists' concern is not with the actual existence of such objects, but only with their status as phenomena for mental deliberation. Attention can be directed to abstract, merely possible, or even impossible objects. Thus, the realm of possible investigation is increased to include the conceivable (real) and the inconceivable (imagined).

The link of phenomenology with existentialism is perhaps most strongly through its methodology and emphasis. In considering the possible and the probable, one achieves a means for investigating in depth the conscious world of concrete and lived experience—the *Lebenswelt* (the life-world) (Kurtz, 1966). However, the translation of phenomenology into education and specifically into curriculum is not widely evident. Still, more curriculum persons in tune with curriculum will increase their understandings of this philosophical domain.

Activity 1-1   *Determining Philosophical Direction*

It is important for individuals involved in curriculum decision-making to determine the philosophical views their colleagues bring to the curriculum arena. Engage some of your colleagues in dialogue about the various philosophical realms and determine how these philosophical views have influenced the treatment of content and the learner.

If this is a new area to you, plan a self-reading program to acquaint yourself in it.

CONCEPTIONS OF CURRICULUM

Disciplined Knowledge and/or Subject Matter

Each of the previous philosophical views suggests a particular conception of curriculum. However, there are other more general views of curriculum. Some persons such as King and Brownell (1966) indicate that the curriculum should be considered solely as disciplined knowledge. Only content structured as the disciplines should be brought into the school's curriculum. A similar view interprets curriculum as subject matter. Educators with this view consider the curriculum as knowledge organized in subject form for optimal learning.

The subjects can either be drawn directly from the disciplines such as history, geography, biology, or physics, or from more global fusions of knowledge such as earth science, language arts, world problems, social studies and environmental studies. Numerous organizers exist for creating subjects. Crucial questions, major ideas or concerns of students or members of the public may serve as primary organizers. Events also can structure content organization. Many schools have courses on "Westward Expansion," the Soviet Revolution, the Middle East conflict, the Space Age. The common aspects of the disciplined knowledge/subject matter organizer are that (a) knowledge is the key organizer and (b) the interpretation of reality draws heavily from realism, pragmatism, experimentalism, and naturalism.

Structured Series of Intended Learning Outcomes

Johnson is perhaps the best known spokesperson for interpreting curriculum as a structured series of intended learning outcomes. He argues (1967, pp. 127–139) that there is no educational experience until the individual actually interacts with the content in some type of environment. But, Johnson maintains that when such interaction occurs, one is in the realm of instruction. For Johnson, this series of intended learning outcomes (the curriculum) results from a curriculum development process. Teachers add the experiences, the environments, the materials as well as the methods to the curriculum in the instructional planning phase.

Johnson's definition points up the curriculum-instructional dualism extant in the field today. Popham and Baker (1970) add to this dualism in defining curriculum as "all planned learning outcomes for which the school is responsible" (p. 48). Curriculum becomes only the listing of outcomes, and not even outcomes resulting from curricular activity but as consequences of instruction. To such individuals, instruction refers to the means and curriculum to the ends. These persons argue that teachers will be helped greatly in their functioning if they make this distinction and realize when they are functioning in the curriculum or instructional realm.

But such dualism, while possible in academic discussion, may be dysfunctional in that teachers will try to separate the two from the actual school encounter. In the reality of the school day one cannot separate curriculum from instruction any more than one can separate knowledge from the activities that one engages in to produce or learn such knowledge. It is impossible to divorce ends from means.

Narrowly defining curriculum also prevents educators from delimiting the means by which one will select the outcomes. How will one select content, activities? How shall the content be sequenced and matched with experiences? How shall experiences be sequenced? In part, these are philosophical questions.

Of course, no one conception of curriculum or philosophical view enables the addressing of all the issues requiring the attention of curriculum specialists and scholars. A clearer view of the field and understanding of our tasks will result by considering several definitions of and approaches to curriculum and querying ourselves as to which definition or approach is the most useful in guiding our actions in a special situation. In instances where we are concerned with the selection of content, we might draw upon those definitions that define curriculum as content, or draw upon pragmatism or naturalism. At other times, confronted with the problem of making some already selected content meaningful to students, we might choose to be guided by a definition of curriculum as a type of existential experience. Ideally, the definition and conceptions of curriculum will be adjusted to serve our needs as determined by the situations we encounter at various times. But regardless of the conception of curriculum we favor, it is evident that curriculum will not result without some type of planning.

A System and Educational Plan

Despite the need to utilize many definitions of curriculum in our actual functioning in the schools, we all have the tendency to favor if not a particular definition at least a basic orientation toward curriculum. In this book, while realizing the need for multiple definitions of curriculum, and drawing perceptions of curriculum from all major philosophies the author favors considering curriculum as both a system and an educational plan.

It is a system in that we can identify numerous phenomena that exist and interact with other phenomena. Faix discussed curriculum itself as a subsystem of an educational system sharing a setting or environment with a value system, communication system, and organizational system. Faix presents the curriculum system as subsuming knowledge systems, value systems, personality systems, and communication systems. Each of these systems occupies a setting or an environmental context. Within each setting are various forces, objectives and events. Each curriculum subsystem contains various subparts or components that can either be classed as behavioral, physical or of a mixed type. For example, those involved in curriculum activity are concerned with the behaviors of staff, of students, and even the lay public in many instances. All curriculum specialists have to make decisions regarding the use of physical elements such as books, films, records, and various instructional technology, as well as size and shape of educational space.

Faix also addressed curriculum structure. Structure refers to the arrangement of the various elements or parts of the curriculum in order to perform particular functions requisite for the working of the curriculum system. In curriculum activity, curriculum specialists must be concerned with organizing knowledge, materials, values and persons, in such ways that they function optimally within an educational environment. Functioning optimally means that all the curriculum elements and their interaction within this environment continually facilitate student learning. All curricular components, subject matter, materials, experiences, methods, etc. exist in a dynamic relationship with one another, not only within each system but between these subsystems.

The curriculum system is created to perform a curriculum process, which Faix defined as a system of activities performing a function through time. Curriculum functions are dynamic descriptions of the system's patterns of interaction. The central purpose of the curriculum system being activated is to assess the demands and needs of the clients being served by the system and to translate those types of input into a plan that will increase the probability that such needs and demands will be met. The curriculum plan, in a real sense, exists on two levels. It exists on the management level dealing with the major functions that must be accomplished if educational activity is to occur, and it exists at the level of document creation where educators, teachers included, create a plan to guide classroom instruction. This plan is the curriculum-instructional plan, the familiar resource unit guide found in many classrooms. This plan is the prime reason for the major management plan. The curriculum-instructional plan results from curriculum development and is the program that is implemented, maintained and evaluated.

This curriculum-instructional plan contains three prime elements: content, experiences and environments. The content, often what most lay persons think of when someone mentions curriculum, refers to all of the facts, precepts, concepts, generalizations, principles, laws and theories unique to a particular area or classification of knowledge. It refers also to the procedures (methods processes) by which content or knowledge is generated in specified fields or disciplines.

Experience includes all of the educational activities deemed necessary if individuals are to learn the content delineated. Additionally, experiences include the instructional strategies that teachers can employ to facilitate student learning of both content and process. These experiences may include or exclude the teachers and may occur in or outside the school. A major purpose of curricular experiences is to provide opportunities for students to confront content and be challenged by it, to engage in decision-making, and actually to utilize knowledge learned.

Content learning occurs within particular milieus, usually the school classroom. However, it need not in all situations. The educational environment component, considered in general terms, refers to the place or space in which the content is to be experienced by students. Educational environment must not be taken for granted. Individuals responsible for developing the curriculum educational plan as opposed to the curriculum management plan must view themselves as designers of educational space, for it is within this space, whether inside or outside the school, that learning occurs. In the environment, the curricular components of content and experiences are melded (Hunkins & Spears, 1973).

One can consider curriculum at yet a third level, the actual level of student encounter with the plan. Here students interact with the knowledge presented in the document, respond to the instructional strategies initiated by the teacher, and become involved in the experiences suggested for the lesson. This encounter occurs in the classroom or in some specialized environment either in the school (e.g., a laboratory) or in the community (e.g., at a store, a court room, or in a factory).

Responsible persons dealing with the curriculum in the schools are aware of these levels of curriculum consideration: the curriculum management plan, the curriculum-educational instructional plan (the actual document or resource guide) and the curriculum-instructional arena, the classroom. The curriculum coordinator will be involved at all three levels.

In this book curriculum refers to all those activities necessary for the creation and utilization of a curriculum-instructional plan. It also includes the plan. This plan, the visible curriculum designed for student learnings, possesses the major components of contents, experiences, and environments so organized as to assist students in achieving most optimally the goals and objectives designated by the total community, both professional and lay, and students. This definition considers the total curriculum management system, involving such macro activities as the creation, maintenance and adjustment of the curriculum-instructional plan. The definition also refers to the curriculum-instructional plan. This is the curriculum that people see, that will be taught and experienced in the classroom. The definition allows one to draw on any and all philosophies and/or conceptions of curriculum. But for curriculum to occur regardless of its conceptions, we must be cognizant of and skilled in facilitating educational change. This requires systematic curriculum planning.

Activity 1–2   *Analyzing the Situation*

Analyze your school or educational system to determine the major conception of curriculum present. Note the roles you play in curriculum activities or the roles you wish to play.

Consider the following questions:

1. What is the source of this conception of the curriculum?
2. How well do the persons involved in curriculum activity understand the philosophical stances implicit in their activities?
3. What procedures might you initiate to heighten your and your colleagues' awareness of the various conceptions of curriculum?

SYSTEMATIC CURRICULUM PLANNING

Change is inevitable; even if one chooses to do nothing, change continues to occur. This verity is valid whether we are discussing landscapes, weather, people, or our institutions. Some persons consider change synonymous with improvement. Others categorize it as neither good nor bad. How one classifies change depends upon one's values and the rate and direction of the change discerned. Change is discussed in the next chapter, but at this juncture we need to realize that change is a phenomenon that can be influenced via particular actions and that it can create productive or nonproductive results.

Curricularists are concerned with educational improvement, with positive change. They are joined in their concern by scholars, parents, students, and the general public. However, great diversity of views is revealed upon querying particular groups as to their interpretations of educational quality and ways to achieve such quality.

Goodlad (1975) has argued that curriculum planning primarily occurs via trial and error. At its best, such planning relies most heavily on precepts derived from the folklore of experience. Few curricular actions result from a comprehensive understanding of various philosophical views or phases of curriculum activity. Many of the procedures we follow lack research bases or follow what Goodlad classifies as "dust bowl empiricism" (p. 127). We have been so concerned with doing, with administering the system as we have inherited it from past times, that we have not mounted research to comprehend how curriculum revisions are made or how curriculum-instructional plans are generated and implemented. We even lack detailed accounts on the effects of new curricular content on students' learnings and attitudes. Part of our failings here results from our not considering curriculum from the three levels of involvement mentioned previously.

However, despite our lack of a research base and the diversity of interpretation as to what curriculum is, we are realizing that for the schools to be responsive to the demands of the times, we require some means for dealing with curricular phenomena. The ways in which we develop school programs (e.g., curriculum and instructional plans), and how we implement, maintain, and adjust these programs (the actual school experiences) must result from procedures that are systematic and consistent, procedures that must be delineated prior to the arrival of students in classrooms.

The following model for systematic curriculum development (Figure 1.1) is one means of conceptualizing the curriculum arena and of dealing with the major tasks implicit within this arena. The model at first glance appears to be linear. However, the feedback loop indicates that it is more precisely circular. Additionally, one need not always start at what appears to be the beginning. The major phases of systematic curriculum development involve the principles of human dynamics. Also the various phases of the procedural model once enacted will activate interactions among some curriculum components about which we presently have limited knowledge. It is important to remember that the final product, the curriculum-instructional plan, and the implementing, the maintaining and the adjusting of that plan and the attendant student encounters are more than the sum of seven stages.

This model stresses procedure but, hopefully, does not induce an overreliance on means-ends thinking. The model can facilitate systematic generating of curriculum programs (e.g., curriculum-instructional plans), but the model should not be viewed as a mechanical orientation to education. The model can assist one in creating a curriculum that will reflect any of the philosophies mentioned in this book.

Good planning will not guarantee programs that will satisfy all, for "good" is a normative-philosophical concept. But quality programs do not result from unplanned actions. This model will not suggest a particular curriculum design, a specific arrangement of objectives, content, experiences, activities, and evaluation procedures. The model depicts process, but it is one's philosophical orientations, interpretations of knowledge, acceptance of particular purposes of the school, view of the student and view of society that influence the precise nature of the curriculum program. If one is a realist, this model can facilitate the generation of a realist curriculum-instructional plan. If one is an experimentalist or an existentialist, one can employ this model to generate programs consonant with those philosophical orientations. The values brought to the activation of the model will influence the resultant curriculum program and the suggested human interactions.

Curriculum Planning Model

The curriculum planning model developed in this text primarily relates to actions requisite for creating a curriculum program (curriculum-instructional plan) for students. However, this model also can be employed to create curricula for teachers presented as staff improvement or in-service and also to generate curricula for the lay public. In reality responsive curriculum planners attend to these three groups realizing that the students' curriculum will not be actualized if the staff are not qualified to teach it or uncommitted to the program. Neither will new curricula be implemented if the general public fails to understand the nature of the program or the reasons for it. During the initial enactment of this model, procedures for dealing with staff and the public must be outlined and the reasons for attending to these groups made explicit.

The model has seven major stages: curriculum conceptualization and legitimization; diagnosis; development, content selection; development, experience selection; implementation; evaluation; and maintenance. A schema of the model follows.

FIGURE 1.1   *Curriculum planning model*

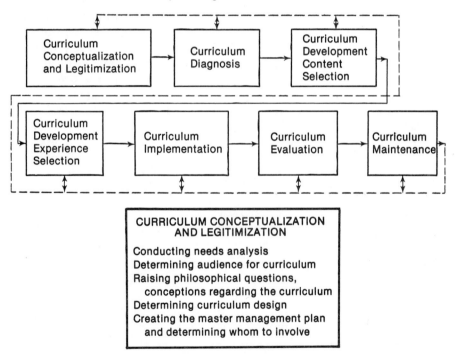

Curriculum conceptualization and legitimization comprise the first phase. As indicated, these two major activities subsume several others. The first activity is that of conducting a needs analysis. At this stage any gaps in the curriculum are indicated and linked to specific individuals in the school population. These gaps become needs when someone feels that they should not exist for one reason or another. This activity relates closely with identifying for whom the curriculum will be designed—the recipients of the new curriculum. The audience might be the entire school population, but, even in such cases, there may be different aspects of the curriculum that would be more appropriate for particular student groups.

Essentially, needs are determined when someone voices a value position or expresses an interpretation of the world, in brief, takes a philosophical position. It is evident that persons involved in curriculum deliberations must raise philosophical questions as well as questions relating to the world at large. Philosophical questions about views of the student in various realities influence curriculum design. To most persons in education, and to many lay citizens, curriculum design refers to the arrangement of curriculum components or elements. Most educators accept the following as basic curriculum elements: (a) aims, goals, and objectives; (b) subject matter or content; (c) learning activities and experiences; and (d) evaluation procedures and experiences. Increasing numbers of curriculum persons are including the component of educational environment also as a basic feature of design.

Creating the master plan is an essential aspect of this first major phase of curriculum activity. In generating this plan, curricularists identify the major tasks requisite for developing, implementing, evaluating, and maintaining the curriculum-instructional plan: the curriculum program. Additionally, they identify who will be involved and their responsibilities. In such planning, constraints to successful programs are noted and means for reducing or eliminating such constraints mapped out. The master management plan spells out the major phases of the model and denotes the substages necessary for the accomplishment of each major curriculum function: development, implementation, evaluation and maintenance.

CURRICULUM DIAGNOSIS

Translating needs as to causes
  and solutions
Generating goals and objectives

Diagnosis can occur during the previous major stage. In some instances, one may have conducted an informal diagnosis to identify needs for reconceptualizing the curricular offerings of the school.

But usually, the first major stage of curriculum activity deals solely with the identification of needs in relation to a curriculum conceptualization. Diagnosis, the second major stage, aims at determining the reasons for the extant needs and suggesting ways (prescriptions) for satisfying such needs. Diagnosis is concerned with recommending means and noting contents for correcting deficiencies noted in the first major stage.

Diagnosis suggests prescriptions. From such prescriptions (remaining mindful of the ways in which the curriculum has been conceptualized), goals and objectives are generated, made precise, and linked to specific aspects of the curriculum program. During diagnosis, the goals and objectives will be prioritized.

In this stage of diagnosis, two levels of objectives are generated, general program objectives and more specific instructional objectives. General program objectives are more precise than goals which are usually broad statements about the purpose of the schools. Goals note the general direction of desired outcomes. "Students will become autonomous learners" is an example of a general goal. A general program objective might be "Students having experienced social studies curricula will understand the political process and relate their understanding to everyday activities." Here one has a little more specificity, but the nature of "understanding" is left open to interpretation.

```
CURRICULUM DEVELOPMENT—CONTENT SELECTION
    Selecting a concept of knowledge, content
    Determining criteria for selection
    Selecting content
    Organizing content
```

Curriculum development, as used in this text, refers to the procedures employed in translating general program and instructional objectives, guided by a basic conceptualization of the curriculum, into contents, experiences, and educational environments. These contents, experiences, and descriptions and suggestions for educational environments are incorporated into the curriculum-instructional master plan commonly referred to as the curriculum guide.

The first major stage under curriculum development deals with content. Drawing on the various conceptions of knowledge and content, one chooses one conception to guide the selecting, structuring, and organizing of content. This task may have been initiated during the conceptualization stage. At this point, criteria for content selection are made specific.

Selecting and organizing content is the central purpose of this stage and these activities will consume a major amount of time. The primary criteria for content selection are that it be teachable and learnable.

```
CURRICULUM DEVELOPMENT—EXPERIENCE SELECTION
    Selecting conception of experiences
    Selecting conception of instruction
    Determining criteria for selection
    Relating experiences to educational environments
    Selecting and organizing experiences
    Creating educational environments
    Melding of curriculum components to curriculum—
        instructional plan
```

The curriculum is more than content; it relates to the objectives, the types of instructional strategies utilized, the types of experiences selected, the types of educational activities planned to facilitate student learning. At this development stage, individuals draw on their definitions of experiences and their philosophical orientations in order to conceptualize this aspect of the educational plan.

After such dialogue, educators and lay members involved must create and/or select criteria for selecting and organizing experiences and melding them with instructional strategies. Where should the experiences occur? This question deals with the environmental component. Should the curriculum be experienced in the "standard" classroom? Should the curriculum be experienced in the community setting? We are now beginning to realize that we need to attend to the educational environments possible and to plan for the utilization and development of various milieus to optimize student learning.

The final substage of curriculum development—experience selection is incorporating all of the results of this and the previous stage into a curriculum-instructional plan—the curriculum program. To a degree, this melding has been occurring since the initial consideration of content. In these two stages, there is much anticipating of possible experiences when selecting content and much referring back to chosen content when dealing with instruction or experience development. The overall planning model facilitates such interaction by feedback and feedforward networks. This interaction within the planning model denotes the dynamic nature of the process model. At the conclusion of this stage, one has a curriculum plan, document, or program ready for trial.

CURRICULUM IMPLEMENTATION

Pilot testing
Delineating types of assistance
   requisite for affected parties
Monitoring the system
Keeping communication channels open
Final implementation

Curriculum implementation is enacting the curriculum-instructional plan produced during the previous stages. However, implementation is not accomplished in one fell swoop. Rather, it occurs gradually and only after the curriculum-instructional plan (the curriculum program) has been piloted in the schools. This is a crucial substage for via piloting one obtains data to validate the new program and to support the program's original justification.

Careful selection of persons to be involved in implementing the program is crucial. Successful programs are those that have been piloted and implemented by competent and committed staff. The level of competence and commitment depends in part upon how one has organized the previous stages and involved both lay and professional persons.

Monitoring the implementation is an obvious necessity. In reality, monitoring has been occurring throughout the total planning process. All monitoring requires open communication channels. Open communication is especially important during the piloting and implementation stage so that students, lay public and all professional staff are aware of the program being introduced. In successful program development, communication is an integral part of each stage of the overall planning and development process.

```
┌─────────────────────────────────┐
│    CURRICULUM EVALUATION         │
│        Formative                 │
│        Summative                 │
└─────────────────────────────────┘
```

Evaluation, although placed toward the end in the model, actually occurs throughout the total planning activity. Determining needs, agreeing upon appropriate content, selecting and organizing experiences and environments, all require evaluative decision-making. Such ongoing evaluation is formative evaluation and relates not only to specific aspects of the curriculum, but also to the processes activated in the overall management plan.

The final evaluation, occurring at the termination of the implementation stage and at selected times after the program has been in operation, is summative evaluation. Such evaluation centers on judging the quality and effectiveness of the total program or curricular plan developed.

As noted previously, evaluation is not an ending phase but fits into a cycle of furnishing data for adjusting the program if necessary and renewing diagnostic, development and research activities. Evaluation comprises the essential component of the feedback and adjustment loop of the overall planning model and is depicted in Figure 1.1 by the broken line. What every educator hopes for is that the results of evaluation will reveal optimal student learnings, competent staff performances, and lay community acceptance of the program.

```
┌─────────────────────────────────┐
│    CURRICULUM MAINTENANCE        │
│  Managing the curriculum system  │
│  Managing the support systems    │
└─────────────────────────────────┘
```

Quite often educators involved in curriculum development of either a total program or aspect of a program express relief when the activities have been completed. Such a view reveals a basic misunderstanding of the nature of curriculum activity. It is impossible to create a program or unit for all time, even a program or unit appropriate for five years. Hopefully, because of the sound thinking and careful development, major changes will not be required during the time a program is active. Nevertheless, students change, new staff members arrive, innovative materials are produced, new needs are perceived and expressed by the public, and new issues, both national and local, occur. Additionally, new knowledge is formulated. These changes require curriculum generalists and specialists to maintain a vigilance over the curriculum as implemented to determine if and where minor adjustment is required.

Managing the curriculum system requires not only noting who will perform certain tasks, but also delineating and coordinating the numerous support systems (people and materials) requisite for keeping the program operational. Maintenance tasks enable one to monitor the goals and needs of the program, the particular objectives being stressed, the actual teaching of the curriculum, and the ongoing evaluation of the program. Well-planned maintenance allows educators to keep the new program functional.

Activity 1–3   *Becoming Acquainted with Curriculum Literature on Models*

An increasing amount of literature is available on systems procedures and model building. Many of the books referred to in this textbook provide excellent in-depth treatments of models and their use in educational planning and curriculum activities.

Check your professional library and/or a nearby college or university library for sources to increase your understanding of models.

Discussion

This chapter presented several philosophical orientations and their relationships to curriculum and various conceptions of curriculum that all educators, specifically curriculum generalists and specialists, need to comprehend. Those who understand the curriculum arena perceive the myriad bases from which they are operating. Comprehending the curriculum theater means knowing curriculum as a system possessing subsystems each containing subcomponents involving people as well as knowledge bases.

The challenge confronting us is to make the schools responsive to the needs of students and society, as currently indicated and as anticipated in the future. To achieve this goal, indeed this mandate, we require precise procedures for dealing with the phenomena relevant to the curriculum field.

The model presented here is developed in greater detail in later chapters. The model should enable curricularists to create, implement, maintain and evaluate curriculum. It is a model that enables the conceptualization of the phenomena we are to manage. It enables us to be more precise and consistent in our functioning. The model does not favor any particular type of curriculum or philosophical approach to education. Persons can incorporate their own philosophical and social-political orientations, their own understandings of content into the model. Some of the subcomponents of the model might be altered. But, the major stages seem to be ones that can allow us to function more precisely in generating and maintaining educational programs that will satisfy all persons voicing their concern with the quality of American education.

References

Blackham, H.J. *Six existentialist thinkers.* London: Routledge & Kegan Paul Ltd., 1967.

Blanshard, B. *The nature of thought* (2 vols.). London: Allen & Unwin, 1939.

Buchler, J. *The concept of method.* New York: Columbia University Press, 1955.

Faix, T.L. *Structural-functional analysis as a conceptual system for curriculum theory and research: a theoretical study.* Unpublished paper, Macalester College, no date.

Goodlad, J.I. *The dynamics of education change: Toward responsive schools.* New York: McGraw-Hill, 1975.

Hunkins, F.P., & Spears, P.F. *Social studies for the evolving individual.* Washington, D.C.: Association for Supervision and Curriculum Development, 1973.

Hutchins, R.M. *The conflict in education.* New York: Harper & Bros., 1953.

James, W. *Pragmatism.* New York: Longmans Green & Co., 1907.

Johnson, M., Jr. Definitions and models in curriculum theory. *Educational Theory,* April 1967, 127–139.

King, A.R., Jr., & Brownell, J.A. *The curriculum and the disciplines of knowledge.* New York: John Wiley & Sons, 1966.

Kurtz, P. *American philosophy in the twentieth century.* New York: Macmillan, 1966.

Marler, C.D. *Philosophy and schooling.* Boston: Allyn & Bacon, Inc., 1975.

Metcalf, L.E., & Hunt, M.P. Relevance and the curriculum. In E. Eisner & E. Vallance (Eds.), *Conflicting conceptions of curriculum.* Berkeley: McCutchan, 1974.

Morris, V.C. *Philosophy and the American school.* Boston: Houghton Mifflin, 1961.

Nagel, E. *Logic without metaphysics and other essays in the philosophy of science.* Glencoe, Ill.: Free Press, 1957.

Neagley, R.L., & Evans, N.D. *Handbook for effective curriculum development.* Englewood Cliffs, N.J.: Prentice-Hall, 1967.

Popham, J.W., & Baker, E.I. *Systematic instruction.* Englewood Cliffs, N.J.: Prentice-Hall, 1970.

Reck, A. *The new American philosophers. An exploration of thought since World War II.* Baton Rouge: Louisiana State University Press, 1968.

Saylor, J.G., & Alexander, W.M. *Curriculum planning for modern schools.* New York: Holt, Rinehart & Winston, 1974.

Tanner, D., & Tanner, L.N. *Curriculum development, theory into practice.* New York: Macmillan, 1975.

Unruh, G.G. *Responsive curriculum development.* Berkeley: McCutchan, 1975.

Wild, J. *The challenge of existentialism.* Bloomington: Indiana University Press, 1955.

chapter

Curriculum Change and Innovation

CHANGE: NATURE AND PURPOSE

Persons involved in curriculum development and related curricular activities realize that one never produces the perfect curriculum for all times. Curriculum developers, implementers, and evaluators appreciate that curricular activities are future-oriented activities aimed at educational improvement.

The twentieth century has been characterized by change. However, as ubiquitous as change has been, it has not made change or the acceptance of it easy for all persons. People react differently to change. Some eagerly anticipate its occurrence and its results. Others, while wishing to be cognizant of and wishing to use the latest in technology, ideas, or approaches, evidence insecurity in confronting change. Other individuals, while not reacting to adjustment with trepidation, remain content with current practices, programs, and customs. Some view change as not always synonymous with improvement. Such a view is valid. Still others strain to lead the way to new frontiers regarding ideas and actions.

Curricular activities (development, implementation, maintenance, evaluation) are change activities. The change is not only with program but also related to making modifications in people. Of course, educational programs may adjust without people precisely understanding the change process or without extensive planning. But, educational alteration occurring accidentally or randomly may not be improvement. *Random change,* or what some call natural change, places the quality of educational programming on a chance basis regarding effectiveness.

Change Typologies

Bennis (1966) has provided curriculum workers with several useful change types. The first is *planned change.* Planned change differs from random change in that the former entails mutual goal setting by involved parties. Often, these parties have equal power and function in prescribed fashion. Planned change requires the identifying and following of precise procedures dealing with the total adjustment process, a deliberateness in approach. The model presented later in this book follows this guide of precision. Not all existing change has resulted from shared decision-making by equal groups or individuals. Certain school modifications have been enacted via procedures of indoctrination which may have resulted from mutual goal setting, but in which the powers of the groups involved were unequal. Adjustments in educational program may be decided upon in general terms with the public sector and educators sharing in goal formulation. However, in attending to the specifics of the contents, the educators often possess the greater power.

A second change type suggested by Bennis (1966) is *coercion.* Such change, an often used tactic, results when one group determines goals and excludes other groups. Additionally, the group formulating the goals wields the major power. Coercion is similar to *indoctrination,* but in indoctrination there is mutual goal setting.

Another typology of change, Bennis noted, is that of *interactional change,* characterized by mutual goal setting and a fairly equal power distribution among groups. However, there is an absence of deliberateness on the part of the parties involved. In schools, interactional change often occurs in which groups of teachers and curriculum specialists get together and precisely define goals with all parties having equal input. But, when it comes to interpreting these goals into precise programs, no deliberate and precise procedures are enacted.

Curricular activities often occur within a well-defined formal structure in which there exists a clear-cut superior–subordinate relationship (i.e., superintendent in charge of curriculum, curriculum specialists, principals, teachers). In this type of setting, we can have what Bennis calls *emulative change.* Such change is enacted or encouraged via identification with superiors or with those with greater status in the system. In certain instances, this type of change is extant when educators try to respond to or emulate those behaviors and/or programs mandated by state and federal governments.

Bennis notes that the opposite of planned change is natural or random change. Such variation refers to those adjustments that occur with no apparent thought and no goal setting on the part of the participants. Often, natural change is the major type evident in the schools with regard to curriculum activity. The curriculum is adjusted not as a result of careful analysis, but is tinkered with in response to unanticipated events. Riots in the streets demanding relevance in the schools or demonstrations for a more sensible use of resources have triggered some permutations in schools' programs. Demands by legislatures for more accountability have triggered additional instances of natural change.[1]

It is evident that most change does not fit into precise categories, but represents overlapping divisions. Modification resulting from reaction to events is called *deficit change*. Change occurring from the anticipation of needs, present and future, is called *creative change*.

Activity 2–1   *Identifying One's Change Typology*

Consider your current situation. Has any major change or innovation occurred recently? How would you characterize the change effort that occurred?

In responding to the above question, reflect on the role/s you played in the change process in your school or educational institution.

The Nature of Change

The certainty of change in education cannot be contested. Persons effectively dealing with curriculum alteration are precise in assessing the current scene and anticipating the future scene in order to determine needed educational change. Leaders in curriculum striving to create and manage new curricula, appropriate for diverse student populations now and in the future, are designing effective plans for bringing about requisite changes. To accomplish this, those in leadership positions, teachers included, must understand the relationships extant between planning and change and must capitalize upon the inherent strengths of these relationships (Morphet, Jesser, & Ludka, 1972).

Being knowledgeable of the nature of change and the various technologies available for activating it, does not mean mounting change efforts just for the sake of change—a criticism often leveled at educators. Wise curriculum persons do not act in such ways that they are accused of changing for the sake of change, of attending to bandwagonism, of adopting fads, gimmicks, or simple answers to complex questions. Curiculum cannot be responsive to present and future client needs if it is haphazard.

Umans (1970) has cited that education is expensive and thus requires systematic management. This does not mean that efficiency in terms of dollars spent ranks as the prime criterion. One is concerned primarily with optimizing learning. The curriculum practitioner faces a challenging complex of tasks in striving to get people to change, in facilitating modifications in programs in order to optimize students' learnings. One difficulty facing curricu-

---

[1]For more detail on typologies of change, consult Bennis, Benne, and Chin (1961).

lum specialists is that precise understanding of or agreement regarding optimal learning is lacking. Persons in the community and in the professional system look at optimal learning from both a social and philosophical stance thus making the creation of optimal programs difficult. People will more easily agree to a definition of change than to one of improvement. Nevertheless, one cannot retreat from systematic and deliberative planning because of the difficulty of the task.

Regardless of the diversity of views, educators frequently strive to obtain consensus among various groups as to the overall goals of the school and its curriculum. Educators develop strategies that allow anticipation of the demands of the numerous publics and diverse student groups. Anticipating events rather than responding with surprise to them is a significant step forward in confronting some of the challenges launched at the schools. More and more curriculum specialists and curriculum scholars are generating blueprints for program development that can be tested as hypotheses and applied in the school settings. Increasingly, educators are seeing the value of planning for orderly, rational, and meaningful change. Figure 2.1 depicts the relative time and difficulty in making various changes.

FIGURE 2.1   *Time and difficulty involved in change*

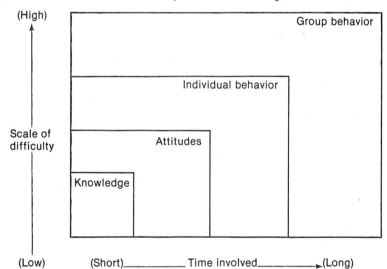

Note. From *Aspects of educational change* by I. Morrish, 1976, p. 34. Copyright 1976 by Allen & Unwin, Ltd. Reprinted by permission.

Models for Change

Curriculum experts can facilitate their change actions by referring to numerous models depicting change. These models denote key components of curriculum, the planning processes and the interrelationships among these components. Umans presents a basic model for educational improvement (Figure 2.2).

FIGURE 2.2   *Educational improvement cycle*

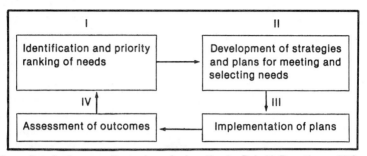

This model presents a logical approach to adjustment. One commences with identifying and ranking needs, proceeding to developing ways to meet the needs, to activating the ways, and finally to assessing their effectiveness thus furnishing data to the identification and ranking of needs stage. Persons in curriculum activity often neglect such a macro view which frequently results in one or more aspects of program change being omitted. Plans for curriculum change often are enacted without a careful delineation of needs. Frequently, plans selected are not chosen as a result of deliberative action, but rather are utilized because persons in the system feel comfortable with such procedures or program plans developed previously. For example, programs in science often are implemented in schools as a result of the persistence of a publisher's representative or the tenured science teacher rather than from a careful identification of needs or the creation of a master curriculum plan. Also, it is not uncommon for the assessment of outcomes to be neglected.

Regardless of the soundness of a specific model, one must realize that a particular model does not assure palpable results of quality education. Whether improvement results from employment of the model shown in Figure 2.2 depends upon the type of data put into the system; the skills of the individuals in processing the data; the philosophical positions of the individuals dealing with or affected by the model; the resources available for supporting the implementation of the program; and the time factor in which the functions extant in the model must occur.

Curriculum improvement is a normative concept. Change to some individuals may signify improvement while to others it may denote a lessening of education quality. It is possible to utilize the model in Figure 2.2 and generate distinctly different curricula. The quality of the resulting product is determined in part by the identification of needs and goals. But systematic planning increases the likelihood that the actions taken will result in achieving the original goal statements. Improvement is tied to the philosophical and educational assumptions extant in these original goal statements.

Figure 2.2 exemplifies a systems model. The systems approach allows one to pursue change in education in a definable and consistent manner.

Umans notes that "the systems approach may be regarded as a functional, relevant, logical, scientific value form designed to test the value of any given concept or structure." (p. 41). Approaching curriculum in this manner enables one to view curriculum change—improvement—from a macro view recognizing the substages of planning, organizing, and controlling the components of curriculum.

The specific natures of the components are influenced by one's conception of curriculum. Thus, persons approaching curriculum from some of the stances depicted in chapter one will center on different components and identify different relationships. For example, persons considering curriculum as just subject matter to be taught will employ the systems approach to identify subject matter deemed requisite for student success in the overall society. Further, their plans will relate only to introducing subject matter content into the curriculum, and to designing ways to evaluate students' learnings of such content.

Individuals viewing curriculum more globally as consisting of content, experiences and environments organized to achieve the goals of the school will consider not only subject matter, but the ways in which the subject matter can be experienced by students and the aspects of the environment in which the encounters with the subject matter can occur. One can systematically design and carry out a management plan regarding these components, finally assessing the effectiveness of their interactions on students' learnings.

But, Umans posits some cautions for those of us dealing with models and procedures for change. One cannot ignore the human condition and its fluidity. Individuals with whom we work and for whom we design curricula are evolving, and this evolution or transcendence is constant but varied in rate of enactment. Thus, mechanisms for monitoring those persons with whom we work are required in order to understand more fully just how the "human condition" can be described, planned for, and dealt with at any particular time.

A second caution relates to the complexity of the educational process. Simple answers to complex situations are to be avoided. The educational process is complex regarding its social dynamics, the interaction of curricular components, the enactment of instructional strategies, the activation of learning approaches, and the utilization of assessment procedures. Additionally, the educational process occurs within an environment that is ever changing and in which there is much "noise" about which we know little as to its effects on individuals encountering the curriculum.

A third difficulty in applying change theory to education is our current lack of educational models that depict different processes and situations. We require models that will identify specific aspects of particular subsystems having relevance to curriculum; we administer people and materials. But such management in the development of curriculum is different than the direction of people and materials in the implementation stage. Models are required that will reveal how change occurs within these two stages as well as at other curriculum stages—maintenance and evaluation.

A fourth difficulty relates to our lack of appropriate instruments to measure just what happens to individuals who experience carefully planned curricula. Often we think of assessment in terms of only measuring student achievement levels. Certainly, we generate new curricula for reasons other than student achievement. We are interested in the quality of interpersonal relationships, the attitude clusters that persons develop, the skills that people attain. But we have a dearth of instruments that will measure how teachers and others react in the curriculum development and implementation phases and how they relate to persons outside the educational system in these two phases. Some measurement people argue that if you cannot measure it, it does not exist or is unimportant. It can be argued that perhaps the most important learnings in education, such as the approach to and joy of learning and the concern for others, are definitely of equal if not greater importance and should be measured to some degree.

But, as Umans points out, our difficulty in measuring the success of what we do rests not solely on a lack of appropriate instruments. We are faced with another problem, the absence of control. Students enter and exit the school's environment being influenced in a legion of ways by the school's curricula and our complicated society. Such complexity presents an almost impossible task of ascertaining whether students' behaviors and knowledge levels are the results of anything done in the schools.

Another caution which we curricularists need to beware of is creating a dehumanizing approach to curriculum in our zeal for being systematic. Certainly, the danger does exist, but being more precise in change strategies should allow educators to create programs which should increase the probability of optimizing education for students. Whether the increased precision creates a dehumanizing curriculum depends upon whether we retain or lose sight of the fact that we are creating programs for people, not constructing an assembly line for marketable goods.

Figure 2.2 presents rather simply a cycle of educational improvement. With increasing introduction of the new technology, additional models have been and continue to be created that can assist one in more effectively conceptualizing and managing change, in assuring educational improvement. Models can describe or reflect an existing structure or they can simulate or generate conceptions of future structures.

Simulation models result from the development of a schema depicting the relationships among the many separate elements of a particular situation or problem and then allowing, often via the use of a computer, the elements to interact and generate myriad possible outcomes. Many of the simulation models are developed from industrial dynamic procedures largely advanced by Jay Forester, a systems leader. Gaynor and Duvall (1977) have taken some of the industrial dynamic ideas and applied them to educational innovation. Such modeling enables one to isolate variables inherent in the total educational change process and to delimit the complex interactions among such factors.

A basic model advanced by Gaynor and Duvall (1977) is shown in Figure 2.3.

This model has some similarities to Figure 2.2, but this model illustrates the dynamics of equilibrium affecting the level of innovativeness within the school system. The model reveals that the level of community demands is

FIGURE 2.3   *Educational change process model*

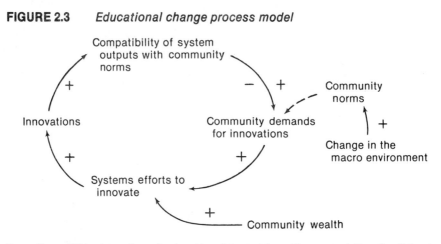

Note. From "The dynamics of educational innovation: Theory and Practice," by A. Gaynor and L. DuVall. Paper presented at the American Educational Research Association annual meeting, April 1977. Reprinted by permission.

related to the degree of compatibility of the systems outputs. The community views the results of the schooling effort and reacts either favorably (+) and urges a continuance of current practice or it reacts negatively (–) and requests that the system activate change efforts. The community's reactions are influenced by the norms it brings to the educational situation. Likewise, norms are affected by the overall changes occurring in the macro environment. The schema reveals that if school systems do enact innovative efforts in response to community demands, the level of the change effort is swayed by the community wealth. Gaynor and Duvall expand this model to explain innovation more accurately.

Curriculum specialists do not always wait until demands emanate from the community before changing programs. Often educators in viewing change in the macro environment feed their perceptions into the system,resulting in both positive and negative influences upon the overall actions of participants in the educational system (creative change). In their expanded model Gaynor and Duvall show that inputs into the total process of innovation result from inputs dealing with past effectiveness of systems efforts to innovate and from ongoing innovation within the subsystem. Figure 2.4 shows this expanded model.

This expanded model of the school system and the community exhibits one causal loop. (Other expanded models can be developed for the political influences on subcommunities in the school system, and for the interactions extant among the school system and its subsystems.)

In the lower left of the model, one can see COMMUNITY NORMS drawn as a loop. Following this loop toward the right side of the diagram, one observes that it blends into a loop identified as SYSTEM NORMS. These norms are those of the professional personnel in the school system. The interfacing of these two loops at the SYSTEM EFFORTS TO INNOVATE suggests the possibility of conflict. This potential impacting of the two norm clusters is shown in the model to have a ripple effect upon the various efforts of the system to innovate.

FIGURE 2.4   *Expanded change process model*

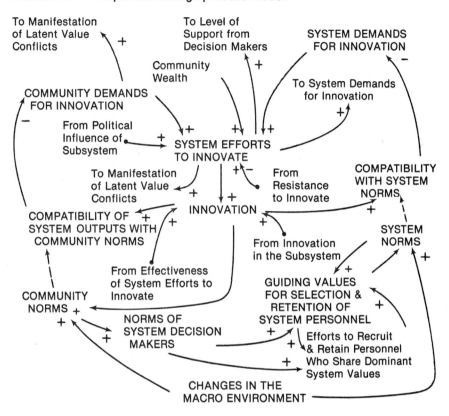

Source: Gaynor and DuVall (1977), p. 13. Reprinted by permission.

Once INNOVATION does occur, it is checked against the system norms and the community norms for compatability. As noted in the model, the system's efforts to innovate also are affected by COMMUNITY DEMANDS and SYSTEM DEMANDS for innovations. These demands do not exist in isolation but are influenced by other factors present in the model (compatability of system norms with systems demands and compatability of systems output with community demands) (Gaynor & Duvall, 1977).

With the use of more powerful models depicting more variables and their interactions, educators will be able to engage in forecasting the effects of various change actions on the school establishment and its program. Such models may reveal areas requiring attention to offset probable conflicts within the educational system or within the interactions between the educational system and its social system (community).

Some models rather than depicting the actual components of the educational system by the similarity of attributes delineate the subcomponents by similarities of operations. The following model developed by Banathy (1973) exemplifies this type (see Figure 2.5).

This model, portraying the interactions extant among and between four major processes, provides educators with a systematic view of the major

FIGURE 2.5   *The motion-picture model*

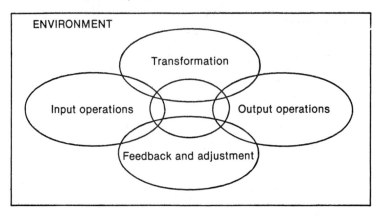

Note. From *Developing a systems view of education* by Bela H. Banathy p. 56. Copyright 1973 by Fearon-Pitman Publishers, Inc. 6 Davis Drive, Belmont, CA. 94002. Reprinted by permission.

educational processing activities and their relationship to the total environment, local or national.

Educators visualizing the total system and all crucial components impacting upon the system can make more effective decisions regarding program change simply because these sub-processes provide necessary information for decision-making. In many current situations, educators lack the total picture of their systems and are unaware of particular components about which data should be gathered and processed. Too often curriculum managers function too hastily with scant realization of the complexity of the system and insufficient data about the numerous subsystems that must be considered.

Umans (1970) presents a model (Figure 2.6) that depicts quite accurately educational reality. This particular model reveals the overlapping of the community and school environments on the student. Here the student is the prime factor in the considerations and deliberations of the program planner, but many persons will or should influence the student. Several major elements within the school and community system impact on the student's curricular experience.

The next model, Figure 2.7, also depicts the student as the central focus. But this model deals with modification over time relating to the student's actual encounter with the curriculum. It portrays a type of evolutionary relationship between the student and various curricular components.

This schema centers on the fact that in creating a responsive curriculum for a student or students, the components of content, experience, and resources must be related to the needs of the students and defined in terms of an encounter occurring within a particular environment. These components, requiring decisions, are adjusted over time partly as the result of the program planner's efforts and partly in consequence to the student's own reactions to the educational encounters.

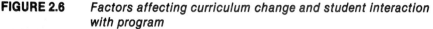

FIGURE 2.6 *Factors affecting curriculum change and student interaction with program*

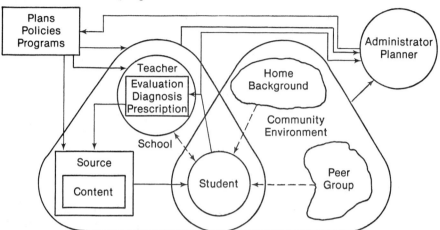

Note. From *The management of education* by S. Umans, 1970, p. 58. Copyright 1970 by S. Umans. Reprinted by permission of Doubleday & Co., Inc.

Model building and utilization are coming into their own as educators are becoming more knowledgeable of sophisticated models and the use of the computer in managing such models. The presence of self-adaptive systems, called heuristic systems, testifies to the increasing awareness of educators to models, systems, and their utilization with regard to educational change. Most likely such models will not be in wide use in the immediate future, for getting "handles" on the specifics of education is extremely difficult. Also, many persons presently within the educational community react negatively to what they perceive as an overuse of machines in dealing with persons. But, it seems evident from analysis of the field and from some of the models presented in this chapter that models and computers are coming into their own in explaining and facilitating the management of change and improvement within the curricular arena.

Activity 2–2   *Model Building and Analysis*

Consider your current situation in relation to curriculum activity. Which of the models presented in this section of the chapter best describes change in your situation?

You may wish to develop another model to depict your situation. How does your model compare with the ones presented in the text? What assumptions are you bringing to your model? What are the implications of your model if one accepts it as describing or prescribing change action?

Relationship of Change to Planning

If quality change—innovation—is the effect, then careful planning is the cause. Rarely does quality educational modification result from accidental efforts of curriculum specialists, from natural change. Of course, program adjustment

FIGURE 2.7 *A model to explain curricular interaction in the classroom*

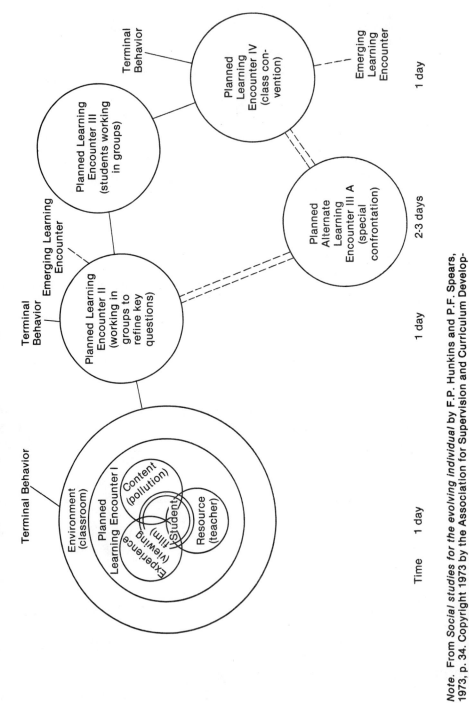

Note. From *Social studies for the evolving individual* by F.P. Hunkins and P.F. Spears, 1973, p. 34. Copyright 1973 by the Association for Supervision and Curriculum Development. Reprinted by permission.

does occur within the school without detailed planning, but much of this change is deficit change and suspect with regard to the school's goals.

Few desire change for change's sake. Most persons wish their efforts to produce quality. But Morphet et al. (1972) indicate that if the processes of planning and change are to be effective and meaningful, the relationships between the two must be carefully considered. Effective planning must relate to a desired and identifiable change. Planning must be purposeful. Change, to be effective, must relate to and result from well-conceived and carefully considered plans.

Duhl (1967) has emphasized the essential kind of relationship between planning and change.

> The planner is an agent of change, and any agent of change is a planner. It does not matter whether he is a politician, a producer, a businessman, an administrator, or an educator. There are many kinds of planner, performing different functions and fulfilling different roles, depending upon the specific problem or situation with which he must deal. What is essential to his definition as a planner is that he be concerned with instituting change in an orderly fashion, so that tomorrow something will be different from what it is today. (p. 780)

Effective developers, managers, and specialists interpret their tasks as largely change tasks. Curriculum leaders apprehend that innovation requires the utilization of clearly defined processes of planning. But recognizing the desirability of change is insufficient in causing it to occur. Change agents, contemplating modification, need to posit many questions and to discover answers for them. Morphet et al. suggest several key questions that curriculum persons should consider.

> How may planned educational change be made to happen?
> Who (agency, institution, organization or person) should be responsible for making the planned change happen?
> What criteria (bases) should be used for determining which changes should be planned for?
> What are the likely or probable consequences of "allowing educational change to happen," rather than making planned educational change happen? (pp. 124–125)

Three kinds of change exist: (a) changes in people, (b) changes in program or processes, and (c) changes in institutions or organizations. Often these three types are interrelated. Additionally, those dealing with any one or all three of these change types must possess contingency plans. If one approach in dealing with a curricular problem, such as making content relevant to a particular student group, proves ineffectual, then a related or contingency plan needs to be activated.

Frequently these three types of change are inseparable, but persons can take one of the three as their major responsibility. Some individuals will feel that if you wish to facilitate change, you must deal primarily with the people. Change the people and you alter the organization. Many persons currently in the humanist camp stress this approach. Others consider that the most effective way to enact modification is to adjust the procedures by which people function within the school. People in this group indicate you do not need to transmute the school or the staff. It is sufficient to provide them with different ways to meet the objectives of the school's program. When unsuccessful in creating program modification using one system's procedure, individuals should utilize another. Finally, there are those who believe that the most effective innovation results from actually adjusting the organization within which people work. Reorganize the environment, vary the way the staff is organized, remodel the room arrangements, and people will adjust in the directions deemed essential by the program manager. Organizational development (OD) currently being stressed within educational administration takes at least two of these tasks—a transformation in the structure of the organization and a change in the people.

Besides considering change from these orientations, one can organize change according to levels of complexity: substitution, alteration, perturbations, restructuring, and value orientation. The first level of change, substitution, depicts alteration in which one element may be substituted for another already extant. In curriculum, the substitution of one textbook for another exemplifies such change. An example with regard to instruction is employing a new method of presenting information replacing an older method.

The second level of change, alteration, exists when curriculum persons, or other educators, introduce into existing materials and programs particular new content, items, materials, or procedures that appear to be only minor and thus are likely to be adopted readily. A curriculum person might encourage teachers to substitute for a reading activity used at a particular point in the curriculum a film-viewing activity in order to meet the needs of students experiencing difficulty in reading. This level of change is easily enacted, but the consequences of such action may not be anticipated, and thus could potentially create conflict in the school system regarding the said program.

Perturbations, the third level, refers to changes that could disrupt the program at first. But, the teacher or curriculum educator with purposeful action can adjust them to the ongoing program within a short time span. An example of this would be the principal adjusting class schedules thus affecting the time allowed for teaching a certain subject. Another example would be introducing new students to the classroom requiring the teacher to adjust significantly the types of materials and methods employed with regard to a curriculum unit.

The fourth level of change, restructuring, refers to those permutations that lead to modification of the system itself. New concepts of teaching roles, such as those present in differentiated staffing, would represent this level of change. A change from graded to ungraded schools also would be an example. At this level, the organization of the curriculum and the diversity of the activities provided must be adjusted significantly. With regard to planning, the involvement of parents and students in the curriculum development phase also can lead to restructuring roles and tasks.

The final level of change, values orientation change, refers to shifts in the fundamental value orientation of the participants. All persons concerned with change in the school are striving for this level. Change at this level has persons becoming committed to the new ideas, programs, procedures, and organizations being advocated. One can argue that if persons don't adjust with regard to their value domain, the change enacted at the lower levels will be short-lived (McNeil, 1977).

Diffusion

Change should extend beyond the local arena. New curricula should spread at least throughout the local school district. Where the program has been developed at a regional laboratory, persons in charge of the development wish to expand the program's influence beyond the local cliental. Change agents are interested in diffusion, a process that must be planned for within the overall change procedure.

Diffusion involves educating individuals regarding the worth of a new program or a program component such as a new content area, or a new type of student material. Incorporating diffusion in the overall change strategy requires that one remain mindful that educational innovation is people-oriented rather than thing-oriented. Katz, Levin, and Hamilton (1963) have provided a most useful definition of diffusion:

> 1) the acceptance, 2) overtime, 3) or some specific item—an idea or practice, 4) by individuals groups or other adopting units linked, 5) to specific channels or communication, 6) to a social structure, and 7) to a given system of values, or culture. (p. 240)

Guba (1967) has described several diffusion strategies: valuing, rational, didactic, psychological, economic, political, and authority. In the valuing strategy, the change agent accepts the adopter as a professionally oriented individual capable of becoming obligated to adopt via an appeal to his or her values. In working with curriculum, one often identifies the value bases of community groups, and then initiates efforts to convince them that the program being suggested is relevant to what they deem important.

The rational strategy or approach is mounted by the curriculum change agent who believes that the potential adopter is a rational individual who can be convinced as to the program's value on the basis of hard data and logical arguments as to the program's feasibility, effectiveness, and efficiency. Persons taking this task gather empirical evidence attesting to the superiority of the proposed plan over the ongoing program. Pilot testing new programs is based on the assumption that the persons within and outside of the school system will be convinced as to the worthwhileness of a program once they have seen the data supporting the new program.

The didactic strategy is utilized by persons who view the adopter as a willing but untrained individual. Once training is furnished, the potential user will be an advocate of the program and will become capable of participating in some aspect of the program whether in development, implementation, maintenance, or evaluation.

The psychological strategy views the adopter as one needing acceptance, involvement, and inclusion in any innovation. If you wish an innovation accepted with future users involved in its development and use, you must identify and appeal to their psychological natures. You must ascertain that their needs for belonging are met, that their needs for contribution are catered to.

Persons approaching change from an economic viewpoint believe that persons can be involved if one provides them adequate compensation. Individuals are primarily economic and if one meets that need, then they will become ready advocates and competent participants in curriculum change and the resulting programs. Presently, as a result of collective bargaining, many teachers are only becoming involved in curricular activity if they are paid for such work in addition to their basic renumeration for teaching. In such instances, curricular activity is viewed as an "add on" activity, not as part of one's regular responsibilities.

Explaining diffusion of innovation and facilitating change from a political approach rests on the assumption that people are primarily political entities who can be influenced to adopt new programs by exerting power pressures. Occasionally, the sole way to get programs adjusted is to threaten educators with loss of program accreditation.

The final strategy mentioned by Guba is the authority strategy. Here the adopter is considered a component in a bureaucratic system who can be convinced to adopt change by virtue of his or her placement in and interaction with the authority hierarchy. Changes in program mandated by legislative bodies exemplify the authority strategy in action. This strategy seems to be increasing with many states having textbooks and particular courses legislated into the schools' programs. Individuals adopt not so much from conviction as to the program's value, but rather because they realize that they must bow to the power of the state or risk losing state funding.

Persons charged with disseminating curricular change rarely approach these strategies as pure types. If one only utilizes values strategies, one may produce a morass of confusion in attempting to process individual values. Approaching diffusion only from the rational viewpoint obscures the fact that people do not always react rationally. Also, empirical data are not without bias, and the values individuals hold will affect their data interpretation. Dealing with diffusion primarily from an economic approach may bring all curricular innovation to a halt if there is a "drying up" of the economic well. Overreliance on the political nature of people may have negative effects for many persons view political motives with suspicion. The authority strategy, utilized alone, will not really achieve great change, for persons complying to a greater force usually revert to previous programs and ways when the pressures exerted by the power sources are lessened. The strategies employed in creating and enacting change, and hopefully improvement, will represent a mosaic of several viewpoints functioning at various levels of complexity. The mosaic will vary as one confronts particular issues relating to curricula in the American school.

It is advantageous for curriculum change agents to consider change and attendant planning from an ecological approach as suggested by Sarason (1971). Change should be considered in the context or contexts of the arenas in which it is to occur. One needs to describe and interpret the physical dimensions of the arena as well as the personalities of the people interacting within the environments.

Characteristics of Innovations

We curriculum experts need to understand those characteristics of innovations (change effort results) that influence the receptiveness of the adopting groups. Rogers and Shoemaker (1971) indicate that the receiver's perceptions of an innovation's attributes are the factors that influence the rate of adoption, rather than the perceptions of the developers as to the value of the innovation. These authors note that innovations judged as valuable by the adopters are those considered high in relative advantage, compatability, trialability, observability, and low in complexity.

Relative advantage is the degree to which an innovation is perceived as being better than the ongoing program. Teachers and other educators who view an innovation as (a) increasing the amount of student interest, generating increased student learning; (b) possessing low initial cost, both short- and long-range; and (c) posing only a low risk to their functional security within the school system will view the innovation as high in relative advantage (Rogers & Shoemaker, 1971).

Compatibility is the degree to which an innovation is perceived as being in agreement with or supportive of the potential adopter's needs and values. Also, it relates to the degree to which the adopter believes the innovation fits into or supports prior educational or curricular experiences.

Rogers and Shoemaker explain that the factor of trialability relates to the degree to which an innovation can be attempted, piloted, on a limited basis. Can we try this without committing too much time, energy, or money to the project? Also, can we obtain maximum data from a limited trial or at least sufficient data to make a decision as to whether the innovation is desired or not?

Just what does the innovation do? Potential adopters of innovation desire palpable results from their efforts. What consequences have occurred from the innovation introduced in different locales? This demand for tangible outcomes has been termed observability by Rogers and Shoemaker. In these days of accountability, this characteristic may take on increasing importance.

Rogers and Shoemaker's final characteristic of innovation relates to complexity, the degree to which an innovation is perceived by potential adopters as being difficult to comprehend and utilize. Faced with a barrage of new ideas, demands, and challenges, educators are not too receptive to innovations that appear to demand an inordinate amount of time to either master new content or to learn new instructional strategies. Many curricular programs proposed in the late '60s did not "take off" precisely because many teachers considered such innovations as too complex to teach, at least too complex to learn with all of the competing demands placed on them as instructors.

Change agents should apply these characteristics to all innovations suggested for acceptance. Regarding program complexity, teachers may be more receptive to complex changes in program if we curriculum leaders schedule inservice to explain those changes to the teachers. Such inservice should not always be an "add on" activity, but should be scheduled during the regular school day. However, this idea is not too popular with many educators at present.

HOW PEOPLE REACT TO CHANGE

Working with change means working with people.

> If the organization's goals are to be achieved, and knowing that both will always strive for self-actualization, it follows that effective leadership is "fusing" the individual and the organization in such a way that both simultaneously obtain self-actualization. The processes of the individual using the organization to fulfill his needs and simultaneously the organization "using" individuals to achieve its demands has been called by Bakke the fusion process. (Argyris, 1957, p. 3)

Curriculum specialists manage, along with administrators, the expectations of the school system and the needs of teachers, principals, and other support personnel. Effective curriculum leaders understand the structure of the system, and perhaps more importantly they apprehend the complexities of the persons within the system. As Williams, Wall, Martin and Berchin (1974) point out, each individual plays a multitude of roles within the system, and each professional brings to his or her role his or her personality. Each person has certain needs which he or she expects to fulfill within the reality of the school or outside of the school. But rarely does one find absolute compatibility between instructional expectations and individual needs. Conflict is bound to exist. Curriculum persons cannot avoid it; they must manage it.

Such conflicts experienced by persons within the system are role—personality conflicts and can be classified into three types: expectational role–personality conflict; actual role–personality conflict; and perceptual role-personality conflict.

Expectational role–personality conflict exists when a discrepancy occurs between what the principal or curriculum leader expects the teacher or educator's roles in the school to be and what the individual perceives his or her roles to be. For example, many curriculum coordinators perceive that teachers should work on curricular matters within the basic definitions of their jobs. However, many teachers in viewing their roles, exclude any responsibility for creating, implementing, or managing curricular programs. In such cases, conflict is likely and must be resolved if teachers are to be included in curriculum activity. Presently, conflict and confusion of roles exist among many teachers. Many are demanding involvement in curricular decision-making if the program is to affect them, while also indicating that such involvement is outside their regular roles, and that they should receive additional compensation for their participation.

Actual role–personality conflict results when the educational leader's, principal's or curriculum specialist's, expectations of a teacher or other educator run counter to exactly what the person has stated his or her need dispositions to be. Focusing on teachers, actual conflict often occurs when teachers rebel or resist or even sabotage the curriculum innovation because it conflicts with their orientations to education, to curriculum, and perhaps even to life.

The final personality conflict, perceptual role–personality conflict, occurs when a teacher or some person in the educational system has an inaccurate idea as to what the curriculum or educational leader holds regarding that individual's role in the system. The teacher's or educator's false perception as to expected role clashes with his or her understanding of role. A teacher may believe that the curriculum specialist thinks that the teacher should be involved in making major adjustments to the content component of the curriculum. This collides with the teacher's perception of his or her major role—perhaps that of teaching. Such confusion can be minimized by maintaining open communication networks in the school system, so that when such conflicts do arise, they can be discussed and the misconceptions corrected (Williams et al., 1974).

Getzels, Lipham and Campbell (1968) have presented a model depicting the major components discussed above and their interactions relevant to personality and organization.

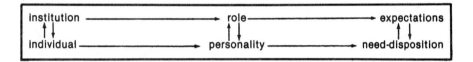

Note. From *Educational administration as a social process* by Jacob W. Getzels, James M. Lipham and Roald F. Campbell. Copyright © 1968 by Jacob W. Getzels, James M. Lipham and Roald F. Campbell. Reprinted by permission of Harper & Row, Publishers, Inc.

Adaptation

No person can totally ignore the change efforts of others. People adapt to change even if the adaptation is dismissing the modification being proposed.

McKelvey (1967) has developed a model depicting four modes of adaptation to change. Two are responses: activity and passivity, and two are attitudes: idealism and cynicism. They can be plotted as follows:

	Activity	Passivity
Idealism	Crusading	Ritualism
Cynicism	Insurgency	Retreatism

Activity is when the individual confronting the modification exerts a concerted effort to alter the school's expectations to fit his or her own. He or she argues that what the school is suggesting, say with regard to a new program, is really incongruous with the general philosophy of the community and the expected and accepted teacher roles. Passivity is when the individual responds to a demand for adjustment by adapting his or her expectations to conform to those of the school.

The attitude of idealism is maintained by the individual who views school improvement as part of the job to be included in school improvement, but also desires involvement in policy-making. The idealist relishes the feeling of being in control of all or a part of the system.

His or her counterpart is the cynic who maintains the view that an individual has scant power in determining educational policy, and improvements are totally within the realm of administration. The cynic feels that whatever he or she might do, it would be ineffectual in influencing the functioning of the system. Thus, he has little interest in any type of participation.

But persons confronted with change demands are not just active or passive or idealists or cynics. People can react to change in numerous ways depending upon the combination of their actions and attitudes. For example, one may be a crusader or active idealist. This educator views the world with confidence and welcomes the prospects of new programs. He or she relishes being involved in the generation of new programs to meet educational needs. Such an individual is constantly striving to bring about increasing effectiveness of curricular programs. Curriculum change agents need to identify these people within the school systems early in any curriculum development activity.

The ritualist, or passive idealist, is one pleased with the existing system. He or she may really believe that some improvement in the program could be exacted, but such improvement is really not worth the effort. It is better to conform to the existing structure of the school. "Why should I be the one to live dangerously and suggest some innovation? Also, why should I get more involved? I am busy enough," he might say. Curriculum persons, attempting to enact curricular improvement, need to convince such people that active involvement, while having risks, is worth the effort in terms of better programs, increased participant excitement, and professional challenge.

The insurgent, the active cynic, is one who expresses opposition to the norms of the school in a negative, and frequently hostile manner. This person exhibits frustration when his or her ideas and views for improvement in the curriculum are rejected. Frequently, the insurgent urges the demolition of the system advocating the phoenix be allowed to rise from the ashes of the ineffectual prior system. Many of the current curriculum revisionists exemplify this individual.

The final type is the retreatist, the passive cynic. He too opposes the school's norms, goals, and programs. He frequently expresses negative and hostile feelings toward the school. But rather than confront the system that is the target of his anger, this person prefers to withdraw from the effort and directs his energies elsewhere. The system is not worth the effort. The retreatist works at a school, but is not part of the personnel. He expends energy only in devising ways to escape from any and all requirements and obligations. Such individuals need to be identified in the system by the curriculum coordinator and or specialist and, if possible, dismissed from the school system (Williams et al., 1974).

Reactions and Resistance

In contemplating types of individuals who may be employed in an educational system, one realizes that in curriculum activities resistance to change is ineluctable but does not occur uniformly. It may be comforting to remember that resistance to new ideas is part of natural human behavior. But, curriculum specialists must understand the reasons for such resistance. Persons may resist variation for their positions may be threatened by it. Savage has presented some common reasons why people react negatively to a change effort:

1. The individual or group may sincerely believe that the change is unwise and will be unproductive in meeting the objectives of the school's program. In fact, the change suggested may cause a reduction in the quality of the program. This is a legitimate reason. All who resist a particular change are not anti-progress or nonrational.

2. An individual or a group may regard and fear the change as a threat to status. Persons who believe that an innovation's acceptance will cause them the loss of recognition and the approval and respect of their peers are certainly going to reject the suggested adjustments. To many people, status is highly desired. It is a worthy goal to which one devotes his or her energies. It is common knowledge that certain professions such as medicine and law have high status. Within the educational community, administrators seem to have a higher status than teachers. Also, teachers at upper grade levels and teaching specific content seem to have higher status than teachers at the elementary levels who are generalists in education.

    Curriculum workers comprehending the "pecking order" within the school system (or educational institution) work to make all feel that their positions are of value, which indeed they are. Attempts at incorporating differentiated staffing, while not eliminating status positions, certainly seem to put more people on equal, but not identical, professional levels. Status also relates to the need to belong and be worthwhile. To enact change, one has to work with the feeling and desires for status rather than posing a threat to persons' statuses. In some cases, curriculum workers may wish to use possible higher status as an incentive to action.

3. Another reason for negative reactions to innovative efforts is that individuals consider such action as having the potential, whether real or imaginary, or affecting their job or financial security. In industry, this occurs if certain workers believe that a new program or procedure will introduce machines that will eliminate their jobs. Teachers sometimes argue similarly in rejecting new educational technology. Many teachers reacted negatively to voucher plan proposals believing the enactment of such plans would deprive them of sufficient numbers of students. Often teachers reject making their courses elective for similar reasons.

4. Another explanation for resisting change is that many educators believe, and perhaps correctly so, that the informal groups to which they belong would be disbanded if particular modifications were introduced into the program. In differentiated staffing, certain cliques might be dissolved as a result of the new staffing organizations. If one were to create a campus school with building clusters, some might argue against the idea primarily

because they would not be able to visit at coffee break time with those individuals who were part of the original school organization. Some argue that the innovation will negatively affect the atmosphere of professionalism and collegiality that exists.

5. Frequently, people resist adjustment because they reject the person advancing the change proposal. It is quite natural for a person to repudiate the ideas of a person whom they do not like personally. This also can occur when the suggesting group is not respected by the professional staff. In curriculum development a group of teachers may cancel a suggestion for curriculum improvement because they consider the advocating group as either too radical or conservative. "What can you expect of those people. They are trying to maintain a repressive society. We need to ignore their ideas; that group has been trying for years to destroy our way of life."

6. One cannot exclude the possibility that the reason a person rejects or resists new ideas, new programs is because of ignorance. Curriculum specialists advocating change must guarantee that persons to be affected by the change—teachers, pupils, lay community members—comprehend the nature of the program change and its rationale. Misunderstandings as to what the modification is really going to do only retards program development. Those championing innovation also must be sure that even those individuals who express agreement with and indicate understanding of the program are completely briefed as to the proposed actions.

   Persons willing to accept an innovation but lacking a clear understanding of it, may incorporate the modification into the curriculum program, but the way in which the innovation is introduced and developed may not be consistent with its purpose and philosophy. In some cases this happened with the curriculum innovations of the last decade. Persons willing to change the curriculum accepted the new programs without complete understanding of the nature of the programs. Thus, many of the new programs while incorporated into the overall curriculum were still taught in traditional manners rather than as suggested or implied in the new syllabi.

7. Most people have traditions to which they adhere and institutions that they cherish. Often times, recommendations for change threaten these traditions and institutions. Frequently, teachers in a particular school are very proud of their school's tradition of meeting the needs of certain types of students. Adjustments that would allow other types of students to be admitted often will be met with resistance. Individuals proposing campus school organizations for more flexibility in the curriculum are many times criticized by individuals who consider the adopting of such an innovation as dooming the "neighborhood school," a worthy tradition. In this author's city, there is a school which has a deep sense of community. Many persons living around this school are reluctant to see other students brought in and their students bussed out, less the school's unique tradition be damaged.

8. Currently, many persons resist change efforts for they feel overwhelmed by what is proposed and the implications such innovation will have for them. Often, new curricular programs suggested are viewed by teachers as requiring them to learn new teaching skills, to develop competencies in curriculum development and management of learning resources, or to learn new skills in interpersonal relations. "I can hardly keep up now without taking on something new" is a frequent reaction.

9. Those educators who feel comfortable with the current educational scene and the ways in which they function within it, may be reluctant to change for they cannot comprehend or see clearly the future. These people feel uncomfortable with the uncertainty that change may create. Bringing in new students or new contents or new ways to organize the program clouds the future for many staff members. Just where will we be in two years if this modification comes in?

10. "Why do we need to change? What is wrong with the way I am functioning at present?" Such questions are repeatedly phrased by those who view the request for variation as a personal attack on their performances as educators. To imply the need for adjustment suggests to such people that what is currently occurring is of poor quality. Curriculum specialists need to educate such staff members that the act of suggesting change does not always mean that present quality is lacking. But, the student population varies, and the demands of the times are in constant flux. Thus, for schools to be responsive to the times in their program offerings, there often is need for program modification.

11. Human beings reject change that they view as just signaling more work for them. "I don't need any new responsibilities or tasks to perform." In curriculum work this is a major obstacle, for at present much curricular activity is "add on" activity. It is something engaged in after the regular day or regular school week or regular school year. Professionals, exhausted by the regular day's responsibilities, may not be enthusiastic about assuming increased work in the name of innovation.

12. A final reason for people resisting change is that they fear that once the innovation is adopted, it will be quickly abandoned when another innovation comes along, thus making all their efforts in vain. This is a very real fear, for there have been many instances of such occurrences happening. Part of this is because many educators succumb to "bandwagonism." Today, we all gather behind this innovation, develop reports and implement programs. Tomorrow, in response to new demands, we throw it all out and bring in the "new," or go back to the "tried and true." Leaders of curriculum innovation need to be sure that what they are involving educators in is not a passing fad, but will represent something that has a high probability of lasting a reasonable time. However, this does not mean that all proposals and work of committees will be accepted and implemented in total, but it does mean that leaders who do reject program suggestions need to furnish valid reasons why the efforts of the committee were not utilized.[2]

Reaction Cycles

In any curriculum development effort, leaders wish to reduce the incidence of resistance to a new program being suggested while increasing the degree of acceptance for it. Change efforts from which positive palpable results occur are conducted by curriculum leaders who comprehend the above reasons people have for resisting modification. Additionally, those in charge realize that innovation efforts move through a cycle (Watson, 1967). At the beginning stage, one

---

[2]From *Interpersonal and group relations in educational administration* by W.W. Savage, 1968, pp. 192–196. Copyright 1968 by Scott, Foresman, and Co. Reprinted by permission.

finds only a few interested individuals. Rogers and Shoemaker (1971) identify these persons as the "innovators." Such persons are venturesome and willing to assume risk taking. These are the staff members who exhibit an eagerness to attempt new ideas. But most people first encountering innovation are not convinced as to its value. Resistance to the new idea or program appears massive, but unorganized. At this juncture, people are suggesting myriad reasons why the innovation cannot work or is inappropriate. Often advocates for the innovation are considered to be persons with wild ideas, visionaries who in many instances must be tolerated.

A second stage occurs when the innovation seems to be catching on (Watson, 1967). "Early adopters" appear and begin to strengthen the ranks of those favoring the innovation (Rogers & Shoemaker, 1971). Such individuals are not too much different in attitude and skills than the mass of individuals in the system. This similarity to the general group is good, for the early adopters serve as role models for others. People consider them as not too unusual and that if they consider an idea good and feasible, then it must have some value. But, opposing forces are also appearing.

The third stage in the innovation cycle is one of direct conflict and showdown. At this point, a third group becomes evident, the "early majority" (Rogers & Shoemaker, 1971). This majority engages in extensive deliberation regarding the innovation. While this group is engaged in discussion, counter groups, termed the "late majority," become mobilized to crush the innovative effort. Here, the major action seems to occur. Here the procedures developed during the planning stages are activated to convince and educate the opposition. The curriculum coordinator identifies and monitors all of the groups engaged in the dialogue and debate and then collates the bases from whence come their arguments.

The cycle's fourth stage occurs after decisive battles have enabled those advocating the change to gain control. Some resistance to the change will

---

Activity 2–3   *Teacher's Perceptions Regarding Curriculum Change*

The previous pages have focused on how people react to change. Interview a random selection of your colleagues (teachers) to determine how they perceive themselves reacting to curriculum change efforts. Use McKelvey's model as a way of recording the four modes of adapation to change.

	Activity	**Passivity**
Idealism	Crusading five persons	Ritualism one person
Cynicism	Insurgency three persons	Retreatism one person

Share your findings with other students of curriculum. Synthesize some conclusions regarding the type of staff you work with from the standpoint of change. Where are you on the chart?

remain for one or more reasons such as identified in the previous section. Now success has been achieved regarding the innovation, but one must continue supporting the innovation's implementation, for any latent opposition could still become mobilized and be of sufficient power to scuttle the alteration. The curriculum coordinator must continue to deal with the power plays of not only the overt opponents, but of those persons (the laggards) who still are not totally convinced as to the value of the change, but who are included in the majority which appears basically to have accepted the innovation (Watson, 1967).

The final stage occurs when most persons in the school system and community have accepted the program shift. However, there are still a few adversaries who now wear the armor of proponents or advocates of change against the innovation which has become the established program. This change demand, change implementation, change institutionalization, change demand is a cycle often repeated. Time, society, and the individual members of that society are in an evolutionary dynamic. This dynamic is monitored by curriculum persons so that they can initiate change as a result of anticipating future needs (creative change) rather than reacting to the anger and disillusionment of particular segments of the society (deficit change).[3] Figure 2.8 shows this adoption process.

FIGURE 2.8   *Adoption as a cumulative curve*

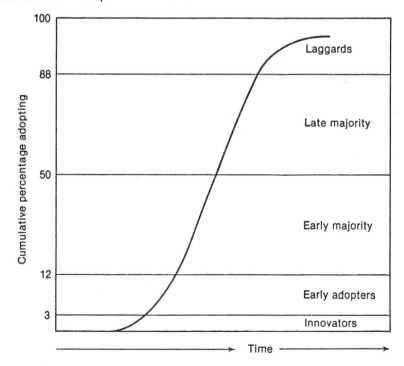

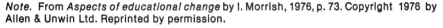

Note. From *Aspects of educational change* by I. Morrish, 1976, p. 73. Copyright 1976 by Allen & Unwin Ltd. Reprinted by permission.

---

[3]Other models of change and diffusion exist, such as the research, development, diffusion, and adoption model; the problem-solver model; the social-interaction model; and the linkage model. Readers interested in these models should consult Havelock, 1970.

Observation of the figure reveals a type of S-curve relating to the reaction cycle. Figure 2.9 shows the degree of involvement of an individual during this adoption process.

FIGURE 2:9   *Involvement of an individual during the adoption process*

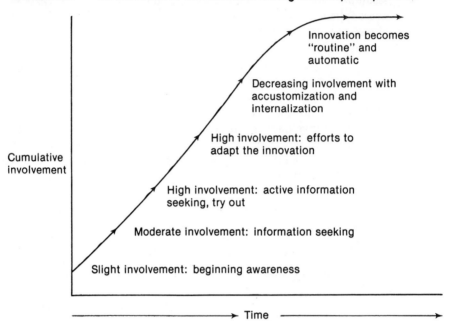

Note. From *Aspects of educational change* by I. Morrish, 1976, p. 74. Copyright 1976 by Allen & Unwin Ltd. Reprinted by permission.

Increasing Receptivity to Change

If we believe that something can be accomplished, usually it can be. Likewise, if we testify to the impossibility of something being done, the prediction usually materializes. But to augment the likelihood of successful innovation occurring, we require more than a positive attitude. Savage has provided some useful guidelines for increasing the receptivity of individuals to curricular innovation:

1. The curriculum effort must be cooperative. Change must be viewed as ours rather than theirs. Even though the plan may originate with the curriculum coordinator, he or she must be sure that the program becomes the property of all those who will be affected by it.
2. To assure that the program being advocated becomes ours, the curriculum coordinator should involve as many persons as feasible in the necessary deliberations and actions. Such involvement, not only stimulates attachment to the program, but also allows persons to understand the suggested curriculum more completely, to apprehend the consequences of the program's introduction, and to be able to keep the innovation on the intended track.
3. Resistance should be anticipated and procedures for dealing with it delineated. Persons managing the change should raise questions such as the following: How will people affected by the change feel about the change?

What explanations can one give to assist us in understanding why people are reacting as they are? What can be done to remove the negative reactions of individuals? How can we lessen the anxiety levels of individuals who will be affected by the change? What types of in-service would need to be provided to reduce resistance both within the professional and lay communities? In those situations where the change most likely will be viewed as threatening to certain individuals, the curriculum change agent should design opportunities so that threatened staff members can express themselves and discuss their concerns. Additionally, such members should be able to avail themselves of various in-service programs that will address some of the needs they express in consequence to the contemplated adjustments.

4. It is important for all to realize that innovations introduced are not to become rigid programs, never subject to change. In the initial stages, innovations are essentially experimental in nature. Even after initial piloting, during the implementation managing stages, adjustments will be required. Also, periodic evaluation of the program will furnish information as to whether the innovation itself should be discarded or redesigned at some future date. This temporality of program is important for the advocates of innovations to remember, lest they feel that once their program has been installed, that it is sacrosanct and cannot be challenged.

5. A final point for the curriculum change agent to remember is that the timing of the innovation is crucial. If one is embroiled with staff division over particular responsibilities, it is not a good idea to introduce the possibility of generating a program that will further strain the educational fabric. However, if the community is demanding that the school meet particular needs, as made evident by national assessment, then it might be most propitious to initiate activities to create a curriculum or a program segment to address the identified deficiencies. Much of the curricular activity creating multicultural, multiethnic and multilingual programs are well timed in that the demands for such programs are common in the general society. Likewise, programs addressing the issue of basics in education will be met with great community acceptance for the foreseeable future.[4]

Social Systems and Planned Change

We have discussed how people react to change focusing mostly on the individuals involved or affected. But contemplated changes are not generated or implemented in vacuums. Working with people is not done in isolation. Curriculum specialists cannot work with people unaware of how individuals relate to groups, social systems or to other structures, whether physical or psychological. Change, whether carefully planned or not, occurs within social milieus. Curriculum coordinators realize that the school is a social system subsuming other systems such as personality systems, values systems, content systems, and organizational systems.

Perhaps the first realization we should have is that social systems have an inherent tendency to resist alteration. This is partly due to the fact that social systems tend toward internal equilibrium, an internal balance. Balance

---

[4]From *Interpersonal and group relations in educational administration* by W.W. Savage, 1968, pp. 192–196. Reprinted by permission.

also means that if equilibrium in one particular system or subsystem is acted upon, the resulting pressure or influence will exert pressures on other systems to either reject the input or to make some type of adjustment. In an ongoing system, the forces for change and for permanence are balanced in such a way that the system maintains a steady state. Interpreting this from a standpoint of force-field analysis, we have in a system driving forces pushing in a particular direction, fostering the initiation and continuation of change. Countering these driving forces are restraining forces acting as barriers to the change demands. When the driving and restraining forces are equal, we have a steady state in the system (Jenkins, 1961). To initiate modification, one has to either increase the driving forces or lessen the restraining forces.

The equilibrium extant in most school systems can be termed as dynamic equilibrium as opposed to static equilibrium. Homans (1950) defines dynamic equilibrium as being achieved to the extent that the interaction among subsystems is flexible enough to allow for changes. The system responds to inputs and makes adjustments which may appear minor at first glance, but which may alter the system extensively over a period of time. Only such a dynamic system can make the necessary adaptations to varying environmental demands. A system that lacks equilibrium is not really a system and becomes impossible to manage either from the standpoint of maintaining a steady state relating to consistency of curricular offerings or from the standpoint of introducing change to the system. Social systems exhibiting static equilibrium eventually deteriorate due to their increasing dysfunctioning in an evolving society.

But change within the school cannot be understood by looking only at the school system. Schools and their activities are influenced by the larger environment in which they exist, the suprasystem. Often the demands from this suprasystem generate pressures which can either enhance or diminish the incidence and effects of desired adjustment. Communities, in voting for special levies for school operations, can either encourage or prevent the introduction of innovation in the curriculum program. Legislation from either state or national bodies can often facilitate change in particular avenues while restraining or eliminating innovation in other dimensions. Certain content is stressed as a result of demands for basic education and bilingual studies while other content is excluded or at least receives a lesser emphasis. Presently, legislation dealing with children within the special education category is providing a fertile environment for diversifications in programs dealing with these students.

Responsible efforts to improve schools result from analyses of their actual, contemporary properties as social systems. Miles (1967) states that in spite of the current interest in educational innovation, educators have not really engaged in any extensive analyses of the schools or school systems. This lack of analyses has prevented educators from discriminating school systems from other types of systems, such as agricultural, medical, and industrial. Many educators are fond of using the three previous areas as sources for educational metaphors, but we have not analyzed our system to the degree where we can compare it precisely to those other systems for similarities and differences. Miles advances the notion that perhaps the school is unique in that it is a social organization existing for the purpose of facilitating desirable changes in students. Of course, one can debate what domains are involved in the changes. Some might argue that the modifications the school is concerned with or should be concerned with are changes dealing with the cognitive dimension, the rational component of individuals. Others might argue that the transformations should cater to the emotional and affective domains of individuals.

But, increasing numbers of curriculum workers, regardless of their philosophical orientations, are realizing that the school is tied to a number of institutions and organizations in the larger society. Curriculum workers are becoming cognizant of and understanding fully the nature of the linkages of the school system to these other systems. If change in one system affects other subsystems, then change in either the school system or in one of the subsystems in society will most likely affect the school and the other systems. Curriculum persons unaware of these linkages, encourage public criticisms and often put the school in a posture of defending its actions rather than advancing proposals for increasing the responsiveness of school experiences to the needs of students.

As Miles posits, the American public school is currently in the midst of a rapidly changing, highly complex environment manifesting change in a legion of ways. There exist adjustments in social-class membership, in attitudes and values, in information bases, in political realms, and in the total economic structure. All of these changes impact upon the school system either directly or indirectly.

Implications for Education

The school as a system is not the only type of system in which change is difficult. Morphet et al. (1972) indicate that all social systems tend to resist planned change, but that educators and other persons need to realize that the cumulative effect of the interrelatedness of many social systems does tend to transmit change from one social system or subsystem to other systems or subsystems. Often these effects are unplanned and unanticipated. The demographic shifts in the nation's population have affected the types of programs required in the schools. The vast migrations of persons from rural areas to the cities have caused programs to be created not as a result of careful planning of their need, but in response to a largely unexpected happening. Mainstreaming children from special education classes into regular classes resulting from action in the legal-political system is certainly impacting school program development. The decrease in numbers of children is affecting schools in ways that can be anticipated and in ways presently unknown.

Pressures to create new types of elementary schools and new elementary curricula will influence demands for new types of secondary schools and resulting secondary curricula. The interrelatedness of these various systems necessitates monitoring systems both within and outside of the school so that educators can process the demands and can engage in creative change. With the technological revolution, the cultural changes, and the knowledge explosion, a key question facing educators—in our instance, curriculum persons—is how to deal rationally and realistically with these pressures. Also, curriculum leaders need to generate procedures for creating pressures to change themselves. Schools and institutions of higher learning need not always maintain a responding posture; they also can initiate demands. Educational institutions can create pressures not only for new programs, but for new types of human interactions within the educational experience.

Many curriculum specialists in the schools and in the universities are developing means for anticipating, identifying, and dealing realistically with the multitude of diverse inputs for change. School systems appear to have four major goals: (a) increased internal interdependence and collaboration; (b) added adaptation mechanisms and skills; (c) stronger data-based, inquiring stances toward change; and (d) continuing commitment to organizational and personal growth and development (Miles, 1967). Educators concerned with change are realizing the need for fostering dialogue and cooperation among the members of educational teams. Procedures for such interaction are being created, perfected, and implemented. Persons working with innovation are realizing that the ideal, absolute educational program is never going to be achieved, but one must continue efforts to approach the ideal. Furthermore, persons concerned with program modification are understanding that decisions must be data-based and that procedures for gathering such data must be part of our repertoire of skills and competencies. What the above suggests is that curriculum innovation requires precision, not just in teaching, but in managing the entire curricular program. But, this is not a false precision in which we believe that we can identify all variables in the curriculum and manage each one with exactitude.

EDUCATIONAL PRECISION IN MODERN SOCIETY

Meadows (1971) indicates that any discussion regarding the adaptive problems and behavior of public education can profit from agreement of what kind of society is at issue. But, he iterates, to characterize correctly our society is most difficult. First, there exists the danger of mischaracterization if one attempts to put one label on the American society in all of its diversity. Such a mischaracterization can be disasterous for the schools, in that part of the school's functioning depends upon correct readings of the society or societies which it serves. To classify and label our society, educators—most likely with the help of sociologists and other social science scholars—will have to analyze it in all of its diversity for common points, and threads of unity.

Meadows has done this and indicates that the United States can be epitomized as "modernity"; the United States of America is a modern country (p. 20). Numerous definitions of modern exist, a useful one being that modernity consists in the realization of humankind's freedom from the bondage of time or practice. In essence, modernity is an attitude or cluster of attitudes. This is important to remember, for curriculum developers and managers wish individuals in the educational system to express modernity. Such expression implies an openness to change, at least a willingness to entertain the prospect of modification.

A contrasting concept is traditionality, a bondage to time or practice. In traditional cultures, humanity is encysted in its cultural milieu; in essence, traditional humanity has either abolished time or has devalued it by emphasizing models that are time free, that transcend time. The traditional person in a traditional society does not worry about adjustment. This person only identifies that which has been valued in the previous generation and strives to maintain it. One can see that having a traditional posture would make change and innovation in education very difficult. The person influenced by tradition would argue that certain aspects of the curriculum are essential to the nature of humanity and to scholarship. The essential aspects of humans are time independent, and therefore there is little need to alter the curriculum.

Curriculum leaders should not interpret traditional persons as simply having deleterious effects upon curriculum innovation while modern persons have productive influences on curriculum change. Indeed, there are aspects of the curriculum that most likely should be continued from one generation to the next. But, there is a difference between continuing aspects of the curriculum or maintaining various organizations of the school in an unquestioning manner because such curricula and organizations have stood the test of previous times and the continuing of such aspects of education as a result of constant analysis and discovery of the ongoing value of such emphases and practices. In the latter case, even though the curriculum may remain constant, the curriculum leader has approached the curriculum from a modernity stance. The person believes in the continued value of the curriculum component, but because its inclusion is the result of careful deliberation rather than passive acceptance, such an individual is not bound by time or previous wisdoms. He may use such time or wisdom, but he is not bound by them. Modern humanity has a multitude of options compared to traditional humanity.

Modern humanity is freed from the requirement to continue to recreate the past in eternal cycles. Modern persons can confront the realities of the present and contemplate anticipated realities of the future with different options about time. Today, those who realize their modernity have released their future behaviors from the shackles of past times. The despair and timidity of their ancestors has been eliminated and there exists no need to continue to repeat past errors. One can formulate various options and different approaches to educational functioning. Modern persons can control their future. But such control and planning for such control requires precise procedures.

Postulates for Precision

Schmuck and Miles (1971) proposed some postulates for functioning more precisely within the curriculum arena. Their first postulate noted that schools are comprised of components (people, curricula, instructional strategies, educational environments) organized into various subsystems. These subsystems are linked via communication networks, decision making pathways, allocation of responsibilities, and procedures of program evaluation. Those persons effective in curriculum planning and management realize that the classroom is a micro unit containing these subsystems.

A second postulate advanced by these authors is that schools that function effectively as systems display the characteristics of openness and adaptability. Even schools classified as traditional are in reality changing, adjusting to the myriad demands being made by students, staff, and public members. This change is most evident when comparing schools of today with those of a half century ago. One discovers compelling differences in types of curricula offered, methods of instruction employed, types of materials used, and even organizations of educational space managed.

The third postulate states that all schools, to a greater or lesser degree, function in accordance with some aims and goals. Such aims and goals, generated by curriculum persons in concert with others in the educational theater, are stated so that students will achieve particular outcomes. The aims and goals selected will determine the major thrust of the curriculum, influence the specifics of its development, and affect its implementation, maintenance, and evaluation.

Curriculum management deals with a multitude of persons and material resources within the various subsystems. Those in charge of curriculum management realize the need to orchestrate these resources. Schmuck and Miles call these resources available for use "on demand" the "variety pool." This last postulate notes that resource acquisition and utilization must be done in reference to the aims and goals of the school, the nature of the staff, and the constraints of the physical environment.

Additional Postulates

Goodlad (1975) in speaking of educational change and the need for increased precision advanced several additional postulates for guiding educators in enacting school improvement. First, he argued that the optimal unit for educational change is the single school with its pupils, teachers, and principal. This is the arena where the change occurs or is to occur. At the local school level one monitors and manages the interactions of the participants, the language they employ, the views and traditions they uphold, the values to which they subscribe. All of these factors comprise the culture, the ecosystem, of the school. The curriculum person brings to his tasks a detailed understanding of the local school as a dynamic system, as the prime arena for change and improvement.

Goodlad's second postulate has been alluded to in previous pages: schools change over the years. They change in appearance, in internal organization, in curriculum, in instructional strategies, in basic purpose. It is possible for schools to continue to adjust so as to be more responsive to the needs and demands of the persons the school serves, namely the students and the public citizenry. However, this implies a change-oriented posture, a view of the modernity of humanity rather than the traditionality of humanity.

A third postulate indicates that comprehensive change models related to education need to synthesize something equivalent to the hub of a wheel which holds the entire system together but allows it to advance over time. Goodlad suggests a central process of dialogue, decision-making, action and evaluation as effective in dealing with change at the local school and total school level. This central process needs to be managed by certain educators, and such management most likely would not occur only in the local school building. It may be located in the office of the assistant superintendent of curriculum and instruction. The point that Goodlad makes is that it is critical that some continuing agency be concerned with internal decision making. This concurs with this author's view that some person or persons must coordinate the decision-making processes if precision and consistency of action are to exist within the curriculum arena, if creative change is to be present.

Defining who will be in charge of and involved in curriculum decision-making allows for the identification of diverse participants. Persons with novel ideas are identified within the system and are allowed to present their cases to the decision-makers and perhaps to become involved in the implementation of their ideas. The school organizes to pick up the drum beat of those different drummers within the system.

In considering educational change (e.g., improvement), one contemplates persons' ideas with regard to longevity. Novel ideas with only a short life span may not be worth the effort to incorporate into the curriculum system. In his fifth postulate, Goodlad stresses that dissimilar organizations or program suggestions must appear to have the potential to be lasting, at least for a respectable length of time. This point was referred to earlier, in Savage's twelfth reason why people resist change. Some agency must be there to assure that continued dialogue and interaction result from the "getting together" of different groups. A continued productive tension needs to be preserved. This tension is maintained by individuals responsible for monitoring the total system so as to prevent the school system from dozing and becoming nonresponsive to demands.

Few persons like to change if they feel that such change will place them in the arena alone. Neither do individuals wish to advocate adjustment unless the likelihood of success is real. For his sixth postulate, Goodlad indicates that for change within the school to be significant and likely to differ from the established practices and norms of the local community, the school will require a supportive peer reference group. Persons advocating change will need to have a cadre of colleagues who can assist both in an educational and psychological sense.

Throughout this chapter the concept of interrelated systems or ecosystem has been stressed. If such a system is to function, is to be dynamic, is to be responsive to the needs of persons both within and outside the system, then networks for relaying messages must be developed and maintained. This is Goodlad's seventh postulate.

His last postulate states that for a school to respond to stimulation for change requires of that school new knowledge, new skills, new patterns of behaving. These new roles, demands, and procedures require of educators commitment to being precise regarding activities within the curriculum arena. The curriculum engineering model presented in Part Three allows one to function with increased precision.

Evaluation and Monitoring of Change

Precise curriculum change necessitates ways of monitoring change processes. Schools can be faulted with being overly concerned with doing rather than thinking about and monitoring their actions. Programs have been created without careful thought as to how one would proceed and how one would evaluate the monitoring of the program. Curriculum leaders often fail to recognize the probable effects, both positive and negative, of their curriculum change efforts. Usually, when curriculum persons have considered evaluation, they have focused solely on evaluating the effects of the new curricula on students' learnings, neglecting assessing the change procedures employed in bringing the new curricula to the students. To be sure, evaluating the effects of the curricula on students' learnings is essential, but one must also inquire as to the effectiveness of the ways in which programs are created and maintained. Goodlad mentions that education as a profession and as an enterprise suffers dearly because of the near absence of research and hypothesis testing within the domain of educational change. This deficiency can be eliminated.

Evaluation efforts should be directed at the change processes employed in creating program modification, at the conditions under which it was enacted, and the consequences of change procedures on all affected parties. Such evaluation plans should be designed at the beginning of the innovation effort.

Program development should be stimulated rather than retarded by assessment efforts. Whether this occurs depends in part on the criteria selected to guide such efforts. Hammon (cited in Umans, 1970) presents a list of six criteria useful to curriculum change agents:

Relevance. The information garnered from the evaluation effort must be relevant to the goals of the change effort and the purposes of the schools. It should be relevant to the types of decisions required.

Significance. Usually in change efforts, one is confronted with legions of data. One must determine if the information culled from the data is of value to the project in question.

Scope. One may obtain information that has relevance and significance to the project at hand, but the information may be too lacking in scope to guide the decision-maker. The information only may relate to a very narrow aspect of the change process and not provide foundations for decision-making regarding the total innovation activity. If one is attempting to select among materials those most appropriate to a particular student population, the data gathered must allow each alternative set of materials to be weighed appropriately.

Credibility. Information in which no one places his trust lacks value. How much trust can one ascribe to the information and the person making the judgment? The person who uses evaluative data and makes a decision must be able to attest to the validity of the information. If the evaluator's data are found suspect, this person will find his or her effectiveness in future change efforts severely hampered if not totally ineffectual.

Timeliness. Information presented after a decision is made is useless no matter how good the quality of the information. Despite this truism, one often finds in change situations that because of poor communications and poor scheduling of activities, data are not forthcoming when required, and frequently arrive after the decision has been made. To increase the precision of the change process, it is necessary to map out the likely times that information will be required and the most likely time that such information will actually be produced and transmitted to individuals within the educational system.

Pervasiveness. This last criterion refers to the nature of the audience to receive the evaluation information. All persons involved in making a decision on some aspect of the curricular change require evaluative information so that it is meaningful. If persons are judging possible materials for piloting, then the evaluative data must get to all persons with this charge.[5]

Discussion

The word "change" produces emotional resistance. It is not a neutral word. To many people it is threatening. It conjures up visions of a revolutionary, a dissatisfied idealist, a trouble maker, a malcontent. (Cartwright, 1961, p. 698)

To change a curriculum means, in a way to change an institution. (Taba, 1962, p. 454)

How do we, as curriculum change specialists, react to change? It is crucial for those charged with managing, in the innovative sense, the schools to realize the complexities of change and how all affected individuals respond to innovation. Change is a constant of these modern times. Those charged with being innovation agents need to realize that change involves values, people; it involves societies and various subcultures. In brief, it builds upon the basic assumptions regarding what is effective education and the good life.

To a certain degree, we have had improvement in our school's curricula, but we have not had much change, much innovation. We still have the basic organizers in the secondary schools as those advocated by the Committee of Ten in 1893. The elementary school in large part has a curriculum organized in a manner suggested by the Committee of Fifteen in 1895. The liberal arts emphasis at the university level is still strong. Certainly, the curricula within these basic organizers has improved regarding the nature of the materials, the methods of instruction, and even the depth of content presented. But, schools have not changed to any dramatic degree in their basic conceptions and organizations. Being systematic regarding change will not mean that schools will become unrecognizable spaces for learning with totally different curricula. But being precise and systematic will enable us to understand why we have what we have and to explain the procedures we used to get here.

Much improvement in education has occurred, but one could argue that even greater improvement in the curriculum arena can be attained if

---

[5]From *The management of education* by Shelley Umans. Copyright ©1970 by Shelley Umans. Reprinted by permission of Doubleday & Company, Inc.

we are more knowledgeable of the change process and more precise in enacting change procedures.

The work of curriculum specialists lies in the realm of change—creating, dealing with, retarding, stimulating, and terminating it. No system that remains static survives. All systems must possess a dynamic quality of adjustment even if such adjustment is the reaffirmation of a previously held position or a previously implemented curriculum. Individuals are beginning to look at all aspects of curricular activities through the orientation of change experts. Such an orientation should enable curriculum workers to process planned change, "creative change," rather than to react to "drifts" in the systems' offerings and emphases, "deficit change."

References

Argyris, C. *Personality and organization.* New York: Harper & Row, 1957.

Banathy, B. *Developing a systems view of education.* Belmont, Ca.: Fearon-Pitman Publishers, Inc., 1973.

Bennis, W.G. *Changing organization.* New York: McGraw-Hill, 1966.

Bennis, W.G., Benne, K.D., & Chin, R. (Eds.) *The planning of change.* New York: Holt, Rinehart & Winston, 1961.

Cartwright, D. Achieving a change in people. In W.G. Bennis, K.D. Benne, & R. Chin (Eds.) *The planning of change.* New York: Holt, Rinehart & Winston, 1961.

Duhl, L.J. Planning and predicting. *Daedalus,* Summer 1967, 780.

Gayner, A., & Duvall, L. *The dynamics of educational innovation: Theory and practice.* Paper presented at the American Educational Research Association annual meeting, April 1977.

Getzels, J., Lipham, J.M., & Campbell, R.R. *Educational administration and social process: Theory, research, practice.* New York: Harper & Row, 1968.

Goodlad, J.I. *The dynamics of educational change: toward responsive schools.* New York: McGraw-Hill, 1975. A Charles F. Kettering Foundation Program.

Guba, E. *The basis for educational improvement.* Bloomingdale, Ind.: The National Institute for the Study of Educational Change, 1967.

Havelock, R.G. *Guide to innovation in education.* Ann Arbor: University of Michigan, 1970.

Homans, G.C. *The human group.* New York: Harcourt, Brace & World, 1950.

Jenkins, D. Force field analysis applied to a school situation. In W.G. Bennis, K.D. Benne, & R. Chin (Eds.) *The planning of change.* New York: Holt, Rinehart & Winston, 1961.

Katz, E., Levin, M.L., & Hamilton, H. Traditions of research on the diffusion of innovation. *American Sociological Review,* April 1963, *27,* 240.

McKelvey, W.W. *Expectational noncomplementarity and deviant adaptation in a research organization.* Unpublished doctoral dissertation, Massachusetts Institute of Technology, 1967.

McNeil, J.D. *Curriculum, a comprehensive introduction.* Boston: Little, Brown & Co., 1977.

Meadows, P. *The many faces of change: Explorations in the theory of social change.* Cambridge, Mass.: Schenkman, 1971.

Miles, M. Some properties of schools as social systems. In G. Watson (Ed.), *Change in school systems.* Washington: National Education Association, 1967. (National Training Laboratory Cooperative Project for Educational Development.)

Morphet, E.L., Jesser, D.L. & Ludka, A.P. *Planning and providing for excellence in education.* New York: Citation Press, 1972.

Rogers, E.M., & Shoemaker, F.F. *Communication of innovation: A cross-cultural approach.* New York: Free Press, 1971.

Sarason, S.B. *The culture of the school and the problem of change.* Boston: Allyn & Bacon, 1971.

Savage, W.W. *Interpersonal and group relations in educational administration.* Greenville, Ill.: Scott, Foresman & Co., 1968.

Schmuck, R.S., & Miles, M.C. (Eds.) *Organization development in schools.* Palo Alto, Calif.: National Press Books, 1971.

Taba, H. *Curriculum development, theory and practice.* New York: Harcourt, Brace & World, 1962.

Umans, S. *The management of education.* New York: Doubleday & Co., 1970.

Watson, G. (Ed.) *Change in school systems.* Washington: National Education Association, 1967. (Published for the Cooperative Project for Educational Development by the National Training Laboratory.)

Williams, R.C., Wall, C.C., Martin, W.M. & Berchin, A. *Effective organizational renewal in schools: a social systems perspective.* New York: McGraw-Hill, 1974.

PART TWO

Sources of Curriculum, Participants in Curriculum Activity

chapter  3

Sources and Forces Affecting Curriculum

KNOWLEDGE

Principal Task of the School

Although educators disagree as to the prime task of the school, most concur that one of the school's foremost tasks is transmitting to each generation the heritage of the human race and providing students with knowledge that will equip them to function effectively in the present and in the future. This task exists at all levels of education, from preschool through postgraduate school.

To perform this function, the school must deal with all types of knowledge. Most educators and educational philosophers agree in general, but disagreement evidences itself when they try to delineate the kinds of knowledge for actual inclusion in the curriculum. In dealing with the issue of knowledge (the cornerstone of the curriculum), two epistemological questions need to be considered. The first concerns the authenticity of the information being organized into knowledge divisions. The second question concerns how consumers of this knowledge come to know these things. Answers to these questions enable curriculum designers to create more effective curricula for students. Curriculum persons need not become philosophers, but they must understand the knowledge realm, as well as the social and political scenes, in order to select and organize curriculum content.

Selection and organization of content are two functions central to curriculum development. Throughout the history of education, individuals have had to designate what to include and, more importantly perhaps, what to exclude from the curriculum. As Doll (1978) points out, schools have always taught subject matter. Subject matter has been the focus of the schools. Most subject matter, even today, is drawn from bodies of organized knowledge, often the disciplines. When educators realize that the source of knowledge is the totality of available, teachable cultural knowledge, they quickly appreciate the magnitude of their curricular tasks. How does one choose from the total world store of knowledge, especially at a time of exploding knowledge production?

Nature of Knowledge

Presently, educators are arguing as to whether the curriculum is drawn from three sources (knowledge, society, and the nature of the learner) or from one prime source (knowledge). This author takes the position that knowledge is the primary *source* of the curriculum and that society and the nature of the learner are really factors or forces that influence the inclusion, organization, emphasis, type and duration of knowledge in the curriculum. This does not mean that only disciplined knowledge is the source of the curriculum. We need to consider knowledge in its broadest possible sense. But, taking a broad view of knowledge requires that we have means of categorizing it.

Taba (1962) described knowledge used in the schools as existing on four levels. The lowest level contains the facts and processes, the next level includes the basic ideas and principles, the third level contains basic concepts, and the final and fourth level incorporates representative thought systems which control the flow of ideas and procedures of inquiry.

Spencer (1885) confronted the question of knowledge selection and organization when he phrased the question, "What knowledge is of most worth?" He identified five kinds of human endeavor as necessary for all to understand: self-preservation, earning a living, bearing and rearing children, participating in social and political life, and enjoying the refinements of culture. The soundness of these categories has been proven several times by groups in this century. In 1918, The Commission on the Reorganization of Secondary Education stressed in its report seven principal objectives or "Cardinal Principles" similar to Spencer's list: (a) health, (b) command of fundamental processes (reading, writing, arithmetic, and oral and written expression), (c) worthy home membership, (d) vocation, (e) citizenship, (f) worthy use of leisure time, and (g) ethical character. More recently, Stratemeyer, Forkner, McKim and Passow (1957) suggested organizing a curriculum centering on persistent life situations: managing money; being accepted in a group; using tools, machines, and equipment; working with different racial and religious groups; using safety measures; and dealing with success and failure.

Dealing with the question as to what knowledge is of most worth requires one to process the prior question of what knowledge is available for selection.

Organization of Knowledge

Processing the question of what knowledge is actually available requires that we curriculum specialists know the present ordering of knowledge, the architectonics of knowledge. Phenix (1964) has noted:

> An architectonic is important for the educator because it provides a scheme for considering in orderly fashion the entire range of what can be known. By having a systematic view of the kinds of knowledge that can be acquired, he gains an essential resource for making intelligent decisions about the content of instruction. He can more easily evaluate existing or proposed curricula with respect to omissions and balance. In the architectonic categories he can also find suggestions concerning the organization of instruction and concerning possible productive relationships between studies in different categories. (p. 44)

Knowledge is complex; it is complex because the range of everyday knowing is vast touching on things, places, persons, and subjects. It deals with information resulting from carefully organized bodies of knowledge and from data gathered by informal and by incidental means. It deals with matters of fact that can be easily seen and matters we can classify as faith, that can only be supported by complex rational procedures.

But the vastness of knowledge is not the only challenge confronting us. We have to realize that knowledge is closely associated with the ways of understanding and controlling nature. The questions raised in the pursuit of knowledge greatly influence the direction of one's inquiry and the resulting conclusions. Knowledge is associated with ideas of contemplation, absorption, and appreciation, and we curricularists need to select knowledge mindful of these ideas. Knowledge is more than descriptive bodies of lore, or great listings of facts. Knowledge in its organizations evidences peoples' standards, ideals, and tastes. Knowledge organizations reveal what people know, and also present a description of them to the world.

We can organize knowledge as to its source. Presently, knowledge is distinguished as being either disciplined knowledge (generated or verified by systematic, precise, and recognizable procedures) or knowledge generated in the common, everyday occurrences (produced as a byproduct, rather than from efforts deliberately intended to produce knowledge).

Disciplined Knowledge

Disciplined knowledge is that produced via deliberate efforts of qualified persons for the purpose of advancing humanity's understanding of particular kinds of phenomena. It is organized to render our experiences intelligible. But, Phenix indicates that knowledge produced and classified in such ways does not mean that the classifications are necessarily inherent in nature. Knowledge divisions, whether formal or informal, represent personal and accepted inventions for making meaning out of reality.

King and Brownell (1966) have identified the disciplines as communities of discourse with ten isomorphic features: (a) a community of persons, (b) an expression of human imagination, (c) a domain, (d) a tradition, (e) a syntactical structure (mode of inquiry), (f) a conceptual structure (substantive structure), (g) a specialized language (h) a heritage of literature and artifacts and a network of communications, (i) a valuative and affective stance, and (j) an instruction community.

Schwab (1964) has discussed the disciplines as to their overall structure or organization, their substantive structure, and their syntactical structure. Their overall structure relates to the question of what knowledge will be included in the family of disciplines. Is chemistry different from biology? Is anthopology different from sociology? Is group behavior different from individual behavior such that we can justify sociology and psychology?

Hirst (1971) deals with this question of inclusion, Schwab's concern for the disciplines' overall organization, by pointing up the need to distinguish three quite different knowledge organizations: forms, fields, and practical theories. The first organization refers to those groups of knowledge that can be distinguished from each other in three interrelated ways. First, forms of knowledge possess distinct domains with unique types of concepts in specialized relationships. For instance, he notes that mathematics has the unique concepts of number, integral, matrix. Chemistry has the unique concepts of hydrogen, atom, magnetic field. Economics has the concepts of scarcity, and market goods. Second, the concepts are organized into specialized networks whose relationships influence the particular types of meanings that can be derived from the form. Marketplace has meaning only if one adheres to particular rules and principles of economics. Third, knowledge can be distinguished by the different types of tests utilized in determining truth or validity of propositions. For example, in science, the tests of observation and experiment are the only valid ones. In religion, rules of reason and statements of dogma are the appropriate tests of validity. Hirst also indicates that forms of knowledge can be further distinguished by their content. Hirst's forms of knowledge are what Schwab and others are naming disciplines.

Hirst's second knowledge division is field of knowledge. Fields represent knowledge organized not according to unique content, conceptual clusters, methodologies, or tests of truth, but rather knowledge systemized around some kind of objective, phenomena, abstract entity or interest. Frequently, school curricula have such an organization. Courses dealing with Social Issues in America, Environmental Studies, Power in the Modern World are all examples of fields. It is evident that a field is a collection of knowledge from various forms which possesses unity simply because of its focus. A field dealing with environmental issues can draw information and methodology from the forms of sociology, anthropology, history, political science, psychology, biology and chemistry. The "glue" which holds the field together in this case is the relevance of the form knowledge to the topic, environmental issues. There is no logic other than this to keep the field together. No unique concepts exist; neither are there any unique means for testing the validity of resulting conclusions.

Practical theories is Hirst's third organization for knowledge. This organization derives its logic from its purposes. Practical theories' raison d'etre is their practical function. People use knowledge organized in this way not to expand the level of understanding, but to apply known information to particular aspects of reality. According to Hirst, education as an area of study qualifies as a practical theory. Education is not concerned with advancing specific knowledge, but rather with using knowledge gained and organized, to determine what should be done in creating viable educational opportunities for students. The clasification is debatable, but Hirst would argue that if one is concerned with advancing the knowledge realm of how individuals learn, one is in the form (the discipline) of psychology and not education. If one strives to advance one's understanding of how people react in curriculum decision-making, one is in the form of psychology and perhaps sociology. Curriculum, following Hirst's logic, also qualifies as a practical theory, a theory concerned with applying knowledge from fields and forms to particular issues and situations pertinent to the realm of curriculum. Rather than striving for complete agreement on whether practical theories are indeed practical theories, curiculum workers need to realize that such conceptualizations of knowledge can exist and such conceptions need to be spelled out.

Schwab's second structure focus is the substantive structure of disciplined knowledge. This structure addresses the inherent nature of the data and conceptions that identify the powers and limits of a particular field of inquiry. Comprising the substantive structure are those crucial concepts and general statements unique to the particular field in question. Knowing the substantive structure of the discipline allows the curricularist to identify the key concepts and concept clusters essential for inclusion in the knowledge organization if the selected knowledge is to accurately represent a particular discipline. Additionally, knowing this structure facilitates the sequencing of particular content clusters in the curriculum. For instance, a curriculum specialist wishing to introduce students to the concept of market specialization in an economics curriculum must have students first encounter the concept of market and initially the central concept of scarcity. Likewise, students cannot grasp the concept of surface tension of liquids in a physics class, unless introduced to the concepts of solution, atoms, molecule, attraction and energy. However, the sequencing of concepts is not as straight forward as mentioned for individuals do not always process information in such "1-2-3" fashion.

In addition to substantive structure, Schwab deals with syntactical structure: "concrete description of the kinds of evidence required by the discipline, how far the kinds of data required are actually obtainable, what sorts of second best substitutes may be employed, what problems of interpretation are posed, and how these problems are overcome" (p. 28). Syntax deals with method, but it deals with more than just procedure. It refers to the problem of determining for each discipline criteria required to determine the appropriateness of the methods employed and the validity and usability of the data obtained. Important to remember is that the syntactical structure provides process models that can be melded with the substantive structures of the disciplines. Much of the concern for process education (inquiry emphases) gained its support from individuals advocating that students comprehend this particular structure. Being cognizant of both structures allows one to intergrate the content and process concerns of education.

Others have spoken of the structure of the disciplines. Phenix (1964) noted that the discipline is knowledge organized for learning. "Disciplines prove themselves by their productiveness. They are the visible evidence of ways of thinking that have proven fruitful. They have arisen by the use of concepts and methods that have generated power" (p. 48).

Broudy's (1961) views regarding the disciplines parallel in part those of Schwab and Hirst. He identified four aspects of a discipline to which curriculum types should attend: (a) the terminology or concepts unique to the discipline, (b) the entire network of data, facts, rules and generalizations and theories developed during the history of the discipline, (c) the method of investigation unique to the discipline, and (d) the rules for evaluating evidence. Points (c) and (d) refer to what Schwab terms syntactical structure, while points (a) and (b) refer to the substantive structure.

Bruner (1963) was another strong advocate of structure. But he was quick to point out, as did Phenix, that the knowledge we identify and create cannot be conceived of in terms of absolute truth:

> Knowledge is a model we construct to give meaning and structure to regularities in experience. The organizing ideas of any body of knowledge are inventions for referring experiences economical and connected. We invent concepts such as force in physics, the bond in chemistry, motive in psychology, style in literature as a means to the end of comprehension. (p. 120)

Bruner (1960) spoke of the benefits of students understanding structure. The message is still important for us to remember. He suggested that knowledge of structure would foster more effectively student learning, would aid student retention, would promote transfer, would increase motivation, and would reduce the gap between instructors and scholars. Awareness of structure could strengthen the bonds of scholarship, the community of discourse if you will, between producers of knowledge and educators.

Not only are there arguments as to whether some knowledge organization should be included in the discipline camp, there are disputes within the camp as to what is the appropriate focus of a particular discipline. Several disciplines process the same phenomena but with different points of view, and frequently with different investigative techniques. Human behavior is the focus of anthropology, sociology, and psychology. However, each generates different questions, resulting in different conclusions. The issue of boundaries between disciplines is likely to increase due to the generation of more hybrid divisions in the realm of knowledge. For example, we have nuclear and solid state physics; biochemistry and molecular biology, political sociology and political science. All have much overlap in both the substantive and syntactical structures. Figure 3.1, adapted from Johnson, presents this overlapping of knowledge domains.

Nondisciplined Knowledge

Nondisciplined knowledge is of several types. Curriculum developers should not think that knowledge in this realm is less useful or of lower status than disci-

FIGURE 3.1   *Three-fold paradigm of disciplined knowledge includes some ambiguities*[1]

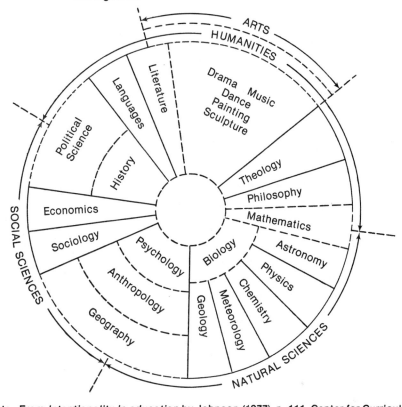

Note. From *Intentionality in education* by Johnson (1977), p. 111. Center for Curriculum Research and Services. Reprinted by permission.

plined knowledge. Recalling Hirst's comments, earlier in the chapter, nondisciplined knowledge has a different focus, a different purpose; it raises and processes different questions and uses other tests to check the validity of its assumptions and its conclusions. Nondisciplined knowledge can be organized as a field of knowledge, drawing content from disciplines or forms in order to allow students to study and understand a particular focus such as Latin American Democracy. There are those such as Martin (1970) who argue that if curriculum content is not to be the disciplines themselves organized for student learning, at least the content supporting the course topics ought to be drawn from disciplined knowledge. Hirst's fields of knowledge would follow Martin's principle; called the SM (subject matter) principle.

But there exist other sources of nondisciplined knowledge. Johnson (1977) has noted that we can draw curriculum content from knowledge

[1]See Phenix (1964) for another way of organizing knowledge. This source shows that various disciplines can be included under different program organizers depending upon the purpose and focus of the knowledge.

associated with various occupational enterprises. This is somewhat similar to the practical theories (e.g., education, medicine, law) identified by Hirst. Here curriculum specialists can draw knowledge from those structured activities that occupy members of various specialities within the society.

Such information is dynamic, for the knowledge explosion is occurring not only within disciplined fields, but also within those realms of work associated with professions and occupations. At certain levels of schooling, knowledge drawn from the field of work will be the primary source of curriculum content. Students in the secondary schools often will experience content drawn from various occupational lore and practice. Students wishing to gain experiences in the electrical trades may experience content delineated from a task analysis of what electricians do.

Activity 3–1   *Conceptualizing a Discipline*

From your previous reading, you should now understand that a discipline has a specialized content and methodology. Additionally, it has a history that records its development and a community of individuals or scholars who have a professional allegiance to it. Select a discipline that interests you and discuss it with a scholar in that discipline regarding the nature of the discipline, the major questions the discipline addresses, and the means by which the questions are proposed.

Select a book dealing with this particular discipline and note your perceptions and understandings melding information gained from the book with information obtained from the discussion with the scholar.

Usually, the knowledge gained from nondisciplined knowledge has more direct and immediate applicability. It is usually more specialized, often being directed at a particular job classification. The student studying to be an electrician is not likely to focus on change theory and its applicability to life in general. If such a student does have understanding and applies it, he or she most likely gained it from those more general aspects of the school's curriculum. The student of nursing who learns survival nursing is specialized. Disciplined knowledge, which seems in the public schools to be foundational, allows students to prepare for evolving futures. History or psychology can contribute to many enterprises. Nondisciplined knowledge (e.g., urban planning or metal working) centers on preparing individuals for assuming known tasks in a defined future.

As Hirst (1971) and Johnson (1977) point out, disciplined knowledge exists independent of its application. Its truth or validity is not dependent upon its use. However, the field of knowledge has content apart from the discipline. The field's content is centered on that segment of a particular enterprise in which knowledge application occurs. For instance, in wood working, there is content unique to the job of wood working. This content is not part of the discipline of biology covering the properties of wood, or of physics, covering the explanation of simple and complex machines. However, the validity of the principles applied to wood working is determined by the validity of the principles drawn from disciplined knowledge. But, the principles are not the focus of study in woodworking.

In addition to the knowledge explosion, this century has witnessed an explosion of occupations. *The Dictionary of Occupation Titles (DOT)* has listed over 30,000 jobs classified into eight major divisions: (a) professional, technical, and managerial, (b) clerical and sales, (c) service, (d) farming, fishery, forestry, and related, (e) processing, (f) machine trades, (g) bench work, and (h) structural work. These job divisions can serve as organizers for particular curricula. But the curriculum person's problem is compounded by the rapidity in which new jobs are being created and existing ones altered or eliminated.

A final source of knowledge still exists: everyday, informal experience. This is knowledge produced not to advance a realm of knowledge or to prepare for a specific job, but rather knowledge gained in incidental and sometimes deliberate fashion solely for the purpose of functioning generally in society. With concern for the total individual, curriculum persons need to determine the major activities of individuals and requisite knowledge for functioning optimally in such activities. Oftentimes, people in their leisure time activities gain particular knowledge that can be classified as cognitive, affective, and psychomotor. If educators wish individuals to participate effectively in leisure time activities, or at least to have the option to participate, then the knowledge components need to be identified and perhaps structured in the curriculum.

Questions Regarding Knowledge

The curriculum person must keep five questions in mind when confronting the realm of knowledge. Initially, the question What is knowledge? must be phrased. Then, in succession, one needs to phrase these questions: What knowledge is more reliable or important? How does knowledge arise? What procedure/s should be used to search for knowledge? How should the knowledge be taught to students? (Scheffler, 1970). This final question relates not only to the teaching (instruction) of the content but to the selecting and arranging of it (curriculum) so that students can learn it in an optimal manner.

Knowledge, the prime source of curriculum content, is in a state of dynamism, a state of flux. It is currently doubling every eight years or so. People are confronted with how to process this knowledge expansion. Additionally, people are confronted with determining what current knowledge is being negated by new knowledge. Curricularists will have to be quite competent in their understanding of knowledge in order to assure students responsive curricula.

Activity 3–2   *Identifying Key Questions Regarding Knowledge*

The questions we formulate influence greatly the conclusions we develop and the directions we take for further study.

Identify five questions regarding knowledge that you consider must be processed by the person involved in curriculum. Then process the questions either alone or with a colleague.

Indicate what conclusions you can make, what guidelines you can develop that will assist you in future dealings with the knowledge realm.

SOCIETY

Debate continues whether society is one of the sources of the curriculum or a force exerting controlling influences on the curriculum. This author takes the position that society is primarily a *force* acting as a filter on the decision-making regarding what will be included and excluded from the curriculum. However, it is realized that when one has society as the focus of curriculum study, the society then serves as a source of the curriculum. But, regardless of how one classifies society, there is no doubting that it has major consequences upon the school's curriculum, both immediate and remote. Societal demands can result in legislation changing current curricular offerings, or in initiating activities that will enact program modification at some distant time.

Ways of Influencing the Curriculum

Tradition

Doll (1978) notes that society and culture at large can influence the curriculum of the school in three major ways: by inhibiting change via the power of tradition, by speeding change as a result of some particular cultural change, and by applying pressures that originate in major segments of American society. Tradition, according to Doll, can be viewed as a retardant. This is not always bad, for it may discourage efforts to discard that which has been proven valuable in the society. Not all change is beneficial, and not all that is maintained is deleterious. There are numerous traditions in American society worthy of retention, and this tendency of tradition to slow the rate of change can serve to our advantage in requiring us to think most carefully about those aspects of society we contemplate changing.

Society has developed mechanisms for monitoring change. The legal structure established in society creates a most effective way of assuring that tradition is maintained. Sometimes the legalities are too imbedded and do prevent needed adjustment from occurring. However, the legal authority can also speed up change as it evidenced by the legislation in the seventies which dealt with civil rights, women's rights and ethnic rights.

Societies are collections of individuals who have organized themselves into groups, and thus societies are influenced by psychological factors. Human beings respond to ideas and to trends in society in somewhat predictable ways. Most persons react to change with some resistance, but with time and effort most can be educated to accept certain changes. Still, some persons will totally resist variation because of their personalities. We in curriculum need to understand human nature and the principles of social action within the overall society. There are some matters in society in which adjustment is most difficult. Morality and religion are areas where people change very slowly if at all. Often times, attempted modification in sex education falls upon difficulties because people tend to view this area as within the domain of morality and total family responsibility.

Tradition has assisted schools, for good or bad, in continuing certain recognizable patterns. Today most schools:

1. have objectives that primarily stress the cognitive dimension of learning
2. have elementary pupils organized in self-contained classrooms and secondary students organized by homeroom and special subjects
3. have the education experience organized in a series of grades
4. emphasize a classical traditional organization of content, with emphasis on the humanities at the secondary level
5. allow students increasing choice of subject matter with advancement through the school system
6. evaluate primarily in terms of achievement, observable phenomena
7. have established neighborhood schools at the elementary level
8. have students compelled by law to attend 12 to 13 years
9. have students attending schools for 5–6 hours per day and 9 months of the year

Societal Flux

Despite the weight of tradition, society is not static. In contemplating the American way of life one hundred years ago with today, we readily see significant changes with regard to individuals' views and their behaviors and understandings. Change extant in society introduces instability which can be tolerated to varying degrees depending upon the total social climate. Currently, many individuals are urging increased diversity within our nation. Perhaps today, American society is changing at a rate more rapid than before. Science and technology are continuing to advance, thus influencing the ways in which individuals perceive their world, both immediate and distant (Doll, 1978).

Attentive curriculum persons understand that society is dynamic and that curricula responsive to one time and people may indeed require major adjustment or actual discardment to meet the demands of another time and different people. Leaders in the curriculum field realize that a society is more than a collection of individuals at a particular time. Individuals become a society when they perceive themselves as "having things in common" which provide them with a realization of membership. These common things comprise the behavior patterns, belief system, artifacts, and other human made components, that furnish the group with an identifiable cohesiveness. It includes peoples' foods, their tools, their clothing, their religion, and their language. Culture is the observable composite of individuals' survival efforts.

Culture is complex. It is in a constant state of flux and its changes, adjustments, frequently bring pressures upon the curriculum. Unruh (1975) notes that, "If planners draw upon more of the total culture, the curriculum development process will respond to the needs and concerns of the persons served by the school" (p. 143).

She points out that the scope of available culture is almost limitless. "It involves societal conditions, knowledge from academic disciplines, professional knowledge about learning and educative processes, philosophical and value bases, futures research, realities in the classroom, pluralistic ethnic backgrounds, and their needs and desires (p. 144). Zais (1976) cautions that we need to consider not only the visible aspects of culture, the language, the artifacts, the rituals, the knowledge produced, but also the psychological aspects of a society, "the interlocking fabric of ideas, ideals, beliefs, values, and assumptions, modes of thought to which individuals in social groups adhere" (p. 157).

In observing today's American society, we can see stereotypes, but we also can observe numerous facts, situations, and organizations all having relevance for the school's curriculum. Today's cultural reality is an age of:

1. the shrinking world brought on by steadily improving transportation and communication
2. bigness, of conglomerates in business and in agriculture, an age of multinational corporation growth
3. rapid population growth in many parts of the world
4. changing family patterns, of serial marriages, or changing family values
5. increased mobility among and between social class groupings
6. increasing control of cultural functions by big government
7. large numbers of youth in stages of "future shock"
8. increasing ethnic identity
9. increasing nationalism, increasing tribalism, and the emergence of mini nation-states
10. increasing concern for human rights
11. slowly increasing world democracy
12. increasing lay participation in educational decision-making

These current societal changes are influencing the curriculum. The shrinking world is causing educators to consider new world cultures for inclusion in the curriculum. The rise in ethnic identity has resulted in legislation addressing the issues of ethnic groups, women's rights, and an unbiased treatment of American culture. The changing American family has resulted in many schools assuming responsibilities once reserved for families.

Increased lay participation has caused educators to assume different postures regarding community involvement. American society has shifted from political and social passivity to intensity of involvement on myriad issues. Paralleling this shift to active involvement are shifts from conservative to liberal and back again. Despite this increased involvement, some individuals feel that citizen input has had little meaning. There exists a feeling that people are becoming lost in the largeness of government, of schools, of industry. There is a feeling overtaking segments of society that the American society is dehumanizing its members. However, these feelings are to be expected in a dynamic society.

At a time when groups are demanding increasing acknowledgement of their diversity, their separateness, their uniqueness, there is a greater mobility among cultural groups within the country necessitating recognition of our commonness. Some 25% of the American population is constantly moving from one location to another. This mobility has changed the character of the schools. Schools of various regions no longer just serve needs derived from local concerns. The vast migration of northerners to the Southeast section of the country in response to industry's move has altered the character of the southern population. Vast shifts of population from the eastern and midwestern regions of the nation to the West coast has brought about a mixing of views and culture traits.

While this mixing has added to the challenge and excitement of the actions of the curriculum developer, it also has heightened his or her frustrations in attempting to meet legions of demands from diverse groups. Schools can no longer, if they ever could, just serve a monoculture. Cultural democracy is in, and this demand is likely to become an increasing force in determining what is added to and subtracted from the curriculum as well as the organization of the content. Cultural democracy assumes that total assimilation of citizens as a goal for the curriculum is out, being replaced with one of partial assimilation and improved communication between and among cultures.

Responding to Pressures

The responsive school is an open system processing and adjusting to societal pressures. Those individuals believing society to be one source of the curriculum, look to society for those objectives requiring attention. Tyler, over 30 years ago (1949), indicated that the school must employ some system for analyzing and selecting from society those learning objectives deemed appropriate for students to learn. He acknowledged that society was a source of the curriculum, but he neglected to note that society also acted as a powerful filter regarding what objectives would be treated and their manner of treatment. Society does influence what objectives are treated, but it also determines to a significant degree who will be educated and who will not.

To which societal pressures should one respond? Thelen (1970) emphasized that those in curriculum must listen to the totality of the culture. Advocating the development of humane individuals, Thelen indicated that the school must allow students to develop "a strong feeling for the human quest, the universal questions that all generations of man must tussle with, the human potential for good and evil inherent in human nature, the problem of availability of rights and distribution of advantages." For Thelen, "all aspects of life should be available for examination, and the aspects most salient at any particular time should be faced" (pp. 27–32). Thus, total society serves as a source, and society in its totality exerts differing pressures upon the school's curricula.

We require procedures for dealing with the societal pressures that influence the functioning of the school. Dealing "with all aspects" of life certainly compels us to not only react to demands, but to "proact," anticipate demands and set up means of processing them prior to their occurrence.

To what pressures should we as curriculum developers respond? The pressures put upon the school vary with the times. Each age has different requests, and therefore the lessons of a previous time may be inappropriate for guiding the development of a curriculum responsive to current times. In the last century, Herbert Spencer (1860) indicated that the classic studies were basically inappropriate for the times, ineffectual in disciplining the minds of students. For this task, science should be incorporated into the curriculum.

In the 1930s, the Progressives urged the schools to adopt the notion of the community school. Such a school's curriculum would address the comprehensive educational needs of the total community. The idea of such a school has persisted into recent times, although the purposes for such a community school have been adjusted. In the 1960s and 1970s community schools were demanded by many pressure groups seeking control of schools. These groups were frequently militant, sought control over the school and its functions: determining curriculum, staffing, and policy. "Give the schools back to the people" was commonly heard. Such demands are still heard.

Today, many pressure groups are faulting educators for their slowness in promoting certain reforms. Ethnic groups are chastizing educators for not incorporating into the curriculum appropriate studies of various cultural groups. Women's advocates are criticizing schools for "dragging their feet" in assuring a nonsexist curriculum supported by nonsexist materials.

Curriculum persons have to respond to these demands. Groups are urging that schools teach the basics, teach or stay away from morality, teach political values requisite to our way of life, provide educational experiences essential for securing meaningful employment, introduce students to those truths necessary for understanding and correcting the ills of the nation and the world.

The demands, although diverse and in some measure not possible to process completely, reveal the diversity of the current American social fabric. American viewpoints are changing: some are shifting from liberal to conservative orientations, others are moving just the opposite. The equivocating of people regarding their views and the resulting inconsistency of positions held are caused to some extent by the complexity of the times and the rapidity of change. People are analyzing and adjusting their views, their values regarding school, government, home, church, and world within a short time frame. Many people are finding it difficult coping; they are indeed suffering from "culture shock."

Some curriculum educators have thrown up their hands in trying to respond to demands. Others have put too much credence into critics' messages. To be sure, the schools have difficulties; the schools must react and proact to the social scene. But a large segment of the population is supportive of the public schools. However, even if 100% of the people were pleased with the schools, (this is really not possible) curriculum persons would need to keep "an ear to the ground" so that the school would adjust to changes occurring and would anticipate and plan for probable social demands.

Trends Influencing Curriculum

In the previous pages, reference was made to various events. Some of these events have been occurring for an extended period of time and can be identified as trends:

1. the explosion of curriculum offerings (ethnic studies, women's studies, photography, computer science)

2. the removing of subject divisions for boys and girls (woodworking for girls, homemaking for boys)
3. the increased involvement of lay persons in curriculum activity (advising, critiquing programs)
4. the use of more community persons in assisting in teaching (use of paraprofessionals)
5. the demands and appropriate legislation for affording all children the "least restrictive environment" in school (this will place many children formerly in special educational classes in the regular classroom)
6. the concern for involving parents in the education of their children (having parents become members of the teaching team and work with children at home on a formal basis prescribed by teachers, parents, and curriculum personnel)
7. the introduction of new types of educational facilities and materials (the use of computers, calculators, new media)
8. the increasing demand for precision in curriculum planning and implementation (represented by much legislation dealing with behavioral objectives production and educational evaluation)
9. the growth of formal testing and national assessment
10. the rising demand for accountability of school personnel regarding the quantity and quality of their functioning
11. the establishment of alternative schools or alternatives within the regular school system. Many districts are creating within the system fundamental schools for parents who wish their children to have a traditional curricular experience. The use of educational vouchers has been suggested as a vehicle for allowing parents to take advantage of various educational options offered by schools. In 1977, Seattle experimented with the "magnet program" which was to offer diverse curricular options to students. Those who wished a program emphasizing the arts could attend one school while students wishing a program stressing science could attend another.
12. the steady efforts to desegregate the nation's schools, primarily via busing
13. the increasing incorporation of values into the educational effort
14. the coordination of educational experience with agencies outside the school (The Schools Without Walls experiment of the Parkway School in Philadelphia is an example.)
15. the increasing power of the labor movement on education (This will have an impact on how curriculum is determined, implemented and evaluated.)
16. the continuing debate between humanists and behaviorists on how to approach schooling
17. the continuing emphasis on process education
18. the increasing awareness of the future as a phenomenon for study and management

Effective communication channels are mandatory for processing these trends.

Linton (cited in Zais, 1976) divided culture into three principal categories: (a) universals, (b) specialties, and (c) alternatives (p. 158). *Universals,* as defined by Linton, are those values, beliefs, and mores generally held by most of the population. The language, goods, religions, and economics of a group qualify as universals. These universals become embedded in the myriad demands currently evidencing themselves. The demand that schools be accountable is tied to some of these universal values. The demand for the "least restrictive environment" for children's learning is related to the universals that citizens hold regarding the rights of individuals within this nation. The elimination of "girls" and "boys" subjects and sex role stereotyping is renewed testimony to the universal of optimum development of all individuals. The increasing growth of (a) the labor movement in education and (b) citizen involvement in decision-making are expressions of beliefs we value regarding our government and principles of individual freedom. By observing our universals, we can describe our nation's basic character. We are Americans, and we can be described in general terms such that we distinguish ourselves from Englishmen, Germans, Nigerians, or any other national group.

Specialties—the second Linton category discussed by Zais—refer to those aspects of culture found only within particular subgroups. In some cases, the values, beliefs, language, customs of our major ethnic or racial groups are specialties. The Spanish-American group form a subcultural group that has elements unique to them. They speak Spanish and usually are of the Catholic faith. Within the dominant culture, specialties also exist but usually refer to vocational subgroups. Educators, doctors, and farm laborers all have different, specific work behaviors. Also they may have different values and specialized languages. These groups may also have expectations as to what is successful and productive behavior for their membership. Specialties can be used to analyze and understand the various social groups within our overall society. What values, customs are used by the groups from which students come?

Lundberg has argued that the American school is a middle class organization influenced by basically middle class values. Prizing the rights of others, valuing formal education, appreciating the arts are primarily values held by the middle and upper classes. Concern for self-protection, anti-intellectualism, preference for practical use of information are values and dispositions by members of the working class. In attempting to respond to demands of working class citizens, the curriculum person has some difficulty for many of these people, according to Lundberg, do not regard highly formal schooling. Many of these people will ask that the schools provide more apprenticeship types of training, more "on the job" training and less of the "classroom intellectual stuff."

"The school must provide alternatives" is often heard in general community dialogue. *Alternatives*—Linton's final category—is the third way in which one can organize culture. Alternatives refers to those beliefs and practices that deviate from the cultural mainstream, that deviate from the universals and specialities. The reasons for such aberrations originate in individuals' attempts to fill needs, solve difficulties, or deal more effectively with some aspects of reality (Zais). Communal living, open marriages, vegetarianism, conducting store-front schools all exemplify alternatives. Illich's (1972) suggestion for de-schooling society fits within this category. With alternatives there may be no one recognizable subgroup that adheres to the alternative. Usually, alternatives are held or suggested by individuals, and these individuals may be members of any culture group.

Activity 3–3   *Trend Check*

Numerous pressures and recognizable trends exist today all affecting or having the potential to affect the school's curricula. Of the trends indicated in the previous pages, note the ones which seem to be the most prominent in your community.

After noting these trends, list and describe the actions that are being undertaken to deal with these trends. What role or roles are you playing in responding to the trends?

Identify reasons that some trends and pressures are not being considered in your school or institution.

The Locus of Curriculum Control

Trends may be national or regional, but the response must finally be local. Curriculum urged at the national level, or created at the regional level in an educational laboratory, is implemented only at the level of the local individual community. Goodlad (1975) advances this point: "The one place . . . where aims, goals, functions, and regularities become one is the individual school. Consequently, the place to begin reform in all of these is the individual school" (p. 22).

Doll (1978) indicates that American communities influence the schools in three basic ways: "through the community's own needs, through the limits communities set on the curriculum of the school, and through the community's decision as to who shall receive education" (p. 91). Communities determine what will be included and, perhaps more importantly, what will be deleted from the curriculum. In numerous communities various subjects and specific curriculum experiences have been eliminated by boards of education in response to local community pressures. In other instances, the opposite is true with pressure groups demanding the inclusion of particular subjects such as women's studies and certain materials that show accurately the contributions of certain ethnic groups.

Most communities possess a most powerful lever to influence the school's curriculum—money. Many communities have voted "no" on operation levies, causing the curtailment of curricular offerings. Numerous districts have refused to fund nursery schools and kindergartens, thus denying certain children these experiences.

A time may come when the local community, both professional and lay, will not hold the major power in curriculum decision-making. Presently, a growing trend exists to have broad educational objectives determined more and more at state levels and even regional levels. Certain national legislation may influence the objectives in local school districts. National assessment already is having an influence on the objectives being addressed by local schools. Recent rulings by the courts as to the unconstitutionality of the local property tax to support public education will perhaps hasten the time when support for all schools will come from state or regional organizations. A centralizing of educational financial support may take the locus of curricular decision-making from the community to state or regional agencies. The shifting of many educational responsibilities from local to regional and to national control may foster the move to more distant places for decision-making. Government funding of curriculum development efforts may be part of this trend away from the local school community. Goodlad states that "the kind of reform likely to be advocated and the principle actors in the process will tend to shift in relation to the ratio of non regular funds to regular funds available" (p. 46). Statewide or national uniformity of curriculum is being advocated by some as a good way to meet the needs of students in a mobile society.

However, it is not likely that the local community will lose too much of its present power in the immediate future. Additionally, implementation has to exist at the local level. But, one must realize that even though districts are making local decisions, the constraints and time tables frequently are being set by centralized govenment. Desegregation is a major example of this.

Presently, most Americans live in communities with populations of 10,000 or less. Within such communities, individuals will continue to find it quite easy to provide input into their schools and to participate, if they wish, in the decision-making requisite for running their schools. But Americans will have to be alert to the possibility that with the future may come a lessening of direct input into the schooling institution. Doll urges Americans to keep active in local educational decision-making. He argues that the total society grows by its participation in the planning processes. Additionally, the involvement of diverse groups in a multitude of communities allows for the generation of creative ideas.

The strength of the American system of education, of its diverse curricula, is that communities have been allowed to experiment, to question, to develop unique curricula. Testing our various curricula in numerous communities allows ideas to be validated as to their worth. Local involvement in the educational enterprise permits the development and prioritizing of options. But regardless of how good local involvement is, the school cannot be considered as the only educating institution in the community. Indeed, many agencies and groups in the community educate: churches, YMCAs and YWCAs, Scouts, volunteer agencies and numerous others all have roles in educating the youth and citizens of the country.

Likewise, curriculum decision-makers must realize that the local community cannot just address local needs. There is a need to balance universal and parochial demands. In some cases, this means that decision-making at the local level will go against some of the ideas held by various pressure groups in the community. It is important to remember that local community control and decision-making in addition to being a strength of the American system has also at times served as a retardant to the progress of American education. Local control has kept many schools segregated and denied groups of children quality education.

We are in a postindustrial society. According to Reich (1971), Americans have passed from a personality stressing the "rugged individualism" through an "organizational personality" conforming primarily to the views and values of others to an "evolving personality" viewing options as totally open. The evolving personality has a new type of inner direction but with the realization of being a member of a greater social system.

Americans can be classified as a modern society compared with a traditional one. This means that the vast numbers of our citizens realize that individuals can change those aspects of society that require adjustment or maintain those aspects that are worthy of retention. We are aware of our options. Traditional societies are slaves to the past or current modes of behaving. They cannot challenge their functioning; they are shackled by time, and they will have difficulties existing effectively within the next century.

In a modern society we can function as evolving personalities. We can consider new options for industrial production, new options for social relationships, new modes of education. This does not mean that we shall overthrow much that is common to the American society. But, it does mean that we will understand our reasons for maintaining our systems, our institutions, our values, our behaviors. Our functioning will not be on the basis of "we have done it this way always."

Managing Social Influences

Effective curriculum workers in a modern society identify strategies for dealing with the forces of society. Society is a force not to be resisted, but rather one to be used to facilitate the creation of meaningful curricula. Doll (1978, pp. 103–105) has identified five guidelines for the curriculum worker:

First, the curriculum worker needs to be as open minded as he can be about the influences that affect the schools. All influences may not be benign, but they all deserve hearing and consideration.

Second, the curriculum worker needs to lead in using social influences. As he welcomes ideas so also must he help school staff square the ideas with theory and practice.

Third, the curriculum worker should fully consider the feelings of Americans about education and should act according to his best diagnosis of those feelings.

Fourth, the curriculum worker should recognize he is operating in a special dynamic. The curriculum worker has the real responsibility for encouraging teachers to move outside their own milieu, so that they may learn from other institutions, agencies, and individuals and many contribute to them.

Fifth, the curriculum leader must realize that he is deep in politics. His is not the politics of the ward heeling variety, but of strategy planning that requires balancing of pressures and cooperative making of policy.[2]

---

[2]From Ronald C. Doll, *Curriculum improvement: Decision making and process,* 4th edition. Copyright ©1978 by Allyn and Bacon, Inc., Boston. Reprinted by permission.

Curriculum workers are responsible for bringing into reality those programs that will prepare and allow individuals to function optimally now and in the future. Effective curriculum workers are those persons who understand the totality of the cultural store of knowledge, the demands and needs of society, and the means by which the total society can participate in the educational planning and delivery processes. Curriculum workers have the responsibility for being in part social designers, social reconstructionists.

Currently, the schools must develop procedures for attending to the major cultural issues of American society. The issues are diverse and pressing: discrimination, minority rights, poverty; urbanization, war and peace; energy use and management, population problems; growth in technology, the shrinking world both socially and economically; rising bureaucracies, individuals' rights, and the food crises. Other issues exist, but these provide us with a general idea of the demands currently confronting curriculum specialists.

Activity 3—4   *Where to Locate the Locus of Power*

Presently, most of the decision-making regarding the school's curriculum is made at the local level. But, whether this should be continued or whether the state and federal government should have an increasing role is becoming a frequently discussed issue. Many persons and some educational organizations are indicating the need for a United States Department of Education that would provide guidance for a national curriculum system. Such a system, it is argued, is necessary to service the needs of a mobile society.

Consider whether you agree with the argument to have the locus of control taken away from the local schools. Defend your position.

How might you strengthen the role of the state departments of education without adversely affecting decision-making at the local school level?

Discussion

This chapter has presented information relating to the prime source of the curriculum—knowledge—and to a major force—society—affecting the ways in which persons develop curricula and the fabric of the program. In an age of rapidly advancing knowledge, those of us charged with creating and managing curricula need to be cognizant of and well versed in the realms of knowledge and those supporting fields essential to the overall design of educational programs.

In addition to being well educated in the field of knowledge, we also need great understanding of society and its influence upon our functioning. We need to be scholars of society or at least well versed enough to interpret societal phenomena and to incorporate such phenomena into our educational planning.

References

Broudy, H.S. *Building a philosophy of education* (2nd ed.). Englewood Cliffs, N.J.: Prentice-Hall, 1961.

Bruner, J. *The process of education.* Cambridge, Mass: Harvard University Press, 1960.

Bruner, J. *On knowing: Essays for the left hand.* Cambridge, Mass.: Harvard University Press, 1963.

Commission on the Reorganization of Secondary Education. *Cardinal principles of secondary education.* Washington, D.C.: U.S. Government Printing Office, 1918.

Doll, R.C. *Curriculum improvement, decision making and process.* Boston: Allyn & Bacon, 1978.

Goodlad, J.I. *The dynamics of educational change.* New York: McGraw-Hill, 1975.

Hirst, P.H. The roles of philosophy and other disciplines in educational theory. In M. Levit (Ed.), *Curriculum.* Urbana, Ill.: University of Illinois Press, 1971.

Illich, I. *Deschooling society.* New York: Harper and Row, 1972.

Johnson, M. *Intentionality in education.* Albany, N.Y.: Center for Curriculum Research and Services, 1977.

King, A.R., Jr., & Brownell, J.A. *The curriculum and the disciplines of knowledge.* New York: John Wiley & Sons, 1966.

Lundberg, M.J. *The incomplete adult.* Westport, Conn.: Greenwood Press, 1974.

Martin. J.R. (Ed.) *Readings in the philosophy of education: a study of curriculum.* Boston: Allyn & Bacon, 1970.

Phenix, P.H. The architectonics of knowledge. In S. Elam (Ed.), *Education and the structure of knowledge.* Chicago: Rand McNally & Co., 1964.

Reich, C. *The greening of America.* New York: Random House, Bantam Books edition, 1971.

Scheffler, I. Justifying curriculum decisions. In J.R. Martin (Ed.), *Readings in the philosophy of education: A study of curriculum.* Boston: Allyn and Bacon, 1970.

Schwab, J.J. Problems, topics, and issues. In S. Elam (Ed.), *Education and the structure of knowledge.* Chicago: Rand McNally & Co., 1964.

Spencer, H. *Education: intellectual, moral and physical.* New York: Appleton-Century-Crofts, 1860.

Stratemeyer, F.B., Forkner, H.L., McKim, M.G., & Passow, H.A. *Developing a curriculum for modern living* (2nd. ed.). New York: Bureau of Publications, Teachers College, Columbia University, 1957.

Taba, H. *Curriculum development, theory and practice.* New York: Harcourt, Brace & World, 1962.

Thelen, H. Comments on "What it takes to become humane." In *Yearbook 1970, To nurture humanness.* Washington, D.C.: Association for Supervision and Curriculum Development, 1970.

Tyler, R. *Basic principles of curriculum and instruction.* Chicago: University of Chicago Press, 1949.

Unruh, G.G. *Responsive curriculum development.* Berkeley, Calif.: McCutchan, 1975.

Zais, R.S. *Curriculum principles and foundations.* New York: Thomas Y. Crowell, 1976.

Psychological Principles of Learning

In addition to understanding the realm of knowledge and social influences upon the curriculum, we curriculum specialists need to be knowledgeable of how individuals learn.

What conditions facilitate learning in individuals? How do individuals actually learn? We need to identify the vantage points from which we consider learning, for our ideas about how individuals learn can influence the curriculum either in a manifest or latent manner. Those of us who believe in the stimulus–response school of psychology will consider optimal curriculum design as affording students opportunities to experience incremental acquisition of simple behaviors which upon combination will contribute to more complex skills and concepts. Those among us who favor the field theory that attributes much of learning to "insight" will arrange curricular elements (contents, materials, experiences) in ways that will allow individuals to encounter fields of experience so that they may discover complex skills and concepts by insight, by integrating parts into comprehensible wholes.

Although we currently have no scientific "truths" regarding learning, much data abounds about learning from the research activity that has occurred since 1885 when Ebbinghaus published his study on memory. Learners have been studied as individuals in "cross-sectional" approaches involving studying thousands of individuals at specific ages and then generalizing about their physical, mental and behavioral characteristics germain to these ages. Psychologists have studied individuals over extended periods of time, examining them at intervals during their development from childhood to adult. Psycho-analysts have probed individuals to gain understandings of their personal feelings and how their experiences have impacted their development. Additionally, a plethora of research exists on efforts to study individuals from sociological viewpoints and from the vantage points of developmental tasks at various stages in life.

DEVELOPMENTAL STAGES

Piaget (1960) is perhaps the best known investigator of developmental stages related to intellect. He has investigated children and has identified four major levels of development: sensorimotor, preoperational, concrete operational, and formal operational. At the sensorimotor level, lasting from infancy to 18 months, the child apparently assimilates sensations and interacts with unfamiliar objects. At this stage, the child is only concerned with success of action, and not with knowledge as such. He or she learns to do things for the sake of being successful in doing, not in understanding what is being done. At this level, intelligence deals only with real entities, and the focus of action involves very short distances between subject and objects.

From 18 months to about 7 years, the child develops his or her perception. He or she passes from a symbolic and preconceptual thought system (from ages 1½ years to 4) in which symbols are developed via imitation and notions are attached to beginning verbal sounds to and through a stage, which Piaget calls the state of intuitive thought (from ages 4 to 7). In this later stage, the child achieves a gradual coordination of representative relations and thus growing conceptualizations. This development leads the child from the symbolic or preconceptual phase to the beginning of the concrete operational stage. At the upper level of this stage, the child can recognize differences in size and increases in number. He or she has command of image use and employs words to symbolize objects and events. But, such intellectual functioning is still not logical. The child operates only on the basis of what appears believable to him.

Logical operations do not occur until the next stage, the level of concrete operations which lasts from ages 7 or 8 to 11 or 12. During this phase of development, the child can recognize several factors at a time. He or she can understand that some things can be combined in various ways to arrive at identical results. He can establish identity when comparing two or more objects or events by engaging in one-to-one correspondence between the elements in each class.

At the beginning of adolescence, around age 12, the child commences formal thought. At this juncture the individual is able to reason on the basis of simple assumptions and can deduce conclusions from the analysis and application of these hypotheses or assumptions.

Piaget has commented that individuals' intellectual development proceeds gradually and continuously. It is thus quite difficult to determine the exact boundaries of the four levels. But, persons proceed through them all. The actual speed at which individuals go through the stages depends upon their maturity, their experiences, and the manner in which they have processed information encountered. A fourth factor contributing to developmental progress is that of equilibration—one's constant striving to achieve a state of cognitive homeostasis and to exert efforts to reachieve this status when it has been disturbed by some situations. This factor of equilibration is central to Piaget's work.[1]

As curriculum persons we need to attend to levels of intellectual development, but we also must consider states of individuals' total development. Havighurst (1972) introduced the concept of "developmental task," which he has defined as:

> a task which arises at or about a certain period in the life of an individual, successful achievement of which leads to happiness and to success with later tasks, while failure leads to unhappiness in the individual, disapproval by the society, and difficulty with later tasks. (p.2)

Havighurst noted developmental tasks from the following domains: biological, psychological, and cultural. All are important to the curriculum developer. Those tasks necessary for intellectual development are: learning to talk, forming simple concepts of social and physical reality (infancy); developing fundamental skills in reading, writing, and mathematic computations (middle childhood); selecting and preparing for an occupation, developing intellectual skills and concepts requisite for social competence (adolescence). Attending to these developmental tasks, the curriculum person gains some idea of the general purposes to which the school's curricula must be addressed. Of course, these tasks also must be considered in light of the social forces extant as well as the understanding of the realm of knowledge.

Developmental Tasks Applicable
to Curriculum Development

1. Attaining an appropriate dependence–independence pattern.
2. Achieving an appropriate pattern of giving–receiving affection.
3. Adapting to and relating to changing social groups.
4. Developing a conscience.
5. Managing a changing body, mastering the psycho-motor domain.
6. Comprehending one's psycho-social-biological sex role.
7. Learning to comprehend and manage the physical world.
8. Relating one's self to total reality. (Tryon & Lilienthal, 1950, pp. 84–87)

As Havighurst identified tasks whose accomplishment was essential, Maslow (1954) has supplied us with a hierarchy of human needs useful to consider when designing curricula.[2]

---

[1]For more information on Piaget's stages of development, see Piaget (1960, 1969).

[2]For information regarding the basic propositions that underlie much of Maslow's thinking with regard to the self-actualizing person, see Maslow (1962).

Hierarchy of Human Needs

Physiological
   A. Homeostasis—balance of internal
      bodily functions
   B. Appetites—food, air, sleep
   C. Sex
Safety
   A. Routines and rules
   B. Stability and security
Belongingness and Love
   A. Intimacy with other people
   B. To be accepted, wanted, and cherished
Esteem
   A. Personal—need for strength, mastery,
      and achievement
   B. Group—reputation, status, dominance,
      appreciation
Self-Actualization
   A. Cognitive—to know and understand
   B. Aesthetic—to perceive and appreciate
      beauty, elegance, and splendor

Those of us creating and implementing curricula must realize that individuals have needs that must be satisfied to some degree in the school program. But satisfaction of a need at one level does not appease needs at all levels. Rather, achieving success regarding one need releases energy that allows a higher level of need to be addressed. The goal for the curriculum is to allow all individuals to satisfy the need for self-actualization. But, individuals must feel safe and a part of the group and furthermore must achieve some appreciation by their peers if the highest level of needs is to be achieved.

Recently, attention has been directed to the moral development of children. This might be in response to the trend of having the school assume an increasingly larger share of responsibility for the "raising" of youth. It also could result from the present flux in the nation's social values. Kohlberg is the individual most associated with investigating the moral development of individuals. In essence he has taken Piaget's stages of intellectual development and translated them into four moral stages. His first is the preconventional stage at which a person responds to human actions as being totally good or bad. At this point persons feel that good will be rewarded and that bad will be punished. The child responds to the pain–pleasure effects of action and the physical power of authorities. He or she does what is right not because of the value of such action, but rather because he or she wishes to avoid punishment and because the other person setting down the rules is powerful.

The second level is the conventional at which the individual attempts to follow rules, initiates behavior to please others, and strives to gain approval by following rules and being "good." Here, the individual considers good behavior to be that which pleases or assists others, behavior that is "appropriate."

The third level as defined by Kohlberg is postconventional—a level having a law and order orientation. Here the individual strives to define valid, moral principles as concepts separated from the authority of individuals or group membership. Right action follows standards generated by careful deliberation.

The final stage is the universal ethical principle level. At this stage, which few individuals ever achieve, one is sensitized to one's conscience—internalized value system—and uses this conscience to guide one's living. The principles of justice and equality become evidence.

Kohlberg's stages can assist curricularists charged with developing programs to foster individuals' moral development. However, some have criticized Kohlberg as being too concerned with the cognitive dimension of individuals and with being too structured. Others have indicated that the case studies Kohlberg has employed to trigger students' responses have presented unrealistic situations, or at least improbable ones in the everyday lives of young children. Still, Kohlberg's work has value for those designing curricula.

Activity 4–1   *Utilizing Piaget's Stages of Cognitive Development*

Piaget has identified four major levels of cognitive development: sensorimotor, preoperational, concrete operational, and formal operational. Matching stages with pupils, identify major activities you would plan for inclusion in a curriculum so as to facilitate student learning.

Indicate the type of learning you would expect from students at each stage.

Activity 4–2   *Kohlberg's Levels of Moral Development in Curricular Decision-Making*

Kohlberg has developed four major levels of moral development: the preconventional, the conventional, the postconventional, and the universal ethical. Each stage has two substages. These stages can assist one in classifying children and in designing curricular experiences appropriate for the moral level of individuals.

Indicate how you would take these four major levels and utilize them for designing curricular experiences.

Note some of the cautions one should keep in mind when applying Kohlberg's ideas. If you can think of no cautions, defend your position.

Nature of the Learner

In order to process the key question of how individuals learn, we must also respond accurately to the related question of how persons develop. Although much current debate centers on the exact nature of humans, and avenues of new research need to be undertaken, there still is a vast body of research that has been done in this century which furnishes us with some descriptions about the growth and development of individuals, the mental capabilities persons bring to their learning tasks, the development of their personalities and self-concepts, and their social learning patterns at various ages. From research already completed, curricularists can conclude that each dimension of individuals' social, emotional, and mental growth is sequential, proceeds from the less mature to the more mature, evolves in cycles, and is organismic (Taba, 1962). Additionally, it is apparent that there exist interrelationships among the areas of individual development. These interrelationships are legion and dynamic. For instance, a student's ability to read is contingent upon his or her intellectual maturity. But this maturity is dependent upon the proper functioning of the eye, an aspect of physical maturity. Listening skills are dependent upon auditory development.

One cannot separate the mind from the body. The body's development affects the development of the persons' intellectual functioning, but the mind also impacts upon the physical development. Those persons experiencing emotional disturbances may have their physical development negatively affected. Back in 1949, Spitz studied the rates of emotional development of children in an institution who were cared for by their mothers and those cared for by institutional staff. Those receiving love and attention from their mothers differed positively in their rates of development over those children who only received the care of nurses.

Analyzing an individual's development enables us to note whether the person is mentally and/or physically able to address some type of learning. Also, investigating human development furnishes us with guidelines for dealing with the problem of pacing material. Just how fast can some students process certain content presented in a particular fashion? We are coming to realize that readiness must be considered within the context of various cultures. We can overgeneralize about the readiness of individuals for certain tasks if we only analyze one major culture. Presently, some educators are inquiring whether all individuals are ready to start the first grade at age six. In schools where the curriculum is sequenced primarily according to the age of students, some of us are beginning to realize that this sequencing and its accompanying uniform requirements are not that successful in accommodating the diverse needs and developmental levels of the student population.

Curricularists are concluding that essential to the designing of appropriate curricula is a vast understanding of the clients for whom we create the programs. We must understand these persons from all aspects of their growth and development. Doll (1978) stresses that we must be knowledgeable about their total functioning drawing on their auditory, visual, tactile, and motor domains. We must consider their verbal and nonverbal functioning. Additionally, we must incorporate into our planning information regarding their emotional development, their personality evolution, and the social histories they bring to the school (Doll, 1978).

Growth and Development Characteristics

How can we describe our clients at various ages?

Pupils in the beginning years of schooling can be characterized in part as follows:

1. developing handedness
2. experiencing a slowing in bone growth
3. experiencing a rapid growth in heart
4. losing baby teeth
5. increasing size of eyes
6. developing motor skills, but with the large muscles more developed than the smaller ones, resulting in some uncoordinated activity
7. exhibiting strong curiosity and eagerness to learn
8. possessing an inclination in their exuberance to be noisy
9. preferring those activities which produce visible tangible results
10. preferring activity which requires total body involvement
11. possessing a strong desire to please the teacher, but frequently setting unrealistic goals for themselves

Requirements

1. Because they are easily fatigued, the children need short periods of activity.
2. Due to their stage of body development, these children should have 12 hours of sleep.
3. Because of their active inquisitiveness, these children should have opportunities for taking some responsibility for their learning.
4. Because of the development of social skills, the children need opportunities to participate in organized groups.

Pupils in the intermediate years of schooling can be characterized in part as follows:

1. improving their coordination due to the continued development of small muscles; eye-hand coordination also is improving
2. slowing of physical growth at this period of prepubescence
3. increasing ability to manage independence and cooperative action
4. developing strong likes and dislikes, and an awakening of sensitivity to social approval from the group
5. expanding interests horizons and a developing capability of completing planned projects independently

Requirements

1. Due to their developmental levels, individuals at this general age stage need a minimum of 10 hours of sleep
2. Because of the expanded interests and also increased ability to manage independence, students require frequent opportunities to continue this development.
3. Students at this age (stage) appreciate consistency in class activities as opposed to continual changes in schedules.

4. Individuals at this stage are very responsive to praise and strive for continuity with their peers as much as possible. They also are searching for meaningful membership in the group.[3]

Students in the grade range of 7 through 9 also share many common characteristics and requirements:

1. This is the beginning of puberty, which is followed by rapid growth but with wide variations occurring between individuals. Girls usually begin puberty earlier than boys and remain taller and heavier than boys during this period.
2. During this stage, individuals are striving to escape from adult domination and become active members of their peer groups.
3. Those individuals who are maturing are beginning to exhibit an interest in the opposite sex.
4. These persons respect good sportsmanship and because of a desire to be cooperative are very interested in team games, outdoor activities.

This also is an age when the radio and television are prime interests. Individuals also are seeking means for earning money.

Requirements

1. Because of the diversity among these individuals regarding interests, developmental levels, the curriculum must have great variety.
2. Clubs and group activities should be provided to meet the specialized and expanding interests of boys and girls.
3. The curriculum should have courses or experiences focusing on the adolescent. This should help these students in understanding the physical and emotional changes occurring within their persons.
4. Educational activities should cater to the increasing need for and capability for independence. Students should be given responsibility without pressure.

Students at the senior high level usually share the following characteristics and requirements:

1. By age 15 most individuals have completed maturation.
2. Toward the end of the adolescent period, the two-year lead of girls' over boys' development begins to diminish.

---

[3]The listing of characteristics and requirements for children in the beginning and intermediate grades is adapted from the Public Schools of Montclair (N.J.), *Language arts guide, kindergarten and grades 1–7.* Used with permission.

3. These individuals are gaining more of an adult appearance. By the end of adolescence, bone growth has been completed, and adult height has been attained.
4. Because of the myriad changes occurring within the body during this period, and the social development occurring, energy levels of individuals vary greatly.
5. Individuals during this period are concerned with discovering their identities and the purpose of their lives. There continues to be a strong striving for independence.
6. In striving for independence from adults, these individuals often exhibit an extreme range in mood, from cooperative to rebellious.
7. The drive for peer acceptance is still strong and individuals are very concerned with being popular, especially with members of the opposite sex.
8. Individuals often experience some problems with making sound judgments.

Requirements

1. A primary need is that of self-knowledge.
2. A knowledge and understanding of sexual relationships and attitudes is essential at this stage.
3. Opportunities need to be provided that allow these individuals to engage in responsible decision-making and to gain acceptance by their peers.
4. Opportunities should be provided to enhance the quality of the relationships that individuals have with adults—family members included.
5. Continued attention should be given to providing these individuals with opportunities to develop their own interests and skills. Attention should also be given to developing in students special skills and talents.
6. Accompanying opportunities for understanding themselves should be opportunities for understanding others as to their feelings, their behaviors, and their knowledge.[4]

Every learner presents an idiosyncratic combination of factors such as personality and mental ability, and unique experiences affected by his or her family and the broader social order. The learner's emotional organization will impact upon his personality, influencing his sensitivity to reality. The ties that an individual has had with adults, both within the family and outside of the family, the successes and failures that he has had, and the current problems he faces all will affect the level of learning.

---

[4]The listing of characteristics and requirements of students in grades 7 through 12 is adapted from Ronald C. Doll, *Curriculum improvement: Decision making and process,* 4th edition. Copyright ©1978 by Allyn and Bacon, Inc., Boston. Reprinted by permission.

Currently, we realize the importance of a positive self-concept to learning. Research results have demonstrated that learners perform according to how they view themselves. Those who view themselves with a positive stance have higher achievement in school than persons with low self-concepts. High achievers in school feel more positive about themselves and their abilities to function in school than do low achievers.

Self-concept is not a unitary factor that can be quantified precisely. Self-concept consists of numerous discreet perceptions—evaluations all dealing with what an individual believes to be true about him or herself and the value he or she places on those beliefs. If I perceive myself as successful, and I highly value success, then I have enhanced my self-concept. However, if I view myself unsuccessful, but still value success, then my self-concept is lessened. The values we place on behaviors, attitudes, knowledge and skills are influenced to a great deal by the values and perceptions held by significant others, those people who are important in our lives (Charles, 1976).

New Learners

Our clients are changing; they are changing continually in biological, intellectual, and myriad other ways. Physically, our students are taller, heavier, and healthier than those of a half century ago. Youth reach puberty and are sexually active at ages much younger than at the beginning of this century. But despite the earlier arrival of puberty, we find that the social context requires extended adolescence in many cases. Many students rebel or are at least extremely annoyed at having their actual adulthood postponed until their mid and late twenties.

A major experiential difference in the learners currently in school and entering school is that these individuals have lived and are living through a period of an excess of knowledge presented via the media and published materials. Our students are emersed in the knowledge explosion, are bombarded with the world's problems, and are introduced to diverse world cultures. These experiences, these confrontations are heightening the intellectual sophistication these students bring to the school. Such experiences and resultant new knowledge also are affecting the talents and creativity of these students. Those of us charged with designing, implementing and maintaining programs will need to utilize all these data as well as to attend to the various learning theories.

THEORIES OF LEARNING

A prodigious body of research has been conducted aimed at determining how individuals learn. While most within the field of psychology agree to the validity of the data gathered, many psychologists and educators disagree as to how such data should be interpreted. Disagreement continues into the present time as to whether the associationist theories or field theories explain the phenomena of learning most accurately. Additionally, much of the research on learning has been faulted by people such as Bruner (1960) for focusing too heavily on the components of short-term learning occurring in highly simplified laboratory situations. Researchers have paid scant attention to the complexities of long-term learning extant in the "noisy" environments of the school and community.

Because of the paucity of research directed to studying the learning process in complex reality some have argued that psychology has little applicability to the issues facing educators (Spence, 1959). Gagne (1962) has noted that the suggestions resulting from psychological research have been of little use in guiding the development and implementation of curriculum. However, most educators and curriculum specialists are optimistic as to the value of psychological principles in guiding the development of curricula and designing instructional sequences. But, it would appear that for optimal use of psychological information, one needs to draw from associationist theories, field theories, and humanity theories. No one theory seems to explain learning in its totality or how we should structure the curriculum to facilitate learning. Currently, research regarding the brain is beginning to supply us with significant insights into its functioning (Chall & Mirsky, 1978). Such new knowledge may require us to adjust our theories of learning.

Learning Defined

How we define learning depends in part upon the theory or theories of learning we support. Gagne (1970) has stated that "Learning is a change in human disposition or capability which can be retrained, and which is not simply ascribable to the process of growth" (p. 13). Gagne has identified eight types or categories of learning, each containing its own rules, and has organized them in a hierarchy from simple to complex. The sequence in which one would have students experience learning of specific curricula is evident from analyzing the hierarchy:

1. signal learning, the conditioned response
2. stimulus-response learning, learning of a connection between a precise response and a discriminated stimulus
3. chaining of two or more stimulus-response connections
4. chaining of verbal associations
5. discrimination of similar but different stimuli
6. concept learning
7. rule learning
8. problem solving

Conley (1973) has defined learning in the following manner:

Learning is a psychological process involving both psychological and psychomotor activities. The process of learning cannot be observed but can be inferred from changes in the behavior of individuals. These changes take place through practice and experience directed toward the satisfaction of needs. Behavior changes include acquisition of knowledge, skills, interests, appreciations, and attitudes. Needs are considered to be intellectual, social, emotional, and psychological. (p. 212)

Gagne's definition refers to learning as an individual's capability to do something, while Conley has defined it as a process, both psychological and psychomotor with some purpose. Gagne's definition is more in line with one offered by Hilgard and Marquis (1961): "Learning. A relatively permanent change in response potentiality which occurs as a result of reinforced practice" (p. 481).

As Conley points out, the process of learning cannot be observed, but its results can. However, all three definitions do not depend or insist on overt, observable behavior as evidence that learning has occurred. Learning, according to these definitions can occur by an internal reorganization that will manifest itself in behavior when a situation occurs in which such behavior is required. However, strict advocates of the behaviorist school would reject such definitions, for, they would argue, it is impossible to determine the presence of learning in the absence of a change in behavior. For those supporting the associationist school, the criterion of "reinforced practice" evidenced by observable behavior is the main support of their views of learning. Conley seems to give partial credence to this view in her definition.

Associationist Theories

Theories included under the associationist category sometimes are termed connectionists, stimulus–response, or reinforcement theories. Whatever the name for these theories, the stimulus–response is the key around which they are built. Individual activity is viewed as being comprised of three basic components: (a) the stimulus situation, (b) the organism's response to the situation, and (c) the connection or link made between the stimulus and response. In essence, these theories hold that a person acquires new responses via a conditioning process. This conditioning process is termed learning. The majority of contemporary associationists believe that stimulus–response bonds develop gradually as a consequence of an individual's trial-and-error behavior. The urge to act is controlled by motivation or drive. Action, the learner's response, is directed by a stimulus, usually extant in the environment. The learner selects one response over another by a combining of various conditioning and psychological drives present at the moment. The result of such action is a response, which psychologists consider as a reward. This reward may be different from moment to moment and from learner to learner.

From such functioning, an individual develops a connection between stimulus and response, a S–R bond. This bond thus determines a person's tendency to respond in a particular way to a given stimulus. The bond's strength is a function of the probability that, provided a certain situation, the person will initiate a particular response. In learning any subject matter, the individual engages in a process or processes of acquiring a large number of appropriately related bonds—a type of chaining, to use Gagne's terminology—which when accumulated constitute the individual's knowledge of the subject.

Behaviorism is a major division under associationist theories. John B. Watson (1878–1958) founded this psychological school. Around the time of World War I he observed that internal mental events readily existed and were available to the individual who experienced them. Watson believed that psychology had to break with the past if it wished to advance the knowledge of learning. Psychology needed to construct a science that would follow the example set by the physical sciences; it must become materialistic, mechanistic, deterministic, and objective. Watson believed that mental processes and consciousness were not inappropriate subjects for scientific study. If a psychologist wished to study another person's thoughts, it was necessary that the person under study translate his interior experience into physical terms such as speech, writing, or observable symbols. These signals were not mental events, but were overt behaviors capable of quantification and analysis. Thus Watson urged abandoning inferential (nonmeasurable) speculation about mental states and attending to overt behaviors that could be analyzed objectively and scientifically.

Gestalt and Field Theories

Theories in this psychological "camp" are referred to in the literature as cognitive theories, organismic theories, or gestalt theories. These theories, rather recent to the field of psychology, originated from attention to visual perception and its influence on human behavior. Learning, although an important aspect of human behavior, was not the major focus of these theories. However, despite this other focus, these theories have provided much guidance to educators and curriculum specialists.

Gestalt psychology development is credited to three general psychologists: Max Wertheimer (1880–1943), Kurt Koffka (1886–1941), and Wolfgang Kohler (1887–). According to Hilgard (1964), Robert M. Ogden—a Cornell educational psychologist—deserves much credit for introducing Gestalt psychology to the American educational community by translating Koffka. Koffka's book (1924/1959) made a significant attack on the associationist's trial-and-error view of learning.

The major assumption of Gestalt psychology is that there is an essential unity in nature. Learning is that process of grasping the relationships assumed to exist among physical, psychological, and biological events. Learning does not emanate from trial and error, but rather occurs as a consequence of insight. But for insight to take place, all the necessary elements of the situation to be learned must be visible (Wertheimer, 1945). To assure the advent of insight, one can make a concerted effort to bring all aspects of the situation into close proximity so that relationships become evident. In essence, learning is a somewhat spontaneous restructuring of the integrated whole. To the Gestaltist, the learner sees things as organized and structured wholes, not atomistically. We view an individual within the context of his entire environment, a person against a background of trees, not a person against a specific number of trees. Human behavior results from a dynamic interaction with environmental forces. Behavior does not eventuate as a consequence of linear occurrence of stimulus and response linkages. Rather, it happens as a result of interacting force fields, clusters of stimuli and responses, which alter a total situation which is recognized by the process of insight. To the Gestaltist, learning is the process of gaining insight, and intelligence is the capacity for insight. The emphasis Gestaltists have placed on organization, meaningfulness, and perception have influenced considerably how curriculum persons have structured educational environments.

Field theory, formulated by Kurt Lewin (1890–1947), developed as an extension of Gestalt psychology. Although not specifically a psychology of learning, it has much information relevant for the curriculum designer. Its central thrust is its concentration upon the individual's perception of the field rather than the objective, physical field only. Lewin coined the term "life space," comprising not only the physical and social reality but also the perceptions the individual brings to the reality as a result of prior experiences. This life space includes the environment, the person, and the interaction between the individual and the objective environment.

As an individual gains insight, the structure of the life space is altered. In essence, learning is the structuring and restructuring of the life space to the extent that problems identified can be solved. For those in curriculum concerned with the environmental dimension of the curriculum, many of Lewin's ideas have much merit. Curriculum persons can consider themselves as designers of potential life spaces in which the properties of the students—their needs, beliefs, values, perceptions, motives—are brought into contact with the objective environment.[5]

LEARNING THEORIES AND CURRICULUM

Curriculum drawn from these various theories will differ markedly. Curriculum specialists adhering to the associationist school will approach curriculum design and organization by primarily dividing curriculum into its simplest components and arranging them so that learners gradually acquire the simple units until all units comprising a complex behavior are attained. Learning is approached in a step-by-step fashion, and curriculum persons are most concerned with the task of sequencing in curriculum development and management.

Curricularists accepting the field theories consider the curriculum from general themes, concepts, ideas and problems. Heuristic questions become key organizers for the curriculum. Curriculum persons design the curriculum elements (content, experiences and environments) so that the individual learner begins to visualize the total and its organizational principles. To those curriculum types attending to this psychological school, it is understood that learning will not occur in a gradual step-by-step fashion. Rather, learning will be sporadic with periodic advances in perception culminating in insight regarding some issue or issues. Interspersed between such gainings of insight will be plateaus in which no really new learning comes about, but information learned will be applied or used in some particular fashion.

---

[5]Counseling theory has made some inroads into the realm of psychological theory. See Rogers (1969) for information on reality therapy and its applications for educators.

The stress on discovery and process learning and on individuals gaining control over their learning all draw heavily from the gestaltist and field orientations toward learning. The thrill of discovery when one finally pieces together isolated concepts into a useful generalization depends in part upon the gaining of insight. The reward to the learner is in the knowing, and this thrill of knowing, this awe of knowledge serves as the prime motivator. This contrasts markedly with the positions of associationists that for learners to be motivated, they must be prodded with extrinsic reinforcers, outside rewards.

However, despite the push for making students autonomous learners, for affording them opportunities to discover—to learn via insight— field theories have not become the dominant influence behind educational practice or curricular activity. Most learning theories within academic psychology have a stimulus–response orientation. Hill (1964) has attributed the success of stimulus–response theories primarily to two factors: (a) stimulus–response theories fit better within knowledge of psychology than do the field-theoretical interpretations; (b) stimulus–response theories focus attention of observable and measurable events in the world of reality. Hill is obviously of the S–R persuasion. Those in the field-theory school would argue the points raised. However, it is evident that S–R theories are easier to manage in that one can identify stimuli and can count responses. One has more difficulty in determining when an individual has had a meaningful insight. With the push for more precision and for more observable results from learning, the S–R orientation most likely will continue to keep its dominance for the forseeable future.

Principles of Learning to Guide Us

In analyzing the myriad research studies and books written on learning, we can only conclude that we still lack scientific truths to guide our actions in education. But, there are numerous fairly well accepted principles we can utilize to direct our decisions regarding curriculum. Goodwin Watson (1963) has attempted to bring together the differing views of psychologists of both the associationists' and Gestaltists' schools of thought. The following list draws heavily on Watson's efforts.

1. Behaviors which are rewarded (reinforced) are more likely to recur.
2. Reward (reinforcement), to be most effective in learning, must follow almost immediately after the desired behavior and be clearly connected with that behavior in the mind of the learner.
3. The simple word "Right," coming directly after a response, will have more influence on learning than any big reward coming much later.
4. Sheer repetition without indications of improvement or any kind of reinforcement is a poor way to learn.
5. Threat and punishment have variable and uncertain effects upon learning.

6. Readiness for any new learning is a complex product of interaction among such factors as (a) sufficient physiological and psychological maturity, (b) sense of importance of the new learning to the learner (c) mastery of prerequisites, and (d) freedom from discouragement or threat.

7. Opportunity for fresh, novel, stimulating experience is a kind of reward which is quite effective in conditioning and learning.

8. Learners progress in an area of learning only as far as they need to go in order to achieve their purposes.

9. The most effective effort is put forth by children when they attempt tasks which are not too easy or too difficult.

10. Genuine participation increases motivation, adapability, and speed of learning.

11. Excessive teacher direction is likely to result in apathetic conformity, defiance.

12. When children or adults experience too much frustration, their behavior ceases to be integrated, purposeful, and rational.

13. The experience of learning by sudden insight arises when (a) there has been a sufficient background and preparation, (b) attention is given to relationships operative in the whole situation, (c) the perceptual structure frees the key elements to be shifted into new patterns, (d) the task is meaningful and within the range of ability of the subject.

14. Learning from reading is facilitated more by time spent recalling what has been read than by reading.

15. Forgetting proceeds, rapidly at first—then more and more slowly.

16. People remember new information which confirms their previous attitudes better than they remember new information which conflicts with their previous attitudes.

17. What is learned is most likely to be remembered if it is learned in a situation similar to that in which it is to be used and immediately preceding the time when it is needed.

18. Ability to learn increases with age up to adult years.

19. Meaningful materials are learned more easily than nonsense materials.

20. Learners think when they confront issues that interest them.

21. Peer teaching both formal and informal is quite effective in introducing students to new information and behavior.

22. Learning is facilitated by the raising of questions at higher cognitive levels. Different types of information can be gained, by consciously asking various kinds of questions.[6]

The above principles are not absolutes, but they are sound guidelines to keep in mind when engaged in curriculum decision-making.

---

[6]For information on how to get students involved with their questioning at various cognitive and affective levels, see Hunkins (1976).

Activity 4–3 *Analyzing the Learner*

Curriculum development requires that we be knowledgeable of the persons who are to receive and interact with the curriculum. We must know our students. We have various learning theories and principles of learning to assist us in our educational decision-making, but we must gather specific information on individuals to ascertain that our curricular recommendations are appropriate for individual students.

Select a student in your class or school and gather information for a "learning profile." Use school records, interviews with the student, dialogue with the parents, and class observations to obtain the necessary data. Focus on the individual's personality factors, his or her cultural background, prior school learning and his or her learning goals.

Note possible types of curricular experiences that should enable the students to correct noted deficiencies or to maintain current strengths in learning.

NEW DIRECTIONS IN LEARNING

The above guidelines are important to remember, but we curriculum designers must also attend to new developments in learning occurring and likely to occur in the near future. In the past, attention was on laboratory experiments designed to determine how individuals learned simple tasks. Even when attention was directed to the classroom arena, researchers focused on how learning occurred as the result of specific programs or teaching strategies. Now, psychologists and sociologists are beginning to comprehend the specific characteristics that influence the development of intellectual capacity. Attention is directed to individuals' socioeconomic status, family environment, and ethnicity, as regards their influences on the cognitive development of children. Walberg and Marjaoribanks (1976) suggest that family environment measures should be considered for inclusion in experimental and correlational studies of educational efforts. "Such measures would be powerful covariates, would remove extraneous variance from achievement, and would allow for more precise estimates of the educational efforts in question" (p. 548).

Attention in learning is being directed to outside influences. "Consider where the individual student is coming from"—a rather common exhortation—is now receiving some serious research attention. Nuttall, Nuttal, Polit and Hunter (1976) have researched the effects of family size, birth order, sibling separation, and crowding on students academic achievement. Working with youngsters in four suburban communities, their research indicated that family constellation triangles such as family size, birth order, spacing of children and crowding were related to academic achievement when IQ was controlled. Boys from small families tended to achieve better than did boys from large ones. First-born girls outperformed later-born girls. Boys in small families seemed to be more oriented toward adult values while their counterparts in large families seemed more influenced by peer groups, and had anti-academic values. Crowding had a deleterious effect on achievement of both sexes; however, the effect was nonsignificant when IQ was controlled.

The implications for curriculum specialists are obvious. In planning and maintaining any program, we must attend to demographic and social data on students and make modifications as to content selected, sequence of content, motivational techniques, values emphasized, support services provided, materials utilized and instructional strategies employed in order to offset any deficiencies students have as a result of their family situation and accompanying experiences.

Learning Styles

Students come to the school possessing various learning styles as a consequence of their prior and continuing experiences in their environments. We as curriculum designers will need to make sure, to the degree possible, that the curriculum and instructional methods complement the learning styles. Dunn and Dunn (1975) have identified four major categories representing ways in which individuals learn: (a) the environmental, including sound, light, temperature, and casualness, as compared with structure; (b) the emotional, involving motivation, persistence, responsibility, and structure; (c) the sociological, involving self, peers, pairs, teams, and adults; and (d) the physical, including perceptual strength, time, intake, and mobility.

These authors have matched four teaching styles to the four categories of learning: (a) the traditional, representing minimum grade level standards; (b) the individualized, in which personal diagnosis and prescription are used to guide student's progress; (c) the open, which allows students opportunities to select their educational encounters within the limits of their abilities, curriculum resources, schedule, and (d) alternative strategies, which allow pupils maximum choice, freedom, in determining how they will learn.

Research on learning style is beginning to reveal that the cultural experiences of individuals greatly affect how they approach learning and the success they have with learning. Ramírez and Castañeda (1974) have done extensive work with Chicano children and have indicated that through socializational practices, children develop preferences for certain types of reward, develop various attitudes and attendant values, and perfect particular social interaction approaches. Learners, because of their cultural experiences, can vary in their cognitive styles which involves variation in styles of learning, incentive-motivation, human relations, and communication.

Research by Witkin (1967) and others has addressed the concept of field dependence and field independence. Investigations seem to indicate that perception of a relatively field-dependent subject is dominated by the overall organization of the field. In contrast, field-independent subjects readily perceive elements as discrete from their backgrounds—they separate them from the totality of which they are a part.

It seems that the average school in the United States reflects an emphasis favoring individuals who are field independent. Individuals having this capability are mostly from the middle class. Thus, those students from various ethnic groups, such as Spanish-speaking, are at a disadvantage. Research being done on the cognitive development of students from various cultural groups has implications for curriculum designers in the ways they design educational environments, the ways they structure content, the ways they design methods of delivery, and the nature of the human encounters they encourage (Ramírez & Castañeda, 1974).

The Human Brain

An exciting area of investigation having crucial relevance to learning is that centering on how the brain functions. Previous theories of learning have not taken into account the actual functioning of the brain, partly because they were developed during periods of limited understanding of the brain. Even today, we do not possess a great deal of knowledge regarding the brain. But our knowledge base is expanding.

The brain consists of the cerebrum, the cerebellum, and the brain stem. The cerebrum has two hemispheres divided by a longitudinal fissure. Researchers have found that information received on the right side of the body is transmitted to the left side of the brain, while information on the left side of the body goes to the right hemisphere.

Investigators have further discovered that the left hemisphere is involved with analytical thinking, especially language and logic, while the right hemisphere is primarily responsible for spatial perception, artistic functioning, body awareness and recognition of faces. However, these functions are not exclusive of each other (Sullivan, 1975).

Individuals are indicating that school curricula contain information and activities that seem to favor the analytic dimensions of the brain neglecting the right hemisphere and the more artistic, creative aspects of learning. It appears, that despite the exhortations for educating the whole child, we have only been stressing cognitive analytic functions. Hart (1978) has noted that:

> the human brain was not "designed" for schools. And schools, dating back far beyond our modern brain knowledge, were not designed to fit the brain. To expect the brain, shaped by eons of evolution, to adapt to schools is of course absurd. We need to design schools and teaching that are "brain-compatible." (p. 393)

Hart introduces several points requiring our consideration. First, at one time we felt that the brain was a blank board, a *tabula rasa* on which instruction was "written." We are beginning to realize that the human brain is intensely aggressive and highly unique, seeking out only that which is meaningful to it. Our increasing emphasis on the active student complements this new knowledge of the brain. Second, the brain is being seen more and more not as a stimulus-response device as advanced in behaviorist theories. A brain will admit only those inputs that it decides to admit, that pass through "gates." What the brain processes has little to do with what the teacher is doing. Rather, the brain at any particular time is more influenced by its total, previous stored experience in relation to a current situation. Third, the neocortex of the human brain does not function well under pressure. Frequently, students are put in pressure situations in school. Such pressure is likely to have deleterious effects upon individuals' learning. Fourth, young students must engage in verbal behavior to learn well and rapidly. It seems that a great portion of the human brain is devoted to language. However, in many schools, the teacher monopolizes the talking. Fifth, we have approached learning by considering the logic of the task. We have attempted to make teaching and the organization of curriculum entirely logical. Current brain research seems to indicate that the human brain does not function physically via a type of logic. Hart indicates that it works not by precision but probabilistically. He indicates that we need to make our schools more brain-compatible. Hopefully, as we in curriculum learn more about the brain, we can increase the compatibility between our programs and the brain.

How does the brain remember? How can information learned at one time be brought back into consciousness? Surely the brain is an awesome phenomenon. The memory process is what enables individuals to learn. Sullivan (1975) notes that two types of memory seem to exist: sensory memory and verbal memory. Sensory memory allows us to recognize what our senses tell us. Individuals recognize a particular taste, the appearance of a person, a particular locale. These sensory memories can be explained by relying upon our verbal memory system. It is this latter memory that enables us to store and express things in ideas and words. This verbal memory also has two levels: long-term and short-term memory. The former handles only a few ideas at a time while we are attempting to determine how to process them. Long-term memory involves permanently storing information which the individual in some way considers important.

One theory on memory indicates that data are stored in vast patterns of interconnections of millions of neurons known as engrams. According to this theory, individuals remember something when they activate one of these patterns. Accepting this theory leads us to believe that there is no one place in the brain where memory is to be found; it exists in several places.

Hart discusses the Proster Theory, which advances the notion that the brain functions by perceiving patterns that are arranged in programs that are arranged into structures, called "prosters." Thus learning appears to be the acquisition of meaningful programs. Prosters are continually arranged in hierarchies allowing for increasingly complex brain functioning. Eventually thousands of programs are stored and the brain functions as a pattern-detecting apparatus.

If this is correct, then when individuals learn some item or content in the curriculum, they are learning a pattern, storing it, and retrieving it whenever appropriate. This recognition of patterns may be what the field psychologists call insight. Hart mentions that a child learning the letter A as distinguishable from B or C is really learning a pattern. Knowing when to say "thank you" rather than "excuse me" results from one recognizing patterns in somewhat complex encounters.

Much remains to be learned about the brain. Presently, we have limited understanding regarding the permanence of long-term memory.[7] Various theories suggest that proteins are responsible in some way for such memory. Research has shown that if production of protein is inhibited shortly after learning, long-term memories are not made. If such protein production is not tampered with after a learning encounter, the person's memory is not adversely affected. The function of protein may be that it facilitates the growing of new connections between the neurons involved in a particular brain pattern. Another is that protein facilitates making available more of the chemical needed to cross gaps between synapses (Sullivan, 1975). Much of this research opens to us the area of chemical functioning of the brain. Perhaps we in education will have to attend to the diets of students as well as the materials they use. Some of this information may seem rather futuristic, but curriculum persons are involved intimately in designing educational encounters that will enhance individuals' learning. To design curricula for stimulating a brain or allowing a brain to function optimally requires of us a detailed understanding of it.

Activity 4—4   *New Directions in Learning*

Presently, much research is being conducted on how cultural factors influence learning styles. Research also is beginning to furnish new data on the brain's structure and functioning. Certainly, educators will be required to utilize new knowledge gained in these areas when creating curricula.

Set up a self-study program that will increase your awareness and understanding of research and writing being done in these new areas. Note how you can use some of this new knowledge when designing and creating curricula.

What directions do you think curricular activity will take as such new information is incorporated in curricular decision-making?

You might engage a colleague in discussing some future consequences of using new found knowledge of the brain.

Environmental Theory and Curriculum

What we know and believe about learning is a powerful force in influencing our curriculum decision-making. But we have tended to ignore the educational environment both inside and outside of the school in which learning occurs. "Man's sense of space is closely related to his sense of self, which is an intimate transaction with his environment" (Hall, 1969, p. 63).

The environment influences individuals in subtle ways and provides them with options. Any spatial transaction between persons and their environments depends upon two variables: their idiosyncratic use of space and the

---

[7]For more information on this, and also for a discussion of the principle of the hologram to explain memory, see Pribram (1971).

environment's structuring. People relate to their world; they place varying demands on their environments. Some people require great amounts of space, while others can function within a limited space (Firt, 1975). Curriculum designers must consider the question "how do changes in the organization of environment affect individuals learning?"

The new field of environmental psychology should provide guidance in curricular decision-making. Proshansky (1975) notes that the major thrust of this field focuses on the complexity that constitutes any physical setting in which persons live, interact, and engage in activities for periods either brief or extended. It is a field aimed at studying the life supporting conditions that are organized in space and time for the function of supporting and mediating the behavior and experiences of individuals either alone or in social groupings. The focus is on the built environment with attention on those dimensions that actually foster, shape and undergird complex human activities that occur in such settings. Attention will be on the role of human perception, thinking, motivation, learning, and feeling in human-environment interactions. This emerging branch of psychology appears to offer an answer to those who say that the results of traditional psychology—gained mainly in sterile laboratories—are not applicable to the environment of the classroom. Environmental psychologists will conduct their research in the physical settings of built environments in which students are functioning. Such research will be conducted in ways that maintain the environment's integrity.

We will need to (a) attend carefully to the educational environment, (b) understand the research regarding this curriculum element, and (c) understand ways in which to plan for and manipulate this element to increase the probability of optimal learning (David, 1975).

Discussion

This chapter centered on learning and psychological principles that have relevance for the curriculum worker. The major theories of psychology were discussed. New areas of investigation related to learning were presented mainly dealing with cognitive style and recent brain research. All of these emphases were discussed with regard to their relevance for those of us with curriculum responsibilities.

The new area of environmental theory was presented as possessing much potential merit for curriculum decision-makers.

These forces influencing curriculum or having the potential to influence curriculum along with the force of society and the source of knowledge all require constant monitoring by curriculum leaders.

References

Bruner, J. *The process of education.* Cambridge, Mass.: Harvard University Press, 1960.

Chall, J.S., & Mirsky, A.F. (Eds.) *Education and the brain.* Chicago: National Society for the Study of Education, 1978. (77th yearbook)

Charles, C.M. *Individualizing instruction.* St. Louis: C.V. Mosby, 1976.

Conley, V.C. *Curriculum and instruction in nursing.* Boston: Little Brown, 1973.

David, T.G. Environmental literacy. In T.G. David & B.D. Wright (Eds.), *Learning environments.* Chicago: University of Chicago Press, 1975.

Doll, R.C. *Curriculum improvement: Decision making and process.* Boston: Allyn & Bacon, 1978.

Dunn, R. & Dunn, K. Learning styles, teaching styles. *Bulletin of the National Association of Secondary School Principals,* October 1975, *59,* no. 393, 37–49.

Firt, S. The individual and his environment. In T.G. David & B.D. Wright (Eds.), *Learning environments.* Chicago: The University of Chicago Press, 1975.

Gagne, R.M. Military training and principles of learning. *American Psychologist,* February 1962, *17,* 83–91.

Gagne, R.M. *The conditions of learning* (2nd ed.). New York: Holt, Rinehart & Winston, 1970.

Hall, E.T. *The hidden dimension.* Garden City, N.Y.: Anchor Books, 1969.

Hart, L.A. The new brain concept of learning. *Phi Delta Kappan.* February 1978, *59,* 393.

Havighurst, R.J. *Developmental tasks and education.* New York: David McKay, 1972.

Hilgard, E.R. *Theories of learning* (2nd ed.). New York: Appleton-Century-Crofts, 1956.

Hilgard, E.R. (Ed.) *Theories of learning and instruction.* Chicago: National Society for the Study of Education, 1964. (63rd yearbook)

Hilgard, E.R., & Marquis, D.G. (revised by G.A. Kimble). *Conditioning and learning.* New York: Appleton-Century-Crofts, 1961.

Hill, W.F. Contemporary developments within stimulus–response theory. In E.R. Hilgard, *Theories of learning and instruction.* Chicago: National Society for the Study of Education, 1964. (63rd yearbook)

Hook, S. *Education for modern man.* New York: The Dial Press, 1946.

Hunkins, F.P. *Involving students in questioning.* Boston: Allyn & Bacon, 1976.

Hunkins, F.P., & Spears, P.F. *Social studies for the evolving individual.* Washington, D.C.: The Association for Supervision and Curriculum Development, 1973.

Hutchins, R.M. *The conflict in education.* New York: Harper & Bros., 1953.

Koffka, K. [*The growth of mind*] (R.M. Ogden, trans.). Patterson, N.J.: Littlefield, Adams, 1959. Originally published, 1924.

Maslow, A.H. *Motivation and personality.* New York: Harper & Row, 1954.

Maslow, A.H. Some basic propositions of a growth and self actualization psychology. In A.W. Combs (Ed.), *Perceiving behaving becoming.* Washington: Association for Supervision and Curriculum Development, 1962. (yearbook)

Nuttall, E.V., Nuttall, R., Polit, D., & Hunter, J. The effects of family size, birth order, sibling separation and crowding on the academic achievement of boys and girls. *American Educational Research Journal,* Summer 1976, *13,* no. 4, 217–223.

Piaget, J. *Psychology of intelligence.* Patterson, N.J.: Littlefield, Adams, 1960.

Piaget, J. *The theory of stages in cognitive development.* Monterey, Calif.: McGraw-Hill, 1969.

Pribram, K.H. *Languages of the brain: experimental paradoxes and principles in neuro-psychology.* Englewood Cliffs, N.J.: Prentice-Hall, 1971.

Proshansky, H.M. Theoretical issues in environmental psychology. In T.G. David & B.D. Wright (Eds.), *Learning environments.* Chicago: The University of Chicago Press, 1975.

Ramirez, M., III, & Castaneda, A. *Cultural democracy, bicognitive development and education.* New York: Academic Press, 1974.

Rogers, C. *Freedom to learn.* Columbus, Ohio: Charles E. Merrill, 1969.

Spence, K.W. The relation of learning theory to the technology of education. *Harvard Educational Review,* Spring 1959, *20*, 84–95.

Spitz, R.A. The role of ecological factors in emotional development in infancy. *Child Development,* September 1949, *20,* 145–155.

Sullivan, E.A. *The future: human ecology and education.* Homewood, Ill.: ETC Publications, 1975.

Taba, H. *Curriculum development, theory and practice.* New York: Harcourt, Brace & World, 1962.

Travers, R.M. (Ed.) *Second handbook on research on teaching.* Skokie, Ill.: Rand McNally, 1973.

Tryon, C., & Lilienthal, J. Developmental tasks: The concepts and its importance. In *Fostering mental health in our schools.* Washington: Association for Supervisions and Curriculum Directors, 1950.

Walberg, H.J., & Marjaoribanks, K. Family environment and cognitive development: twelve analytic models. *Review of Educational Research Journal,* Summer 1976, *46,* 527–551.

Watson, G. What do we know about learning? *Today's Education,* March 1963, *52,* 2–23.

Wertheimer, M. *Productive thinking.* New York: Harper & Bros., 1945.

Witkin, H.A. A cognitive style approach to cross-cultural research. *International Journal of Psychology,* 1967, *2,* 233–250.

chapter 5

Participants in Curricular Activity

> The greatest promise for curricula possessing potential to stimulate in students academic independence lies not within organized national efforts, but in local educators and lay persons assuming new identities, accepting new tasks. (Hunkins, 1972, pp. 503–506)

The above quote addresses in part a central question confronting curriculum developers: Who should be involved in curriculum decision-making? Unruh (1975) indicates that those who have a direct share in curriculum development at some level such as policy-making, producing, or utilizing curricula should be involved. The following figure depicts the various publics that have a stake in curriculum decision-making at several levels of involvement.

MacDonald (1971) also advocates meaningful involvement by all parties affected by curriculum decision-making. He chastizes those educators who consider that curriculum decisions should emanate from experts, be dispensed to teachers, and finally transmitted to students. He presents a model showing several groups all directing their thinking, feelings, and knowledge to curriculum activity. The model depicts persons in continuous interaction. All are challenged to make decisions regarding all segments and elements of the curriculum.

FIGURE 5.1 *Decision-making levels in curriculum planning*

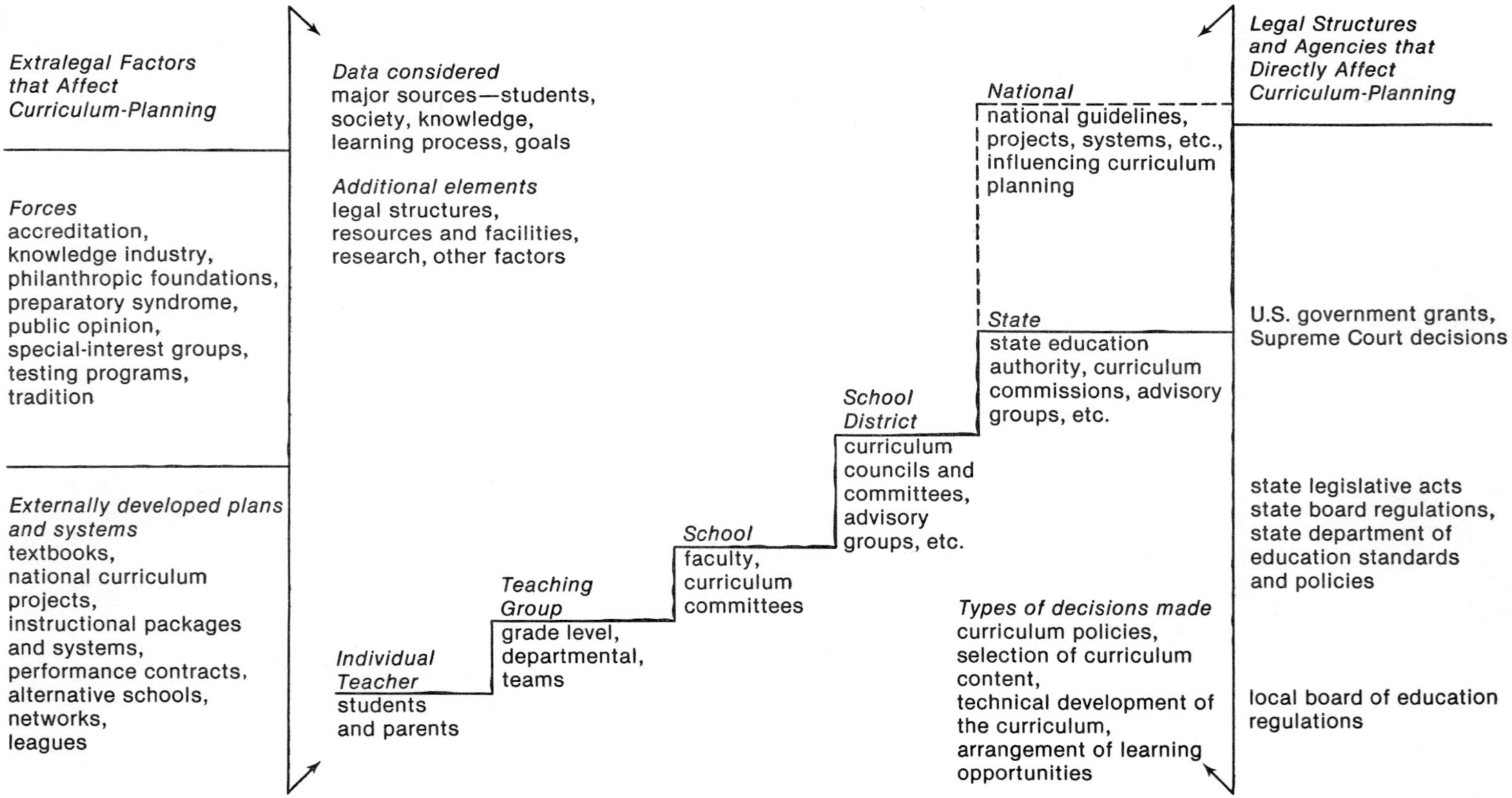

Legal Structures and Agencies that Directly Affect Curriculum-Planning

National
national guidelines, projects, systems, etc., influencing curriculum planning

U.S. government grants, Supreme Court decisions

State
state education authority, curriculum commissions, advisory groups, etc.

state legislative acts
state board regulations, state department of education standards and policies

local board of education regulations

School District
curriculum councils and committees, advisory groups, etc.

School
faculty, curriculum committees

Types of decisions made
curriculum policies, selection of curriculum content, technical development of the curriculum, arrangement of learning opportunities

Teaching Group
grade level, departmental, teams

Individual Teacher
students and parents

Extralegal Factors that Affect Curriculum-Planning

Data considered
major sources—students, society, knowledge, learning process, goals

Additional elements
legal structures, resources and facilities, research, other factors

Forces
accreditation, knowledge industry, philanthropic foundations, preparatory syndrome, public opinion, special-interest groups, testing programs, tradition

Externally developed plans and systems
textbooks, national curriculum projects, instructional packages and systems, performance contracts, alternative schools, networks, leagues

112

From *Planning Curriculum for Schools*, 3rd ed., by J. Galen Saylor and William H. Alexander. Copyright © 1974 by Holt, Rinehart and Winston, Inc. Reprinted by permission of Holt, Rinehart and Winston.

FIGURE 5.2   *Continuous interaction model for curriculum activity*

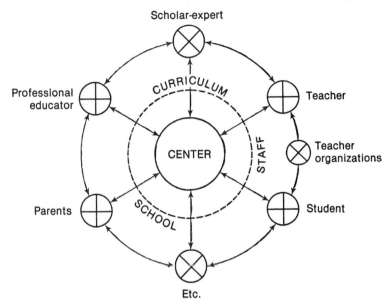

Note. From "Responsible curriculum development" by James B. MacDonald, in E. Eisner (ed.), *Confronting curriculum reform.* Boston: Little, Brown and Co., 1971. Reprinted by permission.

Cooperative action perhaps is the key to producing and managing effective curricula. But just desiring cooperative action is not sufficient for success in multiple group decision-making. In addition to the question of whom to involve are questions directed at determining the special backgrounds, skills, and abilities individuals require for particular curriculum involvement. What talents do participants require? Where can such talents best be used?

Most persons in the community have little or no prior experience in cooperative decision-making. Even many educators lack such decision-making skills and are unaware of the complexities of group functioning. Thus, persons charged with coordinating curriculum development and related activities may have to initiate some type of training of participants regarding their roles and responsibilities. Such training requires time, and frequently both educators and the lay public are reluctant to devote the time requisite for learning how to make careful decisions. Those participants who are already skilled in decision-making may be unwilling to devote large segments of time to serious decision-making. At a period of increasing demands on all persons' time, this problem is likely to increase.

Participant unwillingness to engage in group decision-making is related to a realization that long meetings will be required. Frequently, individuals know that such meetings often get mired in hidden agendas. Also, persons may have had experiences or heard of instances in which communication problems stymied committees. Frequently, such planning committees lack the resources for dealing effectively with curricular issues.

Nevertheless, we as curriculum leaders need local involvement in planning and managing the curriculum to assure its success. Successful involvement presupposes correct interpretations of roles by those to be involved. Not only do we need to understand standard or accepted roles regarding what they entail, but we need to realize and comprehend new roles requisite for confronting emerging needs and demands upon the curriculum.

Social scientists have defined roles in three principal ways: as a position within the organization or hierarchy, as behavior requisite for the performance of jobs, and as expectation concerning tasks to be accomplished by role takers (Gross, Mason, & McEachern, 1958). Currently, the view is to consider roles more in terms of expectations to be accomplished or behavior required for certain tasks than the more traditional definition of position within an organization. Thus, teachers, administrators, lay members and students at times may share similar roles such as analyzer of community educational needs.

In the past, roles of persons in curricular activity have been voluntary, often vague and unassessed. However, the current times demand of education precise functioning. This requires not only that we be aware of whom to include in curriculum decision-making, but be cognizant of the exact manner in which they will be involved as well as be knowledgeable of the rationale for their tasks.

THE PARTICIPANTS

Teachers

The teacher occupies a central position in curriculum decision-making. It is the teacher who decides what aspects of the curriculum, newly developed or ongoing, to implement or stress in a particular class. In most school districts, teachers have this primary involvement of teaching the curriculum. But only a few schools have large numbers of teachers participating in the initial curriculum conceptualization stages or in sharing in the total curriculum development effort. However, this is changing, and organizational schemes such as differentiated staffing are allowing teachers increased opportunities for curriculum decision-making during the regular school day.

Still, much remains to be done to alter the current school organization to allow teachers more meaningful participation. Silberman (1970) and Fantini (1973) had concluded that large numbers of teachers are unable to deviate from rigid curriculum-related specifications developed in the central office. Institutional level decisions, frequently in response to societal pressures, often determine the broad goals for students. Such determination filters down through the system influencing more localized goals, materials used, contents organized, methods employed and even classroom space allowed.

According to Doll (1978), teachers are charged with three major tasks related to curriculum; working and planning with pupils, engaging students in individual study, and communicating curriculum-related experiences with their colleagues. Teachers are in tune with the needs of students; teachers are on the front lines of involvement.

Because the teachers' primary role is implementing the curriculum, they need effective participation in those activities that ultimately result in new curricula or curricular materials. Presently, many teachers are not prepared for such involvement. Teachers' deficiencies in curriculum decision-making result in large part because their prior training in colleges of education stressed only methods of teaching, neglecting curriculum as a realm for concern. Additionally, the school's current organization as mentioned previously, prevents meaningful involvement. For the most part, curricular activity continues to be an "add on" activity for teachers, something beyond their primary responsibility. But teachers need to share in curriculum activity; they need to assume tasks heretofore neglected or managed by others: developing curriculum packages, conceptualizing resource centers, designing educational environments, assisting in piloting curriculum units, and communicating with publics on new curricular projects. Teachers may even be charged with assuming tasks new to the entire educational system such as assessing the myriad actions and decisions of fellow teachers within the school system (process evaluation). Such a teacher could provide reports indicating how particular tasks were approached, approached by whom, and the final outcomes of the tasks taken. Such reporting could provide participants with data suggesting continuance, adjustment or termination of their actions. In this role the teacher serves as an educational "trouble shooter" (Hunkins, 1972). Other educators in the system also can assume such roles.

Such functioning by teachers depends upon competencies not now evidenced by most teachers. Teachers require education for optimal involvement in curricular activities. Some attempts are being made to enable teachers to participate more fully in the curriculum realm. In the late 1970's, the State of Washington supported a program entitled Instructional Theory Into Practice (ITIP) which dealt with an instructional management approach to teaching. Although primarily concerned with instruction, aspects of curriculum decision-making were evident. Teachers were trained to analyze their students, to develop precise program objectives, devise approaches for achieving stated objectives as well as evaluating the effectiveness of instructional efforts. Such state efforts designed to prepare teachers to assume new tasks are likely to increase in the future.

Teachers are beginning to understand the concepts curriculum, curriculum development, and curriculum evaluation. They are learning about curriculum diagnosis, needs interpretation, objectives development, content selection and organization, materials selection and organization, and educational environmental design. They are becoming skilled in writing and organizing curriculum master plans that they and their colleagues can utilize. Some of this new knowledge is gained by on-the-spot involvement in curriculum projects while some is gained in formal course work.

A new role for teachers in relation to curriculum is becoming a member of educational research teams addressing curriculum concerns. Teachers can contribute knowledge about learners and learning processes needed to guide the selection of learning activities and their sequencing. They can assist educational researchers who are searching for optimal ways to sequence particular curriculum elements such as contents and materials to meet the needs of unique student populations. Teachers, as members of research teams can help in diagnosing crucial human factors and significant interpersonal relations. They can aid in delving into curricular variables affecting students' perceptions and attitudes toward particular phenomena.

But if teachers, and other educators as well, are to accept such traditional roles, they must receive training in research techniques and also in philosophical viewpoints about research-based knowledge. This does not mean that teachers will become curriculum researchers, but it does mean that they will have to have sufficient knowledge of research to enable them to be contributing members of such teams. Teachers as professionals have some responsibility for advancing the realm of curricular knowledge as well as allowing students to experience the curriculum (Hunkins, 1977).

Miller and Dhand (1973) have advanced 10 articles relating to teacher participation in curriculum activities.

1. Teacher participation should be used in every phase of the project.
2. Teachers must work cooperatively within a climate of permissiveness, equality, and realization of personal worth.
3. Teachers should be granted time, money, and facilities.
4. Teachers should involve themselves in limited programs, avoiding participation in comprehensive ones.
5. Teachers should attend to specific goals and to useful materials, content and methods.
6. Teachers should learn research methods and acquire a research point of view.
7. Teachers should use a variety of consultant and resource personnel.
8. Teachers should have a coordinating body (central committee) to unify their work.
9. Teachers should develop desirable relationships with supervisors, other teachers, and lay persons.
10. Teachers should evaluate their curriculum work continuously.

The above list provides some useful guidelines. However, point four indicates that teachers should avoid involvement in comprehensive programs. This makes sense only if we continue to organize our schools and staff as we have in the past. It may well be necessary to adjust our staffing, such as that advocated in differentiated staffing. If this were done, teachers qualified in curriculum might well be involved in comprehensive curriculum programs.

In many schools, teachers participate in curriculum mostly when implementing the curriculum in their classrooms. The other most common locus of teacher involvement is the curriculum committee, whether standing or ad hoc. Such committees can be organized by grade level such as the elementary or secondary curriculum committees, or by subject, such as the mathematics curriculum or the social studies curriculum committee. Often committees are by both subject and grade level, the elementary social studies committee or the secondary general science committee. For continuity of programs, committees that cut across grade levels seem preferable to those locked into elementary or secondary categories.

Much of the teachers' involvement will be in ad hoc committees or in informal groups or even in casual dialogue with colleagues. However, for teachers to be contributing members to the curriculum decision-making effort, they require a broadening of their professional backgrounds. No longer can they just focus on methods of teaching, general courses in psychology, and courses in their content majors or minors. Teachers need courses in curriculum development and theory; they need to delve into new fields of knowledge such as futuristics, anthropology, systems theory, philosophy, decision and planning theory, and organization theory. Additionally, they need to read in the field of educational politics.

Activity 5–1   *Teacher Involvement*

Teachers should have significant tasks in the various stages of curriculum activity. In some cases, this will require major adjustment of their teaching roles.

Consider the school in which you now work or if you are not in a school, visit one at either the elementary or secondary level and list the ways in which teachers are involved in curriculum activity. If you find they are most active in curriculum decision-making, indicate ways in which their level of involvement can be maintained. If you discover limited teacher participation in curriculum decision-making, sketch a plan for bringing them into the process.

If you are working in a nonschool setting, analyze it to see how staff are involved in the curriculum process.

Students

Great strides have occurred regarding student involvement in curriculum decision-making. No longer do students just receive curricula created by other persons in the system. Students, especially at the secondary and higher education levels, are taking an increasingly greater and more meaningful share of responsibilities for educational programming.

Much of this increased involvement has resulted from the revolutionary movement that occurred in the colleges in the late sixties. Demands by college students for a voice in what programs were offered affected secondary school students. Additionally, in the decade of the seventies, the courts ruled on several occasions that students have rights and should be furnished opportunities for deciding events and programs that might affect them. This involvement has extended into the elementary level. Increasing numbers of educators are considering the decision-making by students relating to their program an essential element of their total learning.

Currently, the most common type of student participation in curriculum planning occurs at the classroom level. Usually students assume advisory roles informing teachers as to the interest levels, relevance and usefulness of the curriculum being proposed. Many teachers are inviting students to join in planning various curriculum projects such as field trips and the use of community resource persons.

In some schools students have more visible roles in curriculum development. Unruh (1975) reports that Buffalo, Atlanta, and San Diego have paid students for working on curriculum writing and review teams during the summer. Other schools offer students credit in lieu of pay for working on curriculum development committees. At the university and college level, students are sitting as voting members of committees charged with monitoring and developing curricula. Frequently, students are voting on policy matters affecting not only program, but criteria for selecting students into particular programs and the staffing of such programs.

Students can contribute in ways other than sitting on committees. Students can conduct parent surveys, participate in public relations work, and write position papers on aspects of the curriculum. Today's students are much more sophisticated than their counterparts of 10 or 20 years ago. Even so, teachers and curriculum coordinators must ascertain that students have the ability to gain the necessary skills for meaningful involvement in curriculum matters.

Doll (1978) notes that schools choosing to ignore what learners think and feel are indeed acting nonproductively. Ignoring the clients of the school causes anger and neglects opportunities for making the learning experience optimal for the greatest number of students. But, educators should not be carried away with the notion of student participation. Educators must be certain that the tasks in which they invite students to engage are appropriate for their abilities and experience. Some schools will be able to make maximum use of their students' views and expertise. Other schools may only be able to use their students in most general ways such as, What do you think we should focus on in this study? Unruh (1975) notes that it might be propitious for educators to consider student involvement more as a skill to be developed rather than as a right to be granted. Meaningful involvement by students can nurture many crucial learnings: decision-making, group communication, critical thinking, creativity, responsibility, tolerance for ambiguity, tolerance for differing views of others, and a belief in the rational process.

Administrators, Supervisors, Curriculum Specialists

Quality leadership assures quality programs. Earlier in the century, leadership was interpreted primarily as an identifiable position in a visible organization. Today, the leadership concept subsumes leadership as a function. Many members in the educational arena can assume authority depending upon the nature of the situation.

In 1960, the Yearbook of the Association for Supervision and Curriculum Development defined educational leadership as "that action or behavior among individuals and groups which causes both the individual and the groups to move toward educational goals that are increasingly mutually acceptable to them" (p. 27). The definition is still valid. But the actions or behaviors may have become more complex or at least our understandings of them have become more complete. We have become more aware of the educational theater. We have become increasingly sensitive to the variety of interests of our constituent groups, to the styles of learning of our clients, to the variety of motivation of our students, and to the diversity of goals and purposes of both our students and teachers (Robinson, 1977).

Today, numerous challenges are confronting those of us with responsibility for curriculum. Public demands for precision, for better returns on the educational dollar have caused us to realize needs for new skills in decision-making, new competencies in curriculum activities, new management skills, new understandings of group dynamics and organizational theory.

Hilliard (1977) notes that educational leadership has been vulnerable because of the events of the late 1970's. People dissatisfied with what educational leaders had been doing strove to gain some of the guidance roles. Persons in the lay community, from pressure groups, and from various levels of government organized to achieve the initiative in educational decision-making. In the late seventies while lay leaders were on the rise many educators with curriculum responsibilities were dismissed or moved to noncurriculum-related jobs. In the author's home state (Washington state), many school districts eliminated curriculum specialists in subject areas. Numerous school districts reverted to traditional line-staff organizations in which the only leaders were administrators (principals) charged with managing the school and doing whatever needed to be done in curriculum. Because of the demands on their time, most principals could only manage schools. They could not coordinate and maintain development of large scale curriculum projects. Hopefully, a reversal of this trend to eliminate curriculum specialists and curriculum coordinators will occur. As Hilliard noted, educational leadership must come of age.

Administrators and supervisors deal with curriculum at a macro level and have special roles to fill. They are largely responsible for setting the atmosphere in which curriculum activity will happen. Frequently, the central office initiates curriculum action either as a result of perceived needs interpreted by central office staff or from processing inputs from teachers and others at levels nearer the classroom. Regardless of whether curriculum action is introduced by or coordinated by the central office staff, teachers and others affected by the curriculum must be involved.

The Superintendent

The chief administrator of the school system is the superintendent. He is concerned with all educational matters, curriculum included. It is this individual who must set the tone for curriculum activity. This leader is responsible to the board of education for both the curriculum and the manner in which students experience it. Good superintendents inspire change and enable curricula to be responsive to changing demands. Directives from this office can allow individuals in the system opportunities for participation in various phases of curriculum action. Communication networks and supporting services are generated from the management approaches chosen by the superintendent.

The superintendent is directly responsible to the school board for the total educational action in the district. He or she must establish the means for curricular action, must interpret all aspects of the school's program to the board, and must set up communication networks to inform the public of and involve the public in the curriculum process.

The Assistant Superintendent

In numerous school systems, the person with the primary responsibility for curriculum activity is the assistant superintendent. This individual is a line administrator who reports directly to the superintendent. In those districts not having a curriculum coordinator, the assistant superintendent serves the role. Neagley and Evans (1967) list the responsibilities of this person as:

1. informing the superintendent of the major trends occurring in the field of curriculum and how these trends are being processed within the school system;
2. observing the entire program K - 12 and coordinating curriculum activities related to any and all aspects of such program; this role can be shared or assumed by the curriculum coordinators in those districts having such a line position;
3. chairing or serving as council to the general curriculum advisory committee;
4. cooperating with the elementary and secondary coordinators regarding curriculum development, implementation, maintenance, and evaluation;
5. coordinating the utilization and procurement of resources required to support on-going and anticipated curriculum activities;
6. maintaining communication with intermediate school districts or educational service districts on new programs and trends affecting curriculum;
7. determining appropriate budget needs for program development and management;
8. working with educational media and communication specialists in obtaining necessary support materials for ongoing and new programs.

Roles of Curriculum Specialists

Curriculum specialists have been separated from administrators and supervisors in that these persons—in some schools a disappearing breed—are totally involved with curriculum activity. They are not involved directly with total school management. They are not responsible for negotiating teachers' employment terms or mounting programs for bond issues or special levies. Rather, these persons—under the title of curriculum director, curriculum coordinator, coordinator of elementary or secondary education, assistant superintendent of curriculum and/or instruction, or director of some subject speciality—are the major curriculum leaders. The quality of the program development in school districts rests largely on the shoulders of these persons.

Many of these persons have not had a clear mission in mind nor made their presence entirely evident to either their colleagues, the school board or to the general public. Many have been poorly prepared for dealing with the curriculum realm. Frequently, individuals with the title of curriculum coordinator have little, if any, educational background in curriculum, often coming to their jobs with only administrative training. Far too many supervisors of specific curriculum areas such as social studies, general science, or mathematics have training only in supervisory and administrative techniques. Thus, when making curriculum decisions they are unsure about the phenomena with which they are dealing. Curriculum is not instruction, and supervising a teacher as to his or her skill in presenting a lesson—however valuable—is not dealing with curriculum.

It cannot be overemphasized that the degree of skill and level of understanding curriculum specialists bring to their jobs are critical factors in determining the total quality of the curriculum. Curriculum specialists who know their jobs can facilitate the development of programs responsive to changing student needs specifically and public needs generally. Curriculum specialists armed with knowledge of curriculum history, curriculum development, curriculum theory, curriculum evolution, change models, change theory. systems theory, educational sociology, educational psychology, administrative theory and procedures, organizational theory, and educational philosophy will be able to confront the challenges of designing and implementing optimal curricula.

Taba indicated in 1962 that curriculum specialists charged with curriculum development needed skills in identifying problems, planning change strategies, skills in constructing a conceptualization for curriculum development that took a macro view, not a piecemeal approach, and skills in relating curriculum development to the fundamentals of child development and the requirements of the culture. Additionally, the curriculum specialists, Taba urged, must be competent in both diagnosis and curriculum evaluation.

Those assuming curriculum specialists roles have need of interpreting the research of others and of assuring that such research—both action and empirical—is conducted in the school district.

Unruh (1975) notes that the curriculum specialists must be versatile, perceptive, sensitive, patient, and skilled in human relations. Additionally, they need competence in decision-making and leadership. In brief, they need to be able to meld scholarship with practical action.

Unruh has listed roles and responsibilities that define rather specifically the scope of the task for curriculum specialists:

1. defining goals and objectives at various levels of decision-making;
2. conducting needs analysis utilizing subjective and objective means;
3. conceptualizing and implementing models for curriculum development;

4. generating plans, strategies and procedures that encourage people to participate and trust each other in curriculum activities;
5. synthesizing information from fields such as curriculum, subject fields, learning theory, media, and materials development in order to facilitate the total curriculum development process;
6. involving people of different interests, ages, and backgrounds in discussing issues, developing plans, and working toward meaningful programs;
7. coordinating communication networks for the dissemination of information regarding curriculum;
8. providing opportunities for staff to develop greater understanding and sophistication of the realm of curriculum;
9. creating implementation plans for various curriculum activities so that programs can proceed from conceptualization to actualization in the least amount of time;
10. organizing, coordinating and maintaining evaluation processes, both formative and summarative, so that all phases of curriculum activity are assessed and adjusted if necessary; this evaluation refers not only to the products (curricula) being produced, but also the processes, procedures, being utilized in the production.

The previous list makes evident that the curriculum specialist must be a person with specialized competencies, understandings, and skills. No longer can he or she be just an administrator who has been "rewarded" for service with an appointment to a curriculum position. Some change is on the way in that numerous colleges of education are beginning to conceptualize curriculum credentials similar to currently existing administration credentials. One such change is a credential in curriculum administration developed for individuals wishing to become curriculum specialists and/or coordinators in the schools.

Principal

The principal is at the nexus of curriculum activity. This educator is the gatekeeper of the curriculum as well as the crucial administrator in the school system. He or she is in daily contact with teachers and thus knows their needs and their reactions, both positive and negative, to the existing or developing curriculum. This director serves to interpret the local culture to the teachers as well as national trends. He or she is the exemplar of the educator striving to bring to teachers the latest in educational thinking regarding all matters of education including the curriculum. He or she not only sets the stage and provides support for the curriculum elements, but in addition serves as the crucial person, often in the role of supervisor, in assuring that the instructional component of education is viable.

The main functions of the principal are:

1. serving on the curriculum council;
2. serving on various ad hoc and/or standing committees related to the running of the total school system;

3. managing the teachers, determining teaching loads, class schedules, and support personnel required for effective implementation and management of curricula;
4. keeping abreast of current curriculum trends;
5. encouraging teachers to evaluate themselves, and providing assistance in evaluating their effectiveness;
6. interpreting general school goals to the staff;
7. coordinating or working with the curriculum director or specialist in planning and carrying out inservice related to curriculum activity;
8. serving as a spokesperson to the community regarding the essential thrusts of the school's curriculum.

Activity 5–2   *Situational Task Analysis*

Major curricular tasks facing educators deal with determining direction for the curriculum arena, conducting needs analyses, engaging in development activities, managing implementation of programs, furnishing guidance to staff regarding new programs, evaluating new programs, conducting in-service for staff and keeping communication channels open to the public.

Make a data chart listing in the left-hand column the various tasks that should be considered and across the top of the chart the persons who might do them. The chart should look somewhat like the following example.

Persons Tasks	Teachers	Students	Principals	Supt.	Lay Public, etc.
Determining direction for curriculum					
Conducting needs analyses					
Engaging in curriculum development activities, etc.					

Now analyze your current educational situation and note (with a checkmark) which persons in your school or educational institution are involved in the tasks listed. You may add to the tasks noted.

Such a chart should give you an overview of who are involved and how they are involved in the curriculum process.

If you are in a nonschool situation, substitute the names of the persons in your institution for the ones above.

Across the country, the roles and functions of the principal are changing. In many elementary schools, vice or assistant principals are assuming functions formerly handled by the principal. In secondary schools, department chairpersons are taking on many of the planning, supervising, and managing functions formerly held by the principal.

Where differentiated staffing exists, the principal's role in relation to curriculum activities has been greatly altered. Frequently the master or head teacher has been delegated many of the principal's former roles regarding the curriculum. Often these teachers or team leaders manage the creation of conceptions of curriculum programs, assisting in their development, piloting, and introduction into schools. Differentiated staffing also has altered the curriculum roles of department chairpersons. This is not surprising if one considers the school as a system. By adjusting roles of one member of the educational team, all members are affected.

The School Board

Boards of education are the legal agents for the schools. They have received their plenary powers directly from the state legislature. These boards, comprised of lay persons, elected as representatives of the general public are responsible for the overall management of the schools. This group of lay leaders can take any action that is not excluded by specific law. In a sense, the board has greater freedom than the state department of education which can only take those actions specifically spelled out by the legislature.

With regard to curriculum, school boards hold the final accountability for what occurs. Their primary responsibility is to be cognizant of the scope and content of the curriculum. Other responsibilities are to be knowledgeable of state guidelines and regulations regarding all curriculum and instructional matters (textbook adoption procedures); to support and extend the values of the total school system; to serve as the main body for the processing of community values, attitudes, and curricular concerns; to investigate those trends relative to innovations in the curriculum field; to provide communication channels to the public regarding curriculum matters; to determine and administer general policies affecting total curriculum activities within the district; and to be involved actively in the curriculum planning process by voting the funds requisite for putting programs and policies into action, and ensuring that all groups to be affected by the curriculum are meaningfully involved.

The responsibilities for board members are hefty and members thus need to comprehend the complexities of education in general and curriculum and instruction in particular. They also need to understand their roles in relation to others in the curriculum theater (superintendent, curriculum coordinators, curriculum specialists).

Boards must realize the complexities of their task and be sure that all who are affected by educational decisions have a vehicle by which to furnish input. Webb (1977) cites a case in which a school board had a suit brought against it by the local educational association and several private citizens for the board's failure to involve all interested parties in curriculum decisions. In this age of accountability, boards need to realize that they represent the total community and must be sure that the total community feels "ownership" of the curriculum program. With the diversity extant in most communities, this is no small task for the school board.

School policies emanate from the school board. Sumption and Engstrom (1966) note a three-fold function that policies perform: (a) translating goals of education into operational principles; (b) providing ways and means by which educational goals may be achieved; and (c) providing for continuous appraisal of the processes employed by the school to achieve the goals delineated. They further indicate that policies have six characteristics that all educators should bear in mind. All policies:

1. are stated as general principles which have wide application over long periods of time;
2. are stated in such a way as to be readily interpreted and easily applied;
3. permit a maximum of freedom of action to those who are to interpret them and execute them;
4. are consistent one with the other;
5. are stated in such a way as to be understandable by lay citizens as well as to professional educators;
6. are subject to regular review and revision in light of changing conditions.

Table 5.1 is a depiction of a school district's various groups and individuals who have curriculum responsibilities. The figure serves as a useful overview of the major functions these individuals and groups serve.

DYNAMICS OF LEADERSHIP

Leadership is defined in this book not just as a position in an administrative organization but rather as a position of responsibility and guidance that an individual is willing to assume. In working with individuals, one soon discerns great variety in how persons approach their leadership roles. Some are defensive leaders while others qualify as participative leaders. A defensive leader takes an authoritarian, paternalistic or conservative posture while a participative leader exhibits permissiveness in his or her dealings with subordinates, allowing others to maximize their self-determination and contributions to the organization (Gibb, 1969).

The participative authority believes that leaders are not made but emerge from the dynamics of group interaction. Such an individual realizes that as groups proceed with their tasks, controls for optimal functioning will emerge. Gibb believes that optimal leadership allows for joint interdependence, and shared planning. In this time of demands by educators and citizens alike for participation, such an approach seems not only productive but essential for the very survival of the school.

TABLE 5.1 *Function analysis by individuals or groups*

Students, Teachers, Administration, Parents, School Board

1. Initiate action by identifying problem

District General Instruction Committee

1. Establish selection and rotation procedures for articulation committees
2. Approve articulation committee members
3. Recommend adoption of texts, courses, and curriculum revisions to School Board
4. Recommend district curriculum and instruction objectives and priorities to School Board

Principals

1. Provide input during needs assessment
2. Provide assistance in examining alternative solutions
3. Assist in drawing up specifications
4. Provide assistance in determining content and process objectives
5. Provide assistance in resolving controversial issues
6. Provide assistance in implementing pilot* programs and inservice
7. Assume responsibility for implementing and monitoring adopted curricula

Curriculum Specialists/Coordinators (as a group function at Dept. of Instruction)

1. Complete needs assessment
2. Assist in drawing up specifications
3. Provide leadership to articulation committee
4. Serve as resource to District General Instruction Committee
5. Submit problem resolution to Curriculum Director
6. Coordinate implementation of pilot* program and formative evaluation
7. Recommend adoption to District General Instruction Committee
8. Coordinate implementation of adopted program
9. Coordinate program evaluation
10. Coordinate efforts with evaluation specialist and IMSC Coordinator
11. Advise Curriculum Director on curriculum matters
12. Work in conjunction with principal to provide curriculum leadership
13. Recommend adoption to District General Instruction Committee

*Pilots will be an exception and must be approved by the Curriculum Director

Note. From Renton, Washington, School District handbook of procedures for curriculum development. Reprinted by permission.

TABLE 5.1 *continued*

Articulation Committee

1. Assist in determining priorities within subject areas
2. Examine alternatives
3. Abide by administrative specifications
4. Anticipate and resolve controversial issues
5. Recommend problem resolution
6. Assist in needs assessment, pilot* programs, implementation of problem resolution and program evaluation
7. Recommend adoptions to Department of Curriculum & Instruction

Deputy Superintendent

1. Serve as chairman of District General Instruction Committee
2. Assume final responsibility to see that all functions are carried out
3. Serve as secretary to Citizens' Advisory Committee for Instruction

Curriculum Director

1. Make decision following needs assessment and recommended problem resolution and pilot* program as to whether to proceed or not
2. Advise Spec./Coord. and articulation committees of administrative specifications
3. Coordinate the work of curriculum spec./coord.

Research & Evaluation Specialist

1. Assist curriculum Spec./Coord. in formative and summative evaluation
2. Assist articulation committees in establishing criteria for selection of curricula

IMSC Coordinator

1. Work with articulation committee in selection of materials for pilot* and adopted programs

Inservice Specialist

1. Work with Spec./Coord. in designing inservice programs

School Board

1. Establishes policies relating to District philosophy and objectives
2. Ensures that curriculum revision procedures are followed
3. Has final authority in adoption of curriculum & instructional materials

Citizens' Advisory Committee for Instruction

1. Review and recommend instructional goals
2. Review and recommend changes in criteria for selection of instructional materials
3. Review of K-8 learning objectives in reading, language arts, and math

The participative leader approaches his or her tasks on the assumption that McGregor's management Theory Y is the most productive one to follow. McGregor (cited in Seaton & Switzer, 1977), a former professor of management at Massachusetts Institute of Technology (MIT), advanced two theories to explain how individuals approach management, Theory X and Theory Y. Theory Y postulates that first people are not by nature passive or resistant to organization needs. If they behave in such a way, it is because the organization has fostered such passivity. Second, motivation, capacity for assuming responsibility, and readiness to direct behavior toward organizational goals are all present in individuals. These are innate capacities for action. Third, people are self-directed, creative at work, and self-actualizing.

In contrast, Theory X notes that first people lack ambition and dislike responsibility. They prefer to be led. Second, individuals are by nature indolent and only work to the degree necessary for getting by. Third, people are inherently self-centered. Their initial response to organizational objectives is one of indifference, requiring that they must be coerced into accepting them.

Which leadership style or approach is the most effective? The authoritarian model draws heavily from McGregor's Theory X, while the participating model employs assumptions basic to Theory Y. It is not a matter of trying to determine which mode of leadership is the "right" one. Rather, one needs to approach leadership styles with the question of which seems to be the most appropriate in light of the context in which the leader finds him or herself as well as the "climate" of the times. However, it would seem, from an assessment of the current educational scene, that the Theory Y model has more to offer presently.

Assistants in Curriculum Activity

Lay citizens. There is no doubt that the schools belong to the public. Lay individuals in recent years have become increasingly active and visible in determining curricular directions and emphases. Today, few educators challenge the efficiency of lay involvement in curriculum decision-making. Rather, the question is how to involve such individuals optimally.

Sumption and Engstrom (1966) have divided the levels of involvement of lay citizens. At the first level, educators are interested in obtaining a broad base of information as to lay perceptions of need. A major proportion of citizens may be involved indirectly via providing input into Parent Teacher Association (PTA) task forces or directly by working on committees selected by school officials. The second level requires more knowledge of education and how to process information, thus there exists a greater selection of personnel. The final level, at which judgments and recommendations are made, assumes that the personnel involved are qualified for such participation. However, lay citizens should not try to impose their "educational" skills and competencies on curriculum specialists, teachers or other professional educators. Judgments made at this third level are conclusions made by competent lay citizens, not educators. This does not mean that the decisions are valueless, but educators need to realize that the judgments—and especially recommendations—are most often coming from persons viewing the world not as educators.

Ways of Participating

Citizens can provide unique and valuable services, but they must be acquainted with educational matters and also apprised of the possible roles they can play and tasks they might address. Unruh (1975) comments that persons apathetic toward curriculum matters or ignorant of the complexities of curriculum development are as irresponsible as those individuals who misuse power to prevent interaction among referent groups who would make meaningful contributions to curricular decision-making. As to whether lay citizens really comprehend all the complexities of curricular activities is moot. In the Gallup poll of 1977, people seemed more concerned with discipline and integration/segregation—first and second choices, respectively, for major problems facing the schools in 1977—than with poor curriculum. But poor curriculum was considered by the sample to be the fifth major problem in 1977.

Citizen involvement should occur at three levels: societal, institutional, and instructional. Citizens, and this of course includes parents, can assist in long-range curriculum planning, in delineating program goals. Additionally, citizens can participate in long-range planning regarding physical plants (educational environments), materials production and purchase, and financing of school programs, both curricular and extracurricular. Of course, the major responsibility for specific planning in these directions rests with the representative citizens who form boards of education.

The school board is the official policy-making body, but individuals and organizations can contribute to policy development. An individual who holds power in the community speaks out against some educational practice or use of material, and the practice and material are adjusted or discontinued. Groups often have this effect. Parents complaining about the tradition of providing a disappropriate amount of male sports have certainly influenced policy. Teachers listening to the comments of parents regarding classroom practice at parent-teacher conferences often adjust policy as to what topics will be treated in the curriculum and the manner of treatment.

Citizens also can affect policy formally. Usually, this is via the board of education taking some action to revoke or adjust some existing policy, or enact some new policy as a result of community pressure. All school districts have Parent Teacher Associations (PTAs) or Parent Teacher Student Associations and many communities have Rotary and Lions types of organizations. These groups often mount efforts to influence policy.

With the demands for accountability, all individuals who influence or can influence the curriculum and students' encounters with it, should have some means of participating in curriculum decision-making either directly or indirectly. Sharing by residents in all phases of education, but not duplicating educators' roles and tasks, is a necessary foundation for the functioning of our democratic system. Avenues of communication need to be established so that groups can participate.

Laypersons have responsibilities that accompany their involvement. Responsible noneducators recognize and respect the roles of all members, both community and educational. They accept accountability for becoming informed regarding educational issues, curriculum issues in particular. Such citizens believe in the rational process which centers on the gathering of data, the considering of diverse viewpoints, the careful determination of needs, the consideration of possible solutions, the careful selection of such solutions, and the actual implementation and evaluation of solutions.

Vehicles of Participation

Lay persons may participate both formally and informally in curriculum decision-making. Frequently, action by community members is informal and is largely just passive listening and watching what the schools do. The quality of the information the citizens get via the informal means is largely dependent upon the effectiveness of the communication avenues established by the school or available in the community, such as the local radio and television stations.

Informal participation often is on an individual basis in response to particular and transitory needs that arise. Formal involvement usually occurs in group form. Formal groups can be appointed by the PTA or the school board or they can be self-organized, such as various pressure groups, or community groups interested in education such as the YMCA, Daughters of the American Revolution, the Lions.

The most common formal organization formed by schools is the citizens advisory council or committee. This council can exist at several levels in the school. It can be an advisory council for the total district or for a particular school or for even a particular subject area within a school. Such groups can be temporary or continuous. Usually, councils or committees concerned with the total program are continuous, those addressing particular crises are temporary. Regardless of whether the council or committee is permanent or temporary, it has no legal status but is organized by agreement of both school and lay members to function within specified guidelines.

Some advisory committees are not school sponsored, but have solicited community members sharing a certain perception of a current educational situation. Often these groups are protest organizations. They can be either destructive or constructive depending on their goals, needs, and methods. Some committees are organized to advise the school, to pressure it into making major changes in either the curriculum or its means of delivery. Frequently, they are established to influence policy implementation. *Citizens for (or Against) Mandatory Busing* fall into this group. These committees are not school sponsored, but certainly have the objective of providing advice and direction in educational matters.

School-sponsored and individual committees can be divided into overall committees and "phase" committees (Sumption & Engstrom, 1966). Overall committees attend to the total school program while phase committees focus on a particular aspect of education. *Citizens Against Mandatory Busing* is a phase committee. *Parents for Gifted Children* most likely would be an overall committee concerned with the total curricular offerings for the gifted.

Certainly, most school districts will have nonschool sponsored advisory committees, and this is good. But, all schools should have school sponsored committees of both overall and phase types. To ensure effective development and management such groups require rules for operation suggested by the school and adopted by the committee. Membership can be selected by the board of education, or by a committee appointed by the board, or by staff members at the school level. Membership should be rotating to involve the greatest number of lay individuals. A great danger in a citizens' advisory council or committee is that the membership representing the community may not actually be representative of the community. Commonly, lay elites gain control of advisory committees and advocate policies and urge school directions inconsistent with general total community desires.

Effective schools are in communication with their publics, allowing input from citizens. The citizen advisory committee is a most powerful vehicle for enabling schools to respond to the changing demands and needs of society. Sumption and Engstrom (1966) who urge that schools maintain school-sponsored, continuing, and overall advisory committees, indicate several functions such committees can serve. They can:

1. aid in developing educational policy;
2. aid in developing long-range plans to assist in solving school-community problems;
3. assist in evaluating the work of the school;
4. facilitate the maintenance of two-way communication between school and community;
5. stimulate the flow of information to the school.

The citizens advisory committees allow for a multitude of perceptions and expertise to be added to the overall process of curriculum decision-making. Oftentimes such committees stand as the only official link that many community members will use to inform school personnel of pressing needs or perceptions held. Furthermore, such advisory councils often furnish effective links between various community agencies, civic organizations and school liason groups with the main decision-makers within the school system.

Activity 5–3   *Lay Involvement*

Educators and lay citizens have been denoting ways in which lay citizens can be incorporated into curriculum teams. Write a paragraph explaining how you view the involvement of lay citizens in curriculum activities. Indicate the rationales for your views.

Compare your views with the community in which you are located. Are you in agreement or disagreement with the views of the community members?

Assistants Outside the School District

State Department of Education. School districts have the plenary powers for much curriculum decision-making; however, departments of education act as gatekeepers for the entire state regarding educational matters. The state department of education includes the state board of education, the state superintendent of public instruction, and the staff of the state education office. Since the United States Constitution is mute on federal responsibility for education, the states have assumed the major control of education.

For much of our history, states did not accept too much responsibility for educational matters. But currently, states are taking greater roles in educational decision-making. In some states, control is very direct over the curriculum with the state selecting or determining the acquiring of particular curriculum materials, primarily textbooks. Other states have exerted control more indirectly producing lists of guidelines for the management of curriculum rather than delineating specific materials or topics to be considered. However, states achieving greater roles in curriculum decision-making is a noticeable trend.

But inputs from state education offices should be more than simply regulatory. Such offices should be organized to serve the needs of people and society. They should provide some guidance and direction to the educational activities of school districts rather than just gathering statistical data. State offices can set the stage for curricular innovation and can serve as the primary agent of educational diffusion.

Currently, states' education offices are becoming involved in issues of accountability, performance-based teacher education, tenure law revisions, statewide objectives, delineation of basic education, and statewide testing. Schools are responding actively to state mandates that all major curriculum objectives be identified and means for evaluating such objectives specified. There appears to be a strengthening of the belief among the population that the business of education is really under the aegis of the state. Court rulings that the local financing of schools through real estate taxes is unconstitutional have caused many states to begin rethinking their roles and responsibilities not only with regard to financing, but also with regard to determining the directions in which state education should proceed.

Buser and Humm (cited in Doll, 1978) investigated the practices of state educational agencies in 32 states. Results indicated that superintendents, principals and curriculum personnel identified four state practices that had the greatest influence on curriculum at the local level: financial reimbursement on a program or project, granting or withholding accreditation, granting or withholding financial reimbursement because of nonaccreditation, and enforcing state legislation.

Regional organizations. Regional educational laboratories influence school curricula in at least two major ways: first, they are providing guidance in the way of materials and consultants to those involved in curriculum planning and second, they are producing materials for use in school programs. Regional organizations can undertake the development of those materials too large for local districts to produce yet too small to interest commercial publishers.

Research and development centers, usually connected with universities, with funding frequently coming from foundations or federal sources are providing guidance and direction to the area of curriculum. The Ontario

Institute for Studies in Education is a well-known example. Some centers are independent such as the Rand Corporation which attend to some education related issues.

School curriculum leaders charged with greater research roles as well as more precise practioner roles, can well use the facilities and services of research and development centers. Research and Development (R&D) Centers can assist local districts in setting up studies of curriculum variables. Investigations can focus on the effects of the various sequencing of content clusters with particular types of students. R & D centers can provide guidance in analyzing the relationships between the utilization and sequencing of particular types of materials and certain methodologies.

R & D centers can aid curriculum specialists in documenting the effectiveness of particular programs or approaches.

Professional consultants. Educators in the local schools need to make greater utilization of curriculum consultants. Often, schools are reluctant to hire educational consultants for fear that the public will misinterpret such action as educators admitting their inability to perform particular curriculum tasks. However, the judicious use of a curriculum consultant testifies that the educational manager at the local level knows his job well. Often, consultants can provide special expertise that is needed only at a particular time. One need not hire a person full time to address a transitory need. Here, the hiring of a consultant is a wise use of the public's monies.

The judicious use of the professional consultant cannot be overemphasized. Not only can such professionals provide guidance to curriculum decision-makers within the system, but these individuals also can furnish suggestions to and directions for various committees, whether advisory, ad hoc, permanent or temporary.

Consultants can guide and counsel advisory committees as to their purposes, their methods of group functioning, and their restraints, both legal and educational. Consultants can enlighten individual curriculum decision-makers in the schools as to the latest procedures for addressing some curricular issue, or the most recent research to support some particular curricular emphasis. Consultants can present a macro view of the curriculum field and can relate how the functioning of the local school's curriculum fares in light of schools in other parts of the country.

Not all consultants need to come from outside the school system. Many consultants may be from the ranks of the school's personnel. But, many schools are not of sufficient size to have their own consultants on board. In small districts, it usually is necessary to hire consultants from outside the schools, frequently from universities and colleges. These persons bring great expertise with them. But, local districts should not look to these consultants for easy solutions, or ready-made plans of what to implement in the district. The consultant's prime purpose is to provide educators with perspectives of the field, to furnish ideas for possible procedures for curriculum development, implementation, maintenance or evaluation, and to guide individuals in performing those tasks necessary for establishing and maintaining effective curricula. The curriculum consultant enables local school personnel to produce their program, not his or her program.

Producers of educational materials. The textbook still reigns supreme in schools, despite the legions of supporting materials currently available. This is perhaps more the case at the upper levels of education (secondary and higher education) than at the lower levels (elementary and preschool). However, even where commercial publishers have produced systems of materials containing records, audio tapes, films, filmstrips, maps, artifacts, manipulative materials, the textbook usually is the basic structure around which these other materials are built.

The educational market is alive and thriving. The profitability of the market has caused many noneducation firms to enter the educational publishing arena. This was very pronounced in the late 1960's, and the unions that occurred then are still active today.

If the textbook is still the main organizer of the curriculum and influence upon instructional methods, then the test is still the primary means by which student achievement and attitude development is assessed. National assessment and the push for state-wide testing, along with the public's demand for accountability certainly will make testing an even greater part of educational activity in the future. As testing becomes an increasingly significant dimension of the educational effort, there will be added emphases given to certain curricular contents and experiences. In this author's state (Washington), state-wide testing of basic skills at grades four and six is well established. As the public demands why their children are not doing as well as other districts' children, there will be efforts by educators to adjust the content being stressed, and to alter the instructional approaches in ways that will increase students' performances on tests.

Educational organizations. To a degree, we currently have an unofficial national curiculum which has resulted from educators sharing their problems, ideas, and solutions regarding education via the professional literature and professional meetings. Organizations such as the Association for Supervision and Curriculum Development, National Council for the Teachers of English, the National Council for the Social Studies, National Science Teachers Organization, American Educational Research Association, and numerous others exert an influence on education. Usually this control is indirect in that the messages and goals of these organizations are brought back to the school district by an individual member of the organization. However, occasionally organizations take stands on particular issues which directly affect schools' programming often by influencing pending national legislation. Attempts are underway, especially by teachers' unions, to negotiate ways in which teachers will be involved in all phases of curriculum activity. There are educators in the field who argue that the curriculum is too crucial to be an element in the negotiations of any special interest group. You cannot negotiate history in or language out. However, you can negotiate who will be involved in the decision-making relating to the nature of history or language.

Eiken (1977) observed in the late 1970's that curriculum development was becoming more contained as a result of the negotiating processes being concerned increasingly with job security and salary benefits. He also indicated that negotiations were affording teachers more choice in their in-service experience. Thus teachers were taking, and often in a credit buying approach, courses ranging from discipline through assertiveness training to classroom climate. However, few in-service offerings dealt with curriculum development responsibilities.

Benson (1967) has noted that unless public schools are flexible enough in staffing assignments to place the right teachers in the right positions, it is very likely that high priority tasks (such as setting the direction of the curriculum and managing and evaluating it) will be assigned increasingly to private bodies or to public agencies new to education. This author might add that this will occur if educators in the field do not gain the competencies necessary for all phases of curriculum activity. In reviewing a needs analysis of what teachers perceived they required in a particular intermediate school district area in Washington state, it was disconcerting for this author to find that not one interest related to ways to manage or develop the curriculum. The nearest one got to curriculum was an interest in ways of "teaching" the basics.

Negotiations have dealt with issues such as class size and seniority. Persons are moved and removed on the basis of tenure and not on the basis of the skills they possess or their crucialness to the system. As levies fail, staff essential to particular aspects of the program are often released and programs die or are restaffed with "more senior" personnel who frequently are ill prepared for their new roles.

Opportunities for programmatic change and creative decision-making are frequently hamstrung by constraints set down at the bargaining table. Presently the linkage between curriculum specialists and teachers has become dysfunctional as the groups have assumed adversary rather than cooperative postures. The personal needs of teachers, albeit important, have been linked at the bargaining table to the curricular and instructional needs of students. Participants within educational organizations require new conceptualizations that will allow for cooperative decision-making.

Other participants. Discussing educational matters is an American pastime. Often, we relish self-criticism. Frequently, we receive the brunt of the critics' comments, both positive and negative. Many critics are articulate members of various pressure groups. Some are individuals disenchanted with the system for one reason or another who have taken to the pen as a way of making the schools more responsive in their programming.

Colleges and universities also directly and indirectly influence curriculum development. Many of the consultants to the schools come from colleges and universities. However, as the power of teachers' organizations increases, the influence of these institutions of higher learning may wane. In fact, in the late 1970's, the decrease in influence had already occurred with many local associations and intermediate school districts taking the role of marketing professional in-service training for teachers.

Foundations also have participated in curriculum influencing. They have funded projects that have affected the curriculum. They have authorized studies to provide insight into curriculum matters. Silberman (1970) addressed the issues of the schools and their purpose. According to Silberman, schools were more concerned with discipline than with things educational.

WORKING WITH PARTICIPANTS

Curriculum development requires individuals working with individuals, not solely as single units, but rather as members of functioning groups. The effectiveness of working groups is dependent upon its members' knowledge of groups and group functioning, as well as their understanding of curriculum.

The values of the group, the stability of the values, the group atmosphere established, the nature of the conformity, and the sense of purpose all have direct influences upon a group's functioning. The group leader has the responsibility of bringing a collection of individuals into a purposeful group capable of processing information and handling decisions. The leader develops efficient communication networks within the group and provides psychological and material supports requisite for effective group functioning. As the leader must know his or her role, so must group members realize the nature of their organization and their purpose within it.

Likert (1969) lists several roles that individuals can assume in a group:

> initiating—contributing
> information seeking
> opinion seeking
> information giving
> opinion giving
> elaborating
> coordinating: showing or clarifying relationships among various
> > ideas and suggestions
> orientating
> evaluating
> energizing: prodding the group to action or decision
> assisting on procedure
> recording

Effective Communication

Groups functioning effectively communicate effectively. A challenge confronting curriculum types is developing communication networks between and among groups both inside and outside the school system. Groups develop to process information, to formulate messages and to send them to other groups which will receive and hopefully respond to such messages. Thus, the curriculum coordinator and his team of curriculum specialists require understanding of the nature of communication.

It is productive for the curriculum leader to delineate the objectives of communication and define its nature. Communication, put simply, deals with message processing. However, the nature of communication is complex indeed. Communication contains the following elements: (a) a source from which the information emanates, (b) a message to be sent, (c) a medium or vehicle of transmission, (d) a receiver that picks up the message, and (e) a reactor who accepts or rejects the message. The process can be reversed thus making a two-way channel (Sumption & Engstrom, 1966). McCloskey (1960, p. 18) charted the communication model as follows:

A source ———▶ Encodes a ———▶ And tries ———▶ to receiver ———▶ And respond
　　　　　　　　　message　　　　to transmit　　who tries to
　　　　　　　　　　　　　　　　it　　　　　　decode it

Knowing that communication deals with messages and message sending and receiving is not sufficient to assure that communication will be effective or that messages sent will be accurate or of high quality. The curriculum specialist must be sure that the communication network is comprehensive and that avenues for message sending exist in all levels of the school system. Efficacious communication cannot be "hit or miss." The effective system is not rigid but allows varying population members opportunities to and vehicles for furnishing input. Criteria for determining the accuracy of messages are stated. These criteria can deal with the source of the message, the qualifications of the message sender for the type of message sent, the proper use of terms extant in the message, and the appropriateness of the field or aspect of curriculum that the message considers. The public should be kept informed about their school and particular times should be set aside regularly for meeting with the press, with consultants, and with various community groups. Likewise, particular times should be scheduled for communicating with various members of the educational, and particularly the curriculum, staff.

Messages can be presented via various media or transmitting agents. Frequently, the printed word is used to convey messages to several publics both inside and outside the school. However, other vehicles such as pictures or television communications may be more effective in reaching certain groups. The level of education and the backgrounds of the members to which the message is being transmitted need to be considered by the curriculum leader. Additionally, the language in which the message is relayed must be decided. As various cultural groups make their presence known, it may be propitious for education messages to be communicated in several languages.

Not only can messages differ as to the manner sent, they also can vary in content and sophistication of content. What is transmitted can deal with obvious facts or major assumptions relating to the school's functioning. An important point to consider is that currently the world is filled with competing messages bombarding the person. Many of these messages act as "noise" in the communication system and are "cancelled" out by the potential receivers.

Frequently, people cannot handle the information overload extant in competing messages emanating from the various areas of the schools.

Also, certain persons reject those messages that conflict with their existing perceptions or their current behaviors or positions.

Perhaps the greatest detriment to effective communication is that persons within the system are poor or noncritical listeners. This refers to all persons, for senders of messages must also be receivers of messages if the communication is to be a two-way channel. Messages emanate from complex communication systems, and most persons deal with messages from several systems at once. The more people involved in message encoding and sending, the more necessary it is that all be critical listeners.

Most individuals have played the game of having one person start a message and send it around the room and finally have the last person repeat the message. Frequently, what the last person related bears only minimal resemblance to the original message. The cause is poor listening. The reasons for poor listening are many. The points mentioned in the previous paragraphs are some: information overload, rejecting messages that disagree with our previously held positions. Not understanding the nature of the language and the printed word also diminish the listening process.

Objectives of communication. Communication should be enhanced if those in charge and participating in the network realize the general objectives of communication. Sumption and Engstrom (1966) have provided a useful list:

1. to provide information to people about their schools;
2. to provide information to schools about the community;
3. to establish and maintain public confidence in the schools;
4. to secure community support for the school and its programs;
5. to develop a commonality of purpose, effort, achievement;
6. to develop a recognition of vital importance of education in our social and economic life;
7. to keep people informed of new developments, trends in education;
8. via continuous exchange of information to develop an atmosphere of cooperation between school and other social institutions in the community;
9. to secure an unofficial but frank evaluation of the program of the school in terms of educational needs as the community sees them;
10. to develop public good will toward the school. (pp. 104–106)

Vehicles of communication. The printed word is the major means by which messages are relayed. However, even with the printed word several vehicles can be utilized: books, booklets, brochures, bulletins, newspaper accounts, articles, signs, research reports, and scenarios. In addition to the printed word are various audio-visual formats: films, filmstrips, slides, audio cassettes, video cassettes, pictures, charts, graphs, tables, photographs, paintings, educational "realia" (products produced in school programs).

Today, more and more schools are utilizing multimedia approaches to the communication issue. Sound and light shows relating to education have been prepared by some national educational associations to present general messages relating to education. Such approaches, albeit on a smaller scale, are being employed by curriculum coordinators in presentations to school boards or to public groups to justify new programs being created or ongoing programs being adjusted.

But, despite the sophisticated media available, the key to communication is the individual. Communication involves messages among people, not hardware. Phenix (1957) iterated this point in the late fifties, "the real barriers to communication are not technical, but persons" (p. 88). Thus, the curriculum leader needs to create a climate conducive to effective communication among all members of the education staff and community (both person-to- person and mass communication). He or she needs to inform all persons as to the avenues established for communication. He or she needs to inform all persons that their views are welcome and that all have a responsibility to participate in the sending and processing of messages. Quality dialogue is requisite for quality curriculum decision-making.

Cooperative Curriculum Development

Curriculum development is a social enterprise involving diverse individuals and groups. It relies on an understanding of people as individuals and as members of groups. Furthermore, it relies on a comprehensive understanding of communication and of the social roles and responsibilities of persons, both educators and noneducators. For optimal curriculum activities to occur, the atmosphere for personal involvement must be permissive, free and assuring. Educators must feel free to examine, investigate, test, and propose changes that will serve to improve the curriculum. Noneducators must feel free to furnish input, to critique, and to provide their energies for the betterment of education (Verduin, 1967). This atmosphere for cooperative curriculum development is largely created by the curriculum leaders.

However, having groups cooperatively engaged does not mean 100 percent participation by educators and the public. Cooperative curriculum development is optimal involvement, not total involvement. This means that persons will be selected and/or encouraged to participate at various points in the total curriculum development process. But, not all will be doing the same tasks, nor will they all be involved at the same time. Realistically, 100 percent involvement is not possible. We have become far too complex in our society and in our school districts to have "town meeting" approaches to large scale curriculum development efforts. We are a representative democracy, not a participatory democracy. All have a voice in the system, but most will have their messages processed and their contributions made through the energies of representatives. Over a period of years, all may have participated in their own unique ways. In a sense, all teachers are involved in the implementation of curriculum programs, when they start teaching and all lay public members are involved in direct decision-making when they go to the polls. But, not all citizens or educators can sit on all curriculum committees or advisory councils. As Doll (1978) indicates, assign individuals roles or allow them to be considered for various roles and then achieve balance among them. Meaningfully involving the actors in curriculum development requires an orchestration of lay and professional groups and students in a multitude of tasks. The exact nature of the balancing is dependent upon values held by curriculum leaders and assistants and the views of what the school system is.

Verduin (1967) has sketched a continuum of involvement that has meaning for curriculum participants.

FIGURE 5.3   *Curriculum improvement continuum*

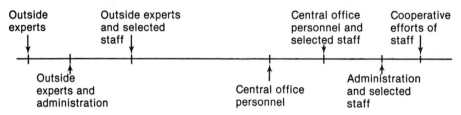

Note. From John R. Verduin, Jr., *Cooperative curriculum improvement,* © 1967, p. 15. Reprinted by permission of Prentice-Hall, Inc., Englewood Cliffs, New Jersey.

The figure indicates the major groups that might be involved in curriculum development. As one proceeds from left to right, more and more staff are involved in the decision-making. One also can incorporate into the diagram an increasing involvement of the lay public as issues of curricular concern become more pertinent to a particular community.

Activity 5–4   *Communication Check*

Effective communication is essential to the management of curriculum activities in any type of educational institution, whether a school or a training program for a business. Assume you are in charge of the communication aspect of educational programming. Indicate what actions you would take to establish and maintain open communication channels.

Communication is somewhat complicated in that it involves perception as well as learning; means as well as messages. You may wish to make a list of self-study materials for outside reading.

PARTICIPANTS AND THE POLITICS OF EDUCATION

For much of this century, educators maintained that the schools were apolitical; they were beyond politics. Part of this push for "noninvolvement" resulted because educators in the early years of this century made efforts to become disentangled from ward politics which had influenced education with corruption and spoils systems privileges. It seems that the early educators overreacted in their zeal to remove the systems from the bickerings and abuses of ward politics. The fears of the spoils systems continued up to present times. Until recently educators interpreted politics in the narrow sense of political parties and influence peddling and thus charted a course of nonalignment with a particular political party as in the best interest of education.

However, in the mid 1950's the attitudes of educators toward the political dimensions of educational activity began to change. No one particular event or major reason explains the shift. However, in the fifties and sixties, the federal government increased its role in education. Court decisions were made that influenced education, the most visible one perhaps being the Brown v. Topeka decision in 1954. Passage in 1965 of the Elementary and Secondary Educational Act also spotlighted the fact that education certainly was influenced by the political processes at all levels from national to local.

During the sixties citizens developed an increased awareness of their rights for participating in their government. The Civil Rights Act of 1964 heightened this awareness. The decade was an age of protests and demands for government responsibility. The schools, as a special type of government institution, received the brunt of many of the demands. Increasing numbers of persons became concerned with the quality of American education, with this concern being fueled by the launching of Sputnik in 1957. The schools belong to the people and the curriculum programs are for the people. The push for cooperative curriculum development intensified through the sixties and has continued into the present.

The Political Process

Curriculum decision-making occurs ultimately to facilitate student learning. It occurs to generate benefits for students. Since it is concerned with the creation and distribution of benefits, it is political. As Mann (1977) indicated, the politics of education is concerned with the question of who benefits and how those benefits are determined. Curriculum is concerned with providing programs to benefit learners. Curriculum leaders and various levels of assistants have to determine what types of curricula will benefit what students, how to select those curricula, how to determine who will receive the benefits of particular curricula and the means of delivering the benefits.

The school is a type of political system subsumed by a larger political system. Easton (1965) has presented a model of a political system useful to curricularists:

FIGURE 5.4   *A model political system*

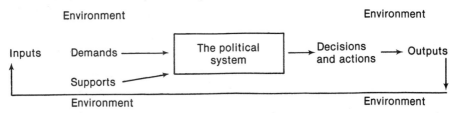

Note. From David Easton, *A systems analysis of political life* (New York: John Wiley & Sons, Inc., 1965), p. 32. Reprinted by permission.

The model indicates that the system exists within an overall environment, and from this environment demands emanate. These demands can take several forms: pressures upon the school or government agency to act in certain ways, to provide particular courses, to deal with particular students; requests for assistance in dealing with particular issues or student populations. To those in curriculum development, it is of paramount importance that someone be in charge of monitoring these demands and ascertaining that communication networks are open to receive such input.

Supports, as depicted in the model, indicate input received into the system that represents a willingness to accept the decisions of the system or a willingness to participate, if called upon, in the decision-making of the school.

In processing inputs, various decisions are made or actions undertaken. However, as in all dynamic systems, there needs to be an evaluative function present. This is shown in the feedback and adjustment arrow going back to the input stage.

Community power systems. The political system and factors influencing it all exist within an environment. In the case of education, this environment is the community in which the school is established. It is imperative that curriculum leaders and those to be involved in curricular activities comprehend the type or types of community in which their school is located. Additionally, curriculum leaders need to realize that the school exists in several communities simultaneously, the local, the county, the state, the regional, and the national. Some decisions necessitate working with persons from all of these communities, while other decisions require only dialogue with persons at one particular level. Adding to the complexities of dealing with communities is the fact that the American community is in a continuous state of emergence. Frequently, the school influences the direction in which the community is moving. Schools and their community are inextricably entwined, thus making it most crucial for school personnel to be aware of the political elements in the community.

Involving community members (at whatever level) in curricular decision-making means being cognizant of the power structures extant in such communities. Power is the central concept of the politics of curriculum activity. Power, in addition to being political in nature, can also be economic and social. The power groups in a community are involved in efforts to influence the decision-makers to act in ways that will enhance the power groups' goals. In a real sense, power groups are selfish; they strive to enhance their positions (Sumption & Engstrom, 1966). This is true whether one is discussing the dominant power groups, or pressure groups representing minorities. All such groups are interested in advancing their positions.

Identifying Power Structures

Know your community! All of us in curriculum should adhere to this guiding principle. Who in the community holds power? What are the objectives of these individuals? How well organized are they to use power? What is the nature of their organization within the community? Are there other groups in the community competing for the power position? What groups exist within the school system? What are the linkages between the power systems in the community and those within the schools? What procedures are evident for making policy decisions? Where is the latent power located in the community? The successful curriculum leader among us analyzes the community with care and assesses whether or not the school as a system is working in tandem or at odds with community power groups (Sumption & Engstrom, 1966).

All communities have one or more power systems, whether latent or manifest. Kimbrough (1970) has presented some organizers by which we can group communities from a power orientation: closed systems and open systems. Closed systems are those designed to process inputs or energy in such a way that the status quo is maintained. Persons in such systems exert energies to defend the current scene and mount strategies to assure the continuance of certain practices and beliefs. Open systems are those that receive input with the purpose of considering that which is useful and utilizing it in such ways as to adjust the system to a changing state. Such systems "fine tune" the input so that the system adjusts as needed, while maintaining a steady state.

Kimbrough has given us two examples of each type of system. One will find few communities as simple as having just one system or having neat divisions between systems. Kimbrough's first example of a closed system is a monopolistic system of power. In such a system, a group of interacting influentials controls more or less extensively the entire establishment. The same people are in the power position from year to year without any serious challenges emanating from the rest of the community. A second type of closed system group is the multigroup noncompetitive group. In this type of community, several groups exercising power on various issues exist, but when these groups contemplate education, they all hold similar views as to its purposes. With such groups, consensus is attained regarding educational matters, and there is little or no change in the educational system.

Open systems can be divided into segmented pluralism and competitive elite systems. The first group consists of fragmented centers of power. Such communities have numerous groups all with diverse views on particular issues, in our case education. However, the groups, usually because of strong leadership, are able to coordinate their energies into effective action. This leadership can either be elected or appointed. The leadership in such groups is able to get the group to achieve consensus regarding issues thus enabling action to occur.

The second open system is the competitive elite system. In this system, several groups are vying for the power position in the community. However, for a community to have such a situation, the power holders must compete for a period that transcends at least two elections or several consecutive public issues. Eventually, one of the groups obtains power causing a new direction to be initiated. The community can become one characterized by segmented pluralism or even one of the closed types.

Working Within the Political Milieu

Effective curriculum leaders and assistants are politically astute. They realize that much of the curriculum theater is political. In a democratic society, people expect to participate, albeit most wish to participate indirectly. But, as the educational stakes become higher, more persons are likely to become actively involved, to strive for control over the situation. Responsive curriculum leaders realize this and understand the means by which people can gain control.

As mentioned previously, total involvement in curriculum decision-making is not possible. Rather, we should strive for optimal involvement. We have become too complicated a society for direct democracy—the "town meeting" approach of one person-one vote. Rather, we have a representative democracy, or what Mann (1977) calls a "polyarchal" democracy. A ployarchy is characterized by (a) elites deciding issues on behalf of masses and (b) the masses having periodic opportunities of changing the leaders via voting. In the case of schools, we have the elites of the school boards and of various community pressure groups and school advisory councils deciding issues affecting the students and the total community. A polyarchy is perhaps the most feasible approach today, but the curriculum leaders need to be aware of possible dangers.

Activity 5–5   *Identifying Power Structures*

Keeping in mind the four types of power systems possible within a community, interview two curriculum leaders within your school to determine what type of power structure they perceive as existing within the community. Ask these leaders the means by which they handle the political aspects of curricular activity.

Now interview at least one person who is active in the community and ask basically the same questions: how do they perceive the power structure within the community, and what means do they utilize to influence their constituents and educators regarding educational programming matters.

If you discover that the perceptions of the educators and the community leaders are markedly different, speculate as to the reasons for the divergence of views. If you discover good agreement, note if you think it accidental or the result of careful planning by the parties involved and effective communication between them.

You may wish to make a self-study plan that gets you more involved with the political aspects of education.

In less complex times, one could have direct democracy assuring the people straight input into the governing system. At the town meeting or school board meeting, persons could tell the authorities what should be done and a vote could be taken that would be binding on the total community. Direct community participation somewhat guaranteed that the interests of the populace would be processed. With the polyarch government, the interests being considered are coming from competing groups, resembling somewhat the competitive elite system defined by Kimbrough.[1]

---

[1]See Mann (1977) for a good discussion of other types of representation.

Informed curriculum leaders and their assistants ascertain, to the degree possible, that the deliberations and dealings with the community groups and professional groups within the school system serve to forward the welfare of the students and the general community. Such educators are responsive to the needs of their constituents. To assure this responsiveness requires a structure for participation that is mutually acceptable to school and community. It requires a precise analysis of the community and an interpretation of the directions of the wider society. The more diverse the constituency, the more difficult it is for curriculum persons to be responsive, but the more crucial it is for such responsiveness.

Discussion

This chapter focused on the roles and responsibilities of the main participants in curricular activity. It noted the responsibilities and the types of expertise requisite for effective decision-making regarding educational programming. It addressed ways to deal with the participants and the needs for careful delineation and consistency of procedures.

Attention was given to the need for understanding group dynamics, and the phenomena of communication. Finally the discussion centered on the politics of education and the necessity of curricularists to realize that they are indeed involved in the politics of education.

To those contemplating managing curriculum or being involved in some aspect of curriculum decision-making, this chapter should serve to point out that curriculum development in all of its phases is a "people" activity. We work with content, with knowledge to be sure, but essentially we deal with people in making conceptions of curricula into student realities.

References

Association for Supervision and Curriculum Development. *Leadership for improving instruction, 1960 yearbook.* Washington, D.C.: Author, 1960.

Benson, C.A. Collective negotiations and the rule of seniority. *Readings on Collective Negotiations in Public Education.* Chicago: Rand McNally, 1967.

Doll, R.C. *Curriculum improvement, decision making and process.* Boston: Allyn & Bacon, 1978.

Easton, D. *A systems analysis of political life.* New York: John Wiley & Sons, 1965.

Eiken, K.P. Teachers unions and the curriculum change process. *Educational Leadership,* December 1977, *35,* no. 3, 174–177.

Fantini, M.D. *Public schools of choice.* New York: Simon & Schuster, 1973.

Gibb, J.R. Dynamics of leadership. In F.D. Carver & T.J. Sergiovanni (Eds.), *Organizations and human behavior: focus on schools.* New York: McGraw-Hill, 1969.

Gross, N., Mason, W.S., & McEachern, A.W. *Explorations in role analysis.* New York: John Wiley & Sons, 1958.

Hilliard, A.G. Near future imperatives, and educational leadership. *Educational Leadership,* December 1977, *35,* no. 3, 163–166.

Hunkins, F.P. New identities for new tasks. *Educational Leadership.* March 1972, *29,* no. 6, 503–506.

Hunkins, F.P., Ehman, L.H., Hahn, C.L., Martorella, P.H., & Tucker, J.L. *Review of research in social studies education, 1970–1975.* Washington, D.C.: National Council for the Social Studies, 1977.

Kimbrough, R.R. Community power systems and strategies for educational change. In M.R. Lawler (Ed.), *Strategies for planned curricular innovation.* New York: Teachers College Press, 1970.

Likert, R. The nature of highly effective groups. In F.D. Carver & T.J. Sergiovanni (Eds.), *Organizations and human behavior: focus on schools.* New York: McGraw-Hill, 1969.

MacDonald, J. Responsible curriculum development. In E. Eisner (Ed.), *Confronting curriculum reform.* Boston: Little, Brown & Co., 1971.

Mann, D. Participation, representation and control. In J.D. Scribner (Ed.), *The politics of education, part 2, The 77th Yearbook of the National Society for the Study of Education.* Chicago: University of Chicago Press, 1970.

McCloskey, G. Principles of communication for principals. *Bulletin of the National Association of Secondary Principals.* September 1960, *44,* no. 257, 17–23.

Miller, T.W. & Dhand, H. *The classroom teacher as curriculum developer.* Edmonton, Alberta: Project Canada West, The Canada Studies Foundation, 1973. (ERIC Document No. Ed. 081 657)

Neagley, R.L. & Evans, N.D. *Handbook for effective curriculum development.* Englewood Cliffs, N.J.: Prentice-Hall, 1967.

Phenix, P. Barriers to academic communication. *Teachers College Record.* November 1957, *59,* no. 2, 88.

Robinson, C. What skills are needed by today's school leaders? *Educational Leadership,* October 1977, *35,* no. 1, 15.

Seaton, M.J. & Switzer, K.D. Educational leadership, no longer a potpourri. *Educational Leadership,* October 1977, *35,* no. 1, 21–24.

Silberman, C.E. *Crisis in the classroom.* New York: Random House, 1970.

Sumption, M.R. & Engstrom, Y. *School-community relations.* New York: McGraw-Hill, 1966.

Taba, H. *Curriculum development, theory and practice.* New York: Harcourt, Brace & World, 1962.

Unruh, G.G. *Responsive curriculum development.* Berkeley, Calif.: McCutchan, 1975.

Verduin, J.R., *Cooperative curriculum improvement.* Englewood Cliffs, N.J.: Prentice-Hall, 1967.

Webb, H.V. School boards and the curriculum: a case of accountability. *Educational Leadership,* December 1977, *35,* no. 3, 179.

PART THREE

The Curriculum Development Model

chapter 6

Curriculum Conceptualization and Legitimization

JUSTIFYING OUR DECISIONS

Ours is a dynamic world with knowledge exploding, social-economic-political patterns adjusting, and intercommunication among and between nations increasing. The flux extant in our world challenges us as educators to make decisions to establish educational programs that will enable individuals to live productively in a world too unstable to describe with precision or predict with certainty.

At one time, the decisions we as educators made went unnoticed in large part and certainly unchallenged. However, today with an increasingly articulate public, we are being requested to justify our decisions relating to the curricular offerings made available to students. Our responses to the public, if effective, will legitimatize our actions and resulting curricula with regard to our times.

Justifying our actions requires knowledge of the realm within which we work. It necessitates documenting our procedures employed in deciding what to include and exclude from the curriculum regarding students' experiences, educational materials and environments and particular realms of knowledge. Responding to this demand means articulating to the public and ourselves the ways in which we plan, maintain, develop, and evaluate curricula.

Few would contest that we legitimatize our actions. But as Scheffler (1970) noted, justifiability can be demanded only in relation to controllable acts or moves. We educators can only be asked to defend those decisions and curricula over which we have control. Parallel to the notion of justifiability is the concept of responsibility. Scheffler argues that our responsibility also rests with that for which we have control. We cannot be held responsible for drought causing hardship among the children of certain workers. We cannot be held answerable for an individual not learning because of protein deficiency.

Faced with the demand to justify our decisions, we must understand the manner in which we can respond. Individuals justify their actions by relating their dealings to more global actions, assumptions, or goals which are held in general approval. Frequently, we vindicate the curricula by noting that it relates to the basic goals which we in a democracy hold sacred. Much educational activity aimed at expanding curricula to address individual needs is warranted on the basis that education is a citizen's right and essential in a functioning democracy. We cite tradition to defend the length of the school day, the duration of the school year, and even the emphasis on the basics. School policy affecting curriculum is often explained by relating such policy to the larger society. School rules frequently mirror society rules.

But in many situations, justifying our actions in education by solely referring to the past tradition or to current demands or legislation is inadequate. In some cases, as Scheffler points out, we are not just asking how broad educational issues mesh with American practice. Rather, we are positing what can be warranted on the basis of basic human or philosophical assumptions. We are faced not only with defining our actions by relating them to rules, but also with critiquing the rules and determining whether the assumptions supporting the rules ought to be maintained or changed. We are being asked to investigate our evidence and to defend its validity and usefulness. Effective rules employed in curricular decision-making are based on assumptions that express our basic beliefs and commitments, that command our acceptance.

Careful curriculum planning assumes participants' knowledge of the rules and their supporting assumptions. It assumes that we have firm bases for defending the curriculum decisions we make, the designs we select, the students we address, and the types of educational environments we create.

Some of the rules are derived logically from philosophical positions. However, other rules are deduced from data obtained via empirical means. In many instances, the inclusion of certain content is justified by its applicability to documented social and individual needs. Social, philosophical, political and economic data also furnish bases upon which various curricular decisions can be justified.

Scheffler notes that perhaps the major guiding principle for all curricular decision-making is that what is chosen and organized should facilitate individuals in attaining maximum self-sufficiency most efficiently. How we can do this requires careful planning and the consideration of data gathered by empirical and nonempirical means.

THE SYSTEMS APPROACH

Systems View

The model developed in Part Three of this book is a systems model that can facilitate curricular planning and allow us to comprehend and justify those actions for which we in education have responsibility. A systems approach to education and to curriculum is a way of thinking, a point of view. It is not a vehicle for dehumanizing education but rather a way of planning curricula to optimize students' learning, to increase their humanness. A systems view can enable us to comprehend curricular phenomena, to visualize curriculum from a macro view and understand it as a complex unity of parts organized to serve a common function—the education of individuals.

A systems view enables us to utilize a systems approach, which has emanated from organizational theory. Kaufman (1972) notes that a systems approach is an overall process by which needs are identifed, problems selected, requirements for problem resolution determined, solutions chosen from alternatives, actual methods and means obtained and implemented, results evaluated, and revisions enacted. These various stages can be divided into two major stages: problem identification and problem resolution.

FIGURE 6.1   *Education as a management process*

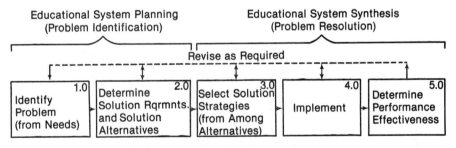

Note. From Roger A. Kaufman, A system approach to education: Derivation and definition. *AV Communication Review,* Winter 1968. Reprinted by permission of the Association for Educational Communications & Technology.

(Even though the diagram denotes identifying a problem as the first major stage, this does not mean that curriculum improvement must await a crisis before being put into action. As mentioned in the preface of this book, the approach is not a negative procedure any more than the problem-solving approach of Dewey was a negative way in which to involve students in their learning.)

We obtain a systems view by noting phenomena that have common characteristics, by identifying relationships between phenomena, by indicating relationships between principles, and by organizing phenomena into conceptual schema that we can display as systems models. Such models can be graphic, as are many in this book. Models are abstractions, representations of reality or expressions of mental images. We as curricularists can utilize models to understand and describe curricular phenomena, to serve as frames of reference by which we can examine and discuss curricular elements depicted.

By activating a systems view and applying systems thinking we can construct new systems or analyze existing ones in ways that will afford us means of improving such systems and systems behaviors and solving problems made evident from such analysis (Banathy, 1973).

Any person's point of view depends upon certain value presuppositions. Our views of reality and of models to represent reality depend upon the values and perceptions we hold. Those situations or occurrences which agree with our mind-sets tend to be accepted more readily into our information bases. Events and concepts which run counter to the way we view things are more likely to be discounted as irrelevant. Boulding (1964) calls such action the "law of perspective" (p. 106).

Boulding advances several presuppositions basic to the systems point of view. This view favors systems, order, regularity and nonrandomness as opposed to chaos and randomness. It has the corollary that the whole empirical world is more interesting, understandable, and manageable when it is orderly. I hasten to add that this should not be interpreted to mean that everything must be accounted for in all of reality, but we should approach reality with the understanding that some order is possible. Some argue that the order is there as an absolute truth of nature for us to discover, while others advance the thesis that we create the order to comprehend phenomena. Which view we take depends in part upon the philosophical positions we support.

Properties of Systems

Boulding's point that a systems view favors order, regularity, and nonrandomness gives us some idea as to the properties of systems. Systems can exist at various levels of generality. We can have all inclusive or suprasystems. Such inclusive systems can be partitioned into macro systems; macro systems can be separated into sub systems, frequently called micro systems. Immegart (1969) has provided a list of general properties of systems. All systems:

1. exist in time-space;
2. tend toward a state of randomness and disorder, the ultimate of which is entropy, or inertia;
3. have boundaries, which are more or less arbitrary demarcations of that included within and that excluded from the system;
4. have environment, which is everything external to the system;
5. have factors that affect the structure and function of the system, factors within the system are variables; factors in the system's environment are parameters.

Definition of System

A system is concerned with the whole of some phenomenon and its parts. The size of the whole is not a consideration in determining whether one has a system or not. What one conceptualizes as a whole depends upon the kinds of phenomena one is processing. We can have a system that organizes persons, atoms, societies, farm machinery or any other phenomena.

Hall and Fagan (1956) define a system as "a set of objects together with relationships between the objects and between their attributes" (p. 18). Kaufman (1972) advances a similar definition, "the sum total of parts working independently and together to achieve a required outcome" (p. 125).

Allport (1955) presents a most detailed definition:

> . . . any recognizably delimited aggregate of dynamic elements that are in some way interconnected and interdependent and that continue to operate together according to certain laws and in such a way as to produce some characteristic total effect. A system . . . is something that is concerned with some kind of activity and preserves a kind of integration and unity; and a particular system can be recognized as distinct from other systems to which, however, it may be dynamically related. Systems may be complex; they may be made up of interdependent substances, each of which, though less autonomous than the entire aggregate, is nevertheless fairly distinguishable in operation. (p. 469)

Schools are systems existing within a large social system. Schools have subsystems, one of which is the curriculum. The following figure notes the major subsystems of the curriculum system.

FIGURE 6.2   *Curriculum system*

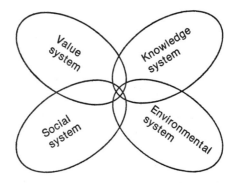

Curriculum as depicted above is comprised of the following subsystems: knowledge, environmental or spatial systems, social systems and value systems. Each can be further divided. It is evident to the curriculum decision-maker that there are various realms about which decisions must be made, about which planning is required.

Curriculum, as Unruh (1975) notes, is not a single system, but a combination of interacting systems and subsystems. The knowledge system refers to the total realm of available teachable content. The environmental system refers to all those elements of the physical and psychological environments about which decisions are made. Educational materials and media would be included in this subsystem. The social system, sometimes called the social environment, refers to all individuals involved in an interface with curriculum: the students, teachers, resource persons, educational planners, and so forth. The value system refers to all information of a normative or axiological nature that impacts upon the other systems. The model denotes that in the reality of the curriculum, all of these subsystems intersect. Planning is done regarding each separately, but also deals with the manner of the various systems' interfaces.

Beauchamp (1975) has provided us with a seminal model for considering curriculum as a system:

FIGURE 6.3   *The systems of schooling*

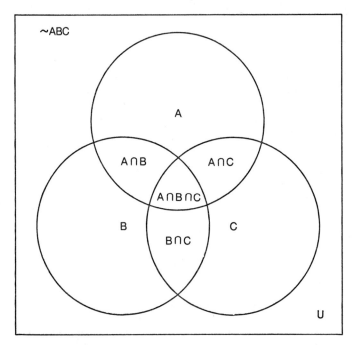

U = universe of discourse (the systems of schooling)
~ABC = all systems of schooling except systems A, B, and C
A = the curriculum system
B = the instructional system
C = the evaluation system
∩ = intersection of systems A, B, and C

Note. From *Curriculum theory* (third ed.) by G.A. Beauchamp (Wilmette, Ill.: The Kagg Press, 1975), p. 137. Reprinted by permission.

Beauchamp's model employs the language of set relationships to explain the interrelationships among the various systems. *U* designates the universal set or the macro system, which in this instance represents schooling. *Subset A* represents the curriculum system; *subset B,* the instructional system; and *subset C,* the evaluative system. Each subset can be divided further. The symbol *U* represents all remaining subsets of systems excluding A, B and C.

Beauchamp advises us to pay special attention to the intersections extant in the model. These intersections denote the continuity and interrelatedness among the three major aspects of schooling: curriculum, instruction, and evaluation. The model indicates that while one can separate curriculum from instruction, and both from evaluation, in the reality of schooling, the three interface in A ∩ B ∩ C as noted in the model. Sometimes, because the three elements of schooling meld, we tend to make them synonymous. The model shows that we need not just focus on one element or the three intersecting. We can attend to the intersections of curriculum and evaluation (A ∩ C), curriculum and instruction (A ∩ B), and instruction and evaluation (B ∩ C). These intersections allow us to identify decision points in curriculum deliberations.

Figure 6.3 depicts the interconnectedness of various major subsystems of schooling. We also can construct models that display the various major processing operations of general systems. Figure 6.4 notes four major operations common to processing information systematically.

FIGURE 6.4   *Model of general systems operations*

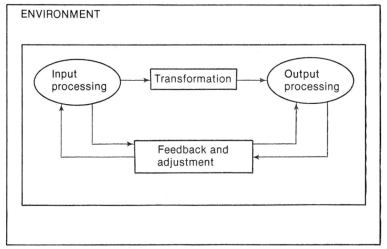

The model depicts four major processes: input, transformation, output, feedback and adjustment. Input processes refers to those operations that enable information to be taken from the environment or suprasystem and introduced into the transformational phase. It separates crucial from incidental data. Transformation refers to those processes that work upon the data furnished the system. In curriculum development, this stage would refer to all those procedures that occur during curriculum diagnosis, content deliberations, experience deliberations, environmental deliberations and implementation. In this stage actions are undertaken that activate the processes and facilitate the processes and make needed changes. Output processes subsume those operations that identify and assess the results of transformation processes and deal with the interaction between the system and the outside environment. Feedback and adjustment activates analysis and interpretation of information such that adjustments can be introduced into the overall functioning of the system if such modifications are necessary (Banathy, 1973).

One can employ the above model to determine specifically the types of data to be processed and the essential tasks for creating, implementing, and maintaining a curriculum.

Figure 6.5 can depict either an open or a closed system. Personal views and the actual decisions made determine to a great extent the openness or closeness of the system. An open system is in a constant state of self-renewal. It is organized so that new data are processed in response to new problems; new complexities are analyzed, and new information employed to adjust the system. Closed systems act on data in terms of some predetermined internal structure and tend to ignore the external or supraenvironment. Such systems accept only input that agrees with the views of the systems' managers. Thus the input does not modify the system, but rather strengthens the status quo. In time, such systems become dysfunctional, for one can only disregard outside demands for only so long.

FIGURE 6.5   *The system*

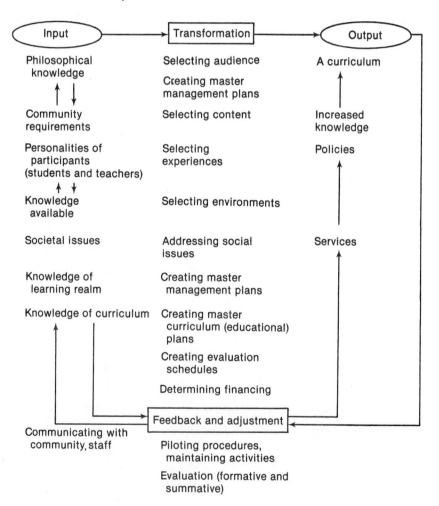

Activity 6–1   *Your Educational Framework*

As noted in this chapter, the systems approach enables one to visualize the essential curricular elements and denote their interactions. Consider the educational environment in which you are presently employed or the environment in which you plan to work. Depict in a schematic the major elements and their interactions.

Compare your model with the models presented in this chapter. If your model is similar, offer some reasons for the similarities. If different, note why you selected another way of displaying such elements within a system.

Disjointed Incrementalism

The previous section dealt with being systematic and employing models for conceptualizing and managing curricular phenomena. Disjointed incrementalism exemplifies a nonmodel; it refers to a random process of decision-making that frequently creates rather than solves problems (Lindblom & Braybroke, 1963). Decisions in this nonmodel often occur as a consequence of a political rather than educational process, usually in response to political pressure brought to bear by advocates of a particular curriculum. The program developed or implemented is to placate the pressures of the particular group. When pressure groups change, the curriculum shifts to confront demands of new groups.

The major features of this process follow:

1. Only marginal changes are contemplated.
2. Radical changes are avoided and only a few policy alternatives are entertained at any one time.
3. Only a few of the possible consequences for any change action are noted.
4. Policy and objectives can be changed at will as new community and staff pressures occur.
5. After data are available from implementation, problems can be reformulated.
6. Changes are made on a piecemeal basis rather than a single comprehensive attack. (McNeil, 1963)

Following such a procedure prevents sound master planning and inhibits program creation. Disjointed incrementalism places us in a reactional posture and surprises us—sometimes with chaos.

INITIATING CURRICULUM ACTION

Curriculum action deals with getting people to assume specialized responsibilities. Frequently, getting persons committed to action and actually to begin is the most difficult phase of curriculum development. Those with experience in curriculum development realize that curriculum improvement is more than just improving the format and relevance of documents. It is more than just structuring a program for students. Curriculum development comprises all of the supportive actions requisite for creating the master educational plan. It incorporates the creation of plans and programs for the staff frequently in the form of in-service programs and also the generation of programs for lay citizens, generally under the umbrella of community public relations.

Attention to all three curricula (for students, for staff, for community) is essential. The staff must be capable of and committed to teaching the curriculum for the students, and the public must comprehend and support the new program to allow such a program to be created and implemented in the community school. Frequently, we ignore the curricula for the staff and community. Many a good program has failed because the staff resisted it or the public fought it for one reason or another. Recall the reasons advanced in chapter two why people resist change. Throughout the reading of this book, one should keep in mind that paralleling the curriculum development for students is the development of these other two curricula.

Frame Factors

Curriculum planning, development, implementation, and evaluation all occur within some context. Johnson (1977) has called these contexts frame factors and has divided them into natural, temporal, physical, cultural, organizational, and personal contexts. Such factors are considered in this first major system stage of curriculum conceptualization and legitimization. Many of these frame factors comprise and/or influence the inputs into the overall transformation process. Other factors provide us with boundaries of the various realms with which we must contend. Johnson's frame factors are explained as the following:

Natural

Time and space are two constants with which we work. Despite their constancy, they can be manipulated to certain limits. Even though a day has only 24 hours, we can juggle how we and students employ the time alloted to schooling. We can modify the emphasis given particular subjects during certain time frames. With increasing understanding of environmental psychology, we are coming to realize that the educational milieu can be managed. We do have means by which educational space can be organized, by which physical elements such as furniture and materials can be arranged. Frequently, we can take learners to outside-of-school space or field trips. The economic resources of an area also can be considered in the spacial realm.

Temporal

In educational activities, time is the most critical frame factor. It is one factor continually passing and always inadequate. We are really in a race against time for all curricular action has deadlines. If we wish to gain on time, we can only do so at some economic cost or expense to some dimension of the program. If you have a task requiring one person's effort for four weeks, you can get it accomplished in one week perhaps by assigning four persons to the task. But, employing four persons removes these individuals from some other actions and also costs the curriculum manager money.

All goals cannot be addressed in the time allotted to formal schooling. Even if life-long learning comes in, all goals cannot be processed simultaneously. All knowledge cannot be included; all students cannot be served. Curricularists must select what to include, what to exclude, whom to involve, whom to leave out. All of this is done within the passage of time.

Physical

Schools exist within physical structures, and these structures exist within communities. Attention to geographic features is necessary in curricular activity. Where is the curriculum to be implemented? Is the school to be an open space structure or the more traditional structure of self-contained classrooms? Is the school existing in a northern urban setting or a southwestern rural setting?

Physical frame factors allow one to identify space as to function, to view space as an educational tool. If a certain type of instruction is desired with regard to a particular curriculum, will the environment suggested allow for optimal learning? Presently, most schools have specialized physical spaces for music, physical education, art work, and eating. However, many other student learnings may require specialized spaces. With modern technology, we may consider designing simulated environments to involve students more completely in particular learnings.

Cultural

Not only do schools exist within environmental spaces, but such spaces are populated with people belonging to culture groups. Each society lives and develops in ways common to and unique from other societies. Curriculum content must build upon the society's values, beliefs, knowledge bases, institutions, and artifacts.

Being in tune with the community culture is one reason for involving citizens in curriculum decision-making. An essential step in curriculum conceptualization and legitimization is determining the audience for the curriculum. This requires analyzing and describing the culture surrounding the school. It also means selecting from the learnable, teachable cultural content those aspects that can be realistically dealt with in the school.

Cultural frame factors cause us to consider the other community institutions that might well contribute to the overall learning of individuals. Effective starts in curriculum establish communication channels with such agencies. Even their educational environments (physical frame factors) might be considered during the creation of the master educational plan.

Organizational

These frame factors are closely related to the physical frame factors, referring to class size, instructional settings, group composition, staff organization, and overall organizational arrangement of the school. Attention to these factors occurs at the outset of curriculum development and also during the experience selection and instructional selection phases.

Personal

Curriculum activity is a people enterprise. It involves students, teachers, administrators, curriculum specialists, lay citizens, interested others. The identification of the audience in this first step of curriculum development and an analysis of community members and staff available comprise the consideration of personal factors. As indicated earlier, the personal frame factors comprise the social subsystem of curriculum.

Activity 6–2   *Determining Frame Factors*

Using the major frame factors or subsystems of curriculum noted in this chapter, list the major components of these frame factors as they exist where you work or plan to work. Describe these frame factors and indicate one or two major questions you will need to raise in order to deal with each one.

What do your questions tell you about your knowledge of curriculum? Your knowledge about your community?

Getting Started

Curricular actions can be initiated from both within and outside the curriculum system. The frame factors previously discussed give us some indication that change or demands for change originate in cultural, organizational and personal frame factors or subsystems. Ideally curriculum action is inaugurated by the curriculum generalists and specialists within the educational system. It occurs as a result of such individuals maintaining an open system and responding to the needs and demands of students, citizens and staff.

But, frequently the impetus for curricular action originates outside the school. Doll (1978) has listed individuals and agencies outside the school that have fostered curricular actions in education.

Bureaus of the Federal Government
private educational testing organizations
private foundations
authors
colleges and universities
Research and Development (R & D) centers
educational laboratories
patriotic organizations
trade associations and industries
political groups

business groups

professional associations

citizen special interest groups

Outside forces always have and always will exist. Rather than lament such forces we should welcome them as means of providing different perceptions (different inputs) regarding education. But we need to determine what roles outside forces should play and the procedures for coordinating their efforts with those of educators. Responsive educators will identify the critical decision points and delimit the consequences of action and non-action regarding curricular activities.

There are myriad ways of commencing curricular action. The model presented in this book provides the first step, engaging individuals, staff and outsiders, in conceptualizing and legitimizing curricula in relation to perceived needs. The crucial point in getting started is that it results not from a once-in-a-lifetime activity but occurs from an ongoing attending to the total community's pulse. The central office, under the guidance of the curriculum coordinator may have established continuing seminars among the staff and the public for ongoing dialogue of current curricular issues. The results of such dialogue can be communicated to others in the educational system and community via newsletters, news broadcasts, regularly scheduled open hearings, and open houses. It is important to have a centrally coordinated approach in which the central office and the schools work cooperatively.

Getting started and maintaining productive action is easier in those districts where a dissemination office is maintained. This office can be responsible for sending new materials to various school staff and community members for their review and critique. This office could also make available the results of piloting various materials and instructional methods.

More and more schools are creating R & D centers charged with experimenting with both the curriculum and instructional realms. Such centers can encourage and furnish teachers with appropriate aid in conducting classroom research. Teachers can become functioning members of research teams (Hunkins et al., 1977). Teachers can participate in testing and experimenting with curriculum materials and educational methodologies, and can develop new curriculum or invent new instructional strategies. Taba (1962) urged, and in much of her work with schools put into practice, the involving of teachers in the total development process. Such a grass roots approach to curriculum assumes that teachers have necessary research and curriculum competencies. Presently, an increasing number of teachers are gaining these competencies. New staff organizations such as differential staffing also are allowing teachers to assume new roles, many of which are within the curriculum realm.

The central curriculum office should be monitoring all ongoing curricular activities. Frequently, data obtained via such monitoring will furnish the impetus for commencing new curricular programs. Also such monitoring will provide for the cooperation and interaction among staff.

How one can commence curricular action varies from school district to school district. Such variation occurs partly due to the diversity among the frame factors. In some districts, the maturity and expertise of the staff allow for more staff initiative and involvement in curriculum development. In other districts, the cultural factors exhibited by the lay citizens influence their levels of involvement in curriculum action.

The central curriculum office in cooperation with the standing curriculum advisory committee or committees should have the responsibilities for making the final decisions about how curriculum action will be started and maintained. It should provide the necessary leadership for all curriculum action. Some approaches for getting individuals involved in curriculum action follow:

1. scheduling continuing brainstorming sessions among staff in which issues relevant to educational programming are considered;
2. establishing district teaching centers attending to curricular and instructional matters;
3. creating committees that will plan and coordinate in-service education;
4. providing in-service on topics that have special relevance to the curriculum realm;
5. allowing staff to attend conventions and to have conference days;
6. releasing staff members to work on special program concerns;
7. establishing liaisons with colleges and universities for continuous curriculum discussion;
8. putting teachers and other staff on 12-month contracts with the additional time devoted entirely to curriculum development, modification;
9. having special clinic sessions addressing unique needs of students as they arise.

The above list is not exhaustive. Few districts or other educational institutions have a clean start in curriculum. Few if any districts or institutions create curriculum where no prior curriculum has existed. Curriculum is not created in a vacuum. Also, once a major curriculum development project is completed, it is not forgotten. New programs must be maintained. Many of the so called "starts" in curriculum are really on-going maintenance activities.

Doll (1978) has presented some principles to keep in mind as we initiate curriculum development and adaptation:

1. Persons in local schools and school systems should accept responsibility for curriculum improvement. The responsibility should be dispersed among numbers of people.
2. Feelings of personal security and worth, as well as satisfactory interpersonal relations, are essential.
3. Adequate time, facilities, and resources should be provided.
4. Curriculum workers should attempt to solve problems that seem real and important.

5. Effective communication about plans, policies, procedures, and achievements should be established and maintained among persons who have a stake in the projects.
6. Curriculum development should be considered a continuous, normal activity and not a stop-and-start activity.
7. All persons concerned in a given project should be involved in it in some way.
8. Nothing of real importance should be undertaken without developing an understanding of its purposes.
9. Continuous evaluation of improvement should be built into the design of each project.
10. Balance must be achieved in both the loci and the types of activities to be performed.
11. Consistency must be maintained between the means and the ascribed ends of each project.

Effective curriculum action is cooperative action among all educators and significant others: administrative staff, instructional staff, curricular staff, students, and various members of the lay public. Such cooperative action can be conceptualized from viewing the following model of a system for decision-making within the curriculum realm.

FIGURE 6.6   *Decision-making within the curriculum realm*

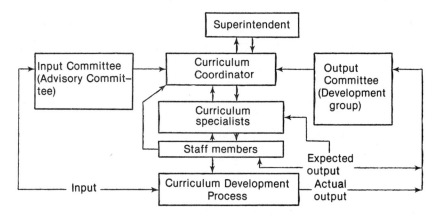

Note. Adapted from C. Jennie Casciano-Savignano, *Systems Approach to Curriculum and Instructional Improvement, Middle School–Grade 12* (Columbus, Ohio: Charles E. Merrill Publishing Co., 1978), p. 12. Reprinted by permission.

This model represents a centrally coordinated organization in that the central office manages the process, but staff are involved in all phases of curriculum activity. Had staff members not been included and the arrows adjusted to depict action coming only from the central office, we would have had an example of a centralized organization.

ENACTING THE CURRICULUM DEVELOPMENT MODEL

The curriculum development model advanced in Chapter 1 is shown again here for easy referral.

FIGURE 6.7   *Curriculum planning model*

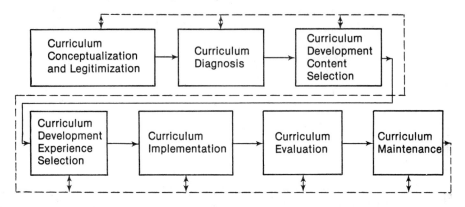

The model denotes a systematic processing of major activities including accompanying decision-making. It represents a systems approach in that it is a way of thinking about the total process of curriculum development, viewing the parts or stages of curriculum decision making as a unit serving a common function—developing programs for the education of individuals.

The initial stage deals with *conceptualizing* the concept of curriculum, *identifying* the audience and its needs, and *legitimizing* the entire curriculum effort to all concerned: students, teachers, lay public. This stage has the following substages:

CURRICULUM CONCEPTUALIZATION AND LEGITIMIZATION

Conducting needs analysis; Determining audience for curriculum; Raising philosophical questions, conceptions regarding the curriculum; Determining the curriculum design; Creating the master management plan and determining whom to involve.

The several steps within the subsystem are related via a feedback network, which allows one to adjust constantly throughout the conceptualization and legitimization phase all plans, data, and perceptions. Also, the model indicates some of the crucial factors that can influence, either positively or negatively, the functioning at each stage. For example, in conducting a needs analysis, the values extant in the community will either foster or retard certain needs being addressed. Likewise, the community demands will either enhance or retard the serving of needs of certain students. At the substage of determining curriculum design, the knowledge individuals bring to the task either facilitates or retards the decision-making. Also information relating to previous district success or other districts' successes with the design being considered impacts the decision-making. Other factors can be added, and effective functioning at this stage incorporates as many factors as possible.

This stage is depicted as a subsystem in the following figure.

FIGURE 6.8   *Curriculum conceptualization and legitimization as a subsystem*

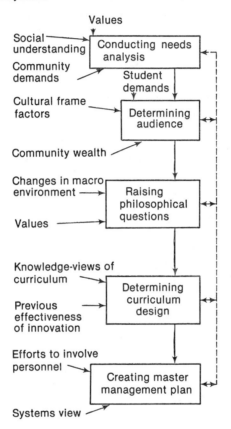

Needs Assessment

Before detailed curricular activity can be enacted, the need or needs for such action must be documented and all frame factors comprising the total situation analyzed. Analyzing and critiquing all relevant needs and frame factors comprise what can be called situational analysis. In such analysis, one gathers information via various techniques, data on student learnings, interests, and attitudes; staff expertise, interests and attitudes and community perceptions of education in general and certain programs in particular.

Situational analysis is an ongoing process extending from the beginning to the ending phases of curriculum development. It comprises the monitoring of existing programs to determine when and where major curricular action is necessary.

Conducting a situational analysis (administering various needs analyses directed to students', staff's, and public's requirements) is the beginning point in curriculum planning. Doll (1978) refers to this phase as problem census, a time for the staff to state their problems, and their perceptions of what needs to be done. The problem census can be triggered by having an expert in the field come to the school and present an overview of some aspect of the curriculum or instruction realm to encourage staff to match their actions and their students' accomplishments with similar accomplishments in other schools within a region or the nation. Situational analysis is a type of evaluation, formative if applied to an ongoing program, and summative if executed at a program's conclusion to ascertain whether a program should be maintained, adjusted or terminated.

Concept of Need

Conducting a need analysis requires the gathering of accurate descriptions of the situation and ideas as to potential audiences and possible program directions. Despite much current dialogue regarding needs, the concept remains vague to many in education. From a psychological stance, a need arises when tensions within a person develop because of a state of disequilibrium between internal forces and external forces. A need denotes a gap or imbalance in an individual regarding where he is and where he should be in terms of some standard. Needs exist at several levels, and Maslow (1968) has created a hierarchy of needs for our consideration as shown below:

> self-actualization
> self-esteem
> love and belonging
> safety
> physiological (survival)

Needs commence with physical or basic needs essential to one's survival and end with mental or spiritual needs. The needs we in curriculum usually address represent the upper levels of the hierarchy and are also social in nature. Individuals need to do this or know that in order to function effectively within the major society.

Needs denote an absence, a gap, but absence alone is insufficient. That an individual has in his or her behavior or knowledge a lack or a gap does not mean that the individual has a need. It is a need only if someone has determined that the gap should not exist. Dearden (1971) presents a fine discussion of needs and stresses that need is a normative concept.

One may note in a needs analysis that an individual lacks an understanding of other cultures. This lack is not a need, unless members of society, students, or staff consider that such an absence of knowledge is to the individual's detriment in today's world.

How do we decide that an individual should possess particular knowledge? Certainly, social norms come into play and this is the reason in curricular decision-making to consider the cultural frame factors. But, since need is a normative concept, it cannot be determined by empirical means. We can document gaps by empirical means, but, we can only identify needs by applying to students' current behavior and knowledge, our values, our perceptions of an educated person.

Thus needs require an identifiable norm. They also require evidence that the norm has not been achieved. Additionally what is needed must be shown to be really relevant for attaining the norm prescribed (Dearden). This last criterion refers to the validity of the curriculum. Will the curriculum offered to meet a specific need actually enable students to learn the called for information? If, for example, students need more competence in reading, will the program advocated really contribute to the improvement of reading? The identification of a need cannot be shown empirically, but the attainment of a need, once agreed upon, can be so determined.

Even though we can identify gaps and determine these gaps to be needs through the application of norms, such labor does not mean that students will be motivated to eliminate the gap noted. Some of us have felt that if we identified the needs, our motivational problems would cease. But, informing a person that he or she needs certain knowledge does not mean that the individual will desire such knowledge. Frequently students will desire information that they really do not need. Our challenge is to make students feel and accept the need for certain knowledge, skills, behaviors, and attitudes. Unless we convince our clients that they have a need for such information, unless we relate to and influence their norms and frames of reference, our being precise in identifying needs will not significantly influence the amount of school learning. We should also remember that in addition to our responsibility for identifying needs, we are charged with creating new student needs. We should foster in students the realization that certain information, skills, attitudes and behaviors are advantageous, are essential to their becoming self-actualized in this world.

The difficulty of our tasks will be lessened somewhat if we are students of society. From what major and subcultures do students come? What are the expectations of those individuals within a particular culture? What perceptions do persons within a culture have of the school? Do they consider the school as a vehicle for transmitting the culture, a force to preserve the status quo? Do they view the school as a major vehicle for bringing about social change, solving inflation, ecological problems, racial tensions? Do they view the school as primarily a place for giving students basic skills essential to employment?

Oliver (1977) has noted that needs analysis can be conducted on four levels: at the level of the society, the individual school, the individual classroom, and the individual. The first two levels receive the major attention in curriculum master planning. The latter two levels are considered in translating curriculum master plans into specific units and lessons, a responsibility of individual teachers.

Assumptions

Before conducting a needs assessment, one requires both an understanding of the concept of needs and a working definition of needs assessment. English and Kaufman (1975) have provided us with some useful definitions:

Needs assessment is a process of defining the desired end (or outcome, product, or result) of a given sequence of curriculum development. As such it is a "curriculumless" process, that is, it is neither a curriculum itself, nor should it embrace any set of assumptions or specifications about the type of curriculum which ought to be developed to best reach the ends desired and defined.

Needs assessment is a process of making specific, in some intelligible manner, what schooling should be about and how it can be assessed. Needs assessment is not by itself a curricular innovation, it is a method for determining if innovation is necessary and/or desirable.

Needs assessment is an empirical process for defining the outcomes of education, and as such it is then a set of criteria by which curricular may be developed and compared. Which curriculum, that is, which configuration of people, time, and space produces the types of outcomes desired? (p.3)

Needs assessment is founded upon certain assumptions. First, it postulated that reality can be known, understood, and represented in symbolic form. This does not imply a static state of reality, but reality can be defined in relative terms at any particular time. However, we must be cognizant that reality's boundaries are fluid and what we know about reality and the people within it is constantly changing.

Second, since reality is dynamic, assessment must be continuous. Those who forget this tend to create programs ideal for times that no longer exist. Third, perceptual fields can and should be adjusted as we modify our views of educational purposes. How we view reality and the school's place within it certainly attests the type of conclusions we derive from needs assessment. Fourth, everything can be measured. This assumption perhaps causes the greatest displeasure among humanists in education. The argument can be diminished somewhat by indicating that everything has the potential to be measured, but not everything can be measured precisely or directly. We cannot measure greed precisely but we can measure the incidence of behaviors that seem to indicate a posture of greed. Of course, there are many things about which we really have no reason as educators to measure. Certain idiosyncratic views of individual students do not need to be measured by educators. But, that does not mean that we would not build into program opportunities for students to develop such idiosyncrasies.

A fifth assumption is that the aims of education can be made known (English & Kaufman). These aims can be stated precisely, to a degree, or globally. Some might argue that global aims must be broken down into more assessable ones. But, there are aspects of the curriculum that can remain vague. Education is an expanding experience for students, and not all directions or ends can be or need be made exact. If certain students require definite indicators, we can educate them to monitor their own learnings and directions of progress. Combs (1978) notes that we need to cease the either–or mentality and realize that we have need of both precision and planned vagueness. We can think of this planned vagueness as similar to algebra. Combs cites algebra as a planned procedure for dealing with unknowns. In education we require formulas that allow us to deal with planning for unknowns. Only when the numbers in the formula begin to appear, can the unknown be defined. But as different quantities are inserted into a formula, different numbers appear for the unknowns. We can defend out action by pointing to the formula and not to the specific numerical value we get for "x."

English and Kaufman advance four other assumptions, but these relate more to the management aspects of the process than to the process itself. They state that the recipients and supporters of the schools should be involved in determining goals and effectiveness. Second, educators must realize that education is too important to be left solely to educators. Third, we need to attend to the relationships between organizational specificity and productivity. If we lack some indication of where we are going, it is unlikely that we will get there, or if per chance we arrive by accident we may fail to recognize our arrival. Their final assumption notes that productivity and humanization are compatible as dual outcomes of schools. It is spurious to argue that to be precise we must sacrifice humanness or to be humane necessitates vagueness. Being humane means addressing students' needs, their total needs and also allowing students to generate new needs and directions for their learning. Unless we plan options, students requiring such options for optimal growth, may find the curriculum lacking. If we plan carefully, we can be more responsive to the needs of students, staff, and the public and furnish the necessary content, experiences and environments. We can be precise in planning situations that facilitate open-ending learnings and divergent thinking. But, we must be mindful that we are talking of precision within the school's context and not of accurateness within an industrial context striving for decreasing cost and increasing output.

Data Collected

Doll (1978) has provided a useful listing of the types of data frequently furnished by needs assessments:

I. Data about pupils
  A. Data about the pupil population as a whole
    1. The general pupil population
    2. Specific subgroups
    3. Enrollment statistics
    4. Indicators of pupils progress
    5. The incidence and nature of school leaving
  B. Data about the growth and development of pupils
    1. Physical growth and development
    2. Achievement in specific school subject matter
    3. Emotional and social development
    4. Psychological needs
    5. Intellectual and creative development
    6. Personal traits
  C. Data about pupils' homes, families, and community conditions
    1. Conditions of home and family life
    2. The school's adult constituency at large
    3. Specifics concerning the nature of the community

    D. Data about pupil opportunities
      1. For current work
      2. For eventual career
      3. In terms of economic projection and forecasts
  II. Data about social and cultural matters
    A. The need to transmit the culture and to alter it
    B. The need to orient and adjust the young
    C. The need to preserve and to alter the social order
    D. The need to prepare pupils specifically for adulthood
    E. The need to relate the individual pupil to the social and cultural milieu
    F. The need to explore with pupils
      1. Values
      2. Expectations
      3. The political power structure
      4. Community issues
      5. Trends of the times
 III. Data about learning—how pupils learn
    A. What learning is
    B. What it means to be motivated to learn
    C. The nature of learning styles
    D. Problems with self-concept
    E. The nature of readiness
    F. How transfer of learning occurs
 IV. Data about subject matter—what pupils should learn
    A. What subject matter—old and new—is of most worth
    B. Criteria for selecting subject matter content
    C. How to organize subject matter
    D. Criteria for selecting and making instructional materials
    E. Criteria for determining relevance of content (pp. 294–95)

Procedures

Needs assessment begins with an initial step of planning to plan, the enactment of a scheme to develop plans by which a situation or situations may be analyzed and data gathered that will furnish information requisite for educational program building. After this first commitment to action, most procedures of needs assessment have the following major steps: identifying current student learnings and behaviors, identifying major goals, the prioritizing and rank ordering of goals and validating of the list of goals once agreed upon, matching of current student learnings and behaviors with major goal statements, the creation on initial gap or "needs" statements, prioritizing of gap statements requiring attention, reconsidering and perhaps reformulating of goals, and finally the creating and prioritizing of objectives to address the gap or needs statements.

      The last two steps of needs assessment, reconsideration, and reformulation of goals and creation and prioritizing of objectives are included in this book under the major curriculum planning stage of curriculum diagnosis. In essence, needs assessment provides gap statements that educators and others analyze in order to formulate goals and objectives necessary to eliminate the gaps.

Identifying current students' learnings and behaviors. Numerous ways exist in which current students' learnings and behaviors can be recorded. Teacher made, standardized and criterion-referenced tests can be given. Anecdotal records, case studies, sociometric data also can furnish data. Classroom observation reports also provide data as to the current levels of students' functioning. Attitude inventories and results of counseling sessions can supply data.

Data gathered should be accurate and the data gathering instruments should be appropriate for the individuals being tested. Also, the recorded information should be readily accessible to those involved in the needs assessment procedure.

Identifying major goals. This step, which is often done first in needs assessment, usually involves staff and citizens. Commonly, a group is furnished a listing of general goals and then asked to rank order them as to importance. Individuals indicate those which they believe the school is addressing satisfactorily. This approach has been perfected by the Program Development Center of Northern California and distributed through the Phi Delta Kappa Organization.

Another way of delimiting the major goals is to have groups generate the goals. This method, although slower, creates a personalization of the goals list and makes individuals feel more involved and committed to the goals and the resultant solutions suggested.

At this stage, the question of the validity of the goals must be addressed. Are the goals advanced valid with regard to the general and more specific purposes of the school and its community. Goal validation, dealing primarily with face validity, is largely determined by referring to the cultural and personal frame factors.

Since time and resources are finite, goals need to be listed in some order of necessity of treatment. Which goals should be addressed first, which second? Which goals can be left to other community institutions to handle? In order to prioritize goals, one requires a clear listing of the current student learnings and behaviors and a good understanding of the match between these learnings and behaviors and community expectations.

Matching students' learnings and behaviors with goals. Once a list of goals has been created and a list of students' performances and understandings created, individuals then analyze which students' behaviors and learnings are in consonance with which goals. A plus can be noted for attainment of a goal, a minus noted for no attainment. From such a matching, a list of gap statements is formulated. But many of the gaps noted will not become part of the final list of needs statements for school staff and citizens will either not consider it necessary to "fill" the gap or will believe some other agency or group in the community has more responsibility for eliminating the gap. This step and the previous one may, in reality, overlap with the diagnosis phase or curriculum development.

Prioritizing needs statements. Educators and citizens are continually confronted with the press of time and the scarcity of resources. It is not possible to address all needs at any one particular time. Thus, needs must be rank ordered as to which require immediate attention, which can be deferred

TABLE 6.1 *Ranking goals according to perceived performance and prioritized goal scores*

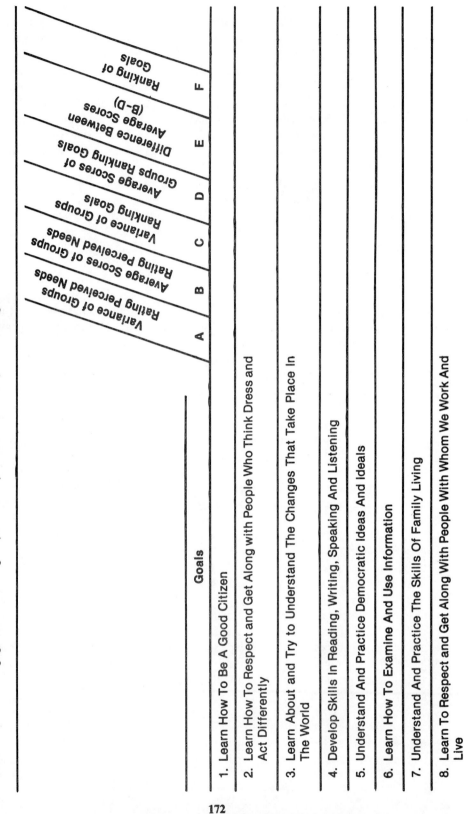

Goals	Variance of Groups Rating perceived Needs	Average Scores of Groups Rating perceived Needs	Variance of Groups Ranking Goals	Average Scores of Groups Ranking Goals	Difference Between Average Scores (B–D)	Ranking of Goals
	A	B	C	D	E	F
1. Learn How To Be A Good Citizen						
2. Learn How To Respect and Get Along with People Who Think Dress and Act Differently						
3. Learn About and Try to Understand The Changes That Take Place In The World						
4. Develop Skills In Reading, Writing, Speaking And Listening						
5. Understand And Practice Democratic Ideas And Ideals						
6. Learn How To Examine And Use Information						
7. Understand And Practice The Skills Of Family Living						
8. Learn To Respect and Get Along With People With Whom We Work And Live						

TABLE 6.1 *continued*

9. Develop Skills To Enter A Specific Field Of Work	
10. Learn How To Be A Good Manager Of Money, Property and Resources	
11. Develop A Desire For Learning Now And In The Future	
12. Learn How To Use Leisure Time	
13. Practice And Understand The Ideas Of Health And Safety	
14. Appreciate Culture And Beauty In The World	
15. Gain Information Needed To Make Job Selections	
16. Develop Pride In Work And A Feeling Of Self-Worth	
17. Develop Good Character And Self-Respect	
18. Gain A General Education	
19.	
20.	

173

Note. From Program Development Center of Northern California, *Phase III of the education planning model.* Bloomington, Ind. Distributed by Phi Delta Kappa, Inc. Reprinted by permission.

Note. See English and Kaufman (1975) for an excellent overview of the major stages of needs assessment. See also Mager (1972). An interesting study using needs analysis outside of education (in the health sciences) is one done by Risley, LaDuca, and Madigan (1976). It deals with an assessment focused approach to curriculum revision focusing on the problem of determining how a student's competence should be assessed at the end of an instructional program.

to the near future, and which cannot be met at all. The prioritizing of needs statements draws upon the cultural and personal frame factors extant in the community. What social understandings are present? What are the demands of the local and larger communities? What are the demands and expressed needs of students? What are those learnings and understandings that are essential, (at the level of developmental tasks) that if left unattended will cause later learning difficulties and problems in the general society?

Reconsidering goals. Often, as a consequence of prioritizing needs statements, groups realize that the initial goal listing needs to be re-thought and perhaps rearranged. This is important, for frequently additional data suggest new problems that require attention as the process continues. If new information were not processed, the direction of the needs assessment ac-tivity, on target at the beginning of the venture, might, because of new events occurring in the general society, be seriously off target resulting in the develop-ment of inappropriate curricula.

Creating and prioritizing objectives. Goals are general statements which usually elicit agreement among groups. In some senses, goals are slogans. But, goals must be made more specific, must become general program objec-tives. General program objectives are not specific lesson objectives stated in be-havioral terms. Creating specific behavioral objectives at this time would not be parallel with the other major stages of curriculum planning. Curriculum planning is making a master curriculum-educational plan for all students. We are concerned with the general behaviors and learnings of these individuals, but it is the teacher in the classroom who is responsible for translating the general program objectives into specific behavioral objectives. Needs assessment at this level of planning gives an overview of the levels of understandings and behaviors appropriate for the total school population or a large segment of it. However, it does not provide an assessment of an individual student. Thus, we cannot create a specific behavioral objective for one student, for we do not know this individ-ual's needs. Teachers will have to conduct their own needs assessment and engage in curriculum planning at the classroom level to create and implement a program for their particular class.

This final stage also requires that objectives be validated. Valida-tion deals with whether the objectives suggested for consideration will in fact elminate the gaps or deficiencies noted. Are the objectives stated consonant with the goals, relevant to the needs? This question of validity here is concerned pri-marily with content validity.

As mentioned previously, these last two stages comprise the cur-riculum diagnosis stage of curriculum development. This points out that fre-quently there is overlap between the general stages of curriculum planning, and that often times there is a going back to previous stages in the actual enactment of the overall planning-development model.

Materials

Table 6.1 shows the document developed by the Program Development Center of Northern California and distributed by Phi Delta Kappa, Inc. This table records the ranking of goals and compares rankings among various groups.

Table 6.2 exemplifies a way one might compile needs data.

TABLE 6.2　*Compiled needs data, with derived needs statements*

Target Goal: To develop skills in reading, writing, speaking, and listening

Compiled Needs Data	Derived Need Statements
Achievement test data—median percentile rank, grades 1–3:	1. Reading skills and performance are not at adequate levels in most schools, drop to unacceptable levels in almost all schools by end of grade 3.

School	Grade 1	Grade 2	Grade 3
1	55	40	47
2	51	44	36
3	65	48	71
4	51	36	30
5	39	40	33
6	35	32	24
7	39	29	24
8	69	59	47
9	44	56	43
10	65	62	30
11	44	40	43
12	44	32	39
13	60	44	47
14	35	44	36

2. Target minority students in many instances are reading substantially below potential.

3. Primary grade administrators, aides and parents perceive as poor or fair district programs to develop reading skills.

Professional staffs in 10 target schools cite unsatisfactory levels of skill in reading and lack of enjoyment in reading.

4. Eighty percent of administrators cite priority needs related to reading: expanded progress, added aides, increased methods/media.

Summarize statements of achievements, by schools:

School 1: 58.4% of students qualify for special funds in reading

School 3: Entering 4th graders have median reading skills 17 percentile points below national norm

School 4: 61% of grades 1–3 students fall below second quartile

School 7: 75% of grades K–3 in 1st quartile

Administrators and teachers cite as major needs: expansion of high intensity reading program into grades 4–6; additional individualization.

5. Teachers cite a need by a majority of students for individualized reading experiences and more help in structured reading activities.

6. A majority of parents of students entering grade 4 do not feel their children are reading at a skill level supportive to adequate achievement.

7. Observations by teachers, resource specialists and parents indicate negative attitudes of many students toward reading activities.

Note. From Program Development Center of Northern California, *Phase III of the educational planning model.* Bloomington, Ind. Distributed by Phi Delta Kappa, Inc. Reprinted by permission.

This form shows that needs data are recorded first and that from the analysis (diagnosis) of such data, needs statements are generated. But, since needs are normative statements, a general target goal is listed.

Activity 6–3 *Conducting a Mini Needs Analysis*

Get three or four colleagues and go through the first three steps of conducting a needs analysis: identification of goals, prioritizing needs statements, reconsidering goals.

Keep your goals list to a manageable number of goals.

Record your perceptions as to the goals that were identified. Indicate your affective response to the actual carrying out of these three stages.

My perceptions: _____

My affective responses: _____

Determining Audiences

Needs analysis provides educators and other parties with a listing of needs statements and identifies students with deficiencies. In some instances, curriculum planning will be for the entire school student population in all subject areas. At other times, it will be for all students but within a specific content area. Frequently, it is for certain students in specific content areas.

Personalizing and optimizing educational experiences for all students necessitates our understanding the various student publics—their characteristics, needs, interests, desires, and motivations. In the past, we have dealt mostly with average students, frequently considering the gifted and intellectually talented students as able to fend for themselves, and students at the lower end of the intellectual scale as belonging in special schools. Today, increasing numbers of schools are creating programs for the gifted and talented, and with current legislation dealing with placing students in the least restrictive environments, schools are creating or adjusting curricula to address the needs of special students.

Cultural frame factors assist us in delimiting the audience for particular curricula. Demands from various pressure or minority groups frequently identify for us our student audiences for particular curricular programs. Much of the bilingual and bicultural education legislation has made it perfectly clear who our students are. In the maintaining of curricular programs, much of the fine tuning (adjusting) of the program will be for particular students. These students will be identified via ongoing testing and informal evaluation techniques.

Determining audiences at the beginning is crucial for the relevance of a program can only be answered by asking the question, relevance for whom? The appropriateness of the content, materials, experiences, and instructional strategies can only be answer when the audience has been identified and described in some detail as to learnings, behaviors, interests and aspirations.

Which audiences we address is determined in part by legislation and also by community wealth. We must educate all students in the basics of education. But, who we address in specialized programs or personalized aspects of programs depends upon how the community views the roles of the school and the level of school funding the community will support. It is only recently that most schools have determined that kindergarten experiences should be for all students. In many schools aspects of music, sports, drama are reserved for only students with major talents or interests.

Still, schooling has long maintained a rhetoric stressing the importance of extending the benefits of education to all youth. In fact, we are the only major country, other than Canada, that has this educational goal. The Brown Decision of 1954 attacked the duality of the American system of education and extended the audience who would receive education. The decision pointed out that we as educators had made decisions that excluded certain individuals from receiving equal access to education. In some instances, we are still making decisions that result in students being excluded. Decisions as to the manner in which we treat curriculum topics may result in excluding students from participating. But, we are working to bring into reality programs that do address the needs of our total American student body.

However, there are groups in present society that indicate that certain student audiences are being denied quality eductional opportunity. These individuals often cite the increasing disparity in achievement among various student populations as evidence that the school is neglecting certain student audiences (Doyle, 1976). This is true to an extent, but schooling should not strive to make people totally common or alike, but rather exert efforts to allow them opportunities to strive, to develop in unique ways. Increasing the range of diversity in achievement and interests should be a goal of the schools. This does not mean excluding groups, but rather allowing members of groups to develop in idiosyncratic ways. Of course, a society requires a certain commonness among learnings if members of the society are to function cooperatively and if the society is to have a recognizable identity.

Philosophical Questions

Creating a long list of needs statements indicating who should receive educational attention is not sufficient for the generation of or adaptation of a curriculum. Lists of statements and lists of objectives are not curricula. One has to have a conception of the phenomena about which he or she will make decisions so as to meet the needs of the intended audiences, whether students, teachers or lay public. The first chapter in this book presented various philosophical views and their relevance to curriculum. All curricularists and those participating on curriculum teams must ask themselves what philosophical conceptions of curriculum they possess.

The major elements of curriculum—the objectives, the contents, the experiences, the instructional strategies, the environments, the means of evaluation—are all couched in a conceptual framework that must be identified at the outset of curriculum activity. Such identification makes evident relationships extant between these elements and notes the assumptions behind the suggested ways of dealing with these elements.

The major philosophical questions are: What is knowledge? What is truth? and What is good and beautiful? How we perceive reality in our curriculum and how we translate it must be addressed. How we interpret and organize knowledge—crucial for the next substage of curriculum design—must be answered. What is valuable and beautiful must be identified, for the values we bring to the curriculum arena influence what we select for inclusion, exclusion and emphasis.

Our philosophical positions influence how we screen the cultural heritage for inclusion in the school's curricula. As knowledge expands and societal dynamics continue, the need for a more precise conception of the curriculum and the answering of philosophical questions becomes even more acute.

In addition to dealing with knowledge, truth and value, philosophical questions also address the issue of comprehensiveness of the educational experience. Such questions also direct our attention to the relationships between schools and society. Should schools work to maintain, adjust, or significantly modify society? The previous substage of determining the audience is related in part to philosophical views held. If you believe that there are certain verities essential for all citizens, then the audience for these learnings is determined. If you believe that education serves primarily as a vehicle for social reconstruction, then certain students may be dealt with in ways that distinguish them from others. Some would argue that revolutionaries should be created in the schools which means that students sharing such beliefs would be singled out to receive the curriculum "message."

The cultural, social and personal frame factors impact on this substage. Careful attention to philosophical questions and to ways to conceptualize curricula will facilitate our advancement to the next substage—curriculum design.

Curriculum Designs

> Curriculum design is a statement which identifies the elements of curriculum, states what their relationships are to each other, and indicates the principles of organization and the requirements of that organization for the administrative conditions under which it is to operate. (Taba, 1962, p. 421)

Curriculum design is very closely related to the previous step of ideating conceptions of curriculum. In most instances, the two steps occur simultaneously. In some cases, design might be considered before conscious attention is given to the macro conception of the curriculum. The order is not that important; the important point is that both must be considered in this overall conceptualization stage of curriculum planning.

Attending to curriculum design focuses our attention on the various theoretical and practical issues of curriculum planning. Design questions are extensions of philosophical questions. Considering the design issue serves to intermix various concepts and data generated in the prior substages (Conley, 1973). Curriculum design is the focal concern of nearly all curriculum contemplation. The results of our thoughts regarding design will influence the overall conception of the curriculum and also the organization of the final product, the curriculum-instructional plan (Beauchamp, 1975). The design characteristics of the final product (the curriculum master plan) are what distinguish one curriculum from another.

Beauchamp defines design as the substance and organization of the goals and culture content so as to reveal potential progression through levels of schooling. Design, an elaboration of a plan or plans, is the bridge between a conception or conceptual model and the actual program. Design, at this stage of curriculum planning, refers to the entire program under consideration. Attending to design at such a global level provides the framework for evolving an optimum configuration of curriculum elements. After a global consideration, attention is then directed to the detailed design of the curriculum elements and their intergration into a more polished design of the total program plan and document.

A curriculum design should (a) identify the elements involved in curriculum, (b) define the relation between the elements and (c) predict and control, in a realistic manner, the educational behaviors of learners. The first two points have to do with the total substance of the document and the arrangements of curricular elements in the documents. The key elements of curriculum are the goals, the philosophical considerations, the objectives, the contents, the experiences, the environments, the instructional strategies, and the evaluation strategies. The third point relates to the mix of objectives, instructional methods, and educational experiences, the management of curricular and instructional components in order to increase the probability that certain student learnings will occur.

When discussing curriculum design we are referring to the written document of curriculum. This document is the output of the curriculum planning-development process. Design indicates what is included in this document, this master plan. A well-developed document contains:

1. a philosophical statement or statements
2. a justification and rationalization for the program
3. the goals
4. the objectives
5. the contents
6. the instructional strategies
7. the experiences
8. an indication of the environment in which the curriculum contents are to be experienced
9. the support materials and personnel required for enactment of particular students' learnings
10. a means of evaluating students progress, both formative and summative

The written document should be developed and constructed in such a way that the above elements and their interrelationships are clear. One should be able to look at the document and realize its major emphases and the ways possible for the students to experience the culture content included.

Curriculum documents of high quality provide guidance in the types of strategies available for teaching particular aspects of the curriculum. Quality documents provide suggestions as to the means for selecting and organizing learning experiences, and the roles that students and teachers can play. Reference to these points is made in the body of the document with specifics included in appendices.

Good curriculum documents are used! There are many who say that to create a curriculum document is not worth the effort, for such documents are put on back shelves and forgotten. There is much truth to this, but I would contend that documents not used are not quality documents and if they are, then the master plan by which such documents were created violated the principles of teacher and community involvement, effective piloting and diffusion strategies.

A carefully conceived and developed curriculum design should enable teachers to know the justification and rationale for the curriculum. It should guide the formulation of the major goals and objectives and provide meaningful guidance in ways to teach and have students experience the major culture content. It also should suggest the environment in which such learning might occur, the type of materials and media to employ in such environments, and the means for the evaluation. A teacher without a curriculum-instruction master plan has little direction of where he or she is going and scant information of how he or she is going to get students to arrive at significant learnings and develop crucial behaviors and competencies.

Crucial Questions

Conceptions of curriculum design enable the curricularist to conceptualize the overall curriculum and to discern the interrelationships among curricular elements. Such conceptions enable the raising and processing of certain questions. Taba (1962) furnished curriculum workers with a meaningful list of questions related to curriculum conceptualization and design:

1. What is a curriculum; what does it include and what differences are there between the issues of a curriculum and those of a method of teaching?
2. What are the chief elements of the curriculum and what principles govern the decisions regarding their selection and the roles that they play in the total curriculum?
3. What should the relationships among these elements and their supporting principles be, and what criteria and principles apply in establishing these relationships?
4. What problems and issues are involved in organizing a curriculum and what criteria need to be applied in making decisions about the patterns and methods of organizing it?
5. What is the relationship of a curriculum pattern or a design to the practical and administrative conditions under which it functions?
6. What is the order of making curriculum decisions and how does one move from one to another? (p. 421)

What is important for inclusion in the school's curriculum? This central question can be answered in part by carefully considering the curriculum design one is advocating. Curriculum design, in addition to raising and providing suggestions as to how to respond to particular questions such as the above, can also make clear to educators the bases for their designs. As suggested by the first question above, design assists one in identifying the subject matter to be used, the classroom procedures to be employed, the appraisal methods to be utilized. Issues of the scope, breadth, depth, and sequence of content can be dealt with more effectively if one is clear about the basic design questions.

Curriculum Design Options

Beauchamp (1975) indicates that most of the argument about curriculum design has centered on the ways in which one should organize culture content within a curriculum. A multitude of designs have been suggested over the years: separate subjects, disciplines, correlated curricula, broad fields, fused curricula, experiences, persistent life situations, problems of living, core curricula. Elaboration of these designs appears in chapter eight.

Design options considered have to be processed in relation to the overall school organization or educational environment. School organization, which has a great deal of influence upon the design features of the curriculum, frequently has not been incorporated into the deliberations of curricularists. Taba in the early sixties indicated that a theoretical vacuum seemed to exist between the requirements of a curriculum design and the administrative arrangements essential to its effective implementation.

A separate subject or discipline design requires a certain type of school organization, a particular type of scheduling. The same is true of the broad fields or fused design. Also, the types of materials necessary are determined in part by attending to the design. If one wishes an experience curriculum design or a design of persistent life situations, one will have to attend to student grouping as well as scheduling. Optimal environments for such a design will need to be identified. Staffing also will be affected by the design selected. In the separate subjects or disciplines design, the most common one currently at the secondary levels of schooling, one has staff members who are content specialists. In fused or broad field designs, common at the elementary levels of schooling, one employs staff who are competent generalists.

Design cannot be ignored; it deals with or accounts for the form and arrangement of the content, which is the foundation of the curriculum. However, design will be more productive if viewed as a possibility for optimizing students learnings, or as a hypothesis for testing rather than as an educational truth which must be followed. Taking the latter view, one becomes a protagonist of a curriculum design taking every effort to defend it as an absolute that must be followed in all instances. Such a stance retards further inquiry into what might be other productive ways of organizing the content available for teaching (Taba).

Curriculum design suggests the central organizing centers for curriculum content around which other curricular elements can be organized. Curriculum deals with the question of what to include, a question that must be processed before dealing with how students will experience the content or who will assist students. But many of the currently available designs defend their appropriateness by a single criterion or principle. Separate subject or discipline

FIGURE 6.9   *A model for curriculum design*

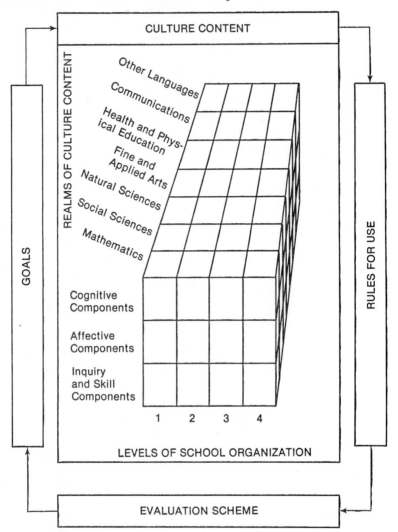

Note. From *Curriculum theory* by G.A. Beauchamp, 1975, p. 129. Copyright by the Kagg Press. Reprinted by permission.

Activity 6–4   *Identifying Existing Design*

Consider your own school district or educational institution. Get a copy of their curriculum guide or any document that indicates how curriculum is to be conceived, developed, and implemented.

Analyze the document to determine what design is emphasized. What rationale is given for the design selection? Engage some colleagues in discussion regarding curriculum design to determine their views of curriculum design and their supporting reasons. Record their perceptions and match them with your own.

designs rest on the single foundation of subject matter or knowledge. Experience curricula base their organization on the criteria of experience and student needs. Persistent life situations or problems of living base their designs on the single criterion of social situation or needs.

Taba warned that such reliance on a single criterion for selecting and organizing curricula content is delimiting. In reality, curricula cannot be based only on content, or on students' experiences, or on social needs. All curricula meld these criteria together. Individuals in their learning encounter subjects, have various experiences, and relate such content and experiences to particular life situations or problems of living. Curriculum design selection needs to draw upon multiple criteria.

A Design Model

Beauchamp (1975) has presented a model (see Figure 6.9) for curriculum design that is most useful for conceptualizing the various elements of design and their interrelations. It also furnishes one with major contextual components such as rules of use and culture content.

Creating the Master Management Plan

Curriculum activity has four major functions: developing, implementing, evaluating, and maintaining. Each requires careful planning, the setting out of definite procedures for acting upon myriad curricular data and creating and managing curricula that will facilitate students' learnings. The curriculum planning model developed in this book identifies the major stages at which specific types of planning and particular types of management procedures can be done.

But, effective curriculum leaders plan to plan; they are systematic in their efforts of developing plans. Planning to plan is the focus of this substage of curriculum conceptualization and legitimization: creating the master management plan. This management plan will furnish the direction as to how to proceed, whom to involve, what resources to select, what finances to secure, and what schedule to set for producing the curriculum-instructional plan. The relationships between the management plan deliberations, the management plan and the curriculum - instructional plan are shown in Figure 6.10. The needs, audience data, and curriculum knowledge are inputs for the decision making regarding the generation of the management plan. Curriculum knowledge is influenced either positively or negatively by knowledge of and commitment to particular designs, particular philosophical orientations, and conceptions of curriculum. However, the frame factors of the school culture, the educational constraints extant in the community, the demands for participant involvement, the time factors and the available community and educational resources also influence the management plan as to its scope and specific steps. Processing these inputs and frame factors, curriculum specialists produce the curriculum management plan. Enactment of the curriculum management plan

FIGURE 6.10 *Creating the curriculum plan*

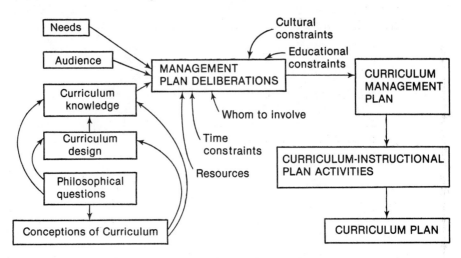

over time guides the production of the curriculum-instructional plan which is the visible curriculum, often presented in document form.

Much work must be done prior to the production of a curriculum-instructional plan. The quality of this visible curriculum document depends greatly upon the initial decisions made with regard to the master management plan at this first stage of curriculum planning. Johnson (1977) calls this stage of planning to plan *meta planning.*

Meta planning by curricularists must be directed to three publics: the students, the educational staff, and the general public. As mentioned previously, most of the attention in this book is dealing with the students' curricula, but we cannot forget the need to plan for involving the staff and the public as well as creating curricula for these groups via in-service education and communication awareness sessions respectively.

Johnson distinguishes between managerial and technical planning, noting that the managerial function exists to assure the correct performance of the technical function. The managerial deals with the planning, organizing, controlling, and administering of people and materials so that they can carry on activities of creating the curriculum, designing instructional sequence, or evaluating the successes of educational activities. Planning to conduct a needs analysis or planning to engage in content selection is a managerial function. The actual conducting of the needs analysis or the selecting and organizing of content is a technical function. The reason for engaging in managerial activities is to improve technical functioning. The reason for devising a master management plan at this stage of the overall curriculum development model is to assure quality technical functioning regarding curriculum diagnosis, curriculum development, curriculum implementation, curriculum evaluation, and curriculum maintenance.

Meta planning, according to Johnson, begins with envisioning the final product, the curriculum document, and even conceptualizing the final result of its enactment—the educated and humane person. Curriculum conceptualization is the beginning step in meta planning. Johnson provides curricularists with a useful list of questions regarding meta planning:

1. What kinds of decisions will have to be made to arrive at the final product?
2. What criteria or factors are to be considered in making these decisions?
3. What prior planning decisions should the planners be aware of?
4. What legal, political, and practical frame factors should they take into account?
5. Are priorities or sequences to be indicated, and if so, on what bases?
6. Who will use the ensuing plan and for what purposes: Who must approve it?
7. When is the plan to be finished? (p. 215)

Meta planning deals with what Kaufman (1972) calls *system analysis.* System analysis is a means of analyzing a situation, by identifying objectives, resources, and alternatives. Kaufman has broken systems analysis into the procedures of mission analysis, function analysis, task analysis, and methods means analysis. Mission analysis states the overall goal and the major milestone events essential to achieve the main objective of the mission (of the meta planning). Function analysis indicates the major tasks to be performed to achieve each milestone event noted in the mission profile. Task analysis delineates the crucial tasks to be done to accomplish each function in the function flow block diagram. The methods means analysis notes the procedures and materials available or needed in order to accomplish all milestone events and related functions and tasks.

Figure 6.7, depicting the curriculum planning development model, is a variation of a mission profile. The relationships among the four tools of systems analysis are presented below:

FIGURE 6.11

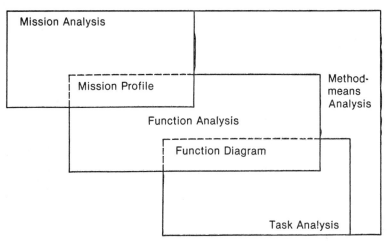

A mission profile of the substages of curriculum conceptualization and legitimization appears below.

FIGURE 6.12

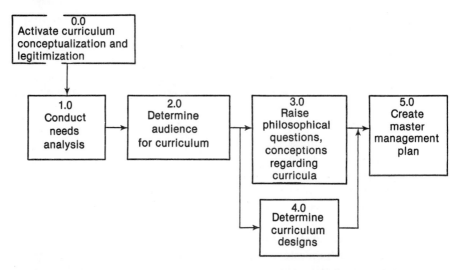

The reason that 3.0 and 4.0 are displayed as they are is because they can be done concurrently rather than sequentially. The mission profile allows one to discern the major tasks required to achieve the mission objective of activating curriculum conceptualization and legitimization. For each major stage in the master curriculum model presented in this book, one could create a mission profile. The function analysis would deal with the specific functions or lower order tasks necessary to perform each milestone event. For instance, what functions would we have to do in conducting a needs analysis? In using master planning, one would break out all of the major things to be done in a needs analysis; the same would be done for each milestone event.

Once we have determined the major aspects of what will be done, our attention turns to whom to involve in creating the management plan and the specifics of the technical enactment of the management plan.

The following questions should prove useful:

1. Who will be involved in the essential tasks and what specifically will be their tasks?
2. What facilities will be provided for the group?
3. What policy procedures will be developed to guide the groups functioning?
4. What types of support services will be provided, including consultants, clerical assistance, background materials?
5. How will these various groups interact with other groups involved in the total educational arena? (Johnson, 1977, p. 215)

When determining the master management plan, one is dealing with both products and processes, with people and materials and situations. The products of master planning refer to the contents to be offered students, the materials to be selected, the facilities to be provided. Products indicated at the macro level will have to be translated at the micro or individual school or class level to meet the needs, interests, demands of specific students.

The processes at the macro planning level deal with all types of decisions and procedures requisite for creating the master management plan and generating and implementing the necessary specific technical plans. Policy involving whom to involve and their manner of participation falls under the process dimension.

In addition to considering products and processes, macro planning also considers the support that can be garnered for carrying out the planning at both macro and micro levels. What budget will curriculum persons have at their disposal? What materials and support will be forthcoming? As noted earlier in this chapter, persons' knowledge of previous efforts to involve personnel in creating master management and technical plans as well as persons' systems views regarding potential participants all influence this substage.

A final consideration regarding the creation of the management plan is the type of organization that exists or is likely to exist within which curriculum deliberations, analyses, and actual curricula-instructional plan creation will occur. This organization refers to both facilities and to personnel. Will separate space be provided persons in which they can engage in curricular activity? Will there be a legitimate leader hired with specific responsibilities for curricular planning? Will specialized groups be authorized to tackle aspects of program development?

Evaluating the Planning Process

Some ways to approach the tasks of curriculum planning and development are better than others. Johnson (1977) develops this point most meaningfully under the topic of managerial evaluation. In a sense, everything that is done regarding curriculum planning must be evaluated or judged as to its appropriateness to the times, to the intended audience, with regard to the staff, in relation to the community, and with regard to environmental constraints. Evaluation is a fluid, ongoing task occurring throughout all curricular activity.

The degree of planning for evaluation depends in part upon whether one is initiating a development of a completely new curriculum program or a revision or minor adaptation of an established program.

Johnson points out that in planning evaluation, one must attend to both the product desired and the procedures requisite for assuring the achievement of such a product. The planning of evaluation focuses on educational results, learning outcomes, and instructional processes. The nature of the evaluative product depends to a degree upon the students and other participants within the curriculum arena, in part upon the decisions that are to result from processing the evaluative data, and in part upon the considerations given the constraints of time, money, anticipated cooperations, and knowledge base of the persons to be involved.

One evaluates not only the management plan, but also develops a plan or plans denoting ways in which the curriculum-instructional plan (the curriculum as document) will be evaluated. This is evaluation that occurs prior to the arrival of students. A plan for judging the soundness, relevance, and feasibility of the content, experiences (with attending instructional strategies) and environments incorporated into the curriculum as document is necessary. Also, at the outset, one indicates those plans necessary for dealing with the eval-

FIGURE 6.13   *Evaluation model*

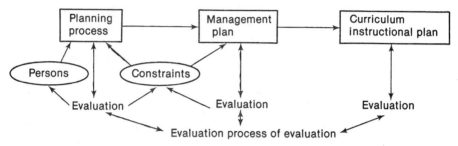

uation of students' encounters with the curriculum to assess the amount of learning.

The master management plan indicates ways in which individuals will be involved in curriculum activity and the time table for such involvement. As a part of the managerial evaluation, one identifies ways of evaluating the procedures employed by persons. One plans for assessing the effectiveness of in-service programs designed to prepare staff to assume new and/or effectively continue roles. One assures that the ways in which curriculum support materials will be selected and incorporated will be subject to a systematic evaluation process or processes. In this planning to evaluate, one attends to the reasonableness of the time schedule for accomplishing the major activities encompassed in curriculum planning.

The curriculum development procedures occurring as a consequence of the enactment of a master management plan will produce curriculum guides, support materials, media, activity packets, public information brochures, and perhaps even various computer programs. All will need to be assessed. The management plan indicates the manner of such evaluation.

Activity 6–5   *Evaluation of Management Plan*

See if your district has a management plan or policy documents regarding how curricular activities are to be conducted within your district or institution.

Engage in some informal evaluation of the management plan. Is the plan clear as to the procedures to be used, the policies to be followed? Is the plan of sufficient detail for staff to follow?

You may find that no such management plan really exists on paper. If this is so, do some informal interviewing to find out how those charged with managing curricula attend to their tasks.

Discussion

This chapter introduced the beginning major phase of a curriculum development model: curriculum conceptualization and legitimization. It presented an orientation to the systems approach with some description as to what a systems approach is, the nature of systems, and what value the utilization of systems concepts can have for curriculum leaders and others interested in curriculum.

The essential point in drawing on systems is that in doing so one's behaviors tend to become systematic; one takes or attempts to take into consideration all the key curricular elements. The process is not just a reaction to problems. Being systematic means that we address all incoming demands made on the educational system. These demands usually are not major crises, but rather are everyday requests from the students, staff, and publics reflecting the dynamics of the times. Problem identification in reality is identifying what programs need to address now and in the future. It does not mean that the educational program is crumbling. Likewise, problem resolution is not really negative action but denotes stages we activate in responding to the requests, goals, and objectives that students and educators have identified as worthwhile.

We in education frequently are challenged by the public as to the appropriateness of our actions, our decisions, the directions we choose for education. Consideration was given to the necessity for justifying our actions and the means by which we can defend and explain educational decisions.

How to get individuals from a concerned stage to an action stage was also considered in this chapter.

The chapter presented in some detail the means by which the various substages of this first major phase of the curriculum development system could be accomplished. Conducting needs analysis was considered along with discussions as to the definition of a need and how needs are made known to school officials. The importance of determining the audience for curriculum was indicated especially in these times in which numerous publics are becoming more vocal and insistent in their demands.

The raising of philosophical questions and conceptions of curriculum was considered as a necessary step leading one into considerations of curriculum design. The concept of design was developed with brief mention of the major curriculum designs available.

The chapter concluded with attention to the creation of the master management plan. This plan was distinguished from the master curriculum-instructional plan—the curriculum document—which guides educators in the school classroom. Attention to such meta planning is essential if all of the remaining stages of curriculum development are to be enacted with the greatest precision possible.

References

Allport, F.H. *Theories of perception and the concept of structure.* New York: John Wiley & Sons, 1955.

Banathy, B.H. *Developing a systems view of education.* Belmont, Calif.: Fearon Publishers, 1973.

Beauchamp, G.A. *Curriculum theory.* Wilmette, Ill.: Kagg Press, 1975.

Boulding, K.E. *The meaning of the twentieth century.* New York: Harper Colophon Books, 1964.

Combs, A.W. Humanism, education, and the future. *Educational Leadership,* January 1978, *35,* no. 4, 300–303.

Conley, V.C. *Curriculum and instruction in nursing.* Boston: Little, Brown, 1973.

Dearden, R.F. Needs in education. In M. Levit (Ed.), *Curriculum,* Urbana, Ill.: University of Illinois Press, 1971.

Doll, R.C. *Curriculum improvement, decision making and process* (fourth edition). Boston, Allyn & Bacon, 1978.

Doyle, W. Education for all: the triumph of professionalism. In O.L. Davis, Jr., (Ed.), *Perspectives on curriculum development, 1776–1976.* Washington, D.C.: Association for Supervision and Curriculum Development, 1976 Yearbook, 17–75.

English, F.W., & Kaufman, R.A. *Needs assessment: a focus for curriculum development.* Washington, D.C.: Association for Supervision and Curriculum Development, 1975.

Hall, A.D., & Fagan, R.E. General systems. In L. von Bertalanffy & A. Rapoport (Eds.), *Yearbook of the society for general systems research.* Ann Arbor: Braun-Brumfield, 1956.

Hunkins, F.P. et al., *Review of research in social studies: 1970–1975.* Washington, D.C.: National Council for the Social Studies, 1977.

Immegart, G.L. Systems theory and taxonomic inquiry into organizational behavior in education. In D.E. Griffiths (Ed.), *Developing taxonomies of organizational behavior in educational administration.* Chicago: Rand McNally, 1969.

Johnson, M. *Intentionality in education.* Albany, N.Y.: Center for Curriculum Research and Services, State University of New York at Albany, 1977.

Kaufman, R.A. *Educational system planning.* Englewood Cliffs, N.J.: Prentice-Hall, 1972.

Lindblom, C., & Braybrooke, D. *A strategy of decision.* New York: Free Press, 1963.

Mager, R. *Goals analysis.* Belmont, Calif.: Lear Siegler, Educational Division, Fearon Publishing, 1972.

Maslow, A.H. *Toward a psychology of being (2nd. ed.).* New York: Van Nostrand, 1968.

McNeil, J.D. *Curriculum, a comprehensive introduction.* Boston: Little, Brown, 1977.

Oliver, A.I. *Curriculum improvement, a guide to problems, principles and process (2nd ed.).* New York: Harper & Row, 1977.

Risley, M., LaDuca, A., & Madigan, M. *Assessment focused approach to curriculum revision.* Urbana: University of Illinois College of Medicine, contract no. 1–24380, U.S. Public Health Service, Department of Health, Education & Welfare, 1976.

Scheffler, I. Justifying curriculum decisions. In J.R. Martin (Ed.), *Readings in the philosophy of education: a study of curriculum.* Boston: Allyn & Bacon, 1970.

Taba, H. *Curriculum development, theory and practice.* New York: Harcourt, Brace & World, 1962.

Unruh, G.G. *Responsive curriculum development.* Berkeley, Calif.: McCutchan, 1975.

Curriculum Diagnosis

The second major stage of the curriculum development model is curriculum diagnosis, comprised of two major tasks: translating needs as to causes and prescribing solutions and generating goals and objectives. This stage continues the systematic approach to curriculum development. Here one defines the problem and the objectives. Remember, however, we are using the word "problem" in a general sense, not suggesting that the system is in a crisis but rather that the system, by its very nature, continually (a) monitors what it is doing and (b) raises questions as to whether the current program is appropriate or in need of modification.

CURRICULUM DIAGNOSIS

Translating needs as to causes
 and prescribing solutions
Generating goals and
 objectives

In the first stage of the development model, curriculum conceptualization and legitimization, needs were identified. But identifying needs is not sufficient; curriculum leaders have to identify the reasons for the gaps—the reasons particular school goals are not being attained. Furthermore, general program objectives and more specific unit (short-range) objectives must be selected that will eliminate the gaps, that will address demands of society.

MEANS OF DIAGNOSIS

Data for diagnosis can be gathered through testing, usually done during the first major curriculum stage. We have at our disposal intelligence tests, achievement tests, attitude inventories, and various interest measures. Intelligence, achievement, and aptitude tests present a series or pattern of items, exercises, or stimuli that will elicit student responses such that one can discern the relative degree of the characteristic under consideration that the individual possesses. Results from such tests can indicate intelligence levels, and from analyzing such results, we can infer the reasons for any gaps extant in intelligence scores between our students and similar populations. Applying norms, both local and national to results of achievement tests and interest inventories enables us to determine gaps in knowledge levels and affective levels.

The use of norm-referenced tests, teacher-made tests, and criterion-referenced tests can supply us with indications regarding students' knowledge levels, attitudes, skills, interests. But, such tests only indicate current levels of student functioning, not the reasons for such accomplishments or lack of accomplishment. One must go to the research literature focusing on both empirical studies and case studies to ascertain why certain students do have learning and knowledge deficiencies. One must go to social research to identify the reasons certain social groups are voicing specific demands. Many theories abound as to why certain students are deficient in school accomplishments (Rosenthal & Jacobson, 1968).

Diagnosis can also be done via actual observation of students in school situations. We can infer what might be some reasons for certain poor performances of students in various aspects of their learning. Community analyses also can furnish information to assist us in determining the causes of students' difficulties or the reasons that the school should attend to certain aspects of the curriculum. Various procedures of sociological analyses can be employed: surveys, questionnaire studies, and fault tree analyses.

Fault tree analysis is a procedure in which a fault or deficiency is noted and prior causes for the fault are identifed which results in a working "backward" for fault to the initial cause. The system is called a tree because the undesired event is located at the apex of the design, and the various contributing events comprise the branches and extend outward and down. In this procedure, failure is defined as the inability of a person or system or portion of a system to perform its or his/her expected function. For each node in the tree, where branches emanate, one can employ mathematical formulae based on the probability of occurrence for the node (individual event). Thus, one can determine which are the most likely contributing branches to the overall fault or deficiency. Upon completing a fault tree (also called a logic tree) one can discern the interrelationships between a terminal fault and precipitous prior events.

FIGURE 7.1　*Example of a fault tree*

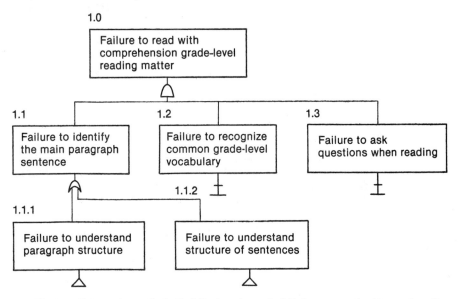

The "and" gate shows that all of the input events it links are required to produce the output event.

The "or" gate notes that the event being considered could be caused by one or more of the input events that are noted in the tree.

The small triangles show transfer in or transfer out of the fault tree.

End point in the tree.

Conducting interviews with students and with parents is another means of gathering data for analyzing the reasons for students' learning needs and demands. Much of the nondirected counseling of Rogers (1969) can be employed at this diagnosis stage.

Those classroom teachers aware of the need for careful diagnosis are always raising questions as to why, and/or how students are performing, not performing, or should be performing. It is just as crucial to know the reasons for successes in learning as well as failures.

Behavior analysis is another means of determining why certain gaps exist and also for delineating what knowledge, skills and attitudes are requisite for success in some aspect of learning or some particular task. This procedure is perhaps more important at upper levels of education, when schooling strives to prepare students for particular jobs.

Originally, this procedure was called job analysis. However, job analysis lacked systematic procedures and was poorly defined. Behavior analysis is systematic and does define its focus and terms. Behavior analysis focuses on these specific activities and tasks which are deemed by professionals in the field to be necessary for the successful performance of a job or task. We at the lower levels of schooling can well ask ourselves what are the necessary tasks a student needs to engage in to facilitate the development of effective reading? If we can agree on some, we can then decide if our students possess them. If they do not, we can inquire as to the reasons for the lack and question where such essential learnings or skills can be obtained. We can then monitor these situations or environments to ascertain that individuals are experiencing or receiving such essential learnings.

Hanna and Michaelis (1977) have provided us with a framework for instructional objectives which can well serve as a means of organizing our diagnostic questions. I have added a fourth major category to the framework, understandings of knowledge, which deals with the substantive structure of knowledge.

TABLE 7.1   *Framework for instructional objectives*

Intellectual Processes		Skills	Attitudes and Values	Understandings of Knowledge
inferring	evaluating prediction	improvising applying mastering	integrating preferring	principles laws rules
generalizing classifying comparing	hypothesizing	patterning imitating	accepting	generalization theories
interpreting	synthesizing analyzing		complying responding	hypotheses facts questions

DATA GATHERING	
Observing	Remembering

Note. From Larry S. Hannah and John Michaelis, *A guide to systematic planning and evaluation.* Reading, Mass.: Addison-Wesley Publishing Co., 1977. Reprinted by permission.

In using this framework, we can obtain data as to why individuals are unable to generalize, or to analyze. We can design investigations to explain why certain individuals lack skills of applying information. We can conduct surveys to document why individuals resist new ideas, new values. We can administer tests to note the gaps in students' knowledge; we can question students and colleagues formally and informally as to why certain understandings of rules of generalizations are lacking. We can also investigate why certain processes, skills, attitudes and knowledge are being requested for emphasis. Prerequisite to suggesting solutions is translating needs as to causes. The solutions we suggest will be incorporated into the objectives we propose and the appropriateness of such solutions will be contingent upon the accuracy of our diagnoses as to reasons for students' deficiencies and community demands.

Activity 7–1   *Conducting A Fault Tree Analysis*

With a colleague, identify what you consider to be a major problem of school learning. Specify it and then work "backwards" to increasingly specific levels in noting the possible contributory causes. Use the symbols in Figure 7.1.

GENERATING AIMS, GOALS, AND OBJECTIVES

Aims

Curriculum activities (conceptualization, diagnosis, development, implementation, evaluation and maintenance), when successful, are purposeful. The terms aim, goal, and general objective are frequently confused and oftentimes used interchangeably. There is a definite relationship among the three, but there are basic differences (Davies, 1976). An aim is a general statement which provides both shape and direction to more specific actions designed to achieve some future product or behavior. Aims of education are often thought of as comprising philosophical dispositions toward educational functioning. Aims serve as starting points, as statements of ideals, as aspirations that express the views of educators, administrators, students, and lay citizens. Aims serve a visionary function allowing individuals to rally behind them. In a real sense, aims serve as slogans which can generate excitement and commitment to various directions of schooling (Komisar & McClellan, 1961).

Because of their global quality, aims should be few in number and clearly stated. An overabundance of aims clouds the general direction of the school leading to confusion and inaction. But, aims should deal with several dimensions of schooling: intellectual, social, personal and productive (Doll, 1978). The intellectual dimension provides direction for dealing with the issues of acquisition of knowledge, communication of knowledge, comprehension of knowledge, and love and desire for knowledge.

The aims in the social dimension relate to person-to-person interaction, person-to-state interactions, person-to-world interaction, and person-to-self interactions. Attention to the total individual is part of this thrust of education. Subsumed in the social dimension division is concern for the physical, emotional and psychological aspects of individuals, and the adaptative aspects of persons with regard to home, family and job.

Presently, much attention is on the school furnishing opportunities for individuals to become self-actualized and humane. The school is challenged to encourage the student to be an evolving individual, one who is literate and capable of functioning both in the present and future. The school also is desirous of providing those types of educational encounters that will enable one to become a productive consumer and contributor to society.[1]

---

[1]Ideas developed here were influenced in part from a list suggested by Downny (1960). That the ideas are still timely is testimony to the quality of the aims. Since aims are so global, they have a tendency to be relevant over extended periods of time. The manner in which they are translated, however, tends to vary with the specific time period under consideration.

Ralph Tyler (1968) is frequently credited with summarizing the aims of American schooling: developing self-realization in individual learners, making literate (fully functioning) individuals, encouraging social mobility in individuals, providing individuals with skills and understandings requisite for productive employment, furnishing individuals with tools necessary for making effective choices in the market place regarding material and nonmaterial services, and finally providing individuals with opportunities to obtain knowledge of and competence in skills essential for continued learning.

Such global lists are useful in enabling one to envision the shape of schooling. Such aims are perhaps common to all schools. But, Doll (1978) brings out that every school exists as a separate institution and therefore should generate its own visions, aims, suggestions for global long-range direction. Specific schools may borrow with alteration some of the more global national aims of schooling such as developing an individual's abilities to think or making a person an enlightened citizen, but schools may wish to modify such aims to fit their student populations. In some instances, a school's aims will be unique to the school or school district.

As mentioned previously aims have a long time span of attention or relevance. The aims summarized by Tyler (1968) are still quite appropriate. Since aims are so long-lasting, persons who will be affected by aims must be aware of them, understand them and be committed to them. Because of the long lasting nature of aims, more and more citizens are requesting involvement in their determination. They wish to make their dreams and aspirations known to educators. This request to provide input has generated issues and debate as to the functions of schooling. Such debate is good; since aims are global and do influence the shape of education, they require a constant monitoring to determine their appropriateness for individual students and society in general. Aims, as they are redefined into goals, objectives and then actual action need clarification to assure that the general aim is relevant and worthwhile in relation to the times. Because schools address the times, the dreams and aspirations of people, continuing debate should be encouraged as to how schools are in tune with the times.

Presently, the place of schooling in the total system of education is receiving attention. Individuals receive education in several institutions in addition to the school. Sometimes we think that the school is the sole educational arena. But, increasing numbers of persons are thinking that education in other places is just as valid and may be more valid in a number of instances. The continuing demand for alternative education both within and outside the school relates to the visions people possess of the educated person and how the school contributes to such a person's development. As different visions are expressed by aims statements, more alternatives for schooling may result.

Open vs. Closed Aims

Throughout most of our history, the American school has advocated the perpetuation of closed-ended aims. Schools and their managers have wished to keep children's and youth's educational activities within the school walls and under the directorate of the school. Presently, most would agree that the basic skills of reading, writing, arithmetic and the teaching of effective citizenship are to be learned primarily within the schools. These basics are in concert with the school aims of producing a certain type of citizen. However, others are bringing new aims to the school, such as the development of the humane person and the politically active individual. Because of these perceptions, some people are requesting that schools assume functions that in past times have been dealt with by other agencies: providing social services for particular citizen groups, providing moral and values education.

Aims of education guide the schools in dealing with questions such as the following: Should the schools conceptualize "the educated person" narrowly and therefore center attention on the basic skills subjects? Should schools aim at creating evolving individuals capable of functioning in future times? Should all individuals be guaranteed education through higher education? Where should the elementary and secondary schools fit into the theme for life-long education?

Goals

Aims provide guidance as to direction, but they do not indicate the actual destination itself. The end point in a means-ends model is noted by goal statements or purposes. Goals are not visionary but rather delimit educational activities so that particular ends or purposes are achieved. Goals are deduced from various aim statements and can be grouped according to whether they relate to social or individual purposes. Derr (1973) indicates that with regard to goals, all debate can be reduced to two essential questions: On whom or what should public school systems have effects? What type of effects should public school systems have?

Goals take the question generated at the aims level, Why is this curriculum being stressed? and translate it into the question, What destination have we visualized for learners who are to experience this curriculum? Goals provide the teacher and curriculum types with broad and general statements of what they expect to accomplish in terms of student learning as a result of a particular course or total school year. Whether the expectation is in terms of a course or total program depends on whether one is attending to a course goal or a total program goal. It is evident that goals exist on a continuum from program general to course specific. Extended further, goals evolve into program or course objectives which are treated in the next major section of this chapter.

In generating goals, one obtains general expressions or desired outcomes that provide substance to educational purposes. The noting of goals can identify the purpose of a particular area of the curriculum and can facilitate the prioritizing of educational actions and the delimiting of educational policies. With regard to goal generation, one has four essential steps:

1. deducing goals (listing) from various aims statements;
2. prioritizing goals as to feasibility, desirability;

3. validating goals as to whether they are truly related to the aims (a type of content validity);
4. reconsidering the goals as to priority.

(Some of this can be started in the curriculum conceptualization stage of curriculum development.)

Justifying Aims and Goals

Why *these* aims and not those? Why *these* goals and not those? Our positions evidenced in our responses are strengthened when we have effective rationales for attending to particular aims and related goals. There will be times when we will be unable to respond with precision, but this should not deter us in attempting to support our directions and emphases. Justification of aims and goals, and corresponding program objectives is done by referring in part to the stage of curriculum conceptualization and legitimization. In that first phase, conceptions of curriculum were delineated, philosophical questions and curriculum designs were processed. Needs also were noted with attention to the societal norms that indicated that such gaps or deficiencies should not exist.

Justifying aims and goals is done on several bases: social, political, economic, moral, philosophical, and educational. One can argue that in reality, there is no educational base unless it relates to one of these other bases. Education for self-awareness and rationalization of self-worth, a frequently expressed aim, emanates from the social base. Education for effective citizenship receives support from the political, social, economic, and moral bases. Aims and goals are justified as to relevancy, worthwhileness, and attainability. These criteria also are employed, along with some others in justifying program objectives.

Where do goals originate? The several bases mentioned above (social, political, economic, moral, philosophical, and educational) all provide areas from which goals can generate. Many pressure groups in society advance goals considered worthy of treatment. Groups within the economic sector also recommend goals to which the school should direct its energies. These sources are processed by curriculum coordinators through various communication channels open to individuals and groups. Teachers faced with implementing a curriculum obtain their knowledge of goals from state and district curriculum guides, sample teaching units, teachers guides, commercial textbooks, and needs assessment reports. Frequently, goals are influenced by the informal dialogue extant among school personnel, students, and lay citizens (Hannah & Michaelis, 1977).

Sample Goals

There are a multitude of goals for educators to process. The following list provides a partial presentation.

To develop in persons procedures for adjusting to life.
To develop in persons positive self-concepts.
To develop in persons critical thinking and decision-making skills.
To develop in persons an appreciation of the arts.
To develop in persons competence in the basic communication skills (both verbal, [written and nonwritten], and nonverbal).
To develop in persons competence in basic information processing skills and procedures.
To develop in individuals a critical, inquisitive attitude.
To develop in individuals competence in utilizing questions and questioning techniques.
To build in individuals empathy for their fellow humans.
To develop in individuals an openness to new ideas.
To develop in individuals an appreciation of and awareness of what is necessary for good physical and mental health.

Activity 7–2   *Justifying Goals*

With several of your colleagues, create a "Justifying Committee." Select three or four major goals that are addressed in your district. Put into writing the rationales behind attending to these goals. Use a format similar to the following.

Goals	*Justification*
_____	_____
	_____
_____	_____
	_____

Objectives

Most, if not all, human behavior is purposeful. Even if we opt for inaction, we have stated an intent of engaging in relaxation or inactivity which in reality is the activity of resting. All phases of curriculum activity also are purposeful at least to the degree that we want the curriculum to do something as opposed to nothing. Thus we bring to the curricular arena certain objectives. Sometimes these are not verbalized and sometimes they are.

While goals deal rather generally with anticipated ends, objectives deal with tactical behaviors and intermediary end results that facilitate the attainment of anticipated ends. Objectives are more specific than goals and this specificity is increased as one advances from program objectives to unit objectives to lesson objectives. Objectives are statements that are designed to communicate to involved parties—teachers, students, lay public—an intent of a particular action. Mager (1962) notes that a meaningfully stated objective is one that communicates effectively to the reader of the objective, the instructional intent of the objective. Its meaningfulness is dependent upon the degree to which it conveys to others the educator's or objective writer's intent of what the successful learner will do. This meaningfulness becomes more exact as one moves from general program objectives to specific lesson objectives.

Objectives, being tactical, require specificity and organization such that one can see in the objective indications of the types of student behaviors and products to be exhibited or produced as a consequence of experiencing the curriculum. However, there are other objectives that must receive attention—the teachers' objectives. Teachers confronted with both curriculum development and actual curriculum implementation have need of delineating what content they will teach, what behaviors or methods they will employ, what time constraints they will face, what criteria they will utilize to judge their teaching and managing of the class. All other persons involved in the several stages of curriculum activity have objectives they can set for themselves. Those who determine curriculum design set objectives dealing with the actual production or selection of the design and also the types of behaviors engaged in during the process.

In this section of the book we are primarily talking of students' objectives. Teachers' objectives can easily be inferred from analysis of students' objectives. In generating students' objectives, one attends to the elements of the curriculum—the content, the experiences, the environments—and the means for assessing how involved parties interact with such elements and the benefits of such interactions. Care must be taken in objective generation less the experiences suggested be trivial, the content valueless, and the environments nonproductive.

Objectives and the Planning Process

Objectives, along with goals, are indications of end points to be achieved. Thus, objectives comprise an integral part of a means-ends perspective of curriculum planning. The defense for objectives is that by having some delineation of end points at the beginning planning stages, the means—the curriculum to be offered, the experiences to be planned and organized, and the environments to be suggested and planned—can be selected and arranged more systematically and purposefully. To be sure, some critics of objectives have argued that such precision is not only impossible, but undesirable. But there has been research that has indicated that the employment of objectives has been instrumental in increasing students' learning and motivation.[2]

The model presented in this textbook incorporates objectives into one of the major initial stages of curriculum planning. Without objectives identified and articulated, one cannot engage in systematic planning; one cannot identify meaningful content, motivating experiences, or optimal educational environments. Davies (1976) points out that planning is really anticipatory

---

[2]For information on the effectiveness of specific objectives compared with general objectives, see McNeil (1967), Jenkins and Deno (1971) and Cardarelli (1971). The following studies have compared the use of specific objectives with no objectives with the results seemingly in favor of objectives: Bryand (1970) and Schneiderwent (1970).

decision-making regarding what to do and how to do it before any actual action is commenced. It directs persons' attention to the elements of the total curriculum and learning process and points out the nature of the relationships between suggested ends advanced and articulated means available.

Objectives as used in this curriculum development model allow one to focus on both educational ends and means prior to beginning major stages of curriculum development. Thus objectives and the means can be critiqued as to worthwhileness, feasibility, appropriateness, relevance, and cost. This does not prevent the inclusion of divergent or evolving ends. More is said about this later in this chapter. But, without an overview of the total curriculum, which in essence was begun in the conceptualization stage, one has difficulty in setting up a systematic planning process. Davies (1976) has adapted the ideas of several educators in creating a figure which depicts rather well the means–ends model and the place of systematic planning.

FIGURE 7.2   *A means-ends perspective of planning*

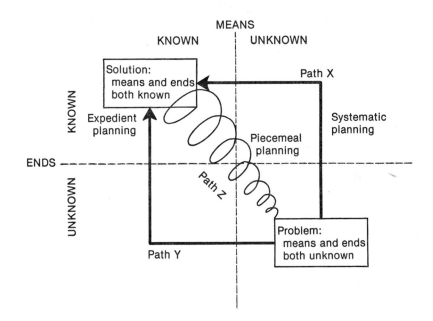

Types of Objectives

We can create various types of obectives throughout educational planning. We can create somewhat general program objectives relating to long-term outcomes as well as more specific unit and lesson objectives attending to more immediate outcomes. However, even when dealing with the specificity of a lesson objective, the effective teacher approaches the objective as still being a guide. He or she realizes that it will have to be adjusted to the needs and interests of the individuals in a class.

The only way an objective can remain exactly as planned is if we at the outset would not wish for variation among our students regarding their learning, their behavior, and their attitudes. Also, we would have to know with certainty that our end product is relevant to the times, to the needs of students. But, individuals approach schooling with their own perceptions regarding learning. Furthermore, learning is multidimensional, and therefore we really cannot list all of the permutations of behaviors. We can certainly indicate levels of performance and particular knowledge and skills to be learned by individuals, but at the same time most of us realize that other learnings not indicated in the objective are also occurring. Presently, we have no way of monitoring such learnings or perhaps even of influencing them. Some would argue that we have no need to regulate all variables affecting learning, only those which we consider to have the greatest impact upon students' education.

In diagramming the relationship of aims to goals to objectives, one can identify objectives at various levels directly related to the program being considered or developed and those only tangentially related. The diagramming also suggests spinoffs from objectives at various levels. Not all objectives need to be noted at the beginning, but the major ones capable of stimulating spinoffs should be identified.

What one calls these various levels of objectives is less important than realizing that objectives do exist at various levels of generalization. Program objectives can be called educational objectives or first level objectives. Unit objectives can be identified as instructional objectives or second level objectives. Lesson objectives can be called behavioral objectives or third level objectives. Conceivably the levels of objectives are limitless. Objectives that one might find within a learning activity packet within a particular school lesson might well be ranked as four level objectives (Clark, 1972; Hannah & Michaelis, 1977).

Vroman (1975) has depicted objectives at three levels: institutional, managerial, and teaching. Institutional objectives, at the apex of the generalness hierarchy, are concerned with innovation and are future-oriented. These objectives can be equated with program objectives. Managerial objectives relate to more immediate action and can be considered parallel with unit objectives. Teaching objectives are concerned with the most immediate action and are another name for behavioral or third level objectives. The relationship between objectives and levels is presented in Figure 7.3.

It is evident that one can generate objectives from the aims of education and the noted goals. The quality of the objectives and their validity depend to a great extent on the quality of the original goals, the accuracy with which the goals reflect and address the central aims of education, and the validity of the resultant objectives with regard to the goals and aims. Also, goals and aims are influenced by the conceptualizations one possesses of the total educational process and the philosophical and design orientations one holds.

FIGURE 7.3   *Relationship between objectives and levels*

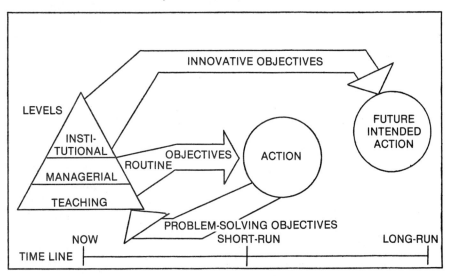

Note. From H. William Vroman, "Educational systems and the problem solving process." In S.D. Zalatino & P.J. Sleeman, *A systems approach to learning environments.* Roselle, N.J.: MEDED Projects, 1975, p. 298. Reprinted by permission.

Experienced program designers and developers realize that just stating technically perfect objectives does not mean that they automatically have value. Objectives do not guarantee quality education and curricula. One can have precisely worded, technically perfect objectives about inconsequential content and valueless behavior. One might even have objectives that note behaviors deleterious to the total learning performance such as accepting the views of authorities without questioning (Durio, 1976).

Advantages

Why should one generate objectives at general levels? Why not construct objectives at the specific lesson level? Clark (1972) has provided a useful listing of advantages for the employment of general educational objectives:

1. General objectives provide guidelines for a group of specific objectives.
2. General objectives can provide the relevance for specific instructional objectives.
3. General objectives can provide teachers with a more encompassing and complete picture of their efforts and thereby prevent them from intentionally omitting desirable instructional objectives not readily apparent.
4. General objectives facilitate communication with nonprofessional people.

5. The values of society and the community, as well as their priority, are more easily incorporated into general educational objectives than they are into specific instructional objectives. (p. 42)

Hanna and Michaelis (1977) provide a similar listing of advantages for instructional objectives. Basically, such objectives provide a general overview of the directions of the total educational process. They provide a guide to understanding, selecting, and modifying objectives at other levels in the program. Such objectives also assist in relating the program to the determined audience for the curriculum and in articulating the levels of students' competencies. Such objectives provide guidance as to the content to be selected, its manner of sequencing, the experiences to be contemplated and their possible sequences, the instructional strategies available and places for possible utilization, possible environments that would facilitate particular students learnings, and types of materials appropriate for these students with regard to the curriculum contemplated. Such instructional or program objectives allow one to judge whether the direction of the total program is meaningful and in concert with the overall purposes of the school as determined by both educators and the society at large.

Program objectives provide direction in the writing of the behavioral objectives at the unit and lesson levels. If one ignores the more global and long-range objectives, one would have difficulty in explaining how a specific lesson objective fits into the overall educational program. Why must a student do this in five minutes and do it verbally? One can only answer such a query by relating back to the general program objectives and even the goals and aims and conceptualization of schooling. For example behaviors stressed in one course such as being able to pick out the correct answer when presented with a list of options, might negate an instructor's efforts of getting students to develop divergent thinking behaviors (Hannah & Michaelis).

Open vs. Closed Objectives

Much of the debate relating to objectives has been that their specificity is more relevant to training activities than to educational activities. Objectives, stated precisely, can only relate to specifics that are known at the beginning of planning. We can be very specific about training persons for particular tasks in certain job-oriented situations and also training persons to attain and use certain skills. Creating behavioral objectives (lesson objectives level) is rather easy when dealing with the skills subjects of reading, writing, and arithmetic. But, to be as specific in the areas of art, social studies and general science is more difficult. Just what distinctive behaviors and content should students know in social studies? We can list map skills, but can we be as precise in noting levels of empathy for others and tolerance for diverse cultural ways? Likewise, in certain subjects, it is rather easy to note with precision "essential" content and behaviors that students should know and demonstrate in short-term situations. But, it is decidedly more difficult to note with exactitude what individuals should be doing at the end of five years of schooling or even what they should be demonstrating five years after graduation.

Precision does have a place in our thinking about the ends of education. But, effective curricularists also entertain divergence, openness, and generate objectives that indicate that students will explore within certain content areas, but which leave open the results of such exploration.

Closed objectives. There are certain objectives that we wish all students to attain to certain levels. Hanna and Michaelis call these standing instructional objectives, and they are closed objectives. Such objectives are statements of standards that students are expected to attain. Often these standards have been generated during goal analysis and the diagnosis of needs. These standards can be determined to be the minimum requisite for individuals if they are to function effectively in our present and future society. These standards are common to all, that is, all students must demonstrate a level of expertise, understanding or performance in order to achieve success in the school program. Such closed objectives in reality are prescriptions. These contents, behaviors, experiences are prescribed for the students' success in the general society. Certainly, we can debate the adequacy as well as the accuracy and appropriateness of the prescription. Examples of closed objectives follow below:

1. Given 10 lists of 2 digit numbers, students will write the correct responses in a 10-minute period with 90% accuracy.
2. Given a globe of the earth, students will determine the correct air mileage between three major Eastern U.S. cities and two West European capitals. This will be done with total accuracy within a 5-minute period.
3. Given a paragraph of seven sentences, students will in three minutes underline the words serving descriptive and naming funtions. Students should attain 85% accuracy.

Open objectives. In contrast to the closed, prescriptive type of objectives, open objectives are descriptive, divergent, and can vary regarding the content, experiences, behaviors, and criteria applied to students. Open objectives allow us to personalize the educational experience. Such objectives often are determined essential as a result of our diagnosis of needs statements. Using open objectives should enable us to still adhere to the idea of creating objectives, but also address the criticisms of those who say that the use of objectives is limiting, misleading, and at worst damaging to individuals. Open objectives are well suited to areas of the curriculum in which the learning is at the conceptual, emotional, and attitudal levels rather than at the skills levels. Examples of such objectives appear below:

1. Students will synthesize generalizations from the sets of primary sources dealing with current conservation legislation.
2. Students will, after reading a report on energy use, develop a plan for reducing our dependence on fossil fuels.

3. Students, given various types of wood, will design a type of furniture.

Note that the exact process and end products are not indicated in the objectives. Neither are the criteria for determining the effectiveness of action. These elements of the objectives will be determined by the instructor considering the unique interests, potentials, and goals of the student. In some situations, instructors would work with students in generating such objectives.

Educational programs require the listing of both open and closed objectives.

Cognitive, Affective, and Psychomotor Objectives

Bloom (1956), Krathwohl (1956) and Harrow (1972) have done extensive work in identifying three types or realms of objectives: cognitive, affective, and psychomotor. The cognitive objectives emphasize mental processes ranging from simple recall to the synthesizing and evaluating of ideas. Affective objectives stress the domain of emotions and feelings. Frequently these objectives emphasize student appreciations, attitudes, interests, values and emotional sets. The third domain of objectives, the psychomotor, is concerned with muscular skills, manipulation of materials or actions that require neuromuscular coordination.

These three domains are not independent from each other. However, attaining success in one domain does not guarantee accomplishment in other domains. One can have students attaining certain knowledge without developing appropriate attitudes and interests. At one time in curriculum development, it was believed that if students were successful in the cognitive aspects of schooling, the other domains would take care of themselves. But, we are realizing that if all domains are to function effectively, we must consciously plan objectives that address all domains.

Components

All objectives whether open or closed, general or specific have the same components—the differences are only in degree, not in kind. Baker and Schutz (1971) mention three: environmental conditions, operations performed, and behavior mode. Environmental conditions refer to the givens of the educational environment in which the student will learn or demonstrate via his or her behavior the attainment of some aspect of learning. This component notes the environmental factors or constraints which exist because of the nature of the school classroom or because of teacher design. An example of this component is contained in the following objective:

> The student will identify the types of paintings in the accompanying series using the descriptions provided in an explanatory list.

The series of paintings and the list of descriptions are two environmental condition components. They set up the physical constraints and direct student performance and action in predetermined directions.

Operations performed refers to the behavior component of objectives. This component depicts what the learner must accomplish under the constraints set by the teacher. Thus, this component notes the types of behaviors that in essence, will be accepted by the teacher as indicating student success in achieving the objective. Referring to the above example, the operation performed is the act of identifying.

The third component noted by Baker and Schutz is the behavior mode. Basically, this component makes more specific the operations noted in the objective. Frequently it is the adjustment of this component that makes a rather general program objective into a unit and finally a lesson objective. Behavior mode refers to the actual behavior the student would demonstrate. In our example, the actual behavior that would be performed is the act of identifying. Identifying can be accomplished by pointing, written circling, verbally noting, written underlining, and verbal explaining. In our example, the objective when translated to a unit or more commonly a lesson objective would note just how the identifying would be done.

As a part of this basic behavior mode is the behavior performance level. Performance level, as Hanna and Michaelis (1977) point out, refers to the level of action the student must demonstrate within the environmental constraints set forth. What is successful behavior or high-level understanding? In the case of our example, one would at the lesson level note perhaps that the students would have to identify five out of eight types of paintings correctly by placing the letter of the correct description under the examples of the paintings.

Hanna and Michaelis also discuss two other elements of objectives of which we should be mindful: target individuals and time. These elements are usually implicit in objectives, but at the lesson level we should make them explicit. Just which students are to identify the types of paintings and how much time will we provide them for demonstrating such behavior? Often the student audience has been defined somewhat precisely in the first stage of the curriculum planning model. Time is a major element to consider for time is one frame factor of which we have a perpetual deficiency. But, students require realistic time intervals, realistic in terms of the task, in terms of their capabilities and prior experiences and levels of understanding. The time factor will vary as the student population fluctuates. In fact, one might adjust all of the objective's components when personalizing the objectives. Considering all of the components and making the necessary adjustment to our earlier program objective, our objective now reads as follows:

> The students in the introductory art appreciation class will identify types of paintings by matching and identifying letters noting painting types with descriptions provided in a written list. For successful performance, students will identify five of the eight types in a fifteen minute period in the art classroom.

The various components of the objectives are underlined. In order of their appearance the components are: target individuals; operations performed; behavior mode; environmental conditions; performance level; and time constraints. Note that the objective required more than one sentence.

In the preceding example, the criterion level of performance was identified in relation to the product that would result from student behavior—five of the eight types correctly identified. One also can note the standard of performance by attending to the percentage of students who would achieve the performance level. In our example, we could have indicated that 85 percent of the class will identify five of the eight types of paintings. If we are accepting mastery learning, we might require 100 percent of the students to achieve the noted performance level.

Baker and Schutz (1971) provide us with examples of standards that we can incorporate into our objectives. We can note the percentage of accuracy as discussed above. All students will score at least 90 percent correct responses in a multiple choice test. We can also note performance on a scale. Students will write a paragraph from a story and achieve a score of seven or higher as measured on the calligraphy writing scale. We can note the number of errors that will be allowed. Students will solve at least five of the ten problems in division presented. A final standard we can apply is the qualitative attribute. The student will write a composition that will be neat with legible writing. How we actually write the objective will depend in part on our conclusions resulting from the diagnosis of student gaps, and also the demands of the community.

Creating Objectives: Cognitive and Affective

Cognitive. The elements of an objective suggests a sequence of requisite tasks. First, identify the intended audience. This has been done in the first stage of curriculum development. Usually we develop general objectives for the students we have in our school district. But, in analyzing needs, we can identify those particular students who might require particular objectives. This first step is really done at two levels.

> Determining the audience for the general objective—long-term objective. Determining the audience (from general audience) for a more specific unit or lesson objective—short-term objective.

Second, one identifies the operations performed, the terminal behavior. At this stage, one also attends to the actual behavior mode. Can we state the behavior in such a way that it is clear to both instructor and student? Also, is the behavior mentioned really a valid indication that the basic intent of the objective has been met. In some cases with open ended objectives, the actual behavior mode will be decided by the student. Instructors will accept numerous behaviors as appropriate for the objective: writing, listening, talking, demonstrating, etc. However, even with open-ended objectives, instructors have some definite ideas as to possible actual behaviors that fit the intent of the objective mentioned.

Third, one lists the performance level desired or expected to occur as a result of the curriculum. The selection of the performance level depends in part on the nature of the learning behavior and what we have learned from diagnostic data on the students and the community. In some cases, one either does the behavior or does not. One either gets the basketball through the hoop or does not. One either spells the word correctly or not. In these cases, one might list the standards as getting a percentage of baskets completed. But, determining which number represents competence or skill is difficult. How many baskets should a student get in physical education? Ten baskets out of ten tries? Five baskets out of ten tries? A lot depends upon the purpose of the exercise. Is it to build up psychomotor skill so that a student enjoys sports? Is it to enable the student to make first string on the varsity team? Obviously the levels of performance will fluctuate. Frequently, the norms are arbitrary and influenced by local community norms and teachers' expectations. If one were writing objectives dealing with oral speech, one would strive for a performance level of 100 percent. All students would use correct grammar in their speech one hundred percent of the time. This would be a goal to strive for. In most classes, the majority of students would not have flawless English.

Fourth, one notes the environmental frame factors. What will be the constraints under which the teacher will work and the students will learn? What are the givens? Which environmental frame factors are put into objectives depends in part on the educational environment in which one finds oneself and in which students will have to function. It also is contingent upon the types of environments and types of situations in which students need to learn to perform. Diagnosis provides guidance here. Sometimes, the nature of the overall task or the general goal of the entire unit, will suggest the types of constraints to be incorporated into an objective. If students are to demonstrate a certain performance or understanding in the outside world, it may be propitious to incorporate such contacts into the objective. Thus, the students learn to function in a situation analogous to the reality outside of the school. Too often, educators are faulted for testing students' behaviors in situations that only vaguely resemble the actual situation in which such a learning or behavior will be required in the real world.

How much time do the students have to learn and finally demonstrate that the objective has been achieved? This question is addressed in the fifth step in developing objectives and is answered when we consider the nature of the terminal behavior, the audience identified, the level of performance desired or deemed necessary, and the constraints built into the environment, either consciously or unconsciously.[3]

Affective. Cognitive objectives deal with the intellectual dimensions of individuals' learnings. Affective objectives focus on the attitudes, feelings, values and interests of learners. In actuality, one cannot separate the two domains and their objectives. But, as noted previously, the existence of one behavior in the cognitive domain does not mean that a corresponding positive behavior is present in the learner. To assure our addressing the attitudes, feelings, values and interests of students, we will write into our master curriculum plans affective objectives. These objectives deal with behaviors suggesting emotional and attitudinal reactions. All of education is concerned with stimulating in students a love of learning. Love of learning is hard to quantify, but we can note behaviors or statements that indicate, however vaguely, that students have or are developing such a disposition toward learning. Objectives which ask

---

[3]The following researchers have investigated the relationships between objectives and learner characteristics: Cook (1969), Keuter (1970), Merrill and Towle (1971).

TABLE 7.2 *Stages for generating objectives*

Stages	Tasks
1. Identify audience (done during curriculum conceptualization and legitimization)	Conduct community surveys, situational analyses Conduct needs analysis Conduct goals analysis
2. Identify operations performed, terminal behavior noted	Analysis of needs data Analysis of the nature of the content, subject area being considered.
3. Listing performance levels.	Analyzing the nature of the tasks. Generating criterion levels. Matching criterion levels to levels of students Noting students' areas of interest
4. Noting and incorporating environmental elements	Doing environmental survey. Noting the types of environmental frame-factors required for actual performance, achievement of the objective
5. Determining the time factors	Noting time available. Noting the time required with regard to nature of tasks, learnings, nature of student audience
6. Formulating the finished objective	Going back over the previous stages to determine if the objective is feasible, relevant, worthwhile.

Activity 7–3 *Creating Objectives*

With several colleagues select two general program objectives. Write your defenses for these objectives.

General program objectives: _____

_____
_____

Defenses of these objectives:_____

_____

Now take these program objectives and make two specific teaching objectives for each program objective. Share these objectives with your colleagues and indicate the reasons for selecting these objectives. Also underscore the essential criteria of student performance in each objective.

Teaching objectives	*Defense*
_____	_____
_____	_____
_____	_____
_____	_____
_____	_____

students to note in writing the types of books or learning activities they have read or engaged in during a period of time give us some indication of the affective aspects of students' behaviors.

In developing affective objectives, one can first develop a model of a person who possesses or demonstrates the affective quality in question. What does such an individual look like, how does he or she behave? Baker and Popham (1973) note that such a person can become our model, our "attribute possessor."

Once we have identified an attribute possessor, we can then generate a "model" person lacking these qualities, the "nonattribute possessor." In essence, we are noting negative behaviors or attitudes or the lack of certain behaviors. But to be this precise in reality is not likely; most probably, we will have to settle for an approximation.

The third step is noting the situations in which these two hypothetical individuals would actually behave differently. At this stage, we are attempting to define the behavior modes, both positive and negative and the environmental conditions under which such behaviors would occur. These conditions can be natural (not under the control of the educator) or manipulated (under the management of the educator.)

The next step is describing those situations that would enhance or retard the affective actions of the student in specified ways. What conditions can we create that will foster students' love of learning? What experiences can be introduced in school or presented in a natural situation that would reduce the love of learning? In answering these questions, we determine environmental frame factors essential for enhancing the affective response desired. But we must remember that more often than not our findings will have to be modified to meet the uniqueness of individuals.

The final step in creating these objectives is making sure all the objective's elements are clear and agreed upon by all affected parties: curriculum specialists, teachers and in some cases, students. Hopefully, the objectives as finally developed would be feasible, worthwhile, and relevant to the needs of students and the general society (Baker & Popham).

Appropriateness of Objectives

A central question when developing objectives is Why stress these objectives rather than some others? Curriculum development activity is constantly confronted with variations of this question. Why these contents rather than those? Why these materials rather than those? Why these students rather than those? The diagnosis substage of this major step in curriculum development allows us to process such questions.

Key questions. Can the objective be attained by the school? Can the student learn it, can the teachers teach it? Is there adequate time available, sufficient materials purchased, appropriate educational spaces present?

Another question queries the objective's relevancy to the student and to the overall community. Relevance is concerned with what is useful and important. We can identify objectives and behaviors as relevant if we can relate them to a use in the real world, if we can relate them to human concerns.

However, different groups of individuals are likely to have idiosyncratic views regarding relevance. What may be pertinent to learn for an individual in one community may be irrelevant for another. The question of appropriateness is answered in part by attending to the targeted audience for the objective and the nature of the times. Diagnosis regarding students' actual performances and community (both local and national) demands furnishes data by which we can process this question.

Closely related to relevance is the question of worthwhileness. A certain activity while related to the real world of individuals, may have its value to the individual found wanting over an extended period of time.

Indeed, some behaviors or learnings relevant to a particular time may be deleterious to students in the future. For instance, some learning might relate to gaining a particular job and performing it well. But the job may not exist in ten years, and therefore the learning of the job is really not as worthwhile as learning how to adapt to a changing job market. In our society, some learnings and behaviors have more value than others. It is more important to develop adaptative behaviors and a willingness to tolerate change than to develop dependence upon authority and a rigidness of action. Worthwhileness is a fluid concept, but it still requires our attention. We cannot divorce the question from the time in which we do live and will live.

One can advance the thesis that worthwhile things tend to be long-term rather than transitory. Such activities and behaviors are more likely to challenge higher levels of thinking and higher stages of affective behavior. Such activities would be major rather than trivial in contributing to the learning of individuals. Activities and behaviors that add to one's total view of reality are more essential than those that contribute a disintegrated world view. But, still, one will have to hammer out the specifics of just what is worthwhile to a particular time and student audience (Davies, 1976).

Relevancy and worthwhileness relate to whether the objective provides motivation for the student and addresses his or her needs.

Since objectives do not exist in isolation, one needs to query whether the necessary prerequisites to the objective in question have been attained.

There are numerous other key questions that require our attention:

1. Is the content of the objective evident so that one can be guided in the content selection and development aspects of curriculum development?
2. Are the behaviors noted in the objective clear?
3. Are performance criteria clearly stated?
4. Is the objective capable of being modified to address changing times and student populations?
5. Is the objective valid? Will it enable the student to obtain the behavior implicitly or explicitly stated in the objective?
6. Are instructional materials and experiences suggested in the objective?
7. Is the objective supported by existing research data?

8. Is the objective consistent with the philosophical positions of the staff and community?
9. Is the educational environment implied in the objective?
10. Is the objective capable of stimulating multiple learnings in both the cognitive and affective domains?

Discussion

This chapter dealt with the second major stage of curriculum planning and development—curriculum diagnosis. Attention was placed on the meaning of diagnosis and distinctions were drawn between aims, goals, and objectives.

Objectives were presented as being at various levels: program, unit, and lesson. Objectives also were discussed as to their degree of openness and closedness. The role of objectives in the total planning process was considered. Elements common to all levels of objectives received attention.

The latter third of the chapter dealt with means of creating objectives and criteria to consider in the generation of objectives.

From this chapter, it is evident that curriculum quality is dependent upon actions taken during the stage of curriculum conceptualization and this second stage in which aims can be noted, goals identified, and objectives developed and organized. Being precise in creating objectives does not mean that the objectives are relevant or worthwhile. We can make technically perfect trivial objectives. However, if we realize the complexity of objectives and accept the basic rationale for having objectives—both open and closed—we increase the probability of generating curricula that will be responsive to the needs of students. Additionally, we will have some significant ideas as to ways in which we implement such objectives and evaluate resultant student learnings.

Again, the actions suggested in this chapter are drawn from a systems orientation in which one notes phenomena having common characteristics and identifies the relationships between noted phenomena. One cannot optimally diagnose curriculum or translate needs unless one discerns what does indeed exist in the school and/or in the community. Additionally, as one deals with this stage of curriculum development, one is beginning to anticipate what content and experiences might be appropriate in light of the results of this diagnostic phase.

References

Baker, E.I., & Popham, W.J. *Expanding dimensions of instructional objectives.* Englewood Cliffs, N.J.: Prentice-Hall, 1973.

Baker, R.L., & Schutz, R.E. (Eds.). *Instructional product development.* New York: Van Nostrand Reinhold, 1971.

Bloom, B.S. (Ed.). *Taxonomy of educational objectives, handbook I: cognitive domain.* New York: David McKay, 1956.

Bryant, N. *The effects of performance objectives on the achievement level of selected eighth-grade pupils in four predominantly black inner-city schools.* Unpublished doctoral dissertation, Indiana University, 1970.

Cardarelli, A.F. An investigation of the effect on pupil achievement when teachers are assigned and trained in the use of behavioral objectives. (Doctoral dissertation, Syracuse University, 1971). *Dissertation Abstracts International,* 1972. (University Microfilms No. 72-6562, 112.)

Clark, D.C. *Using instructional objectives in teaching.* New York: Scott, Foresman, 1972.

Cook, J.M. Learning and retention by informing students of behavioral objectives and their place in the hierarchical learning sequence. *USOE Final Report,* 1969, ERIC # Ed. 036 869.

Davies, I.K. *Objectives in curriculum design.* New York: McGraw-Hill, 1976.

Derr, R.L. *A taxonomy of social purposes of public schools.* New York: David McKay, 1973.

Doll, R.D. *Curriculum improvement, decision making and process (4th ed.).* Boston: Allyn & Bacon, 1978.

Downny, L.M. *The task of public education.* Chicago: Midwest Administration Center, University of Chicago, 1960.

Durio, H.F. Behavioral objectives: where have they taken us? *Clearing House,* January 1976, *49,* no. 5, 202.

Hannah, L.S., & Michaelis, J.U. *A comprehensive framework for instructional objectives: a guide to systematic planning and evaluation.* Reading, Mass.: Addison-Wesley, 1977.

Harrow, A.J. *A taxonomy of the psychomotor domain.* New York: David McKay, 1972.

Jenkins, J.R., & Deno, S.L. Influence of knowledge and type of objectives on subject-matter learning. *Journal of Educational Psychology.* 1971, *62,* 67-70.

Keuter, R.A. *Instructional strategies: the effects of personality factors on recognition learning using statements of behavioral objectives as opposed to no statements of behavioral objectives prior to instruction.* Unpublished doctoral dissertation, Indiana University, 1970.

Komisar, B.P., & McClellan, J.E. The logic of slogans. In B.O. Smith & R.H. Ennis (Eds.). *Language and concepts in education.* Chicago: Rand McNally, 1961.

Krathwohol, D.R. (Ed.) *Taxonomy of educational objectives, handbook II: affective domain.* New York: David McKay, 1964.

Mager, R.F. *Preparing instructional objectives.* Palo Alto, Calif.: Fearon, 1962.

McNeil, J.D. Concomitants of using behavioral objectives in the assessment of teacher effectiveness. *Journal of Experimental Psychology.* 1967, *36,* 69-74.

Merrill, P.F., & Towle, N.J. Interaction of abilities and anxiety with availability of objectives and/or test items on computer-based task performance. *Proceedings of the 79th Annual Convention of the American Psychological Association,* 1971, 539-540.

Rogers, C.R. *Freedom to learn.* Columbus, Ohio: Charles E. Merrill, 1969.

Rosenthal, R., & Jacobson, L. *Pygmalion in the classroom.* New York: Holt, Rinehart & Winston, 1968.

Schneiderwent, M.O. *The effects of using behavioral objectives in the instruction of Harvard project physics.* Unpublished doctoral dissertation, University of Northern California, 1970.

Tyler, R.W. Purposes of our schools. *Bulletin of the National Association of Secondary School Principals.* 1968, *52,* no. 332, 1-12.

chapter

Curriculum Development:
Content Selection

SELECTING CONCEPT OF KNOWLEDGE

Knowledge refers to the end results of active inquiry and reflection. It incorporates the theories, laws, principles and generalizations with their various supporting rules, concepts, values, attitudes, and myriad facts. In addition to being the recording of information resulting from inquiry, it furnishes the basis for additional investigation. Some argue that the record of knowledge is content, but in this book, the totality of information chronicled is knowledge. In contrast, content is defined as the specialized arrangement/s of knowledge for purposes of instruction within a structure or structures commonly called the curriculum.

Knowledge can be organized as disciplines, such as history, chemistry or psychology, as nondisciplines such as environmental studies, social studies, or home economics, or as practical theories such as medicine or education. Regardless of the major organization of knowledge one selects, there are some components common to all divisions. We can arrange all knowledge by major concepts, the building blocks of the structure of knowledge. Concepts refer to categories of phenomena systematized according to particular common characteristics or attributes. Concepts serve as organizers of reality for purposes of making reality intelligible (Bruner, 1956).

Concepts can be organized as to the level or degree of abstractness and concreteness. A concrete concept can be learned via the senses and perceived in reality, such as boy, mountain, and house. Abstract concepts are not observed in reality but are inferred from analyzing reality or ideas, such as revolution, honesty, power, relationship. Often these concepts are learned as definitions and then applied whenever such a definition is appropriate for comprehending a particular situation.

Concepts also can be classified as conjunctive, disjunctive, and relational (Bruner). *Conjunctive concepts* are those defined by the presence of two or more attributes that contribute to the concept's meaning. Examples of this concept type are international conflict, fire power, chemical reaction.

A *disjunctive concept* is one in which there must be one or another set of defining attributes present for the concept to exist in meaning. The attributes are not additive, but each can contribute equally to the concept's meaning such as creative genius or political activist. Any number of attributes can describe both concepts, and there is no set number or particular properties that must be present. Bruner uses the example of a strike in baseball as a disjunctive concept. A strike can be a pitch that is across the plate and between the batter's knees and shoulders or it can be a pitch at which the batter swings and misses. It also can be the third foul ball hit into the stands or field. There is no apparent relationship among the attributes, and such arbitrariness causes difficulties in using this type of concept classification. This variability of contributing characteristics makes precision difficult when teaching such a concept, for students may be centering on differing attributes while still indicating that they understand the concept.

The third major concept classification is *relational.* These concepts are defined by a specifiable relationship between defining attributes. Bruner presents effective stimulus as one example. Such a stimulus is defined as an energy change at a receptor surface capable of discharging the receptor, thus noting a relationship between these two states. Year is another example of such a concept noting a dependence of time and number of days. Mental age is such a concept noting an association between a level of intellectual functioning and chronological age.

Concepts are created by clustering or organizing facts. Facts are statements of the particular, of the observable, the quantifiable. They frequently denote specific phenomena or events considered true, that can be checked for validity via observation. A fact is Mt. Rainier is 14,410 ft. above sea level. Another is that the major gases comprising air are oxygen and nitrogen. Facts do not necessarily have to be one word statements. Laws that have received the support of a group of persons or are believed true by a group of persons can be considered facts. The law of gravity passes as a fact, for most persons do accept its validity.

As facts support concepts, concepts underpin generalizations, statements noting the relationships among two or more concepts. Generalizations can be descriptive such as "There are numerous social groups in the United States," or they can denote cause and effect such as "the location of a nation on the earth influences the degree of its political importance." Generalizations have varying degrees of universality. Statements can be created that are valid only for the United States, "There are numerous native American tribes in the United States," or valid for the entire world at the cause and effect level, "The cultures of people influence the values they hold."

Somewhat related to generalizations are laws and law-like statements. Laws contain concepts so stated that they have high explanatory and predictive powers. Such statements also can be used to regulate or guide individuals' behaviors in working with knowledge. The laws of motion can guide a physicist in his work. Laws are statements indicating that certain natural phenomena are consistent in their behaviors irrespective of time and place. In this way, laws differ from certain generalizations which can be influenced by time and place.

Knowledge also can be organized as values and attitudes. Attitudes are expressions of psychological states, dispositions or tendencies to act or respond in particular ways to certain situations or phenomena. Attitudes are views that individuals may possess regarding the merit of something. They convey information to others as to what the holder of the attitude is for or against.

Values, quite often, are difficult to distinguish from attitudes. Indeed, attitudes are frequently influenced by the values individuals have. Values, however, contain normative criteria employed to guide one's judgments and behaviors, to assist one in determining the goodness or appropriateness of particular behaviors (Raths, Harmin & Simon, 1978).

FIGURE 8.1 *Knowledge—source of curriculum content*

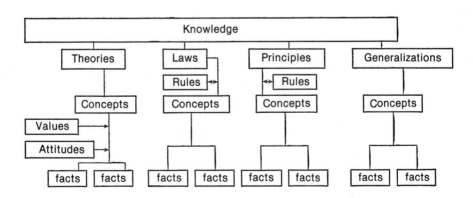

Content. As knowledge is the source of the curriculum, so content is the foundation of the curriculum. All curricula have content. Even those curricula titled experience curricula have students engaged in experiences in order to learn content. School content is extracted from all types of knowledge: disciplined, nondisciplined, and incidental. Frequently, persons forget that content is the central dimension of the curriculum, often becoming only concerned with how students will learn and process information. But, before processing the "how" in education, a question relating to the experience aspect of curriculum and the instructional component of education, one has to address the "what." Realizing that content is the central curriculum dimension does not diminish our concern for the individual student. Content selected, organized, and sequenced is all done so that particular students will become fully functioning individuals.

> When the school specialist speaks of content, he refers to the compendium of information which comprises the learning material for a particular course or a given grade. The information may consist of a related body of facts, laws, theories, and generalizations, as in a traditional science course, or a description of events as in a history course, or in any other predetermined arrangement of a particular segment of man's knowledge. (Parker & Rubin, 1966, p. 1)

Content can be considered as that which is presented to students or that which is made available to students for possible use.

Today, many educators are indicating that it is more important to learn process rather than content. Such a statement dichotomizes content and process when in reality they should receive equal emphasis in the school's curriculum. Indeed, the methods that students can learn are really a type of specialized content—content relating to methodology and procedures. Parker and Rubin note:

> Process refers to all the random or ordered operations which can be associated with knowledge and with human activities. There are a variety of processes through which knowledge is created. There are also processes for utilizing knowledge and communicating it. (p. 2)

Emphasis upon process does not reduce the value of students assimilating knowledge, but rather acknowledges that students need to be active in their learning. Furthermore, such underscoring on process indicates that students must progress beyond the simple acquisition of knowledge; they must use the knowledge, if they are to gain appreciation and understanding of it. Content selection requires not only the designation of the laws, principles, generalizations, concepts and facts, (the substantive structure), but also the specifying of the procedures, methodologies, techniques, and evaluative tests requisite for using the content (the syntactical structure).

In reality content and process coexist. It is only in discussion and reflection on curricular matters that we can separate them. But, we should realize that even though they do coexist in education, they are not identical. By keeping the two separate in our planning, we can perhaps more efficiently deal with the difficult decisions relating to content and process selection.

Comprehending content and its knowledge source allows us in curriculum development to deal with the explosion of knowledge. Making the concepts and generalizations the focuses of the content incapsulates vast amounts of knowledge for student learning. Stressing facts in the curriculum presents teachers and students with the impossible task of teaching and learning all facts extant. Organizing content around conceptual loci enables one to decide useful topics and to select pertinent facts. For instance, in selecting content for economics, it is more useful to organize a unit around the concepts of scarcity, market place, needs and wants, than around the legions of specific facts relating to how many goods are produced in the United States or the money flow in the total U.S. economy.

In contemplating subject matter or content, we might conclude that content really is another term for knowledge. It is true that content (subject matter) is a compendium of facts, concepts, generalizations, principles, rules and theories similar to disciplined knowledge. Additionally, school content incorporates the methods of processing information, also an aspect of disciplined knowledge. But knowledge, whether disciplined like chemistry or nondisciplined such as population control, is concerned with the advancement of understanding, the exploration of the unknown reaches of the various realms of knowledge. Content and processes arranged in school subjects are not to provide students with opportunities for advancing the fields or forms of knowledge, but rather for learning, for discovering, knowledge that is new to them but known in the communities of scholars and practitioners outside of the school. School content is distinguished from fields of knowledge by its purpose.

Organization of content. Determining what knowledge to incorporate into school content, still leaves one with the challenge of organizing it in ways that will facilitate student learning. One can arrange content drawing directly from the organization extant in disciplined and nondisciplined knowledge. One also can organize content on the basis of societal institutions and activities such as government, agriculture, medicine, theology, and philosophy. Further, one can generate content in response to articulated social needs, environmental studies, race relations, population control. Attending to tradition also assists one in determining how to map the legions of knowledge.

The prime reason for organizing anything is to render it comprehensible. We systematize and classify our reality so as to understand and manage it; conceivably even to extend it. Perhaps it is more productive to judge our content classifications useful and feasible rather than truthful. In grouping content we are concerned with the validity of the content, but validity only in terms of the assumptions extant in its organization. The validity of mathematical formula rests upon the agreed upon primary assumptions. If we alter the assumptions we threaten the validity. The truthfulness of the concept of mountain depends upon a set of attributes that geographers agree describes a mountain. Change the attributes, and the concept is altered. But the truthfulness of the concept of mountain is not dependent upon its actual presence in reality, but upon the usefulness of the criteria accepted by certain persons (geographers) who have agreed to define mountain in a particular way. Tamper with the criterion of height, and we may have our mountains made into hills.

Content is organized both logically and psychologically. Logically, content is organized via certain rules to make it manageable. Certain concepts are deeded central to the content, and particular concepts are prerequisite to other concepts. In economics, the concept of scarcity is the central conceptual organizer. Without this concept, one cannot understand the meaning of wants and needs or market. Also, if one focuses on the concept of market, there are certain concepts connected by the logic of the discipline, such as diversification, capital, and labor. This grouping of content has no relationship to how individuals might actually learn economics, a psychological logic. The concept of structure of the discipline discussed in chapter three relates to the logic of content organization.

Psychological organization relates to how we perceive that persons learn or process information. In social studies we have worked for many years on the assumption that content should be organized going from the immediate environment of a student to a more distant environment. Such advice was based on the assumption that the immediate was more concrete and within the experience of the student and therefore easier to learn. We have assumed that children have to deal with the concrete before they can process the abstract. Psychological organization is based on what we know, via empirical studies, about how individuals learn and process information rather than on what we know about the structure of the discipline. Of course, these organizations are moot. Discussion continues as to the substantive structures of disciplines as well as the optimal sequence by which persons learn. The wise curriculum designer manifests an experimental questioning posture when considering the issue of content organization.

CRITERIA FOR CONTENT SELECTION

Crucial to content selection are the tasks of developing and accepting the selection criteria. Frequently, these criteria will be influenced by one's conception of the curriculum formulated and/or articulated in the first stage of curriculum building. Scheffler (1970) posits that the prime guiding principle for content selection is that of assisting the learner to attain maximum self-sufficiency in the most economical manner. He elaborates three types of economy: economy in terms of teaching effort and educational resources; economy in terms of students' efforts; and finally economy in terms of subject matter's extent of generalizability. One can decide subject matter economy drawing on empirical data that state that particular learning facilitates other learning. One can attend to the logical organization of the content itself. Content logically central to a subject or knowledge area is more efficient in the sense that it relates or allows the learner to relate to wide bodies of cognate issues or problems. Scheffler's central point is that content should be such that learners after experiencing it will be able to make personal and moral decisions and fully understand the knowledge to which the school subject refers.

The criterion of economy of effort is often assumed rather than stated in curricular dialogue. But two criteria that loom large in educational discussions are *significance* and *validity.* Significance refers to the essentialness of the content to be learned. Content to be learned is significant only to the degree to which it contributes to basic ideas, concepts, principles, generalizations etc. Significance is related to the matter of breadth and depth of curriculum content.

Significance also pertains to how the content or experience contributes to the development of particular learning abilities, skills, processes and attitude formation. Taba (1962) has noted that one should not just select content based on the cognitive aspects of learners but also on the affective dimensions of individuals.

The import of content also concerns the issue of durability. Significant content will last over time or at least over an extended period of time. Content relevant to current times, but unlikely to be of interest in five years is not as meaningful as content that is likely to be of use in the year 2025.

Validity refers to the authenticity of the content selected. In this time of information explosion, knowledge selected for school content can quickly become obsolete, and even incorrect. As new knowledge is discovered, content assumed valid is discovered to be misleading at best and false at worst. Validity as a criterion is applied at the initial selection of curriculum content, but also needs to be raised at regular intervals through the duration of the curricular program to determine if content originally valid remains so.

Validity also pertains to whether the content selected is sound in relation to selected goals and objectives. For example, if one has an objective in the program that indicates that students will learn the nature of the relationship between one's cultural approaches to life and the possibilities extant in a person's environment, then the content chosen will be valid to the extent that it shows this relationship in a form which can be comprehended by students (Nicholls & Nicholls, 1972).

Another criterion is *interest* which is frequently misunderstood by educators who assume that curriculum content should be selected solely on the basis of students' interests. This argument often is manifested when persons are discussing the humanistic approach at the elementary level of schooling. Certainly, content must be selected with students' interests in mind, but we in program development also are charged with selecting and organizing content in ways that will generate and broaden students' interests. Attending to this criterion is difficult for students' interests often are transitory and frequently reflect cultural bias. A much easier task is noting those casual and immediate interests of students. A question to keep in mind in addition to the one Is this content potentially interesting to the students? is a question Are students' current interests of long-lasting educational value for both the students and society? Dealing with this question is difficult for it assumes we possess some degree of perception regarding the future and students' places in that future. The weight of the criterion of students' interests should be adjusted to allow for students' maturity, their level in schooling, their prior experiences, and the educational and social value of their interests.

Students frequently want to utilize immediately gained information, skills, and processes, or at least discern how such information contributes to other learning that has a clearly identified application. The criterion of *utility* attends to content usefulness. In elementary and secondary schools, utility frequently is defined as useful to the performance of adult activities. Such a use puts the school primarily in a preparatory posture. Certainly, the school has this role, but students also exist in a reality paralleling their school experiences, and therefore content should have some degree of immediacy of use.

Persons applying the utility criterion can draw on empirical data regarding how persons outside of the school perceive certain contents as necessary for effective functioning in the overall society. Employers can identify those tasks and competencies requisite for successful employment. In these situations, content selected can be judged as having utility if it corresponds to that content which employers say graduates require. However, this application of the utility criterion relates only to the current scene. It is far more difficult to decide the future utility of present content.

Learnability, an essential criterion, might be reacted to as suggesting the obvious. However, schools are coming under increasing criticism for stressing content and organizing it in ways that make its learning difficult for large segments of the population who are field dependent while favoring selected students who are field independent (largely from the middle class). The learnability criterion relates to the issue of optimal placement and appropriate organization and sequencing of the content. Further, it addresses the issue of appropriateness for the intended student audience.

Feasibility addresses the question Can the content selected be taught in the time allowed, with the resources available, with the expertise of the current staff, with the political climate extant in the community, with the current legislation, and with the amount of monies allocated for curriculum and instruction? Often, valuable content is deleted or not even seriously considered for constraints affecting feasibility appear insurmountable.

Selecting content also requires our attention to *human development.* Content selected should be appropriate for the particular developmental level of the students; it should be within the capabilities of the students to process. Content that is value laden or requires sophisticated thinking must be matched to the intended audience. Of course, Bruner (1961) has postulated that any content can be taught at any level of schooling in an intellectually honest way. But, that does not mean we can ignore adjusting content to the developmental levels of students.

Other criteria for selecting content can be and should be generated by curriculum developers. The emotional dimension of content needs attention. The criterion of transferability should guide our choices. Ideally, all content specified should satisfy all the criteria mentioned above and any other criteria developed to guide content selection. However, at certain levels of schooling, particular criteria will receive more weight. Such weighting will be influenced in part by the conceptions of curriculum and schooling we bring to the content selection activity.

TABLE 8.1   *Checklist for content selection criteria*

Criteria	High	Medium	Low
Economy of effort	_____	_____	_____
Significance	_____	_____	_____
Validity*	(Yes)	– – –	(No)
Interest	_____	_____	_____
Learnability**	_____	_____	_____
Feasibility	_____	_____	_____
Human development***	(Yes)	– – –	(No)
Other	_____		

*Can only be considered as binary: either content is valid or it is not.

**High learnability would relate to content that can be learned by most students; low learnability may indicate content learnable by only a small segment of the student population.

***Must only be considered as binary: either the content contributes to or agrees with our understanding of human development or it does not.

Activity 8–1   *Assessing Content*

Obtain a curriculum guide in your educational institution and, using the criteria in Table 8.1, assess the major topics in the guide.

Record your general reactions to the content in the guide or master plan.

SELECTING AND ORGANIZING CONTENT

During the curriculum conceptualization stage, we attended to curriculum design somewhat globally, striving to obtain group design consensus as to what is curriculum design and its basic components. The conception of curriculum design decided upon at that juncture becomes the input for the actual designing of the curriculum.

That the output of a previous stage becomes the input of the next stage points out that the major steps in the systematic curriculum development model are in fact a series of interconnecting subsystems. Each major stage accepts input, transforms or acts upon it using various procedures, and produces an output. All the while the various processes are monitored via a feedback and adjustment loop. In our instance, the outputs of curriculum conceptualization and curriculum diagnosis become the inputs of the major stage of content selection and organization.

Design deals with the elements of the curriculum (the objectives, the content, the experiences, the environments, the resource materials and even persons) and the manner or manners in which they are structured so that the parts functioning together create an autonomous curricular content system. Curriculum design exists along two basic organizational dimensions: horizontal and vertical. Content elements organized horizontally involve the concepts of scope and integration. Vertical organizations (referred to by the concepts of sequence and continuity) are concerned with the arrangement of curricular elements over time. More will be discussed regarding these issues later in this chapter. At this point, it is necessary to mention that in most school operations, overall macro curricular designs receive scant attention. Most school curricula, regardless of school level, are not really closely related either vertically or horizontally. Curricular elements frequently exist as disjointed clusters of content organized as particular subjects that often duplicate and/or conflict with other elements in the school program. To bring about an internal consistency in a program requires that a master curricular design be created (at the conceptualization stage) which depicts the key elements of the total program and their interrelationships. Such a plan can allow for more effective decision-making, for persons charged with such deliberations will be cognizant of the impact of their judgments.

FIGURE 8.2   *Conception of curriculum design*

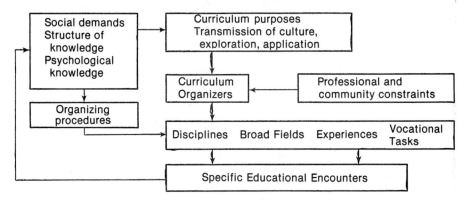

There are several common designs extant in today's schools from preschool through graduate schools: separate subjects, disciplines, broad fields, correlated designs, culture epoch, interests, experiences. All of these designs can be subsumed under the category of either subject- (or content-) centered designs or learner-centered designs. Those designs within the subject-centered camp do not exclude experiences, and those within the learner-centered design camp do not ignore content. The differences lie in the degree of emphasis of the various curricular elements.

Subject-centered Designs

Subject Design

The subject design has the distinction of being the oldest school design (practiced even in classical Greece), and of being the best known by both educators and the lay public. In this design, content is arranged by specific subjects representing a specialized and common area of content. Frequently, educators supporting this design have received their professional training in a particular subject area, or discipline.

This organization assumes that subjects are systematized primarily on a chronological basis with (a) prerequisite learnings carefully noted, (b) stress on whole-to-part mastery, and (c) deductive learning. The teacher assumes the active role, that of teaching, while students take on a somewhat passive role, that of receiving information to be memorized and related back to the teacher via a test or immediate application. Such a design rests heavily on verbal activities and the utilization of logic.

Advocates of this design postulate that for each subject there exists a single and distinctive kind of content. Furthermore, this content is arranged in subjects that possess a hierarchy of value. Certain academic subjects are deemed superior to certain practical subjects. The academic subjects make up the core of the curriculum. The following list shows such an organization as suggested by Aristotle (Schwab, 1964). The organization is not far different from many curricula in current high schools.

Theoretical Disciplines
  (Stress on knowing, advancing knowledge)
  Metaphysics
  Mathematics
  Natural sciences
Practical Disciplines
  (Stress on deliberate choice, decision, action)
  Practical sciences
  Ethics
  Politics
Productive Disciplines
  (Focus on making)
  The fine arts
  Applied arts
  Engineering

Certainly a design so popular cannot exist without well articulated advantages. A prime advantage is that this design allows the introduction to youth of essential cultural elements. Also, textbooks and support materials on the educational market are organized frequently in this format. Additionally, tradition supports the continuation of this design. People have become comfortable with the design and regard it as depicting what school is all about.

Attempts at individualizing are not made by adjusting the content, which remains a constant, but by modifying the instructional strategies, the educational activities, and the myriad types of assignments given students. Further alteration can be given by manipulating the amount of time scheduled for various subjects.

But all designs have deficiencies. Perhaps the greatest disadvantage to this easily administered design is the lack of integration of the curriculum content. Learning tends to be compartmentalized with a stress on mnemonic skills; subjects tend to be detached from the reality of students. A major criticism is that the design stresses content to the neglect of students' needs, interests, and experiences. Finally, critics of the design indicate that it fosters a passive learner.

Disciplines

The disciplines design is an extension of the separate subject design, but a major difference is that this design allows students to be active in processing information. School subjects do not just have a content dimension (substantive structure), but subjects also have a process dimension (syntactical structure) (Schwab, 1971). Discipline designs also identify specific realms of content, but unlike the subject design, the rationale for content selection is made known, selection criteria are identified, and the crucial concepts of the discipline are delimited in a clarification of the content's structure.

The structure of disciplined knowledge is the key aspect of this curriculum design. Content selected is determined in part by identifying or creating a discipline's structure and using this foundation as a guide for selecting the school content and organizing it for learning. This emphasis on structure makes the content realm more comprehensible to both teacher and student. This stress on understanding and utilizing knowledge to advance one's comprehension is a significant difference between this design and the previous one which considered learning primarily as memory learning. In the disciplines design, students are encouraged to analyze content organization, to generate additional information from known information, and to perceive the interrelationships among the key concepts, ideas, generalizations and principles.

This design, which received a great deal of support from scholars involved in the curricular activities of the fifties and sixties, has today taken over much of the position of the separate subject design (Tanner & Tanner, 1975). Persons have realized that the design has the advantage of being systematic and does allow the crucial dimensions of the culture to be transmitted. Furthermore, many materials currently available from commercial publishing firms also follow this design.

However, the design can be criticized and for many of the same reasons that the separate subject design was challenged. Separate disciplines can also fragment students' curricular experiences. Frequently, the relationship between schooling and life is neglected. Often, the interests and needs of students are ignored, and educators assume that students must adapt to the curriculum, rather than the curriculum adapting or being modified to meet students' requirements. Additionally, the design rests on the supposition that most students have a common or at least similar type of learning style. Presently, this design, still strong at the secondary and higher educational levels of schooling, is undergoing some modification in that adjustments are being made in the procedures suggested for processing the content, and the design is being melded with other curriculum designs.

Correlation

Reducing fragmentation of curricular content is the thrust of organizing content by correlation. In correlation similar topics or subjects are scheduled for simultaneous study, but still retain their separate identities. Frequently, one might have students studying colonial history and also studying colonial literature. A unit from biology might be related to a unit in mathematics dealing with quantifying observable phenomena.

This content organization evolved from the subject-centered tradition and thus shares some of the weaknesses of that specific design. Over the years, this design, also called the correlated core, has evolved into two rather distinct forms. The first form links two separate subjects, with each subject taught by a specialist. Thus, in our above example, the unit in biology would be taught by the biology teacher with reference made to mathematics, and the mathematics would be taught by the mathematics teacher with information related to biology. The second form melds subject matter according to a common theme or general problem. A theme such as wise use of energy sources would draw content from both the social sciences and physical sciences. This particular form is extremely close to the next curriculum design, the broad fields design.

The correlated design is not widely used in schools. Its limited used is due in part to the fact that many teachers do not feel comfortable breaking away from the separate subject organization, or if they do they find the fused curricular design more to their liking. Also, few educational materials are organized to support the correlated organization.

Broad Fields

This design, commonly called a fused design, goes a step beyond the correlated design. Here, subjects that are logically related are clustered together, often around some shared organizer, to overcome the fragmentation and compartmentalization of subjects. Thus, melding subjects into a single broad field (e.g., social studies, language arts) allows students to comprehend the interrelationships among content and also fosters in students the relating of school content to their daily world. This design, most evident in elementary schools, also is becoming increasingly common at secondary and higher education levels, often in response to demands by students that content be relevant to their current and anticipated needs.

The main advantages of this design are that it provides for an orderly and systematic exposure to the essentials of the culture. Furthermore, it allows for the integration of related contents into meaningful clusters. It can meet students' interests and furnish students with diverse experiences. Frequently, concepts, general principles, generalizations or general issues function as the organizers. In social studies, westward expansion, political power, social problems, environmental issues are employed as organizers drawing data from the social sciences and even physical sciences. Figure 8.3 gives a graphic representation of this type of design.

FIGURE 8.3   *Broad fields design*

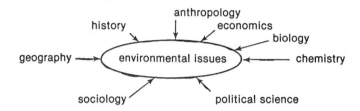

But, even this design has potential shortcomings. Content so organized can be superficial, it can lack depth of treatment. Also, such a content structuring can still be fragmented and not relate to the actual world of the student. Furthermore, it may not, due to its stress on content, meet the current or future interests of the students. Because it has a subject matter orientation, teachers who use the design tend to become more concerned with students' cognitive learnings than students' process or affective learnings. This potential shortcoming is shared by all designs that evolve from the subject matter focus. Regardless of the design selected, one must attend to potential dangers less the content as organized be dysfunctional.

Learner-centered Designs

Learner-centered designs are not content-free, but they do emphasize the learner. Attention is given to individuals' development, their organizational patterns, their needs, their interests, their reasons for attending to particular subject matter. For this design we draw on what we know about human growth and development and learning. We accept, in extreme instances, the assumption that all individuals are idiosyncratic thus preventing us from planning any curriculum in great detail prior to the arrival of students. Upon students' arrival we can identify their concerns and then generate appropriate topics and address meaningful problems. This extreme was popular in the experience curriculum of the thirties. More moderate positions do exist indicating that the curriculum should respond to students' needs and interests, but we do know enough about human growth and development and learning to plan, prior to the arrival of students, the global aspects of the curriculum, the general topics, the sequencing of some general topics, and even the types of materials that might be appropriate.

The rationale for this design has been stated by Taba (1962).

> People learn only what they experience. Only that learning which is related to active purposes and is rooted in experience translates itself into behavior changes. Children learn best those things that are attached to solving actual problems, that help them in meeting real needs or that connect with some active interest. Learning in its true sense is an active transaction. (p. 404).

One strength of this design is that students' needs and interests are considered in the selection and organization of content. However, the basis of this approach rests upon the assumption that students' needs are valid organizers and that their interests and needs are long lasting. One can challenge this assumption with various degrees of vigor depending on what level of education one is discussing and also the types of students one is considering.

The design focuses on the student being active in his or her learning. It is process-oriented. As students confront challenges to their learning, they mount strategies to overcome their difficulties and in so doing learn not only new knowledge, but new procedures, and a more realistic and confident attitude toward themselves as learners and as people. Such positive encounters with difficulties motivate students to continue their learning.

Another advantage of this design is that since needs and interests are primary organizers, the subject matter is relevant to the students' world. Also, the design allows learners to be active, and to apprehend skills and procedures applicable to the outside world. Many in the humanist camp subscribe at least to the basic principles of this type of curriculum design.

But the design, as with all the others, does have deficiencies. The major one, already mentioned, is that students' interests and expressed needs may not be valid or long lasting. Also, students' interests may not reflect those areas of knowledge requisite for successful functioning in the general society. Students' immediate interests may in reality be irrelevant to the general society. Also, students coming from certain environments may have had inadequate experiences to be able to discern their needs and interests. Furthermore, educators are charged with generating needs as well as responding to them. Another problem relates to the continuity of learning experiences based on students' interests. Students' attentions do shift over time, often having an extreme range just within a week's time. Perhaps a more practical limitation of the design is that commercial materials are not available and cannot be produced if one assumes totally that individuals bring idiosyncratic needs and interests to the school. A final limitation is that the design also can contribute to superficiality of coverage.

Other Curriculum Designs

Several other types of designs exist. Stratemeyer, Forkner, and McKim (1957) suggested a design organized around persistent life situations. A greatly reduced version of Stratemeyer's key organizers is shown as:

I. Situations calling for growth in individual capacities
    A. Health
    B. Intellectual capacity
    C. Moral choices
    D. Aesthetic expressions and appreciation
II. Situations calling for growth in social participation
    A. Person-to-person relationships
    B. Group membership

III. Situations calling for growth in capabilities for processing environmental factors and forces.
   A. Natural phenomena
   B. Technological phenomena
   C. Economic-social-political structures and dynamics

Berman (1973) has presented a design undergirded by the concept of communication. Another organization is that of the culture epoch. In this design, a period in human history is the central focus for the curriculum. Content introduced into the curriculum serves to help students apprehend this period. A variation of this is the contemporary problems core in which current problems serve as the organizer for content emanating from many sources (Vars, 1969).

These above designs are hybrid types that may be grouped under problem-centered designs. As to which designs are correct, one's response is "all of them." In reality we do not need to seek the true design, but only the most useful. The usefulness of the design can change as the students change, as the times adjust, as new knowledge is discovered and as professionals within various knowledge realms urge adjustment in their field's organizations. The essential point is that prior to the action of selecting and organizing content, the design issue must be resolved to the satisfaction of the majority of those members charged with curricular planning and development.

The design issue will influence not only the content selection and organization but also the experience and environment selection discussed in the next chapter. Design is not an issue that is dealt with at one time and forgotten. Rather, it is constantly contemplated and used in determining if what is being suggested for inclusion in the educational program supports the design initially selected in the conceptualization stage. As indicated previously, the model design shows the relationship among a number of curricular elements. In addition to content suggested, design indicates the types of possible experiences, the roles of teachers and other personnel in both the planning and activation of curricula, and also the types of materials requisite for implementing the curriculum design.

Activity 8–2   *Curriculum Design Determination*

Analyze the curriculum master plan or major curriculum document in your educational institution and note which design is present. Determine if there is any rationale given for the design selected. Are the major assumptions of the design attended to in the document and are there suggestions as to how to avoid some design weaknesses?

Record your general reactions to the design utilized.

Design Problems

Scope

The selecting and organizing of content requires contemplating several key problems. One such problem is that of scope, the breadth and depth of content.

What content from the disciplines, from the nondisciplines, from the occupational activities should be included in the curriculum? What content should be mandatory for all students? What content should be considered as electives? Our processing of such questions is guided in part by our conceptualization of curriculum and our selection of a particular curricular design.

But, the problem of scope is not eliminated by listing content and the major topics to be covered and noting likely materials. Scope is a continual issue, for knowledge production is dynamic. Certain content areas because of increased information can become unmanageable. General science at the elementary level currently has a much greater knowledge base from which to choose than was true at the beginning of this century. Some individuals are reacting to the expansion of knowledge by advocating that the school redefine, usually in a limiting fashion, its purpose, that it narrow its curricular scope. Some are advocating attending only to basics, ignoring such issues as socialization and morality. How much detail and how much emphasis should be given particular curriculum content has to be answered. Our schools function within a finite time period. Also, students can learn only so much during any particular interim. How much detail do students require at various levels of schooling? At the elementary level, where the broad fields design exists, educators interpret scope to mean that the key concepts and generalizations should be experienced, but the actual number of specific content focuses can be rather limited. Giving students an understanding of the concepts of globe and region does not require students to study all countries in depth.

The scope of curricular content is regulated in part by the goals and objectives generated during the diagnosis stage in curriculum planning.

Sequence

Content selected must be arranged in time. Sequence deals with the question of, What content and experiences are to follow what content and experiences? Sequence addresses the problem of ordering the curricular offerings so as to optimize students' learnings. Posner and Strike (1976) note that before dealing with the question of how content should be arranged, curricularists need to posit a prior question of how curricula can be placed in time. They note that currently we have little empirical data regarding the consequences of particular content sequences.

Johnson (1977) informs us that there has been a long standing controversy regarding whether the logical sequencing and organization of curriculum content is sounder than a psychological one. Sequence based on psychological principles draws on our understanding of and research on human growth, development and learning. Piaget's (1960) research has provided a framework for sequencing content and activities and relating expectations to what we know about how individuals function at various cognitive levels. Kohlberg's (1971) research has provided a similar service regarding the moral development of individuals and the ways in which individuals process types of moral issues and concepts.

Certainly, in organizing content into a productive sequence one cannot totally disregard how individuals develop and learn. But one also can organize and sequence content drawing on the substantive structure of the content, the logic of the discipline. Here content is arranged on the basis of key concepts and the order of learning is determined by what concepts are prerequisite to the learning and comprehending of other concepts. However, stressing the logic of disciplines does not diminish the essentialness of psychological principles of learning as guides to sequencing curricular content. In reality, we require both logics.

An experimental posture regarding sequence should provide answers to our present questions. What subject matter can be handled by students at this particular level of schooling? What subjects should be moved down the school grade scale? What subjects should be postponed until students are more mature?

Frequently, curricularists faced with sequencing content have drawn upon some fairly well-accepted principles. Smith, Stanley, and Shores (1957) introduced four such principles: simple to complex, prerequisite learnings, whole to part, and chronology. The first, simple-to-complex, indicates that content is optimally organized in a sequence going from simple subordinate components or elements to complex components depicting interrelationships of components. It draws on the idea that optimal learning can proceed when individuals deal with the easy material, often in concrete form, and proceed to the more difficult material, often abstract.

However, some curricularists comment that optimal sequence is that which presents the content in an overview (abstract) fashion initially, thus furnishing students with a general idea of the information. After such a global encounter, students can learn the particulars. Ausubel (1963) in his discussions on verbal learning exhorts educators to consider this approach to learning content. Phenix (1964) in discussing the various realms of meaning indicates that dealing with the abstract first, the global picture, may indeed be the optimal approach to learning content.

In contrast, urging prerequisite learnings approaches sequence from a part to whole approach, works on the assumption that there exist bits of learning that must be comprehended before other bits of learning can be apprehended. In learning to read, one masters the sounds of the letters of the alphabet prior to processing initial blends in words. After learning blends, one can attack word pronunciation. Learning to pronounce words leads to the act of reading. Of course, this approach is debatable. In economics, one might urge the learning of the essential concept of scarcity as prerequisite to understanding the concepts of needs and wants. In mathematics, we follow the logic of the discipline. Addition is taught before multiplication; algebra and geometry prior to calculus.

Chronology is another organizer for sequencing content. Frequently, history, political science, and world events are so organized. At times, we employ a reverse chronology, suggesting that students study present content, and then via "flashback" techniques investigate prior events that led to the current event. This type of sequence is defended on the basis that it facilitates understanding the causality of events.

Posner and Strike (1976) present five organizers for determining sequence: world-related, concept-related, inquiry-related, learning-related, and utilization-related. World-related sequences organize content as it seems to or does occur in the world. The content structure reflects the empirical relationships among events, people and things. History and geography would employ this organization.

The concept-related sequence organizer draws heavily from the structure of knowledge focusing on the interrelationships among and between concepts rather than on the real world. Mathematics and logic are in large measure organized independently of world reality. However, even with this organization, concepts may not be divorced entirely from reality.

The arrangement of content drawing on how individuals, or how we assume individuals learn content, is another organizer. This learner-related organizer provides those basic principles of going from simple to complex, concrete to abstract, and from near to the distant.

Determining sequence by attending to the inquiry procedures employed in processing and/or advancing knowledge is somewhat new. This approach is derived from the nature of procedures employed by scholars in the field. Scholars working inductively gather facts, develop concepts, test concepts for their interrelationships, and develop generalizations. Resulting generalizations are tested for validity and if valid often elevated to rules and principles. The ultimates in knowledge production are theories and laws.

The utilization-related sequence organizer also is somewhat new to curricular use. This rationale for sequencing content has one select content as to its social, personal, and career utilization and sequences it as to what is needed and its order of use. Drawing on this sequence organizer, the curricular specialist would incorporate as initial content that considered most important. One would have students study simple interest before getting into compound interest. One would teach values prior to comparative cultures. This organizer draws from the idea of proceeding from essential content to tangential content.

Double sequence. The previous discussion has primarily dealt with content sequencing. But, Taba (1962) has advocated a double sequencing as essential for creating a meaningful curriculum. Both content and cognitive processes need to be planned into the curriculum sequence. One might also add affective and psychomotor processes into the sequencing task. Some educators would posit that if one attends to the sequencing of the content, these other dimensions will take care of themselves. But, we are discovering that frequently our imprecision as to which cognitive processes we are stressing and our manner of treatment have caused us to ignore certain processes now considered crucial for comprehensive understanding. The inquiry-related sequence suggested by Posner and Strike (1976) attends to some of this in that cognitive processes are at least implied in the steps for processing data and generating conclusions.

Continuity

Sequence and continuity are usually considered in tandem. Continuity refers to the continuousness with which individuals will experience content at various levels within an educational system. It deals with vertical manipulation of curriculum elements. It also can be considered as a horizontal concept if one thinks of the continuousness of particular topics or experiences at any particular time, for instance during a certain day or days.

Curricularists often extend themes vertically throughout an entire curriculum. The spiral curriculum organization exemplifies continuity in that the key concepts are experienced successively by students throughout the curriculum. "Persons have basic needs" can be a theme that might extend through 13 years of a school curriculum. Having two years of algebra and having history for three years—dealing with the history of Europe from 1000 to 1500, from 1500 to 1750's, and from 1750 to present times—exemplify continuity.

Continuity deals with the *continued* presence of curriculum elements (content topics or concepts or issues) and relates very closely with the concept of articulation.

Articulation

Articulation refers to the interrelatedness of various aspects of the curriculum. One can have vertical articulation depicting the relationships of certain aspects in the curriculum sequence to topics appearing later in the program's sequence. It also can refer to the association between or among elements occurring simultaneously, defined as horizontal articulation. Correlated studies exemplifies horizontal articulation.

Articulation is difficult to achieve and few school systems have mapped out procedures by which the various interrelationships among varied and distinct parts are made evident to the planners and/or to the instructors and learners. However, the question of how these elements relate to other elements and the effects of these relationships to students' learnings is a paramount one.

Oliver (1977) notes that curricularists usually confront three problems relating to articulation. The first relates to the interrelationships among subjects. As noted earlier in this chapter, often curricula arranged as subjects are not related causing students to experience such content in a disjointed manner. At the elementary school level, we have the separate and distinct skills subjects of reading, mathematics, and language usually with no attempt to relate them, to articulate their component elements. Another articulation problem is that often theory is presented in courses as distinct from practice. Much of school learning is focused on interpretative learning to the exclusion of applicative learning (Broudy, Smith & Burnett, 1964). A related problem is the bifurcation of the nature of school learning and school curriculum with the current life outside the school. The issue of articulation causes us to consider means by which school learning can be made applicable to outside reality.

Improved articulation should result if present subject boundaries can be modified so that interfaces between one content area can be related, either with the teacher's assistance or the student's own efforts, to other content areas.

Balance

The Association for Supervision and Curriculum Development (1961) describes a balanced curriculum as the following:

> A balanced curriculum implies structure and order in its scope and sequence (means) leading to the achievement of educational objectives (ends). . . .
> The problem of balance has two dimensions. First, . . . there is the balance sought in the curriculum provided by the school . . . subjects to be offered and required and programs of studies to be recommended . . . time allotments for various subjects and activities . . . the use of books and other educational aids . . . the respective amounts of general and specialized education to be provided.
> The second . . . dimension of balance is that part of the curriculum actually selected by and/or experienced by each individual pupil. . . .
> Ideally, balance is attained in the individual's own curriculum as he or she develops an optimal level of competence in each of the areas for which provision is made in the curriculum. (pp. 4–7)

Conceptually, an ideal balance exists for each student regarding all curriculum elements. Globally, there is an ideal equilibrium among general education, special education, gifted education, application education, interpretative education, among required courses and among electives. But, to achieve such a curricular state requires more precision in diagnosing our students than we currently exhibit. However, falling short of our mark should not cause us to diminish our striving toward optimal balance such that a wide range of goals is addressed.

One way of broaching the problems of balance is to involve the student more extensively in the selection of curriculum elements (contents, experiences, environments) so as to achieve a meaningful mix in light of his or her goals and levels of development.

Most likely true balance is unattainable due to the simple fact that curriculum and the persons experiencing it are in dynamic interrelationships. Content diversifies; individuals change. Experiences or content ideal for an individual or individuals today may be inappropriate tomorrow because of alterations in the individual's goals and perceptions caused by his or her intervening experiences. Doll (1978) argues that true balance is more likely approached in those schools where a system of flexible scheduling exists and curriculum content and experiences are varied.

Integration

A final concept relating to incorporating content into particular designs is that of integration. Those confronted with designing curricula hopefully realize that learning is more effective when content from one field is related meaningfully to content in another field. Integration, sometimes seen as emphasizing horizontal relationships among various curricular areas, attempts to interrelate content themes, ideas, and facts in order to assure students perceiving a unity of knowledge. Thus, what is learned in language study may be related to study within a social studies unit on communication in modern times. What is learned in science may be further interpreted within the realm of mathematics (Taba, 1962).

In attending to integration, the curricularist generates ways of assisting students in creating a comprehensive understanding of that content experienced in the educational setting. Program developers look for integrative threads. Bloom (1958) defines an integrative thread as "any idea, problem, method, or device by which two or more separate learning experiences are related" (p. 91). It is evident that the concept of integration is used by persons engaged in designing curriculum according to broad fields design and correlated design. The concept is closely related to articulation, but frequently in integrating content, the content areas lose their separate identities.

Activity 8–3   *Identifying Design Problems*

Study the curriculum document in your educational institution and determine if any design problems exist. If so, suggest some ways to correct the problems noted.

Procedural Steps

As has been stressed in this chapter, effective curriculum planners and developers contemplate the possible designs extant, the means for addressing design problems, and the criteria for content selection and organization. The major steps for this stage of curriculum planning appear as in Figure 8.4.

This flow chart of the procedural steps draws from the realm of systems in that the systems concept of input is noted, the concept of transformation is depicted via the various milestone events (1.0 through 5.0), and the concept of output is in evidence in the curriculum content in some type of sequence. Additionally, the general system function of feedback and adjustment is present.

Breakouts of each major milestone activity appear in Figures 8.5 through 8.9.

It is essential for curricularists to realize that regardless of the design selected, the design problems must be contemplated continuously. Considering design problems guides one in actually selecting and organizing the content for students.

As a consequence of this stage of curriculum development, a tentative listing and suggested organization of content are available for incorporation into the next major stage—experience selection and organization. However, content selection and organization may be done simultaneously with experience selection and organization rather than as a sequentially distinct step.

FIGURE 8.4 *Selecting and organizing content*

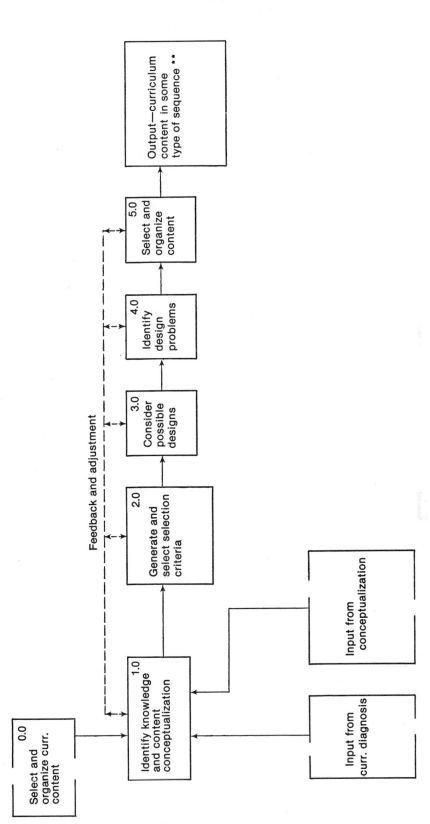

**This output will be input into the experience selection and organization stage.

FIGURE 8.5 *Identifying knowledge and content conceptualization*

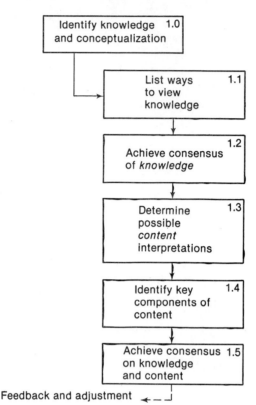

FIGURE 8.6 *Generation and selection of criteria*

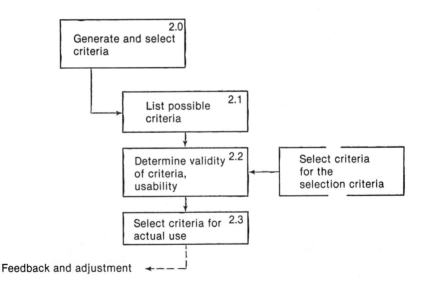

FIGURE 8.7   *Considering possible curricular designs*

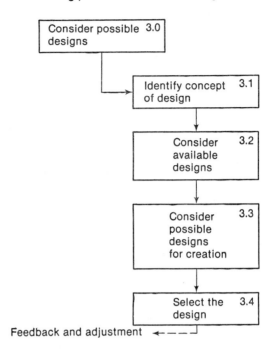

Feedback and adjustment ←– – –⌐

FIGURE 8.8   *Identifying design problems*

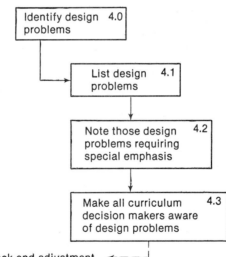

feedback and adjustment ←– – –⌐

     This listing is considered tentative since the content arrangement will not be finalized until the completion of piloting. Even then, teachers are encouraged to make adjustments in content organization and emphasis to cater to the unique needs of their students.

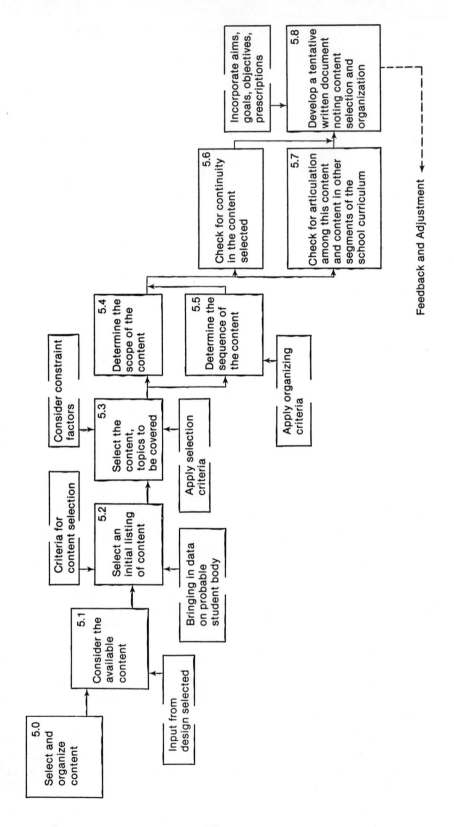

FIGURE 8.9 *Selecting and organizing the content*

5.0 Select and organize content

Input from design selected

5.1 Consider the available content

Criteria for content selection

5.2 Select an initial listing of content

Bringing in data on probable student body

Consider constraint factors

5.3 Select the content, topics to be covered

Apply selection criteria

5.4 Determine the scope of the content

5.5 Determine the sequence of the content

Apply organizing criteria

5.6 Check for continuity in the content selected

5.7 Check for articulation among this content and content in other segments of the school curriculum

Incorporate aims, goals, objectives, prescriptions

5.8 Develop a tentative written document noting content selection and organization

Feedback and Adjustment

Activity 8–4   *Selecting and Organizing Content*

Take a topic or subsection of a topic and following the profile for selecting and organizing content actually engage in this major task.

Check out your work with a colleague.

Note: This activity will consume a considerable portion of time.

Posner (1974) in discussing curriculum structure has provided us with a cogent organizer for addressing the major sub-stages under selecting and organizing content (see Table 8.2).

TABLE 8.2   *Dimensions of curriculum structure extensiveness*

Temporality		Commonality		
		Repeated	**Related**	**Unrelated**
	Contiguous			
Vertical				
	Noncontiguous			
Horizontal				

Note. From G.J. Posner, The extensiveness of curriculum structure: a conceptual scheme. *Review of Educational Research*, Fall 1974, *44*, no. 4, 401. Reprinted by permission.

Commonality deals with the degree to which parts of curricular elements (content) are identical as opposed to independent. Content exists along a continuum going from content that is closely identical with other content to that which is quite distinct from other content. The chart allows us to note those common elements as repeated, as related, and as unrelated.

When organizing content, one considers when persons will experience it—the temporality dimension. As the chart notes, elements can be related in time either vertically as one element prerequisite to a later one, or as horizontal, one element related to another but not in a linear sequence. Vertical elements can be further bifurcated as either contiguous (one element related directly to another element in a tight sequence) or noncontiguous (one element related to another, but separated in time from the first element by one or more unrelated elements) (Posner).

This schematic allows not only a selection and organization of content, but makes clear the various design concepts that require attention: scope, sequence, continuity, articulation. The temporality dimension deals with sequence (vertical) and scope (horizontal). Articulation is considered when dealing with the repeated and related segments of the schematic. Integration also is considered on this level.

Using this type of organizer, one could generate the following table:

TABLE 8.3

Temporality	Commonality		
	Repeated	**Related**	**Unrelated**
Vertical	Repeating biology until all units passed	Chemistry after biology	English literature after study of grammar rules
Horizontal	Sociology and economics	Studying poetry of early New England along with the history of the area	Contemporary art and Physical Education

From such an arrangement of content, one can construct a content outline that besides indicating content to be encountered, denotes where meaningful branches can be developed in the curriculum. One would look carefully at those content elements depicted as unrelated, asking why such content was arranged vertically initially or why such content was being considered in tandem with other content elements.

Relating Functional Tasks to Personal Competencies

The functional breakouts attending to major stages in content selection and organization will be done by individuals both within and outside the educational system. As to whom to involve is a decision required of the curriculum leader. As noted in chapter five, there exist numerous parties interested in participating in curricular decision-making.

Whom to involve depends in part on the particular functional task under consideration and the accompanying level of curriculum decision-making. Content selection and organization can be on a macro level involving the total school program in one or more subject areas or at a macro level referring to curricular decisions for a particular course or even a unit within a course organization. The general steps for content selection remain the same regardless of level, but the specifics of the decisions and the persons to involve are adjusted in manners appropriate for the level of focus.

The following table, relating functional tasks to persons and noting types of support necessary can be employed at this stage in curriculum planning.

TABLE 8.4   *Functional task—personnel matching*

Functional-Task	Possible Personnel	Time Estimate	Support Required
Conceptualizing knowledge and content	Curriculum director, teachers, lay public	3 months	Materials on realm of knowledge Curriculum consultant meeting rooms
Selecting criteria for content selection	curriculum director teachers in a team lay advisory board members	1 month	Curriculum materials Criteria lists Criteria for criteria selection

Such a listing can be created for each milestone function and related subfunctions. The chart allows the recording of what needs to be done, the matching of personnel to particular tasks, the scheduling of appropriate time, and the arranging of requisite support for personnel.

Discussion

Content selection and organization deal with the heart of the curriculum. This milestone event, as evident by the various profiles and breakouts of functional tasks, can be very involved consuming resources in terms of persons' time, material, and money. Whether the end product of this phase of curriculum development, the actual tentative draft of the content to be taught or experienced by students, is of quality depends in part on the qualifications of the persons involved in the curriculum decision making.

Careful planning of this stage should provide a firm foundation for the curriculum. If the major stages as noted in Figure 8.4 are followed, then one increases the probability that the curriculum produced will be relevant to the present and future needs of students and demands of society.

References

Association for Supervision and Curriculum Development. *Balance in the curriculum.* Washington, D.C.: Author, 1961.

Ausubel, D.P. *The psychology of meaningful verbal learning.* New York: Grune & Stratton, 1963.

Berman, L.M. New curriculum designs for children. In R.T. Hyman (Ed.) *Approaches in curriculum.* Englewood Cliffs, N.J.: Prentice-Hall, 1973.

Bloom, B.S. Ideas, problems and methods of inquiry. In National Society for the Study of Education, *Integration of educational experiences, 57th yearbook.* Chicago: University of Chicago Press, 1958.

Broudy, H.S., Smith, B.O., & Burnett, J.R. *Democracy and excellence in American secondary education.* Chicago: Rand McNally, 1964.

Bruner, J.S. *The process of education.* Cambridge, Mass.: Harvard University Press, 1961.

Bruner, J.S. *A study of thinking.* New York: John Wiley & Sons, 1956.

Doll, R.C. *Curriculum improvement, decision making and process (4th ed.)* Boston: Allyn & Bacon, 1978.

Johnson, M. *Intentionality in education.* Albany, N.Y.: Center for Curriculum Research and Services, 1977.

Kohlberg, L. The concepts of developmental psychology as central guide to education: examples from cognitive, moral and psychological education. In M.C. Reynolds (Ed.) *Proceedings of the conference on psychology and the process of schooling in the next decade: alternative conceptions.* Minneapolis: University of Minnesota, 1971.

Nicholls, A., & Nicholls, S.H. *Developing a curriculum, a practical guide.* London: Allen & Unwin, 1972.

Oliver, A.I. *Curriculum improvement, a guide to problems, principles and process (2nd. ed.).* New York: Harper & Row, 1977.

Parker, J.C., & Rubin, L.J. *Process as content: curriculum design and the application of knowledge.* Chicago: Rand McNally, 1966.

Phenix, P.H. *Realms of meaning.* New York: McGraw-Hill, 1964.

Piaget, J. *The psychology of intelligence.* Paterson, N.J.: Littlefield, Adams, 1960.

Posner, G.J. The extensiveness of curriculum structure: a conceptual scheme. In *Review of Educational Research.* Fall 1974, *44,* no. 4, 401–406.

Posner, G.J., & Strike, K.A. A categorization scheme for principles of sequencing content. In *Review of Educational Research,* Fall 1976, *46,* no. 4, 665–690.

Raths, L.E., Harmin, M., & Simon, S.B. *Values and teaching (2nd ed.).* Columbus, Ohio: Charles E. Merrill, 1978.

Scheffler, I. Justifying curriculum decisions. In J. Martin (Ed.) *Readings in the philosophy of education: a study of curriculum.* Boston: Allyn & Bacon, 1970.

Schwab, J.J. Problems, topics, and issues. In S. Elam (Ed.), *Education and the structure of knowledge.* Chicago: Rand McNally and Co., 1964.

Schwab, J.J. Structures and dynamics of knowledge. In M. Levit (Ed.), *Curriculum.* Chicago: University of Illinois Press, 1971.

Smith, B.O., Stanley, W.O., & Shores, J.H. *Fundamentals of curriculum development (Rev. ed.).* New York: Harcourt Brace Jovanovich, 1957.

Stratemeyer, F.B., Forkner, & McKim, *Developing a curriculum for modern living (2nd. ed.).* New York: Bureau of Publications, Teachers College Press, 1957.

Taba, H. *Curriculum development, theory and practice.* New York: Harcourt, Brace & World, 1962.

Tanner, D., & Tanner, L.N. *Curriculum development.* New York: Macmillan, 1975.

Vars, Gordon (Ed.) *Common learnings, core and interdisciplinary team approaches. Scranton, Penn.: International Textbook, 1969.*

chapter

Curriculum Development: Experience Selection

> Perhaps the first important consideration in achieving a wider range of objectives is the fact that the learning experiences, and not the content as such, are the means for achieving all objectives besides those of knowledge and understanding. (Taba, 1962)

The above quote testifies to the importance of experience to the education of students. Indeed, curricularists would have difficulty in conceiving of learning in a manner other than via experience. Yet, despite its centrality to the planning process, Johnson (1977) points out that educators and lay public members frequently misunderstand what experience is.

Dewey (1938) wrote extensively on educational experience, but some educators have misinterpreted him to mean that to be meaningful, all learning had to be experienced directly. In his book, Dewey did advocate a more active approach to learning utilizing direct experiences. But he did not say that all activity had to be overt, nor that the only valuable experiences for students were direct and familiar. He advocated reflection on experience as well as the actual participation in it. Dewey called attention to the fact that experience involved an interaction between an individual and some aspect of his or her environment. The quality of the learning, the actual levels of understandings gained from the experiences, depends in part upon the level of interactions extant in the experience provided and lived.

Experience selection is a crucial stage in curriculum planning, dealing with the question of "how." How shall the students experience the content selected in the previous curriculum planning stage so as to achieve the goals and objectives unique to the schools program and consonant with their own aspirations? Experience selection proceeds through several stages.

Substages of experience selection:

CURRICULUM DEVELOPMENT: EXPERIENCE SELECTION

Selecting conception of experience
Selecting conception of instruction
Determining criteria for selection (of experience and instruction)
Relating experiences to educational environments
Selecting and organizing experiences
Creating educational environments
Melding curricular components into a curriculum-instructional plan

---

STAGES OF EXPERIENCE SELECTION

Selecting Conception of Experience

Our conception of experience depends in part on our philosophical views as well as our understanding of curriculum. If we believe curriculum to be primarily the listing of content and knowledge for transmission to rather passive learners then the experiences we opt for will be those of listening, writing, and memorizing. If we hold that curriculum is a melding of knowledge and an expanding of students' comprehensions of their worlds, then the experiences we gather will be of a more active nature, perhaps student initiated or student managed.

In the majority of schools experiences have traditionally centered on reading, listening, and responding to teachers' verbal moves. Learners primarily have been passive receivers of knowledge. Because of this passiveness, teachers could, did, and do assume that experiences can be planned for all students with little variability necessary. However, today, increasing numbers of educators believe that students are somewhat unique in their interests, backgrounds, aspirations, capabilities, and that they should be more active in their learning. This demand for more student activeness is considered at the experience selection stage of curriculum planning. When students are involved in their learning, educational activities usually evolve in an almost unlimited variety.

To cater to the requirements of the energetic student several things must be kept in mind. First, we must have an awareness of the different behaviors involved in the legions of objectives being suggested. Kilpatrick (1925) phrased it rather nicely. "To each thing to be learned belongs its own way of being learned . . . To learn how to form judgments, we must practice forming judgment—under conditions that tell success from failure. To learn to think independently, we must practice thinking independently" (pp. 5–6).

Presently, much attention is centering on having students gain skills in value formation and utilization. If we select this objective, then the experiences we design in our master curriculum plans must furnish students opportunities not only to discuss the concept of values, but situations in which individuals question their own values, perhaps form new ones, and apply value to situations which have meaning and relevance. In this day of humanism, much attention, at least at the verbal level, is directed to having students develop an understanding of and empathy for persons from different cultures. Do we have in our schools experiences which allow students to encounter such persons, to utilize materials written by others in foreign cultures? Frequently, students learn of foreign cultures primarily by reading and discussing their reading—a rather passive approach.

An objective that is currently receiving emphasis is that of involving students in inquiry within the various subject realms. Are the experiences planned actually conducive to this activity? Frequently, lessons masquerading as inquiry are little more than students responding to teacher's questions. Within social studies, we may desire that students learn the history of a certain movement but often we only have students reading history books with scant opportunities to experience data as an historian.

Relationship of content and experiences. Despite the fact that content and experiences are inseparable, the process of curriculum planning has bifurcated content selection from experience selection. Zais (1976) makes a case for separating content and activities (experiences) in the planning process. In isolating them we avoid two common curricular problems. First, we avoid matching highly appropriate content with inappropriate activities thus avoiding dysfunctioning learning or inappropriate products resulting from the experiences. For example, if we have content that relates to understanding the complexities and contradictions of a society, having to listen to a lecture on this topic with no opportunities for questions may result in diminishing student interest in the said culture, or even fostering a disenchantment with school in general.

Zais' second point is that one, by not separating the content from the experience realms, may be guilty of selecting highly effective activities in themselves and mismatching them with insignificant content. Curriculum planners might incorporate into a master curriculum plan a marvelous inquiry activity in which students employ a formal method of inquiry but then have students employ this strategy with learning some insignificant bit of information containing little relevance or value. Having students investigate why many men wear silk ties exemplifies such a mismatch. However, when we separate experience from content in our planning we are more likely to avoid this for we will be employing specialized sets of criteria for selecting the experiences. As will be shown later in this chapter, these criteria are different from, albeit related to, the criteria employed in the selection of content.

Selecting Conception of Instruction

Experiences planned for students really involve two major components of instruction: educational methods and educational activities. Those planning experiences actually are making decisions as to what teaching methods to employ with various students and what educational activities to provide.

Teaching Methods and Techniques

Teaching is what teachers do. That is, teaching refers to the behaviors exhibited by teachers in the classroom for the primary purpose of inducing student learning. Defining it as behavior specifically activated to influence learning distinguishes such teacher behavior from other teacher behaviors that might relate to the management of the classroom which could be classified as disciplinary behaviors (Haddan, 1970). Teaching is an observable behavior. It can be studied as both an independent or dependent variable by researchers.

Teaching methods are not random behaviors; such methods have form and consistency. They have form in that they have definite steps, stages or subbehaviors that are recurrent and applicable to various subject matters. Additionally, they have a form that is recognizable and usable by other teachers. These subbehaviors are recurrent in that they can be repeated over time depending upon students' needs. Berliner and Gage (1976) mention that teaching methods can be described as patterned behavior.

Teaching methods refer to general procedures that are applicable to the teaching of various subject areas at various levels of complexity. Ascher (1966) lists common methods under the divisions of telling, showing, and doing.

TABLE 9.1 *Common types of methods*

Telling	Showing	Doing
lecture	demonstration	role-playing
discussion	modeling	practice
exposition	pictures	exercise
debates	written words	inquiry procedures
panel discussion		simulation

It is obvious that some of the methods under the common types are really not methods of teaching but more appropriately refer to educational activities or educational techniques. To have a teaching method, one requires the presence of the teacher. With a lecture or a discussion, the teacher's presence is requisite. However, students could engage in a simulation or drill session without the teacher assuming an active role. This does not mean that the teacher is not involved, but the involvement might be more along the lines of managing and arranging the learning encounter.

Techniques are specific aspects of methods. Frequently these are subject specific. A technique of teaching reading is using "words in color". A technique of lecturing may be that of modulating the voice and adjusting the pacing of speaking to generate attention of students. We have techniques of manipulating various educational apparatus. Using multimedia presentations with slides and sounds and then perhaps stopping in the middle for reflection is a technique used to trigger higher levels of thinking. There is the technique of questioning that presents a key question initially followed by a brief period of reflection. Working with cuisenaire rods in mathematics is a technique for getting students to apprehend certain number relationships. We have techniques of employing learning activity packets in certain subjects that get students into active learning roles (Haddan, 1970).

In educational dialogue, teaching methods receive disproportionate attention in relation to elements in education. Certainly, in most schools teachers are concerned more frequently with deciding about methods than deciding about content for the curriculum or even activities for the students. Methods are important, but they need to be considered in relation to all other elements in the curriculum planning process. It makes little sense to be precise in determining *how* we shall do something if we are vague as to *what* we shall do.

At this experience selection stage when we are selecting methods to incorporate into the curriculum-instructional master plan, we need to avoid arguing which methods are better than others. Much research in education seems to have been motivated by desires to prove some method superior to some other method. In reality, all methods are potentially productive. Curriculum planners need not spend their time in determining the generic best method, but in matching methods which seem appropriate and productive for certain students learning particular content. Effective curriculum planners in preparing for instruction take into account the content that has been tentatively selected, the range of methods and activities available, the types of students identified, the grouping procedures known, and the types of pupil-teacher relationships possible. Additionally, ideas as to the potential learning environment, whether within or ouside the school, are contemplated.

Certain methods will require greater variety of content, more time for processing the information, greater space and flexibility of space than other methods. Important to remember is that all students do not learn from the same method, neither do particular individuals learn continuously from the same method (Nicholls & Nicholls, 1972). An orchestration of methods, techniques, and experiences is planned at this stage of curriculum creation. Certainly, teaching methods are complex. The following diagram may prove helpful in identifying the variables that require attention.

This model shows that the teacher has responsibilities for both curricular and instructional decision-making. The decision-making and planning about subject matter refer to the content selection aspects. Subject matter form refers to the stage of content organization. Lesson form deals specifically with types of teaching methods and possible educational activities. Media ties in

FIGURE 9.1   *A teacher's task*

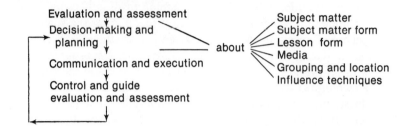

Note. From D.A. Perea, Teachers: Selection, initial and subsequent training. *Curriculum Theory Network,* Winter 1968-69. Reprinted by permission

to both content selection and experience selection. The grouping, location and influence techniques deal with the motivational and management procedures planned for and utilized in a classroom (Perea, 1968).

Bretz (1975) has also provided a useful schematic relating to the components of instruction.

FIGURE 9.2   *Flow chart of instruction*

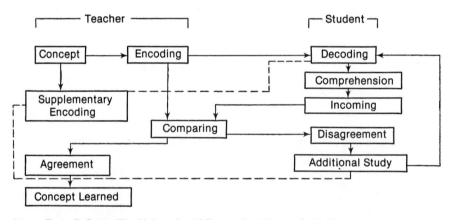

Note. From R. Bretz, The University of Texas dental branch clinical encounter system. In S.D. Zalatimo & Sleeman, *A systems approach to learning environments.* Roselle, N.J.: MEDED Projects, 1975, p. 352. Reprinted by permission.

Activity 9—1   *Identifying Concept of Instruction*

Engage colleagues in a dialogue as to the nature of instruction. Note if their views and yours are similar to the ones expressed in this textbook—that instruction comprises both teaching methods and educational activities. If your views and theirs are different, indicate where the differences exist and how such views affect one's consideration of instruction in general.

Another activity is to critique curriculum guides in the school to determine what conception of instruction is implied in the documents. Do the documents have sufficient detail regarding teaching methods and educational activities so that educators can use intended strategies and manage suggested activities? Share your critique with other colleagues.

The diagram explains the key elements in teaching methods and how students are responding to and interacting with the methods. The schematic clearly points out that teaching methods are specialized communication procedures.

Criteria for Experiences Selection

Experiences incorporated into curriculum master plans differ from many activities found in out-of-school reality. Experiences for inclusion into the curriculum are purposeful rather than random; they are contrived rather than natural. In fact, many of the experiences designed for school are planned for the very reason that they are absent in the everyday occurrences of individuals (McNeil, 1977). Thus, one brings the belief to this task of experience selection that if such experiences were not generated and afforded individuals, individuals would be deprived of other opportunities to experience them. Of course, the experiences that are created are done with a realization of what types of experiences the general public desires. This fact causes one to think back to the first stage of curriculum development, curriculum conceptualization and legitimization.

The experiences and methods to incorporate into the curriculum can only be determined by asking what content has been tentatively selected and determining the intended audience. A clear understanding of various criteria and their application to the experience selection task facilitates the selecting of experiences for the master curriculum plan.

Criteria

The central criterion for any educational experience or activity is that it contributes to the attainment of the curriculum goals and objectives. If one has the objective that students learn inductively about the concept of power, then the experience or experiences selected should be such that there exists a high probability that students will learn, via inductive methods, the concept of power. If one selected the lecture method or the activity of listening to an audio tape, then one has missed the intent of the objective and only focused on the end product of attaining the content. For such an objective, one would incorporate experiences of an inductive teaching strategy and/or experience in which students could employ an inductive information processing method.

Another crucial standard for experiences is that the activities indicate that the planners have a respect for the preciousness or integrity of human beings. The activities also should allow students to develop an appreciation for themselves and others as humans (McNeil). Related to this is that the experiences allow individuals to develop empathy for others.

Many of the criteria suggested for content selection can also be employed in experience selection. One may wish to reread the section in Chapter 8 on this. Certainly, as mentioned above, experiences selected for inclusion in the curriculum plan must be valid in the sense of contributing to the objective. Also, the experiences should be learnable in the sense that they are appropriate for the age and experience levels of students. Taba (1962) speaks of the adaptability of experiences to students. When selecting experiences, keep in mind the necessity of adjusting the experiences as well as the content to the learning abilities and experiences of students. Getzels (1975) speaks of the adaptative environment as opposed to the selective environment. The adaptive environment approaches the learner as one with diverse abilities but abilities that can be taught and improved via the type of curriculum and experiences offered. The selective environment rests on the postulate that persons possess unalterable abilities necessitating selecting students with particular abilities and matching such individuals to particular sections of the curriculum. This author favors considering students' abilities as modifiable. But, to function in such a manner requires our going back to the audience identified in the conceptualization stage. In actuality one continually goes back (feedback) to prior planning stages and in a real sense reprocesses the information making those modifications deemed essential for matching the curriculum to the intended student audience.

Keeping students' backgrounds in mind is essential. If we assume that students have prior experiences and knowledge which in actuality they do not, we run the risk of selecting and organizing experiences which will be dysfunctional.

Experiences also should be economical in the sense of enabling students to learn the maximum amount with minimum expenditure of energy. Somewhat related to the criterion on economy is that of feasibility. Can one actually involve students in the experience giving the constraints of time, school resources, staff expertise, community expectations, and maturity and experiential levels of students?

Expansiveness—another essential criterion to apply to experience selection—refers to the extent to which an experience contributes to multiple student learners. Those experiences contributing to myriad learnings are more appropriate than experiences relating to a narrow specific learning. Experiences that contribute to the learning of specific content, specific processes or strategies of investigation, particular attitudes and values are certainly of greater value than an experience that only allows students to learn a list of facts relating to significant generals of a certain war. Related to this multiple learning aspect is the criterion of economy. An experience that can cause many learnings to develop simultaneously certainly uses time more efficaciously than an experience of equal duration but addressing only one or a few learnings.

An example of an experience meeting the expansiveness criterion is a group investigation into the cultural interpretation of resources. The experience puts groups of students into a situation in which they examine specific case studies noting how various cultural groups at certain periods of time interpreted and utilized the resources of their regions. The student groups approach these cases with the challenge to identify key questions for investigation. In order to meet this challenge, students have to identify the key questions, translate such questions into hypotheses, map out an information processing strategy, actually carry out the data gathering and analyze and interpret the resultant information. Furthermore, the students have to perfect their management of time and design effective means of working with other individuals and groups.

Such an activity not only teaches about the concepts of culture and resources, but students also learn, via such an experience, how to process information and work with groups. Additionally, the students have gained learnings in the affective domain: the learning of appreciation of others, a tolerance for diverse views, an empathy for others, and perhaps an appreciation for democratic ways. A most important aspect of such knowledge might be an appreciation of intellectual activity.

In identifying experiences, one soon realizes that compromise is necessary. Frequently, we trade off certain values of experiences for others. The above activity relating to multiple learnings certainly requires much time, thus there may be a need for downplaying the economy criterion. Also, for particular students, activities having too many learnings embedded within them might be confusing. Thus, these criteria must also be related to the characteristics of the selected or anticipated student audience.

Certainly, learning is complex and multidimensional. As we apprehend more about how individuals learn, we will be able to select and organize activities appropriate for triggering desired learnings. As we seek out more data on how the brain functions, we will be able to select experiences that are functional rather than dysfunctional to brain activity.

Questions to Consider

To reiterate, the essential question of experience selection is, Will the experience do what we wish it to do in light of the overall aims and goals of the program and specific objectives of the curriculum? The following questions are specific extensions of this central question. Are the experiences:

1. valid in light of the ways in which knowledge and skills, will be applied in out-of-school situations?
2. feasible in terms of time, staff expertise, facilities available within and outside of the school, community expectations?
3. optimal in terms of students learning the content?
4. capable of allowing the students to develop their thinking skills, their rational powers?
5. capable of stimulating in students greater understandings of their own existence as individuals and members of groups?
6. capable of fostering in students an openness to new experiences, a tolerance for diversity?
8. such that students will develop awe, wonder, and reverence for the world of knowledge and ideas? (Phenix, 1974)
9. such that they will facilitate, motivate students to continue learning?
10. capable of allowing students to address their needs?
11. such that positive multidimensional learning is generated?
12. such that students will broaden their interests?

13. such that the content planned can be learned in optimal ways?
14. such that they will foster the total development of students in cognitive, affective, and psychomotor domains?
15. such that students will encounter various types of curriculum materials and educational media?

The list, while not exhaustive, does indicate that numerous questions can be posited to assist us in our selecting experiences to make students' encounters with curriculum meaningful, relevant, and stimulating.

Activity 9–2   *Applying Experience Selection Criteria*

Employing the criteria suggested in this section of the textbook, assess the experiences provided in the teacher's editions of the textbook currently employed in your subject area and also the experiences proposed in the curriculum guide for your particular subject.

If the experiences recommended do not meet most of the criteria, generate a list of reasons for such a failure. Discuss your findings with a colleague.

Experiences and Educational Environments

We would have to worry a lot less in our schools about "motivating" children, about finding ways to make good things happen if we would just provide more spaces in which good things *could* happen. (Holt, 1975)

Educational space is crucial to meaningful educational experiences. Curtis and Smith (1975) note that children who experience a creative environment are much more likely to be stimulated to realize their potential and to have a heightened excitement about learning. Space, as Holt notes, creates activity; it allows students to generate places and moods.

All behavior occurs within space. Despite this verity, scant attention has been given to educational space and to the things within such space. Literally for centuries education was envisioned primarily as people in interaction. Where such interaction occurred was basically ignored. But, today, we are coming to realize that the environment of the school or the out-of-school educational setting may be as important as the types of experiences we schedule into the master curriculum plan (Castaldi, 1977). Educational space and the physical phenomena that bounds such space can be considered as an educational tool. Effective educational space should be capable of supporting a wide variety of learning experiences related to a vast array of curriculum content offerings. The design, creation, and management of such space is receiving attention from persons within the field of environmental psychology.

These specialized psychologists are concerned with the physical environment focusing primarily on the complexity that constitutes the physical setting in which people live, interact and engage in activities for varying periods of time (Proshansky, 1975). These new educational specialists are analyzing the role of human perception, motivation, thinking, learning and feeling in man-environment interactions. Since, designers of curricula are in effect creating master plans for stimulating multiple learnings in man-environment interactions, an understanding of this new field and how it can assist us in our curricular decision-making is requisite for successful curriculum development.

In a way, environmental psychologists are looking at educational space from a "geographical" orientation as well as a behavioral stance. By looking at educational space from a geographical perspective, we may be able to make suggestions as to what types of spacial settings are most appropriate for fostering certain experiences resulting in particular learnings. Certainly, these data will facilitate our decision-making. Much of the attention with open education deals with educational space. Openness of space should allow for openness of time, choice of activity, variety in the educational methods employed, and multiplicity of content offered (Proshansky & Wolfe, 1975).

Environmental Psychology and Educational Facilities

Understanding environmental psychology and realizing that in curriculum development we are determining the design of the educational arena should enable us to plan educational milieu that will support, stimulate, and enhance the level of student learning. We are beginning to realize that educational space that is flexible has more power as an educational tool than space that lacks such pliability.

Castaldi (1977) states that educational facilities should address social needs, feelings of security, feelings of belongingness, the development of inner awareness and appreciation, and an increased empathy for others.

Presently, much attention is on personalizing the curriculum. Individuals differ from others in myriad ways: interests, capabilities, backgrounds. But individuals also share similarities with other persons. We can infer many of these similarities from what we know about psychology, and even sociology. All individuals seem to progress through the same developmental stages of cognition. All individuals certainly need food, air, liquid, activity and rest.

The environments that we design at this system stage of curriculum development should facilitate students attending to the experiences and content we have selected and organized. If we wish students to reflect on the concept of matter and energy, the environment should facilitate such reflection. Environments should facilitate the transfer of learning. "Transfer of learning exists whenever a previous learning has influence upon the learning or performance of new responses" (Blair, Jones & Simpson, 1962). Such transfer is likely to occur when the person is confronted with a situation or environment in which a new situation is recognized as being similar to other situations for which the behavior or knowledge has been appropriate. Castaldi (1977) notes that the greater the similarity between school experiences and the anticipated real-life experiences, the higher the level of transfer of learning.

As we design educational spaces, this concept of similarity of educational space to the reality space needs to be employed. Often times, schools have been criticized as having nothing to do with reality and putting students in unreal encounters within unnatural learning spaces. Much of the discussion about deschooling, taking students outside the formal school walls addresses the need of making learning spaces for experiencing the curriculum more real.

The environments we design should stimulate purposeful student activity. They should allow for the depth and range of activities that facilitate content learning. Educational milieu should do more than provide warm environments for "book type" learning. Getting students involved in their learning should be a guideline for us as we work through this aspect of curriculum planning. Spaces should facilitate active learning. For example, in science learning we may wish to design educational space so that we have a projection counter, hot and cold running water, sand tables, space for aquariums and terrariums. Spaces should be provided to allow students to conduct experiments requiring several days or even weeks. So often students' meaningful inquiry is inhibited for they have to "clean up" at the end of each day or period. The environments we design should be rich in the visual, the thermal, the textual, and in the possibilities they allow for students' learnings (Spivack, 1975). Environments will be rich if we keep in mind the type or types of behaviors we wish to stimulate or encourage. Spivack's listing of polar paradigms of behavior tendencies is useful to consider as we design educational spaces. We should strive for elements in the right-hand column.

TABLE 9.2   *Behavior tendencies*

Disorganization, Disintegration, Randomness, Rigidity, and Ritualization	Organization, Integrated, Function, Purposiveness, Synthesis, Learning, and Flexibility of Response
1. Stimulus-avoiding	Stimulus-seeking
2. Relatively rigid	Relatively fluid
3. Ritualized, closed	Evolving, open
4. Unique-event	Repeated-with-variations
5. Transient	Enduring
6. Inappropriate-to-context	Appropriate-to-context
7. Erratic-unlinked	Flowing-linked
8. Functionally fixed	Functionally flexible
9. Solitary-self-absorbed	Social-other-oriented

Environmental Literacy

Environmental literacy is essential knowledge for curriculum designers. As David (1975) notes, "Developing environmental literacy will enable us to analyze our living and learning spaces more critically and to function as intelligent environmental consumers" (p. 161). We as curriculum environment designers need to have an ecological awareness, an awareness of persons in interactions with other persons and with the physical dimensions of their natural surroundings. With assistance from the field of environmental psychology, we can become aware of how people behave in certain environments. If students have difficulty seeing or hearing, how does their learning behavior change? Individuals can learn with all their senses. We are beginning to talk about multisensory learning, but often our school environments are geared only to learning via the perception of the written symbol and the hearing of the spoken word. Individuals need cognizance of how their senses of touch, smell and hearing can enhance their various learnings.

It may be that we need new words for communicating to each other about educational milieu. We require concepts that relate to the grouping of spatial phenomena and how students and teachers relate to such groupings and adjust to them. Environmental literacy, as David pointed out, means the translating of our awareness into critical, problem-solving and problem-seeking attention towards one's surroundings. With such understanding, we as designers and students of curriculum can make effective choices regarding educational environments or design experiments to ascertain optimal environments. "Environmental literacy is the application of the generalized vocabulary of awareness to one's immediate physical surroundings in a problem-solving fashion" (David, p. 165).

Being aware of the dimensions of educational environment means that we understand the types of potential interactions a person can have within educational space. Frymier and Hawn (1970) write of actors and artifacts when discussing educational arena. David notes that one can define a person as an actor and the environment as the actor's surroundings, lying outside the boundaries of the social system. But he noted that one also can consider the surroundings as the actor and the student as the environment.

In order for students to learn and grow, they must provide themselves continually with opportunities to be taught by the environment, both the human and the nonhuman elements. Often we talk of the hidden curriculum. This curriculum is the result of the unplanned and often uncontrolled elements (both people and things) extant in the environment interfacing with students. Any effort to develop environmental literacy must assure that the "invisible" forces present in the environment are really considered in the curriculum development process (David).

Nature of Learning Environments

When dealing with learning environments we are in reality considering three environments: the physical, the social, and the psychological. The physical greatly influences the social and the psychological. Much of the previous discussion dealt with the physical and the social and some attention has been given to the psychological.

The physical is perhaps the easiest to deal with for it is observable. It contains the physical facilities, the furniture, hardware and the materials. The architecture, the space, and the equipment varies with schools as a result of monies allocated, philosophy of the educators and the public, conceptions of curriculum, and the culture in which the school finds itself. However, the environmental factors are considered from the standpoint of flexibility. Today, increasing numbers of the schools are equipping their environments with multimedia instructional equipment to deliver or have the students encounter the curriculum content in meaningful ways.

Engaging in decision-making related to processing the physical environment requires consideration of the variables of student types, class size, actual physical characteristics of the school, the types of media equipment available, and the number and type of accessory facilities present. These variables are embodied into the planning, and suggestions about the management of such variables are incorporated into the curriculum-master plan. In a sense, environmental designers consider the educational environment as a Gestalt designed for students. The objects and events as well as the content, prepared for the stimulus situation for learning will be adjusted according to the objectives selected for a particular aspect of the curriculum.

The social environment is palpable whether we plan for it or not, for individuals rarely function as isolates. In planning for such environments, we draw on our understanding of group dynamics. Suggestions dealing with the social environment provide guidance to educators regarding how to optimize students' social intercourse. Educators often incorporate into their objectives that individuals will develop cooperation, will manage competition, will accept themselves and others, and will formulate role expectations for themselves. All of these objectives are achieved in consequence to the functioning of the social environment.

Effective planning of this environment takes into consideration the teacher's behaviors. Suggestions are given to teachers as to how they can optimize the interactions within the social educational milieu to benefit learning. Also, suggestions address ways in which students can achieve a better understanding of themselves and others in social interactions.

The psychological environment, considered really in tandem with the other two types of environment, can be defined as the complex of stimuli that impact upon the individual causing some type of response. It refers to those factors that influence the psychological boundaries of individuals. Such concepts as personality need, the internal press or force of the individual, and environmental presses, the external counterpart of personality need, are useful to bear in mind when considering this environment.

When planning environments for individuals we note that each person brings with him or her a private world, a unique stance in relation to others and to phenomena. There is a level at which a person's private world interfaces with the worlds of others. Although we perhaps cannot be exact at this time in planning for such interfaces, we can have some ideas as to how what we plan regarding content and experiences will impact upon people as individuals and as members of groups (Conley, 1973).

Criteria

Castaldi (1977) has suggested the following three criteria when contemplating and designing educational space: adequacy, efficiency and economy. Adequacy refers to both the number of spaces as well as their size. Is the space planned of sufficient number to accommodate the students who will be using it in regard to some aspect of the curriculum? If one plans to have 30 percent of the students inquiring into specific content clusters, is there sufficient area to allow such activity? If one schedules into the curriculum that 25 percent of the time, at least half of the students may be engaged in independent study, is the space effective? Has one planned for the inclusion of study carrels or "quiet corners" where one can interact with curriculum content or read a book in quiet reflection?

Castaldi notes that the number of spaces required for groups depends on the size of the groups as well as the nature of the curricular program. He has developed a formula that can be used as a guide:

$$T = 1.25 \times \frac{E}{C} \cdot \frac{n}{N}$$

Where T = Number of areas needed
E = Total number of students requiring space
C = Number of students in a given group or class
n = Number of minutes that a given group size meets per week
N = Number of minutes in the school day (p. 36)

Example: Assume that a program in general science calls for 200 students to take this segment of the curriculum. The school day of 5 hours equals 300 minutes. During the week, students would be divided into teams of 4, for 60 minutes per week. Given these statistics, and employing the formula one can determine requisite spaces for these groups:

$$T = (1.25) \frac{200}{4} \cdot \frac{60}{300} = (1.25) (50) (0.2) = 12.5 \text{ or } 13 \text{ spaces}$$

Caution should be noted. Quantifying information can lead us to believe that we can always act with precision in curricular matters. It seems more propitious to accept such mathematical calculations as guides as to how much space is necessary rather than as a precise dictum. Additionally, one needs to remember that flexible space is necessary and there may be times when only 5 spaces might be required or other times when 17 spaces might be necessary. Adequacy is constantly being considered in light of ongoing student activities. In the curriculum master plan, ways of monitoring the adequacy of the learning environment are suggested.

Adequacy can also refer to environmental controls. Is the lighting adequate for ease of reading; are the visuals satisfactory in terms of size so that students can see them? Are the materials serviceable in terms of the learning styles of the students. Are the acoustics sufficient in terms of being able to hear the teacher and other students. Such points are noted in the curriculum guide.

Closely related to adequacy is suitability (Castaldi). In many schools, all classrooms have the same shape and size, a rectangular shape that can accommodate approximately one teacher and 35 students. However, the shape of the environment should be modified to suit the function intended for it. In present-day education, the modern classroom allows for demonstration and discovery, as well as exposition. Optimal educational environments are suggested in the planning stage to facilitate the lessons' main thrusts. Environmental suitability may be influenced by the color combinations within the classroom (Faber, 1955), the lighting design, the textures of the interior surfaces as well as the types of classroom furniture. In curriculum development, these factors are considered. Such attention is important for as mentioned previously, the environment acts upon and teaches the students.

The last point under adequacy is the adequacy of the relationships between the various spaces within a school. How do spaces designed for individual investigation relate to spaces planned for the storage and retrieval of educational materials? How do spaces created for small group investigation relate to spaces designed for small group viewing of educational media? Will students be able to get from one area to another without disrupting other students? Many new schools are organizing spaces in clusters determined by the types of activities planned and the contents selected. It makes sense to have science discussion activities planned for spaces near the laboratories where students can conduct experiments. It is more effectual to have reading activities, especially individual reading, scheduled for spaces near the learning resource center.

The second criterion regarding educational space is efficiency. As Castaldi notes, this criterion refers to those characteristics of educational space that are likely to improve its instructional effectiveness or operational characteristics. Does the environment as planned allow the educational activity (whether large group, small group or individual) to be initiated and accomplished with a minimum of effort. Will the environment as planned facilitate the greatest amount of learning with the least amount of effort. Will students and teachers find functioning within the educational milieu convenient?

The final major criterion is economy. One aspect of economy is the actual savings in terms of capital outlay that can be achieved by initial architectural design or by modification of an existing environment for a particular aspect of the curriculum. Economy raises the question, How much does it cost to teach this content, to provide this experience, to maintain this environment? Certainly, in planning a curriculum one must at some point consider what it costs in terms of materials, salaries, and operation to implement the curriculum master plan suggested. This consideration, while essential, is not done earlier in the curriculum planning process.

Before considering cost, we first ask what are the students' education needs. Such needs are identified by processing data obtained from students, educators, and the general public. Once needs are delineated we can determine the cost of meeting them. At this time, we also estimate the costs in terms of negative consequences of not addressing particular students needs.

Such cost determination is extremely difficult for we frequently lack specific data or precise enough instruments to measure or forecast what inaction or the nonoffering of some aspect of the curriculum is in terms of social or economic consequences. It may be that by not releasing money for a curriculum that deals with values, valuing, and inquiry procedures, we run the risk of having to spend future monies for remedial education for those citizens who have made inappropriate choices with regard to their own lives resulting in an overall negative impact upon the general society.

Economy, however, does not just refer to saving money (Castaldi). It also relates to economy of students and teachers' efforts. Time is a resource, and we design curricula to take as little time as possible to achieve the maximum benefit in terms of attainment of our basic program goals and objectives. This is not advocating the short and cheap curriculum as best. For students to develop empathy for others, extended encounters with persons of varying views and cultures are required. But the extended period of time should only be as long as necessary to achieve the goal. There is little defense for prolonging an activity or experience just to fill time. But the difficulty is that we frequently are ignorant of how long an activity should be in order to allow students to attain the greatest amounts of understanding. We need to play this "by ear." We should monitor activities once implemented and then note what seems to be sufficient time for meeting our objectives.

In the planning stages, before actually selecting and organizing experiences and then placing them in possible environments, one needs to ascertain that all members in the curriculum development process understand what is meant by learning environments. From the previous sections it is evident that this curriculum element is complicated.

Activity 9–3   *Describing an Educational Environment*

Drawing on what you have read about educational environments, critique the environments extant in your educational institution.

If the environments are not of high quality, map out a means to upgrade them.

Creating Educational Environments

Up to this point, we have discussed selecting a conception of experience and instruction, the criteria necessary to consider when dealing with experience selection, the nature of educational environments, the relationship of experiences to such environments, and the criteria to employ in selecting potential educational environments. After such consideration, one develops a plan for actually selecting and organizing the experiences and creating or suggesting particular educational environments. This section delineates the steps in processing such information ending with the actual creation of the final curriculum-instructional master plan (the curriculum guide).

FIGURE 9.3 *Guide to curriculum development*

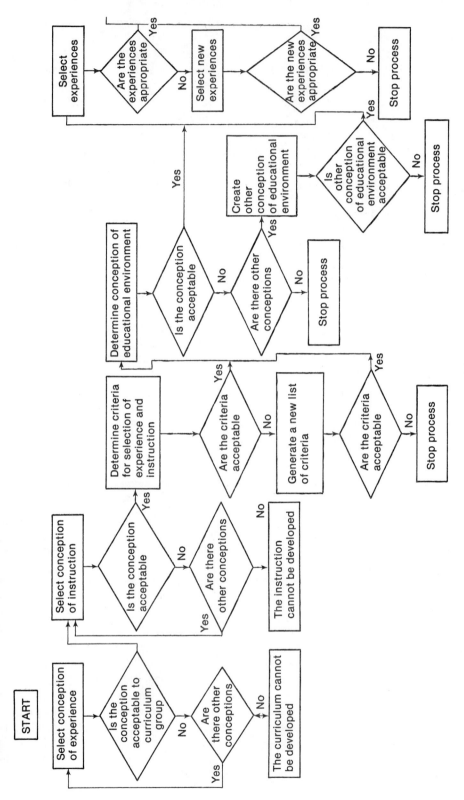

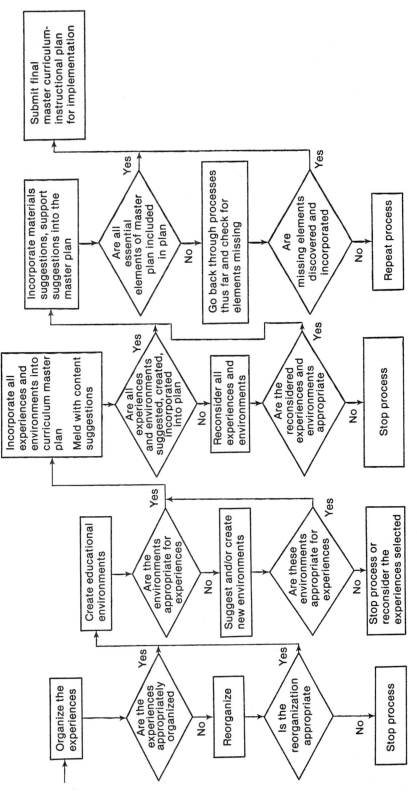

FIGURE 9.3 *continued*

263

Figure 9.3 depicts the major substeps dealing with this major milestone stage of curriculum development. This model can be employed as a guide. The rectangles represent activities that need to be accomplished. The diamond-shapes denote decision points throughout the system process.

Figure 9.3 represents a suggested rather than an absolute procedure. Also, the sequence one might go through may not be linear. Some individuals will have good ideas about environments and will work "backwards" to the experience and instructional decision stages. Other persons may come to this stage of curriculum development with ideas about potentially exciting student experiences and will suggest places where such experiences might be utilized. These people would have to go back to the stages that deal with criteria for selection as well as the junctures dealing with the sequencing of the experiences. Regardless of where people start in this major stage, they all will have to refer back to the previous milestone stage of content selection to determine if the experience and environment are appropriate in light of the content tentatively selected. Such content and the experiences and environments are all tentative until their worth has been determined in the piloting substage.

That persons charged with this phase of curricular activity will have to refer back to prior stages and will need to keep in mind the upcoming stages points to the unity of the total process of curriculum development. It also addresses what has continually been referred to as a systems approach to curriculum activity. Essentially, this is an attitude, an orientation to the total task of curriculum activity. It is not a narrowing of our approach to program development or a diminishing of the scopes of the programs that result from our deliberations. Rather, it is a viewing of our actions in their totality, witnessing where such actions impact within the total educational theater and realizing how all of our decisions relate.

The Curriculum-Instruction Master Plan

Essentially, curriculum development is concerned with the production of a curriculum master plan (a latent curriculum) that will be available to instructors to assist them in conducting the business of education (activated via the functional or manifest curriculum). The curriculum master plan is the goal for which educators and curricularists work. Of course, as suggested in this book, the work of curricularists and educators is not completed with the production of the curriculum master plan. The plan has to be implemented, its effectiveness has to be evaluated, and it has to be maintained over time with necessary modifications.

Frequently, curriculum master plans created in the form of curriculum guides are not used by educators. Many of these educators feel such plans are not useful or are cumbersome to employ. They also argue that the process of curriculum development is really of greater value than any product produced by such development. Persons involved in creating plans or segments of plans have opportunities to learn about the nature of curriculum, update their knowledge of certain content fields, become skilled in the creation and management of educational activities, and become familiar with the latest materials. In short, participants have opportunities to growth by being involved in the process.

Surely, participants do have great opportunities for professional and intellectual growth by being involved in the curriculum development process. But this does not reduce the importance of the guide. As Neagley and Evans (1967) point out not all teachers who will use the guide will have been furnished the occasion to participate in its creation. Additionally, staff new to the school or educational institution will require a guide or master plan to be able to function effectively with regard to the schools' major goals.

That guides have not been used is not an argument for their discontinuance. Rather, it is a challenge to curricularists to create master plans that are interesting, comprehensive, and truly facilitative of quality curriculum implementation and educational instruction. The curriculum master plan enables the school or educational institution to have a means of making sure that the program is activated as conceived and that over a period of time the program's key components and ways of having students encounter certain knowledge areas remains somewhat constant. Educational programs that are not the result of following a curriculum guide have the tendency to lack consistency of purpose and frequently are so general as to have vague and imprecise instruction.

Form

Just what form does a master plan assume? Earlier in the book it was mentioned that two plans are created in the curriculum development process: a master curriculum-instructional plan and a master management plan that relates to how one will manage resources and people during the curriculum development phase. Master plan is a relative term. It can refer to the entire curriculum plan for all subjects and all grades in a school system. Additionally, it can refer to an entire series of courses in a particular subject area for all grades or levels of schooling. Or it can apply to a particular subject area for just one year. Which plan level we are discussing depends upon the scope of our curricular efforts. Certainly, educational institutions do not engage in creating simultaneously master plans for all subjects at all grades on a frequent basis. But most schools do create master plans for a particular subject area for all grades on a regular cycle, often every five years.

Frequently master plans are called course guides or curriculum or instructional units. Course guides usually cover entire years while instructional units cover time segments within a year usually making up divisions in a course. But instructional units may also be used synonymously with course guides at levels of schooling where mini courses are offered as electives. The important point to remember is that regardless of the level of breadth, whether a guide for an entire district or a guide for a particular class unit, the major categories remain basically unchanged.

As a rule of thumb, guides created at national or state levels contain less detail than those created at the school district level. Some national and state guides are only suggested outlines with some sampling of possible materials. These guides are then taken by school personnel and more detail is added in the form of content suggestions and suggestions for teaching methods and educational activities. However, guides, regardless of level, address the basic elements of curriculum (content, experiences, and environments) as well as means of evaluating the effectiveness of the curriculum and suggestions for appropriate materials and media.

Approach to Guide Use

A guide is just that—a guide. It is not a document requiring one to teach only certain content or commanding that it be taught in specific ways. A guide or master plan (synonymously called a resource unit) is suggestive; it presents myriad methodological procedures and educational activities as well as numerous content clusters potentially useful for achieving, in general, school goals and objectives and, in particular, course or subject area goals and objectives. When first looking at guides some teachers exclaim, "I can't teach all that in the time I have scheduled!" Teachers are not supposed to teach "all that." Rather, they should select from the noted content, experiences, and environments those deemed appropriate for the particular students they now have taking into consideration the constraints extant at the time of implementation.

A curriculum guide should facilitate, not limit, creative teaching. Teachers require freedom to make those types of professional decisions relating to the implementation of a curriculum master plan within the framework furnished by the guide. Certainly, teachers are not free to disregard the guide's basic orientation or thrust. A teacher cannot state that since he or she considers a certain content or unit topic of limited value, he or she will disregard it. If a school has coordinated the creation of a cooperative guide on the topic of conservation of resources, a teacher cannot decide to ignore teaching such content. The teacher's freedom lies in selecting specific content from the guide to address the topic of resources and then determining what teaching methods and educational activities to employ with particular groups of students. Also, the teacher decides what types of materials to use and their manner of use. But, again, if certain basic commercial materials have been selected to complement the curriculum master plan, a teacher cannot refuse to utilize such materials.

Components

To be useful, guides should have the following major components:

1. A title page.
2. A table of contents.
3. An introduction to the guide noting its nature and purpose. The guide's format can be discussed at this juncture.
4. A rationale statement noting the justification or reason for offering or requiring students to experience this curriculum.

5. A philosophical statement advancing one's view of education in general and the particular ways a teacher is to teach and a student is to experience this course or unit. Frequently philosophical statements are too general, informing the reader only that the persons responsible for the guide believe in the abilities of students to learn. The philosophical statement, whether made under the rational section or its own section, should be specific enough to inform the reader whether the creators of the guide are traditional, progressive, or eclectic in philosophical orientation.

6. Listing of major generalizations for the course, unit, or guide. Often generalizations are selected from lists created by scholars of the various disciplines. Educators can then take such lists and modify them to the specific goals of the guide.

7. Listing general goals of the guide.

8. Listing of the general objectives of the master plan. These objectives denote in general terms what the curriculum developed expects students to gain from experiencing the unit.

9. The content outline. The outline should note the essential content topics to be considered in the entire unit or master plan. The detail should be sufficient to furnish the reader with an idea of all the major topics and subtopics. With regard to the major content topics, the teacher would be expected to deal with them all. However, the teacher has greater choice as to what subtopics to stress.

10. The body of the master plan. This section melds the objectives, content, experiences, teaching methods, educational environments, and educational materials into relationships such that the teacher can relate the content of the outline to particular objectives, to particular content, to specific activities and methods, and certain materials. The body also arranges the lesson into some type of sequence usually introductory activities, developmental activities, and concluding activities. It also contains suggestions as to how to evaluate the effectiveness of both the teacher's instructional behaviors and the students' learning behaviors.

11. End matter. Frequently curriculum guides suffer from the quality of "generalness." For example, teachers dealing with group conflict might be advised to get students to discuss the topic of group conflict and answer questions relating to such conflict. This advice, while perhaps on target, tells the teacher little that is meaningful. What type of discussion method should one use? What type of grouping procedure should one employ? What types of questions should be raised? Which questioning strategy might be effective at this point? There are specific types of teaching methods available, and they do have names. The Taba method is fairly well known. If one were to inform teachers that the Taba method would be useful in getting students to generate some generalization regarding group conflict, the teacher has a specific

recommendation. Also, when new staff come into the school, they, upon reading the guide, know specifically what method they might use. The same is true of questions and questioning strategies. There are specific ways to sequence particular types of questions, and the manner in which questioning is enacted can influence student learning.

But, such detail is cumbersome in the body of the guide. However, we can note in the body the strategy or activity by name and refer the reader to the unit's end matter for a more detailed explanation. The level of detail depends upon the backgrounds and experience of the teachers. But, it should be sufficient so that the teacher can correctly use the strategy or activity in question. Depending on the background of the educational staff, it may be useful to incorporate in the end matter a brief explanation of the nature of a resource unit, less teachers err in thinking they need to teach all that is contained within the curriculum master plan.

A detailed listing of generalizations appropriate for development in the unit may be listed in the end matter. Frequently, in units that are multi-disciplinary, the list of generalizations is fairly extensive.

Teachers frequently find it of value to have a scope and sequence chart of all the basic skills to be covered in the unit. Teachers can then visualize how what they might be doing at a particular level relates to what is done at other levels. Annotated bibliographies may also be included in the end matter.

These bibliographies may be for both students' and teachers' materials.

Information on techniques of evaluation also may be included in an appendix. It might be useful to have at the end of a unit a descriptive profile of the community in which expected students live. In an age when many teachers do not live in the community in which they teach, such information can prove most useful when attempting to individualize the program.

The unit's format is not absolute. There will be variations of format from one subject area to another frequently due to the nature of the content and the types of learning experiences. A guide for physical education might well differ in format from one in mathematics. However, the guides, even with format variability should still have the same basic components. All guides should have objectives and content outlines regardless of whether they are dealing with science or drivers education or human psychology.

Evaluating the Master Plan

Curriculum master plans can be evaluated before implementation as well as during and after implementation. First, we can evaluate the master plan to de-

Activity 9—4   *Assessing Curriculum Guide*

Take the curriculum guide for your major subject or a subject in the grade you teach and critique it for inclusion of the basic components of a guide. How inclusive is your guide?

   Note how often you use your curriculum guide. If you do not use it often or ignore it completely, indicate the reason or reasons for such limited use or nonuse. What would have to be done to increase the guide's usefulness to you?

termine if all the essential components are present. Then we can assess the value of the content suggested in the outline. We can assess the utility of the goals and objectives. We can determine the validity of the content and the logic of its organization. We also can assess the appropriateness and specificity of the experiences (instructional strategies and educational activities) in light of the content suggested. We can critique the feasibilities of activities suggested in terms of cost, time, facilities, and staff. Much of this evaluation occurs during the guide's creation, but a final (summative) evaluation is essential before the master plan is entered into the piloting and final implementation stages.

   Guides should also be pleasant to look at and easy to use. The art work within the guide can be judged as to artistic quality. The guides should be printed in a type size and shape that makes for easy reading. Also, it is recommended that guides be bound in loose-leaf form, so that pages can be deleted and added as necessary. Guides should contain blank spaces so that teachers can jot down ideas and modifications.

   Participants in the curriculum development process should also evaluate the end matter in the guide to assure that it will be of value. If not appropriate, there is a likelihood that it will not be used, or if used may lead to poor utilization of the curriculum or a disenchantment with the program suggested.

Synthesizing the Master Plan

Synthesizing all the elements of a curriculum guide is no easy task. Unless a district or educational institution has a resident expert on board, a consultant should be called in to assist in the synthesizing of all the data and information resulting from the previous stages. Most likely, a district or institution engaging in curriculum development would have secured the services of a consultant at the commencement of the process.

   Up to this point in systematic curriculum development, one has been gathering segments of the essential curricular elements and making decisions as to possible ways to organize these elements to increase the probability of students' learning the information contained within the program. Now, one confronts a compositional task of getting the final document ready for piloting and ultimately final implementation. Here, one takes the tentative listings and sequences of content and experiences and, remembering the nature of the curriculum master plan, composes a written document (either a master plan, a course plan, or a unit plan). At this juncture one also may create support materials to complement commercial materials related to aspects of the curriculum-instructional master plan.

Following is a flow chart listing the milestone events requisite for creating the final master plan for piloting and eventually final implementation.

At first glance, the profile gives the illusion that creating a curriculum master plan (curriculum guide) is uncomplicated. But, in order to accomplish each milestone event, many other steps are required and much knowledge needs to be brought to the tasks. For example, 8.1 notes that one is to match and sequence the content to the objectives and outline. But, all of the substages listed in the previous chapters have to be considered in order to do this. The next events, 8.2 and 8.3 really require all of the substeps noted earlier in this chapter, from determining how one will perceive the meaning of experience to actually making specific selections and organizing them logically and psychologically and then recommending them for activation within particular types of educational environments.

After completing this, one has a document ready for piloting, a latent curriculum having the potential of meeting the aims, goals, general and specific objectives of the educational institution.

Activity 9–5   *Implementing Curriculum Development*

Following the flow chart listing the milestone events for creating a final curriculum master plan, create a tentative curriculum guide for one subject. (Note: This activity will take a considerable time period, and you may wish to work with a colleague.) If your educational institution is about to engage in curriculum development, volunteer your services and apply the information gained in this book.

You might keep a record of the procedures you employ and the decisions you make at the various milestone stages in the curriculum development process.

Discussion

Experience selection and the previous major curricular task of content selection comprise the most visible activities of curriculum development. These activities result in some tangible document that can be used by other educators to facilitate and enhance students' learnings.

However, these visible activities depend upon the previous major stages of curriculum development as well as those that are to follow. It is important to view experience selection and content selection as essential parts of a total process—curriculum development and management. Having such a global view assists one in relating what one is doing to the total purpose of education, to increase the likelihood, in many cases to assure it, that particular types of student learnings will occur.

FIGURE 9.4 *Creating the master plan*

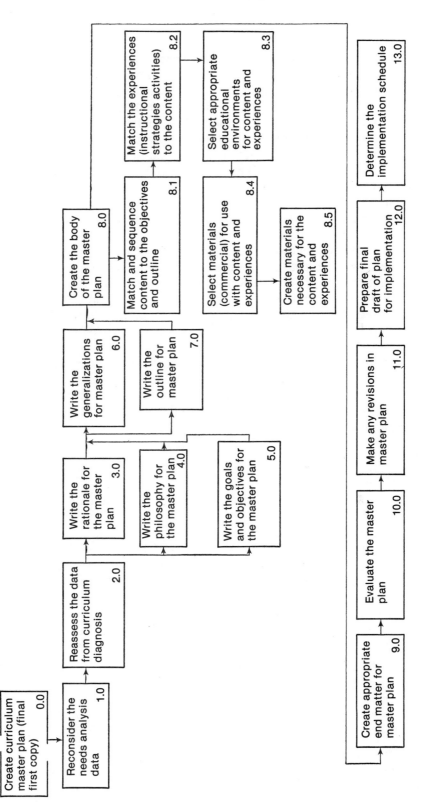

Those of us involved in curricular activity soon realize that the phenomena about which we are making decisions are indeed complex. Also, we comprehend that even though we can be systematic in our approach to curricular and other educational phenomena, we often only crudely approach the tasks. Currently, our lack of information inhibits our precision of action and prevents us from stating with certainty that specific aspects of the curriculum arranged in particular ways will have predictable effects.

We certainly can draw on tradition, our knowledge of society, our understanding of human growth and development and learning, our understanding of the field of curriculum and curriculum theory, and our knowledge of the field of knowledge, but most curricularists among us approach their tasks mindful that they engage in curriculum development with only partial views, partial understandings. We really know little about how people learn. As noted previously, most of our theories of learning were developed prior to any research on the way the brain actually functions physiologically. Also, much of what we bring to the curricular tasks in this major step or in the previous ones is based on tradition or social demands rather than on any sound curriculum theory. But, we can take the best of that which we do know and work with it to create quality curricula. We cannot wait until all the information is in before building programs. But, if we realize that we are functioning with only partial knowledge of the process and curricular elements, we will maintain an inquiry posture and make modifications in our master plans as we attain new information, new insights, and process new demands from the community at large and students in particular.

References

Ascher, R.S. Methods and techniques in teacher development. *Educational Technology,* November 1966, 30, 1–2.

Berliner, D.C., & Gage, N.L. The psychology of teaching methods. In N.L. Gage (Ed.) *The psychology of teaching methods, the 75th yearbook of the National Society for the Study of Education, part 1.* Chicago: University of Chicago Press, 1976.

Blair, G.M., Jones, R.S., & Simpson, R.H. *Educational psychology (2nd ed.)* New York: Macmillan, 1962.

Castaldi, B. *Educational facilities, planning, remodeling and management.* Boston: Allyn & Bacon, 1977.

Conley, V.C. *Curriculum and instruction in nursing.* Boston: Little, Brown, 1973.

Curtis, P., & Smith, R. A child's exploration of space. In T.G. David & B.D. Wright (Eds.) *Learning environments.* Chicago: The University of Chicago Press, 1975.

David, T.G. Environmental literacy. In T.G. David & B.D. Wright (eds.) *Learning environments.* Chicago: The University of Chicago Press, 1975.

Dewey, J. *Experience and education.* New York: Macmillan, 1938.

Faber, B. *New horizons in color.* New York: Rinehold, 1955.

Frymier, J.R., & Hawn, H.C. *Curriculum improvement for better schools.* Worthington, Ohio: Charles A. Jones, 1970.

Getzels, J.W. Images of the classroom and visions of the learner. In T.G. David & B. D. Wright (Eds.) *Learning environments*. Chicago: The University of Chicago Press, 1975.

Haddan, E.E. *Evolving instruction*. New York: Macmillan, 1970.

Holt, J. Children are sensitive to space. In T.G. David & B.D. Wright (Eds.) *Learning environments*. Chicago: The University of Chicago Press, 1975.

Johnson, M. *Intentionality in education*. Albany, N.Y.: Center for Curriculum Research and Services, 1977.

Kilpatrick, W.H. *Foundations of method: informal talks on teaching*. New York: Macmillan, 1925.

McNeil, J.D. *Curriculum, a comprehensive introduction*. Boston: Little, Brown, 1977.

Neagley, R.L., & Evans, N.D. *Handbook for effective curriculum development*. Englewood Cliffs, N.J.: Prentice-Hall, 1967.

Nicholls, A., & Nicholls, S.H. *Developing a curriculum, a practical guide*. London: Allen & Unwin, 1972.

Perea, D.A. Teachers: selection, initial and subsequent training. *Curriculum Theory Network*, Winter 1968–1969, 9, p. 58.

Phenix, P.H. Transcendence and the curriculum. In E.W. Eisner & E. Vallance *Conflicting conceptions of curriculum*. Berkeley, Calif.: McCutchan, 1974.

Proshansky, E., & Wolfe, M. The physical setting and open education. In T.G. David & B.D. Wright (Eds.) *Learning environments*. Chicago: The University of Chicago Press, 1975.

Proshansky, H.M. Theoretical issues in environmental psychology. In T.G. David & B.D. Wright (Eds.) *Learning environments*. Chicago: The University of Chicago Press, 1975.

Spivack, M. The exceptional environment: strategies for design. In T.G. David & B.D. Wright (Eds.) *Learning environments*. Chicago: The University of Chicago Press, 1975.

Taba, H. *Curriculum development, theory & practice*. New York: Harcourt, Brace & World, 1962.

Zais, R.S. *Curriculum: principles and foundations*. New York: Thomas Y. Crowell, 1976.

chapter  10

Curriculum Implementation

Curriculum implementation, comprised of piloting and final diffusion of the tested program, is a critical phase in curriculum development. At this juncture, the curriculum-instructional master plans—the results of the previous curriculum development phases—are put to work. The actual substages comprising curriculum implementation can vary from school to school influenced in part by each school's unique situation. However, there do exist several generic stages, and these optimally are mapped out at the beginning of the overall curriculum development effort.

CURRICULUM IMPLEMENTATION

Piloting the curriculum
Delineating types of assistance
   needed
Monitoring the system (keeping
   communication channels open)
Final implementation

Neglecting to delineate these stages at the beginning of the total curriculum process increases the likelihood of the project failing to go from planning to operation. Successful implementation requires trained educators and support personnel. It necessitates a physical and psychological school environment that will make teachers comfortable with and committed to the new curriculum. Implementation merges the latent or planned curriculum with the manifest curriculum, the curriculum actually to be used in the classroom as a stimulus for student learning.

Hopefully, many teachers in the system have been involved in the earlier phases of curriculum development, thus gaining requisite expertise and knowledge for teaching the curriculum. Ideally these early stages also have furnished administrators with opportunities to gain understanding of and commitment to the new program. In instances where administrators and teachers have worked cooperatively on the program, the likelihood of successful implementation is heightened. But, teachers' enthusiasms for a new program is not accidental. Such zeal occurs in schools where the leader has worked systematically to prepare teachers for piloting and finally incorporating the new curriculum. Despite the fact that the teacher is the individual who must implement the curriculum, teachers as a group are usually not the initiators of curriculum development or implementation. This is due partly to the fact that most teachers do not view curriculum development as their major responsibility. However, there are signs that this attitude is changing.

To get teachers, learning resources people and supervisory staff involved in all phases of curriculum development requires a program of professional education. Such a program comprises part of the curriculum for educators that was mentioned briefly at the beginning of this book. The quality of this curriculum for staff will influence significantly the effectiveness with which the curriculum for the students is piloted, revised, and finally totally implemented. This staff curriculum requires funding. Ideally, such monies were perceived as necessary at the outset of the curriculum development effort and now can be obtained with little difficulty.

Bishop (1976) notes that implementation requires restructuring and replacement. It requires a reorganization in that personal habits, ways of behaving, program emphases, organizations of learning spaces and existing curriculum and schedules need to be adjusted. It means getting educators to shift from the current program to the new program. Such modification can be met with great resistance. The reader is encouraged to refer to chapter 2 dealing with the reasons why persons might resist change. The ease with which the curriculum leader can trigger such behavior changes in staff depends in part upon the quality of the initial planning and the precision with which the previous curriculum development phases were enacted.

Experienced leaders of curriculum activity realize that implementation is an essential aspect of the total effort of systematic curriculum development. It cannot be divorced from other program development phases. The interrelationships of implementation to other phases of the total effort must be carefully delineated. Also, implementation must be considered in relationship to those phases that are to follow—curriculum evaluation and curriculum maintenance. One will recall that with regard to a system all parts or stages are interrelated and that activity in one stage permeates the entire system affecting it either positively or negatively. When one is significantly modifying the existing situation, one not only is adjusting the realm of curriculum, but one also is altering the administrative realm, the supervisory realm, and the public relations realm. Curriculum development, implementation notwithstanding, requires of the curriculum leader great skill in orchestrating persons, contents, materials, environments, monies, and time.

This orchestration of events and subevents is easier to accomplish for the curriculum leader who has approached his or her task from a systems view noting the system's subsystems and their interfaces. Essentially, the curriculum master plan is the input of the implementation phase. Diagrammatically, implementation can be shown as follows:

FIGURE 10.1   *Implementation*

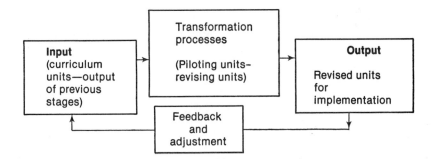

The output of the piloting phase of curriculum implementation becomes the input into the final implementation phase. Diagrammatically it is shown below.

FIGURE 10.2   *Final implementation phase*

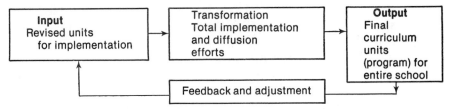

The feedback and adjustment activities refer to the fine tuning done during diffusion.

The above systems models depict the school district as an open system—a system that is related to its environment and readily exchanges matter, energy and information with its environment (Casciano-Savignano, 1978). Openness of system is basic to the entire model for systematic curriculum development. It will be recalled that if a system is closed, (not making exchanges with its environments) it eventually becomes dysfunctional and ceases to be a system.

Viewing implementation from a systems stance keeps us aware of the relationships between and among all elements impacting upon curriculum development: curriculum elements (objectives, contents), instructional elements (methods and activities), various noninstructional and noncurricular support elements (school facilities, policy statements). Attention is directed to educational personnel and the lay community membership. All phases of implementation are considered with regard to research and development efforts that may follow the program's incorporation. Additionally, consideration is given to the means of record-keeping requisite for all phases of this stage of curriculum development.

The curriculum leader has the responsibility for managing implementation. This requires, as noted by Bushnell and Rappaport (1971), attending to several primary tasks, the first being the setting up of the major steps in the implementation system. The second task is that of reviewing the existing system and noting existing networks and places where new networks are required. The third task is allocating budget for the various actions of implementation. The fourth step is the assuring that a management plan for this substage of curriculum development is created. Optimally, this stage was at least conceptualized during the initial stage of curriculum development. The management plan should note the person or persons in charge of implementation, both the piloting and the final diffusion, the roles of all involved personnel, and especially the roles of those individuals in the central curriculum office. The fifth step is developing means of synchronizing all the support systems requisite for successful piloting and final implementation. Often in both small and large districts, orchestration of support systems is either not done or done so poorly that various support and information systems within the district operate at cross purposes creating frustration among staff and inappropriate modification of the new curriculum. The sixth step relates to the preparation of the curriculum for teachers—staff training. Optimally this step was planned from the outset of the curriculum development process, and this step only activates these prior plans.

Ideally, staff training is for all staff who will receive the field-tested curriculum. Special training for persons who will pilot the program should have been begun before reaching the implementation stage so that qualified persons are on hand when required. If one delays training pilot personnel until curriculum implementation, the overall curriculum development effort is halted until such individuals gain the requisite skills and competencies.

The final step is that of identifying all staff required for the technical implementation of the field tested program.

Bishop (1976) posits some basic questions regarding staff to be involved in piloting and final implementation. What new staff knowledges and skills are essential for program implementation? What are the new roles and responsibilities that staff will have to assume in both the piloting and the final implementation? The level of expertise a staff possesses will influence the answers to the previous questions. This level should have been ascertained at the beginning of curriculum development, and the central curriculum office staff should have been working from that point on correcting staff deficiencies regarding particular curriculum responsibilities. At this juncture, the question is not what expertise do staff require, but where are the staff currently with regard to required expertise. Related to staffing is the question of staffing patterns and the actual physical organization of the school. With some new curriculum, staffing patterns will be adjusted and new environments suggested resulting in actual modification of physical educational spaces. From the beginning the curriculum leader has plotted all stages of systematic curriculum development on a time frame. At the implementation stage, the final time requirements are noted and judged as to reasonableness. Implementation is always a race against time, since new programs remain new for only short periods because of the knowledge explosion and the dynamics of society.

Activity 10–1   *Matching Piloting Tasks with Reality*

Piloting requires the listing of several essential tasks. Ideally these tasks are noted at the outset of curriculum development. Interview some person or persons responsible for curriculum development in your institution to determine if piloting is usually considered at the beginning of program development and if a listing and sequencing of tasks are formulated. If a listing exists, match the steps noted with what has been presented in this book. You may also recheck these steps after reading this chapter.

Note your conclusions regarding how persons in the field perceive the piloting function.

PILOTING THE CURRICULUM

Piloting is the vehicle by which the new curriculum's validity is established. The data gathered from this effort are used to substantiate recommendations made by the curriculum staff to those publics affected by or likely to be affected by the final implementation: teachers, the students, the parents, and other interested lay members. Piloting deals with the question, will the new program or new units within a program do what we say they will do? If through piloting, one discovers that the programs or the new units will not enable intended learnings to occur, then the need for revision is made known. In essence, piloting furnishes data that denote the degree and nature of revision requisite to make the curriculum valid in light of its goals and general objectives.

Essentially, piloting is an evaluation activity, specifically formative evaluation. It is formative in that if at any time during the piloting phase materials or units are found wanting with regard to particular objectives, then necessary revisions can be made. Piloting contains a self-correcting aspect. Kaufman (1972) brings out an important point in noting that via piloting, teachers come to realize that they have a right to fail. This right is part of the responsibility for exploring what is appropriate or not. For many teachers, such a right is not believed. In fact, many teachers and administrators as well are only interested in "fail-safe" programs already tried and true. But, such programs will not be generated unless some educators dare to take educational risks, to develop avant garde programs and then assess their effectiveness.

Piloting is part of an experimental posture, an inquiry stance that allows curricularists to experiment with curriculum elements. Piloting requires clear delineation of the major program objectives, clear conceptualization of curriculum, and the identification of rationales for all program elements. Once piloting starts, it is essential that information be efficiently and accurately gathered, and that it be reported systematically and periodically to all curriculum decision makers. This demand for accurate reporting of information (subsumed under feedback and adjustment) has been essential throughout all the stages of systematic curriculum development.

Steps in Piloting

Developing Units

Taba (1962) in the sixties outlined several steps in piloting which are still useful. The first step—that of producing the pilot units—has really been active since the major stage of curriculum analysis. The important point to remember is that the units generated from systematic curriculum development are experimental units, units destined for field testing.

The number of units created for piloting depends on the scope of the curriculum development effort. Few schools will undertake the development of a total curriculum in all subjects at all grade levels. However, schools frequently do develop a curriculum for one subject for one grade level and sometimes mount curricular efforts for one subject at all grade levels. The specific magnitude of curricular activity has been determined by those persons involved in the curriculum conceptualization and legitimization stage and the curriculum diagnosis stage.

Testing Experimental Units

The most evident substage of piloting is the testing of experimental units. These units have been created either by special staff, curricular personnel committees, central curriculum office personnel, or by individual teachers working alone or in small groups. Who actually has created the units depends on whether the efforts have been centralized (only involving the central office), centrally-coordinated (involving the central office staff working with teachers and significant others), or grassroots (teachers taking the major initiative for the curriculum unit development).

These units are developed with the realization that they are not as yet perfect exemplars for others to use. These units will require testing in different classrooms, with different pupils, under different conditions in order to establish their teachability and validity. Additionally, such testing will identify optimal student audiences for the units noting the abilities levels of students who would most benefit from these units. During piloting, involved staff consider all of the curriculum elements: the contents, the experiences, the environments, the materials. In many cases, there will be experimental manipulation of these elements to ascertain which contents are appropriate with certain students, which content and experience sequences seem to optimize learning of particular concepts, and which environments facilitate learning among various student personality types. From the piloting, teachers will identify which content coverage is adequate for particular groups of students, and which content requires greater scope or a rearranged sequence in order to address the intellectual needs of particular students. Piloting furnishes data that will allow the final units to cater more expeditiously to the unique as well as common needs of students.

Another important learning derived from dealing with the experimental units is the determination of which teaching styles work effectively with which units or program elements. Teachers are individuals and vary greatly in their approaches to learning and teaching. Thus, data furnished by field testing may indicate that professionals with special talents in small group instruction may find certain experiences in particular units complementary to individual teaching strengths. Other teachers who find large group demonstration their strong point, can be advised of those content aspects in the units which can be taught effectively via this approach. Piloting also will furnish teachers with ideas as to how to blend certain instructional strategies with particular content clusters and educational activities.

Baker and Schutz (1971), in dealing with the procedure for instructional product development, have provided some useful rules for testing experimental units. Their first rule indicates that curricularists should avoid an extremely small or extremely large number of learners when engaged in field testing. The exact number to involve depends in part on the breadth of the curriculum effort, is it for one subject at all grades, or one subject at just one grade level? If the number of students is insufficient, then one will gather unreliable information about a particular unit's appropriateness. However, if the student sample is excessive, then the piloting effort would be inefficient in the uses of time, personnel, and money. But, the sample should be representative of the total school student population.

The second rule is that the procedures employed should allow for replication of the treatment. During the field testing, one may discover that certain instructional approaches make the unit somewhat dysfunctional in regard to general program objectives. Or, it may be found that directions for the employment of a particular teaching method are too vague resulting in nonuse or inappropriate use of the method. Some materials may be found to be too difficult for intended students. Materials suggested in the units may be invalid with regard to the goals and program objectives, thus requiring deletion or extensive modification.

The third rule relates to communicating results. Data summarized from field testing should be comprehensible to those essentially responsible for the final unit revision. The need for open and clear communication of field testing efforts also is important for relaying results to the school board and the lay public. This information will be employed, along with information regarding the necessary revisions, in building a case that the new curriculum or new units are indeed educationally sound and that any deficiencies have been discovered and corrected. Because such message sending is essential, plans for it optimally are made at the generation of the master management plan (stage 1). If procedures for summarizing data are delayed until the time of field testing, there is a greater likelihood that much important data will not be relayed to significant others.

The fourth rule advanced by Baker and Schutz is that those involved in field testing the product, in our case the curriculum unit, should not engage in drawing inferences from the data. This is a moot point. There are those, such as Baker and Schutz who advocate this separating of data gathering from data interpretation on the belief that such separation prevents persons from yielding to the temptation to make sweeping generalizations regarding how the unit worked in the classroom setting. They note that there is a vast difference between an observed phenomenon and the inferences which can be derived from such phenomenon. In piloting, data should be carefully recorded on a form for use by later developers and curriculum experts who will draw inferences from the data. However, one can argue that if the use of a pilot unit is video taped, the person who developed the unit and also taught it can observe the tape and make accurate recordings of what is occurring and can later interpret these data. If the developer is teaching the unit, one can surmise that he or she would be professional enough to record accurately the success of the unit in an earnest desire to improve the unit or product before final implementation.

Piloting is a very visible part of the feedback network in systematic curriculum development. The nature of the feedback depends greatly on the expertise of the persons involved in the several aspects of piloting. Hopefully, educators engaged in this major curriculum stage are knowledgeable about curriculum, curriculum development, and especially about field testing. The persons concerned with supplying feedback during piloting are focusing on the interactions of learners with the curriculum elements, the total curriculum context. Also, these persons are attempting to obtain data not only from viewing interactions extant within the class environment, but also from interviewing students who have experienced the curriculum. Students also can respond to questionnaires. To get a total picture of the curriculum unit in action, observers of the curriculum will attempt to gain data regarding the perceptions of the teachers who taught the experimental units. Knowledgeable curriculum experts strive to get feedback from a variety of perspectives: from teachers, students, administrators, supervisors, and even from public members (Berman & Roderick, 1977).

Feedback can address how the performers within the classroom (the teachers and students) are reacting to and dealing with the unit's key curriculum elements: the contents, experiences, environments and materials. The feedback can record students' performances over time as well as the level of learning, indicated by achievement scores on teacher-made and criterion-referenced tests. Inferences drawn from interpreting classroom observation schedules can comprise an integral part of feedback. Feedback can also provide discriptive information about the physical learning space: the materials within the space, the arrangement of furniture and resources, the amount of time provided for action within space, and the significant other persons brought into the educational environment. Feedback will indicate the effects, both positive and negative of these curricular dimensions.

Feedback furnishes educators with a picture of the effects of teachers' behaviors on the actions of students, and the influence of students' actions on teachers as well as significant others. It provides a panorama of the interactions, both positive and negative, extant in the educational environment. Feedback is an essential aspect of the inquiry stance that all professional educators have to assure that educational programs are continuously meaningful over time. In processing such information, educators can determine the immediate and long-term value of the units.

The central purpose of feedback is to allow the developers and potential users of curriculum to determine whether or not students are learning and modifying their behaviors, attitudes, and skills in ways deemed important and indicated in the programs' goals and general objectives. For feedback to have value, it must be used. As noted previously, the data must be summarized in forms that are interpretable and usable by staff. Feedback allows educators opportunities to function as group investigators and students of curriculum. It supplies them with prods for scrutinizing the philosophical assumptions they as educators bring to the educational arena—to analyze the bases upon which they operate in the classroom and within the total school structure.

Feedback also requires careful interpretation. Educators involved in this stage are challenged to isolate reasons that explain what and why something has happened to a student or students in confrontation with some curriculum element. We must sort out the relationships between student behaviors and curriculum elements and the bearing between students' behaviors and teachers' behaviors. Educators concerned with advancing the knowledge of education, and curriculum development especially, will search the data in order to develop generalizations that will guide persons in various phases of curriculum activity and that will generate questions requiring additional investigation.

There are numerous ways to record feedback data. The following form (p.284) provides one example.

This form, albeit incomplete, does provide one with an idea of how feedback information addressing curriculum elements might be recorded and interpreted. Quantitative data from tests may be recorded as well.

Revision and Consolidation

The final step in piloting is utilizing the information gained to revise the units as necessary (Taba, 1962). As Kaufman (1972) notes, revision results from the performance data that denote where modifications are required to address the needs of students and associated requirements of the program. The exact nature of the changes should be noted with revisions delineated.

It is during this stage that the suggestions of the piloting personnel are translated into concrete modifications so that the units are appropriate to diverse student populations, classroom teachers, and educational en-

TABLE 10.1   *Curriculum unit observation form*

Curriculum Element Observed	Student/Teacher Behavior Recorded	Inference Made
Content: Topic dealing with growth of cities	Looking carefully at teacher Listening Asking questions, notetaking	Meets students' interests Content is concept oriented Students knowledgeable of inquiry process
Experiences: Teaching method inquiry strategy	Student attending to task Teacher raising initial questions	Students comfortable with this approach to learning Appropriate strategy Experiences advanced in nature Examples used at the appropriate level of complexity for students
Environment: Classroom with learning center	Students using learning center, class library Space for library books and learning center Lighting provided, audio equipment set up	Space somewhat small for learning centers, may retard some processing of information Number of library books and other materials might be expanded More books at this same level of difficulty needed

vironments. One examines the unit outlines for consistency and to ascertain that modifications recommended will address deficiencies noted in the field testing. All curriculum elements are reanalyzed using the criteria developed earlier in the curriculum development process. Materials are rechecked for validity and feasibility in light of available resources. The rationale, the theoretical and philosophical considerations relating to the program, is again considered in light of the interpretation garnered from studying the field test data. The units are assessed as to how well they address the demands of teachers, the needs of students and the requests of lay public members.

Activity 10–2 *Conducting a Mini Data Gathering Task*

Select some class or situation in which a curriculum is being followed. Either using the observation form (Table 10.1) or utilizing your own, observe the program for a week's duration to get some indication of its effectiveness.

You will need to note the aspect or aspects of the curriculum you will observe, the means by which you will gather data, how you will record the data, criteria you will draw upon, and then finally make some judgments as to whether program objectives are being achieved. Obtaining the curriculum plan or course syllabus being used by the instructor will assist you in this activity.

Even the most carefully conceived curriculum master plan or specific unit requires some revision. But if the curriculum plans are carefully thought through and developed systematically, then fewer major revisions are likely to be revealed as necessary from the field testing. Whenever a revision is made, it should be supported by the interpretation of the field test data. Such revisions should note the expected effects of the revision on the students' and teachers' learnings and behaviors. Such effects will be considered during the final evaluation stage when the implemented program is critiqued. The feedback and revision aspect of program development is really ongoing throughout the life of the curriculum program. This continuous monitoring and adjusting, developed in more detail in another chapter, assures to a great degree that the program will be responsive to the changing times and the evolving needs of students.

Implementation of the total program may be facilitated if the conclusions obtained in the piloting subphase are recorded in a handbook to accompany the finished units and/or master plan. This information can be used to provide answers to questions that other staff may have as to why certain contents are stressed in certain units, the reasons for particular sequences and stress within units, and the rationale for suggesting particular educational activities and materials for use at certain unit junctures. This handbook can be developed by supervisors, curriculum coordinators, curriculum specialists, and representative teachers, working cooperatively.

DELINEATING TYPES OF ASSISTANCE NEEDED

In order for piloting stages to be enacted effectively one needs assurance that support systems for such piloting activities are functional.

Support Systems

In essence, curriculum development is a systematic and purposeful attempt to transfuse a school system or a segment of a school system with a new and hopefully creative program for student learning. As noted in this book, such an effort requires a carefully engineered systems approach. The success of such a scheme depends not only on the enactment of the essential curiculum development stages, but also on the creating of conditions to facilitate action at the various stages. Curriculum development at each stage, including the piloting stage, needs supportive management. Curriculum leaders, other educational leaders, and teachers involved in the curriculum development and/or piloting activities will be required to work cooperatively to generate new ideas and foster new practices.

During the piloting of experimental units, support systems relating to preparing the total staff to teach the field tested units need to be undertaken. Reference already has been made to providing teachers with in-service relating to aspects of the new content in the curriculum or to new methods to employ in the program. Such in-service hopefully will encourage teachers to engage in self-examination as to their professional goals and their roles within the educational system.

Furnishing teachers with opportunities to become acquainted with the new curriculum being developed and field tested usually increases the staff's levels of commitment to the new program. Furthermore, it fosters in teachers feelings of competence to mount the new curriculum in ways intended by the designers. Effective support services attend to the human relations phenomena extant among staff. Directors of piloting realize that all persons within the educational system, especially the instructional staff, exert influences on the environment. Thus, the needs of all persons must be addressed in the types of support services and materials provided. Huckins and Bernard (1977) note that persons responsible for innovation need to focus on the individuals within the system and how they influence all members in the group. Analyzing the staff will provide curriculum leaders with information that will guide them in providing appropriate types of support services and/or materials. As noted by these two authors, the successful curriculum implementer is cognizant of the operation of cliques, the status of various persons within the system, the dominance hierarchies. The implementer also realizes the existence of both formal and informal interaction systems and provides support so that in reality both function effectively and for the good of the overall curriculum effort, in this case the piloting and implementation phase.

Huckins and Bernard point out that the curriculum implementer must not assume that the informal systems are nonexistent or that they coincide in structure and organization with the formally delineated staff organization. These authors urge innovators to keep two points in mind: first, the higher the rank and the greater the responsibility of an individual, the more important is his or her role in providing support and direction for the overall curriculum effort. For this reason the communication directives emanating from his or her office must be critically clear. Second, the greater the power and influence of a curriculum leader, the greater will be the difficulty in establishing and maintaining open and meaningful channels of communication. Thus, the curriculum leader in providing and communicating support has to realize that his or her position requires clear communication. However, the very fact that he or she has that position may interfere with others accepting or hearing clearly the message emanating from the curriculum office. This difficulty occurs partly because persons view people in power positions as a type of threat, of questionable motives, and as exhibiting self-serving behaviors. Thus, the challenge to the curriculum leader especially during piloting and dissemination is to present himself or herself in a way that promotes trust (Huckins & Bernard).

As noted above, successful piloting and implementation requires of the curriculum leader accommodation to the individuality of all persons affected by the new curriculum: the teacher, support personnel, administrators and students. The providing of support services addresses the need of accommodation. Examples of support services that have proven effective in schools are as follows:

1. The development of training programs for school's staff and central office personnel. One can have teacher teams created and educated to attain the competencies and knowledge requisite for teaching a new curriculum. In some instances, the training programs can be staffed by in-district personnel. In other situations, it may be more propitious to have outside experts speak on particular aspects of the program. Outside experts can be most useful if the units being piloted have been essentially developed by an outside agency and the school's role has been that of piloting them to determine what adaptations if any are necessary to make the units and support materials appropriate for the school district's particular student population.

2. A related support service is that of establishing demonstration centers where new units can be piloted and observed by staff. Time can be allowed for debriefing sessions so that staff concerns and questions can be responded to at the time such concerns occur.

3. Related to demonstration centers are workshops in which persons charged with particular roles or likely to assume particular roles can meet to discuss problems relating to such roles and to map strategies for learning those skills requisite for successful role assumption.

4. Another support service is allowing staff to engage in case studies or role playing relating to aspects of the new program under development or consideration so that staff begin to feel comfortable with the new roles they will be required to assume.

5. A standard type of support service provided teachers for assuming new roles and teaching behaviors is the course, lecture, workshop, and/or seminar offered within the district for in-district or university credit or on a college or university campus for university credit. More and more colleges are amiable to creating problem or district specific courses that address immediate needs of teachers confronting a new curriculum.

6. Another support service is that of providing staff with materials, both reading and audio visual, and allowing staff time for reading these materials that address the emphases of a new curriculum. Hopefully, well informed teachers and other school staff will be motivated to increase their own professional libraries and become committed to the practice of systematized pro-

fessional reading. Debriefing sessions on professional readings can furnish opportunities for staff to discuss their readings and relate their findings to the particular curriculum efforts being undertaken in their district.

7. Another means of supporting the curriculum effort is by providing staff with continuous information regarding the curricular development and piloting efforts. Such information can be relayed via newsletters and bulletins.[1]

COMMUNICATION CHANNELS

Open communication is essential in all phases of systematic curriculum development. It perhaps reaches peak importance during the implementation stage, not only during piloting but also just prior to and during the final dissemination of the field tested units. New and existing staff have to be oriented to the program to be disseminated. In familiarizing the staff to the new program, all aspects of the curriculum are communicated. The nature of the content, the types of new experiences, the incorporation of novel methods, the utilization of new materials all are spelled out. Staff are encouraged that the utilization of the "new" in the field tested program can be accomplished with great skill by them. The reader may recall that in the chapter on change, it was noted that an effective way to get persons to change their behavior is to indicate that they will not have to make major changes in the way they are already functioning. The curriculum leader communicates that the changes will not be of great magnitude, and that he or she has great confidence in the abilities of the staff to be highly effective with the new program.

The means of communication available are via scheduled meetings, individual reading, bulletins, debriefing sessions and in-service sessions focusing on particular aspects of the program. In essence, one can consider all of the support services noted earlier as vehicles of communication.

The curriculum leader is a believer in open communication. Huckins and Bernard (1977) have drawn from Combs and others some suggestions useful when considering communications. First, the feelings of persons should be in central place during the communication process. Second, persons' feelings of frustration and anger that result from feeling threatened by the innovation need to be aired. Three, communication must foster the feelings of personal security and importance among all staff members. Fourth, the curriculum leaders should rec gnize the diversity extant among staff in their abilities to implement various asp cts of the new program. Fifth, all staff should be made to realize that they are members of a system, and that their actions influence actions of others within the system. Sixth, curriculum leaders should employ straight line, open, and explicit communication models. Keeping these points in mind, the curriculum leader should increase the probability of the new program being introduced successfully with minimum disruption of staff functioning.

---

[1] Several of these ideas were noted by Scanlon (1977), as well as the thinking and experiences of this author.

FINAL IMPLEMENTATION

Implementation is the making real that which has been planned. It is the "time of truth" so to speak. In most schools or educational institutions, implementation will be managed by the curriculum staff in the central office, working with staff at other levels throughout the system. This is the centrally-coordinated model of curriculum development. As Doll (1978) notes, the central office in cooperation with other staff during the implementation stage will be likely to foster effective coordination and assure that the program is implemented under uniform conditions and with a great economy of time. The central office staff can assure that the program is implemented into an educational system rather than just a series of components that may or may not be related.

A reason that it is more likely that the central office will coordinate a smooth implementation is that systems experts, if found within the school district or the educational institution, are most likely to be housed in the central office. If such experts are not employed by the district, it is still the central office that has the power and responsibility to hire such personnel. Also, the curriculum leaders in the central office are most likely to have a macro view of the total curriculum program and can see where dissemination efforts tie into the total system. But, this does not mean that the central office does everything. In this book, it is the centrally coordinated approach that is being advocated, not the centralized model. The difference is that in the centrally coordinated approach curriculum leaders assume only those responsibilities and charges which are theirs and leave to other staff and school agencies those tasks that can best be done by them. The central office does not usurp those activities that rightly belong to individual schools. There is room even for some grassroots curriculum development in which innovative ideas and units emanate from instructors in the classrooms.

Stages of Implementation

Two phases of implementation have been outlined by Bishop (1976): the preoperational stage and the operational stage. In the preoperational stage curriculum leaders and staff have been concerned with establishing the procedural steps essential for the piloting and also for diffusion of the field tested program. Educators have been interested in those activities related to the training and recruitment of staff to participate in the piloting of units as well as the teaching of the finished units. Attention is directed to the realignment of staff, the assignment of students, and the selection of staff for particular grades or specialized functions. Preoperational activities also attend to the developing of schedules for both piloting and final implementation, the preparation of physical facilities to accept the new program units, and the preparation and purchase of materials necessary for the successful activation of the program. Also, curriculum leaders at this juncture complete policy and budget preparations, note and finalize the means of communicating to the public, and make arrangements for activities that will occur during the next major phases of curriculum evaluation and maintenance.

The operational phase occurs when all plans for dissemination are activated. This stage involves those decisions and actions that guide the actual placing of units in school classrooms and the use of these materials by total staff. It deals with the managing of the support services noted earlier. Actions begun at this juncture will carry over into the next two major stages of curriculum development, the stages of evaluation and maintenance. One can see that throughout systematic curriculum development, the boundaries of the particular stages are not always clear. One does not think just of one thing, and then when that is completed, advance to the next. Usually one contemplates several phases of development simultaneously.

Points to Remember

Successful implementing depends upon whether the administration has commitment to the new program, whether the teaching staff considers the new program worthwhile, whether the necessary reeducation has been provided for existing staff and newly hired staff, and whether allowances have been provided for involving teachers, students, and lay public in total program development.

Scanlon (1977) has noted several facts known about dissemination which are useful to those charged with implementing curricular innovation. The following list draws on much of Scanlon's and this writer's thinking.

1. An innovation stands little chance of successful implementation and maintenance if no diffusion strategy exists, regardless of how excellent the new program might be.
2. Any diffusion strategy, if it is to be successful, must be people-oriented. It must address the needs, concerns, fears, and aspirations of staff and students alike.
3. School boards in local school districts will continue to have the legal decision-making responsibilities regarding all district innovations. This being the case, those charged with creating new programs need to develop effective arguments as to why a new program should be authorized for total implementation.
4. Variety of programs and approaches to curriculum matters should be allowed and encouraged within school systems.
5. Curriculum development at the school level should not duplicate the efforts and materials of commercial publishers or educational laboratories. The curriculum leader should provide the means by which commercial materials and those from outside agencies can be incorporated into the curriculum master plan and school-developed materials.
6. Assistance must be provided, both formally and informally, to local school personnel in matters relating to curriculum development and curriculum implementation.
7. Curriculum officials should generate avenues by which outside agencies, both state and private, can participate either directly or indirectly, in the curriculum development effort.
8. The success of a curriculum development effort, although requiring money, is more effected by the clarity of purpose and precision of plans than with the actual amount of allocated monies.

9.   The most effective projects are those which are managed by well qualified leaders, knowledgeable of curriculum, curriculum theory, educational philosophy, systems, group dynamics, administration, organizational theory, educational evaluation, educational sociology, community relations, and educational politics.

It is evident that few individuals will be expert in all of these areas, thus necessitating the utilization of the concept of curriculum "headship." Such a "headship" will involve several individuals expert in various aspects of curriculum functioning. Any curriculum effort requires curriculum scholars at both the district and university level working in unison. Scholarship is requisite if the programs to be implemented are to have intellectual rigor, if the methodologies suggested are to have validity and sound psychological underpinnings, if aspects of programs are to be designed realistically, and if management procedures for programs are to be founded on effective management and curriculum development principles. Individuals keeping these points in mind should be creators of and participants in successful curricula.

Discussion

This chapter dealt with two major phases of curriculum implementation: the piloting phase and the final implementation phase. It has oriented the reader to the nature of and specific steps in piloting.

Attention also has been given to the types of support requisite during the piloting and implementation stages. It was noted that in addition to such support services such as in-service training, providing educational materials, etc., that the curriculum leader during this phase needs to set up communication channels and keep them open to deliver, when necessary, messages to staff, students, and interested and affected publics.

The chapter concluded with attention to the final implementation stage. Points to keep in mind were presented that have proven useful in the diffusion of new curricula throughout school districts and educational institutions.

References

Baker, R.L., & Schutz, R.E. (Eds.). *Instructional product development.* New York: Van Nostrand Reinhold, 1971.

Berman, L.M., & Roderick, J.A. *Curriculum: teaching the what, how and why of living.* Columbus, Ohio: Charles E. Merrill, 1977.

Bishop, L.J. *Staff development and instructional improvement, plans and procedures.* Boston: Allyn & Bacon, 1976.

Bushnell, D.S., & Rappaport, D. *Planned change in education, a systems approach.* New York: Harcourt Brace Jovanovich, 1971.

Casciano-Savignano, C.J. *Systems approach to curriculum and instructional improvement, middle school-grade 12.* Columbus, Ohio: Charles E. Merrill, 1978.

Doll, R.C. *Curriculum improvement, decision making and process* (4th ed.) Boston: Allyn & Bacon, 1978.

Huckins, W.C., & Bernard, H.W. Organizing for innovation. In L. Rubin, *Curriculum handbook, administration and theory.* Boston: Allyn & Bacon, 1977.

Kaufman, R.A. *Educational system planning.* Englewood Cliffs, N.J.: Prentice-Hall, 1972.

Scanlon, R.G. Building relationships for the dissemination of innovations. In L. Rubin (Ed.) *Curriculum handbook, administration and theory.* Boston: Allyn & Bacon, 1977.

Taba, H. *Curriculum development, theory and practice.* New York: Harcourt Brace & World, 1962.

chapter

Evaluation

EVALUATION—NATURE AND PURPOSE

> Evaluation is the process of delineating, obtaining, and providing useful information for judging decision alternatives. (Phi Delta Kappa, 1971, p. xxv.)

Evaluation is a process or cluster of processes enacted to provide data so that decisions can be made as to whether something should be accepted, changed, or eliminated. Implicit in evaluation is the process of ascertaining the relative values of whatever is being judged. The general purpose of evaluation aims at determining whether the expected, the planned for, has occurred or is occurring in relation to the intended. When applied to curriculum, evaluation is the process or processes used for discovering the extent to which the curriculum as designed, developed and implemented is producing or can produce the desired results (behaviors, knowledge) in students. Thus, evaluation focuses on the strengths and weaknesses of the curriculum master plan before implementation as well as its effectiveness during and after active use. Such information is used by decision-makers involved in this aspect of curriculum activity.

      The evaluator posits several key questions (Phi Delta Kappa). What are the needs, problems, and opportunities extant within the program to be evaluated? What decisions must be made to respond to identified needs? What possible alternative ways can be generated to address identified needs? How reasonable are the bases for opting for a particular available alternative. Finally, how can one make the selected response—whether an action, program or material—work even more effectively?

The definition advanced by Phi Delta Kappa (1971) focuses on decision-making. Brandt (1978) has noted that evaluation as part of decision-making is a prospective approach requiring the evaluator to furnish timely feedback. He or she has to generate information that can be utilized by the decision-maker. This differs from evaluation solely for accountability, which Brandt classifies as retrospective—a looking back. But, such "looking back," according to Zais (1976) is the dominant evaluation posture. We are looking back at how individuals behaved, academically and socially, as a consequence of experiencing the curriculum or from using a specific educational material. Such retrospection deals with curriculum evaluation in terms of congruence (Phi Delta Kappa, 1971) between the performance and objectives. In educational reality, we need both prospection and retrospection in order to make necessary decisions regarding a newly introduced program.

The Phi Delta Kappa definition is a broad concept of evaluation. It goes beyond equating evaluation entirely with congruence or considering evaluation as solely measurement. It extends one's thinking of evaluation beyond that of professional judgment.

FIGURE 11.1   *Educational improvement through data analysis*

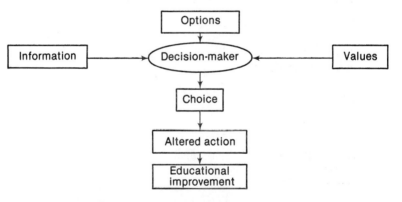

From Phi Delta Kappa National Study Committee on Evaluation, D.L. Stufflebeam (Chair), *Educational evaluation and decision making.* Bloomington, Ind.: Phi Delta Kappa, 1971, p. 39. Reprinted by permission.

Central to evaluation is decision-making. It allows the educator to identify alternative curricular actions and to select those that taken alone or in various combinations have the greatest likelihood of stimulating student learnings in light of overall program goals. In evaluation, the decision-maker obtains data that will allow him or her to select program components that have proven effective. The schematic reveals that the decision-maker considers options, processes information as to the effectiveness of options and matches this information with values, hopefully identified in the first stage of systematic curriculum development. From such deliberations, the decision-maker can make a choice—either to continue the program as planned, to alter it or some of its components, or to eliminate a particular program component or in a rare instance to discontinue the total curriculum. If the judgment is based on the analysis of data during evaluation, the decision should result in an educational improvement (Phi Delta Kappa, 1971). Essentially, curriculum evaluation involves four general classes of decision-making. The first class is the choosing between goals advanced by both the professional and lay communities. The second class of decision or choice-making occurs when a specific goal has been selected with the identification of several possible means of accomplishing it. The third class is in evidence once a plan has been selected, developed and implemented. The final class occurs once the program has been carried out and successfully diffused in the educational system (Gephart, 1978).

These four classes of choice-making occur intermittently throughout the total curriculum development process: 1) curriculum conceptualization and legitimization; 2) curriculum diagnosis; 3) curriculum development-content selection; 4) curriculum development-experience selection; 5) curriculum implementation, 6) curriculum evaluation and 7) curriculum maintenance. The first class of choice-making occurs during stages one and two. The second class is activated during the third and fourth stages concerning the actual development of the program. These two stages also include a part of the third class of choice-making. The majority of the third class occurs during stages five and six (curriculum implementation and evaluation). The last class of choice-making occurs during stages six and seven (evaluation and maintenance).

Making choices, deciding which course of action to take, requires competence in decision-making. Bross (1953) has advanced a schema of the total process of decision-making.

FIGURE 11.2   *Total process of decision-making*

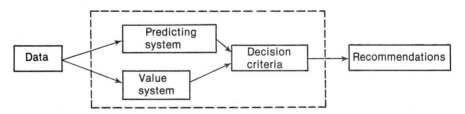

Reprinted with permission of Macmillan Publishing Co., Inc. from *Design for decision* by Irwin D.J. Bross. Copyright 1953 by Macmillan Publishing Co., Inc.

The recommendations which are the outputs of the system are phrased so that one has information to utilize in judging decision alternatives. At the first class of choice-making, we ask Which goals should be addressed? At the second class of decisions we posit, Which content should be emphasized? Our responses are more defensible if we have traced the consequence of each alternative advanced. What are the likely student outcomes to be gained from developing one particular curriculum element as opposed to some other?

Purposes of Evaluation

Evaluation whether done informally or formally provides the bases for deciding whether to address a particular need or not, whether to create a program or not, whether to continue a program, whether to modify a program, or whether to terminate it. It also furnishes one with information necessary for deciding what should be done with regard to the staff's education and the community's education.

Conley (1973) has identifed several general purposes of evaluation:

1. to increase the substantive knowledge base regarding the education process, in our case the total curriculum process.
2. to furnish information that will facilitate making decisions as to whether to continue, adjust, or discard an on-going curriculum.
3. to provide justification for a political-social-and economic action relating to the curricular proglram.
4. to create a report that can be utilized by all appropriate persons in the educational system resulting in the introduction and continuance of effective curricula.
5. to generate information that can be employed in educating the community as to the rationale for a particular program, and the effectiveness of the program (p. 353)

FIGURE 11.3 *Why evaluate?*

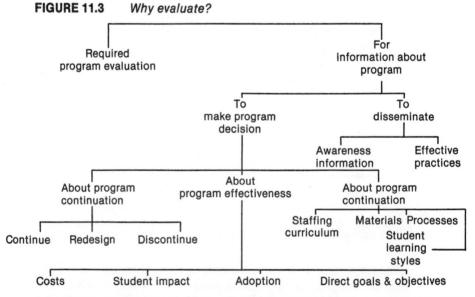

From Barbara Hunt, Who and what are to be evaluated? *Educational Leadership* 35(4): 261, January 1978. Reprinted with permission of the Association for Supervision and Curriculum Development and Barbara Hunt. Copyright © 1978 by the Association for Supervision and Curriculum. All rights reserved.

Figure 11.3 allows us, at a glance, to answer this central question of, Why evaluate? If our response is to make program decisions, then we can, following the diagram, focus on subreasons for our evaluative efforts.

FIGURE 11.4   *Whom do you evaluate?*

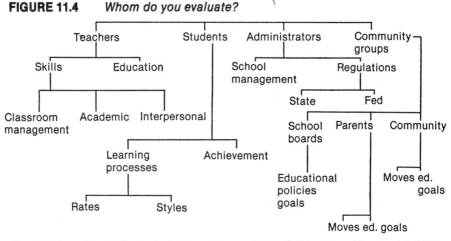

Figure 11.4 also provides us with answers. Additionally, it directs our attention to what we specifically will evaluate regarding teachers, students, administrators, and community groups.

The following diagram (Figure 11.5) notes what we can evaluate within the curriculum realm.

This final schematic furnishes us with a useful guide for identifying what should be evaluated within the framework of curriculum. In surveying this diagram, one identifies what should be attended to and also notes gaps in the evaluative process. Frequently, goals and objectives are evaluated as are student and teacher experiences, but no attempts are made to assess the philosophy of the program or persons' underlying comprehensions of a particular knowledge realm. Likewise, few among us evaluate our environments as to their potential impacts upon a particular curriculum.

Evaluation Roles for Persons

Regarding evaluation, people can undertake four major roles. The first role is that of *doer.* Here the focus is on the behavior of the student, the teacher, the practitioner, the curriculum developer. The second major role is that of *observer.* The observer is the individual who views the doer's actions. The third major role is that of the *judge,* the person who receives and interprets the results as to value and adequacy. The final role is that of the *actor,* the person who acts upon the data gathered. These roles may reside in one individual. For example, a curriculum developer can be the doer. He or she, via the use of video tape, also

FIGURE 11.5   *What to evaluate in curriculum*

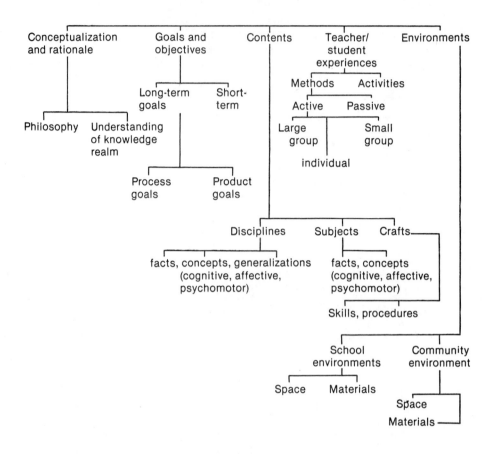

can be the observer. Taking into consideration the observations, the individual can be the judge. Finally, the individual can be the interpreter. Assuming all roles is somewhat unlikely for one individual, but it is not uncommon for persons within the evaluation process to coordinate at least two roles, perhaps those of the judge and actor (Conley, 1973).

METHODOLOGY OF EVALUATION

As noted previously, evaluation is a process of delineating, obtaining, and providing useful information for judging decision alternatives (Phi Delta Kappa, 1971). The basic structure of the evaluation process does not vary with the type of evaluation to be enacted. One would follow the same major steps whether one was engaged in formative evaluation of a particular curriculum element, or in final summative evaluation of a total curriculum.

Components

The first major component of evaluation methodology focuses on the curricular phenomena to be evaluated and the range of evaluation activities requisite. It is the generation of the management plan or procedural design for the evaluation process. At this point, one delimits the setting or settings within which the overall evaluation process is to occur (Phi Delta Kappa). Since this first stage determines the boundaries of the total evaluation system, it is macroanalytic. However, macroanalytic is a relative term, for evaluation can address the total process of systematic curriculum development, or center on just one stage of curriculum development. One can assess the major tasks relating to developing curriculum content, or one can evaluate students' behaviors as a consequence of their experiencing a curriculum for one year.

Substages under evaluation focusing are (a) the spelling out of objectives of the evaluation activity, and (b) the noting of constraints and policies under which the evaluation must be conducted. Attention is given to the level of decision-making necessary for enactment of this stage. After identifying each level of judgment required, the requisite decisions are noted and their cruciality to the overall evaluation process indicated. Also, attention is given to identifying criteria for specifying the variables for measurement and the standards to employ in determining alternative decisions, action paths, and assessing results of curriculum components.

Collecting information is the second major component of evaluation methodology. This involves the following steps:

1. identifying the sources of information essential for consideration and noting the state of current information;
2. identifying the means for collecting the information (tests, interviews, observation schedules, etc.);
3. noting the procedures available, the methods for obtaining the information;
4. developing a mission profile for carrying out these steps.

Once information is collected, it is organized so as to become interpretable to the evaluators and the final intended audience—the specific decision-makers. Here the evaluator attends to the means by which collected data will be classified, organized, recorded, and retrieved. This activity comprises the third method component.

The fourth component is the analysis of the information organized. The planners select and employ appropriate analysis techniques, the specific technique depending upon the focus and level of formality of the evaluation. The techniques can range from computing a group's mean score on an achievement test to factor analysis to isolate factors influencing students' learnings regarding some aspect of the curriculum.

After information analysis, one reports the information—the fifth method component. The nature of the reporting is geared to the characteristics of the audience scheduled to receive the report. Informal evaluation would consist of opinioning, estimating and judging based on general perceptions. Formal evaluation would be more rigorous in the collecting, treating and reporting of the data. Recipients of evaluation reports are board members, superintendents, curriculum leaders, supervisors, instructors, parent/community advisory committee members, students, and various community agents.

Careful planning of these five components at the outset of curriculum evaluation activity increases the likelihood of the evaluation effort running smoothly. The milestone events in the administration of the above components are presented in Figure 11.6. This mission profile reveals that there is much to be done between the first event (1.0), that of determining the five evaluation method components, and the actual activation of such components.

TABLE 11.1   *Evaluation timeline*

Evaluation Tasks	Due Dates	Calendar of Events in months Jly 1 2 3 4 5 6 7–12	Personnel Involved			
			Curr. Evaluator	Curr. Coord.	Inst. Staff	Curr. Consultant
Focus on evaluation	9/18	xxxxxxxxx	X	X		
Selection of information	1/12	xxxxxx	X	X	X	
Organization of information	1/12	xxxxxx	X			X
Analysis of data	3/25			X		X
Reporting of data	6/30		X	X		X

Major Tasks of Evaluation—Another Look

Although the general approach to evaluation is basically the same regardless of the focus or scope of the effort, there can be variations. The mission profile presents one macro approach. The Phi Delta Kappa (1971) committee has provided another cogent work breakdown of evaluation (see Figure 11.7). The work breakdown can be arranged as to major events and key activities in the form of a Program Evaluation Review Technique (PERT) network. Such a network for major task 1.0, delineation of information needs, might be developed as shown on p. 302.

The circles represent events that will occur and the lines represent activities necessary for arriving at specific events. Events do not consume resources in terms of money, persons, time, or space; they simply denote a point in

FIGURE 11.6   *Events in the administration of evaluation components*

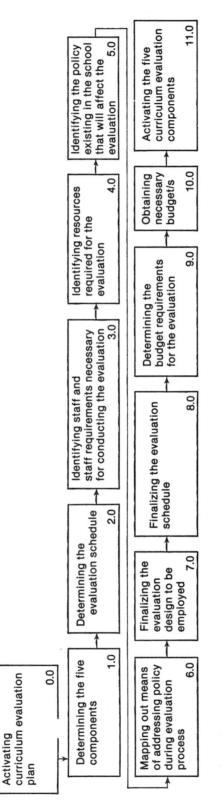

FIGURE 11.7   *Breakdown of evaluation*

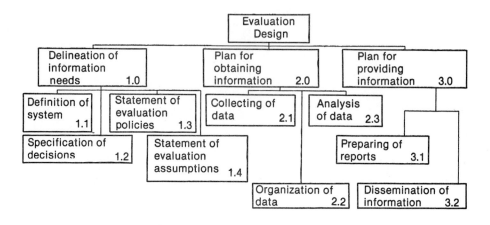

From Phi Delta Kappa National Study Committee on Evaluation D.L. Stufflebeam (Chrmn.) *Educational evaluation and decision making.* Bloomington, Ind.: Phi Delta Kappa, 1971, p. 156. Reprinted by permission.

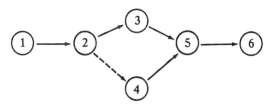

1. Start evaluation design
2. Begin to delineate information needs
3. Begin definition of system
4. Begin specification of decisions
5. Begin statement of evaluation policies
6. Begin statement of evaluation assumptions

time. However, activities do consume resources in terms of persons' energies, time and money. The network as depicted indicates that events 3 and 4 can be done concurrently rather than sequentially. Thus, one group of persons can be defining the system while another group is specifying the decisions that will be necessary. The reason for the dashed line 2–4 (called in network parlance "dummy activities") is that no activity really exists at this point in the network. The dashed line merely keeps the network together logically. The activity 2–3 represents the delineating of information needs, thus there can be no activity 2–4 since one cannot have two different activities with the same beginning. One is either delineating information needs or one is not. One may argue that events 3–5 and 4–5 should not be done concurrently, but sequentially. The actual design of the network is influenced by the logic of the activities, as well as by resources (people, materials, time, and money) available.

Evaluation Design

In addition to referring to all the major tasks of evaluation, design also refers to the conditions and procedures that will guide data collection. As noted by Airasian (1974), the basic question relating to the adequacy of any design is "How unambiguous are the data in indicating that the observed outcomes can be attributed to the program and not to extraneous confounding factors?" (p. 159). Can we say without equivocation that the increase in students' learnings of geographic concepts is in fact caused by the new physical geography content? In processing this question, one usually posits rival plausible explanations for the increase in student learning. Perhaps, it was a teacher's enthusiasm that triggered the learning, perhaps the new teaching method employed was the cause and not the new content of the curriculum unit. Perhaps the natural maturation of the students accounted for the learning. The learning might even be attributable to a significant outside event, perhaps the publishing in the news of satellite pictures of the earth's terrain.

In curriculum evaluation one considers causality. Can we say with assurance, at least to a reasonable degree, that a certain curriculum element actually caused an observed behavior or a documented knowledge? Here, as Airasian points out, one is concerned with temporal precedence of the causative factor to the observed result. Thus, the curriculum evaluator must demonstrate that the presumed cause of some observed outcome or end result did actually exist prior to the observed effect. It is possible that the observed effect may have been present before the causative factor, the curriculum element, or the instructional method, was applied. Airasian advances a second factor that relates to the covariation or to the presence of a statistical relationship between the presumed cause and the anticipated effect. A third factor addresses the point that causality is based upon the demonstration of a one-to-one relationship between a particular outcome and its cause (Airasian).

The curriculum evaluator may never really be able to deal completely with this issue of causality due to the "noise" (other potentially significant variables) in the educational environment and the out-of-school environment. Airasian notes the example that one may introduce a curriculum on environmental studies with the general program objective of increasing students' environmental awareness. At the end of the unit, one might note that students do indeed have heightened environmental awareness. But, such awareness may not be caused by the unit. Perhaps it is the emphasis such a topic is receiving in the overall society that has fostered such cognizance. And perhaps, no increase in awareness really has occurred. Without employing a design with a pretest dimension, one cannot say with surety that the observed effect did not in fact exist prior to the implementation of the curriculum.

Noting cause and effect among curriculum elements and students' behaviors is concerned with internal validity. Such validity centers on determining with adequate precision that a curriculum implemented, or curriculum component stressed, or method utilized, or material used did in fact trigger the observed results in students' behaviors or knowledge. This is the essence of curriculum evaluation. If one cannot promulgate this, then the usefulness, the diagnostic worth, of the data is nonexistent.

Less often do curriculum evaluators address the generalizability of the information gained. They are not as interested in advancing knowledge relating to the field of curriculum evaluation. However, there may be times when the generalizability of information is the focus. This is true especially if the evaluation is being conducted by an educational laboratory or commercial publisher interested in the extensive use of their materials. The evaluators with this focus then confront the problem of external validity. Just how generalizable are the results of the curriculum evaluation effort? To what groups, settings, and schools can these results be applied? Here evaluation has a dual purpose—making decisions regarding the usefulness of the curriculum or materials to a wide student audience and advancing the realm of knowledge about curriculum evaluation and particular types of curriculum programs (Airasian).

ENACTING CURRICULUM EVALUATION

Enacting comprehensive curriculum evaluation is extremely complex, but one can be guided by the numerous evaluation models available. A useful one advanced by Stake (1967) suggests the development of a matrix (see Table 11.2).

Dealing with these variables will be facilitated if the curriculum evaluator has identified four categories of information sources:

1. Intents: What goals various persons affected by the program evaluation have;
2. Observations: What perceptions are recorded related to events occuring;
3. Standards: What curriculum evaluation experts and curriculum development experts consider as the optimal occurrence in a situation like the one under consideration.
4. Judgments: What are the feelings of individuals affected by our program about the curriculum. (Stake, 1967)

Arranging information and variables in the evaluation matrix according to antecedents, transactions and outcomes can guide the curriculum evaluator's decision-making. Again, Stake (1967) has provided some useful guidance in the collecting of information (see Table 11.3).

The evaluation matrix organizes data collection. The function of the first column is to list the categories of data the evaluator will need to consider: antecedents, transactions and outcomes. Data are recorded in each of the 12 cells for whichever item is receiving attention under each of the program variable categories. Intents refer to the goals or objectives noted; observation denotes the descriptive data gathered from numerous sources. Standards refers to what various persons responsible for curriculum evaluation—be they teachers, administrators, curriculum coordinators—have judged to be the level of student performance or attainment in the aspects of curriculum being considered. Judgments denote the feelings of individuals such as students, parents, teachers, and curriculum leaders regarding aspects of the curriculum being evaluated.

TABLE 11.2   *Sample matrix: Curriculum variable to be evaluated in specific physical geography unit*

Variables	Examples
Antecedents	
Student characteristics	Background, abilities, previous geography learnings
Staff characteristics	Background, personal and professional characteristics relating to geography, personality, teaching styles
Educational environment (school space)	Size, features
Curriculum content	Concepts, generalizations, organization, sequence
Curriculum materials	Books, maps, charts, photographs
Transactions	
Curriculum experiences teaching methods presentation of content	Lecture, discovery strategies, demonstration
Educational activities	Independent student investigations, film viewing, simulation, group investigation
	Student-student interactions
	Teacher-student interactions
Curriculum environment	(Actual environment utilized to facilitate the experiences)
Outcomes	
Students:	
Increase in knowledge of geography	Facts, concepts, generalizations, principles
Increase in knowledge of and skill in geographic methods	Regional method, topical method, the asking of questions in information processing sequences
Increase in attitudes toward geography	Relationship of knowledge, skills and attitudes gained
Staff:	
Increase in knowledge of geography	Facts, concepts, generalizations
Increase in knowledge of and skill in geographic methods	Regional method
Increase in skill in teaching methods	Discovery strategies
Increase in commitment to the new curriculum	Positive views, attitudes, insights into purpose of geographic education
Community	Level of commitment of community members to the new program, to overall purpose of the school. Realization of the importance of the program.

Adapted from R.E. Stake, The countenance of educational evaluation. *Teachers College Record*, 1967, *68*, no. 529.

TABLE 11.3   *Matrix of evaluation information on physical geography/unit data for evaluation*

Program Variables	Intent Sources	Observation Sources	Standard Sources	Judgment Source
Antecedents				
Student characteristics	A2			
Staff characteristics				
Curriculum content	A1			
Curriculum materials				
Transactions				
Curriculum experiences	A3			D1
Curriculum environment				
Outcomes				
Students knowledge gain		B1	C1	
Students skills gain		B2	C2	
Students attitude adjustment				
Staff				
Community				

Symbols:

A1 Curriculum content	The content goals as found in the guide, in conversations with geography curriculum coordinator.
A2 Student characteristics	The intent noted as to how to utilize student characteristics or to maintain them, or to make a conscious effort to modify them.
A3 Curriculum experiences	The noted intent of the experiences as planned
B1 Students knowledge gain	Observed situations in which students actually used the new geography knowledge
B2 Students skill gain	Observed situations, case study reports, where geographic skills utilized
C1 Students knowledge gain	Data obtained via the use of a standardized achievement test in physical geography
C2 Students skills gains	Opinions of geography curriculum specialists resulting from correcting standard teacher-made achievement test
D1 Curriculum experiences	Judgment of the curriculum coordinator and the staff as to the value of the intended curriculum experiences

Adapted from R.E. Stake, The countenance of educational evaluation. *Teachers College Record,* 1967, *68,* no. 529.

Approaches to Data Utilization

Stake notes that both description and judgment are essential in evaluation and thus he uses two approaches to describe the utilization of data collected. One approach is to identify contingencies among the antecedents, transactions and outcomes. These contingencies refer to the relationships among the variables in these categories. In seeking contingency, one sorts out the causal relationships. What accounts for the occurrence of observed phenomena? Do certain curriculum contents really precipitate in students a specific type of attitude development or achievement? The challenge facing the curriculum evaluator is that of identifying the outcomes that are contingent upon particular antecedent phenomena activated in specific transactions.

Initially, the curriculum evaluator examines the logical and empirical bases for the contingencies noted. He or she records the contingency between intended antecedents and intended transactions and between intended transactions and intended outcomes. Analyzing these contingencies, the evaluator considers the logical relationships among the contingencies.

But, the evaluator does not stop here. He or she also examines the congruencies between the intended and the observed antecedents, the intended and observed transactions, and the intended and observed outcomes. In dealing with congruence, one strives to achieve a match between what is intended and what is observed. Did what we wish to happen actually happen? If upon analysis, the curriculum evaluator discovers that what was intended—let us say to increase the level of knowledge of concepts relating to physical geography—actually does happen, then we can say that congruence has been achieved between intended outcomes and observed outcomes. A decision can be made to maintain this portion of the curriculum.

Of course, one may not find that complete congruence is achieved among and between the key variables. For instance, one may have had an intended transaction dealing with the sequencing of content according to the logic of a particular discipline. Upon analysis of the observed transaction, the curriculum evaluator discovers that during the action, the instructor significantly modified the content sequence. In this case, the lack of congruence is indicated. If upon looking at the observed outcomes, one denotes that students still achieved the intended outcomes, then one may postulate that the intended content sequence is not crucial to the success of students learning this information. If the intended outcomes do not measure up with regard to performance standards originally accepted, then one may commence a new field-testing making sure this time that congruence is maintained between the intended transaction (sequencing of content) and the observed transaction.

Most curriculum evaluation centers on the congruence of the intended and observed outcomes. This is fine, for by analyzing congruence, one gathers data that can be useful in curriculum review and revision.

The evaluation of intended contingencies depends upon logical analysis. Frequently, curriculum persons do not engage in such analysis and curriculum goes into the field with developers having scant knowledge of its quality. However, let us assume that such logical analysis—evaluation prior to implementation—has occurred. Now, one will focus on the observed contingencies. Such evaluation depends upon empirical evidences. If we are assessing the degree of student knowledge of geographic concepts, we will require quantitative data as to the level of achievement gathered by some type of achievement test, either standardized or instructor made. But, the strength of this evaluation of observed contingencies will be weak if one only evaluates the results of the program at one time. If, as alluded to previously, the curriculum evaluator seeks to determine if a particular content sequence causes a certain level of learning, then the evaluator needs to experiment with the independent variable of content sequence to see just what does happen to achievement levels with each modification.

Figure 11.8 graphically displays the congruence-contingency model.

FIGURE 11.8   *Congruence-contingency model*

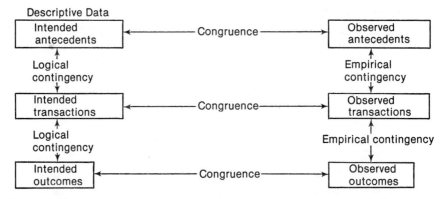

From R.E. Stake, Language, rationality, and assessment. In W.H. Beatty (Ed.), *Improving educational assessment and an inventory of measures of affective behavior* (Washington, D.C.: Association for Supervision and Curriculum Development, 1969), p. 20. Used with permission.

Standards: Student's Performance

Looking at students' behaviors and trying to assess them for level of learning and quality of action requires the utilization of various types of standards. The type of standard employed depends in part upon the intended outcomes noted in the early stages of curriculum development (Zais, 1976). Zais has presented a cogent discussion of four standards for evaluation: absolute maximum standard, the absolute minimum, the relative standard, and the multiple standard.

The absolute maximum standard, set arbitrarily, denotes the level of achievement of all students. Its point of success may be either placed at a maximum or minimum level. When fixed at the maximum level, the standard is obtainable by only a few students. When we employ the percentage system of evaluation in our schools, we are setting success at the maximum level. In this situation 90 to 100 percent performance represents excellence in achievement. Theoretically, this level is attainable by all students if they apply themselves, but realistically, only a few students can achieve it. This standard also has a level below which students theoretically fail. In most schools, scores below 70% indicate failing performance. Many educators accept this benchmark with little question.

The absolute minimum standard, according to Zais, represents a point that ensures success for virtually all students in the program. This canon is employed in programs emphasizing minimum competency. Students unable to achieve competency regarding specific curriculum objectives are retaught or the curriculum is modified as to content and experiences until the individuals are successful. If students continually fail to reach the program's objectives, then the curriculum is judged as uneffective. Zais recommends the use of this criterion in training situations. In such instances, one can be more precise in delineating the intended outcomes and the level of performance necessary for success. Also, in training situations, the competency being measured can be considered binary; it either exists or it does not. The students can either perform the skill or task, or they cannot. This norm might be used in subjects such as spelling or grammar where you either act correctly or you do not.

The third standard, the relative standard (Zais), employs the concept of the "normal curve." In employing this standard, one judges each student against the relative performance of other group members. The group's mean performance serves as a sliding scale against which a person's performance is appraised. Where this norm is employed, high competition exists since top achievement is determined by behavior or knowledge higher than that of most members in the class. A flaw in this norm is that it does not consider the sample's nature. If one had a class of postdoctoral fellows and employed this standard, it is conceivable that some individuals would get the top grades, the A's, while some would be at the bottom of the curve and receive C's and D's. However, one might in using an absolute maximum standard, find that all students in this select group had really achieved within the 90–100% range.

Another difficulty of this criterion is that it assumes that all students are equally capable of successfully competing. Everyone exerting the necessary effort can be the top scorer. But, despite the standard's deficiencies, Zais notes it does have some merit. It furnishes us with a normative base line regarding what are the types of behaviors or performances we can expect in relation to some curriculum element or program unit. For example, if in assessing a chemistry unit, we discover that 60% of the students are getting over half of the final test items incorrect, we have some evidence that one or more of the curriculum components (either content, experiences or environments) is or are dysfunctional. The problem is identified as being with either the program or the instructional staff, not with the students.

The fourth standard discussed by Zais is the multiple standard which measures the growth that each student experiences during the program. This standard provides data on each individual's actual performance at the program's outset and at the point of evaluation. Also, the teacher has information that allows her to plot each student in relation to other students. But, students' grades in a curriculum area cannot be based solely on the degree of student growth. One student may exhibit the greatest growth in the class, but only receive a B because of the intitial level of knowledge or performance. Students who enter class situations with a high level of knowledge will not achieve as great a gain in percentage points as students who enter a class knowing little or nothing about the subject area.

Many would advocate using the multiple standard for it addresses the idiosyncrasies of individuals. However, Zais explains that this standard poses myriad problems. First, any attempt to measure the legions of students' traits at program implementation for the purposes of obtaining base line data is virtually impossible with our current levels of measurement sophistication. Also, such a measurement if indeed possible would take considerable time. Additionally, students rarely proceed in their learning of a particular curriculum unit or series of units at a uniform rate over time. Zais recommends that this standard be employed in those situations which stress highly restricted training. Rather than locking into one standard, the effective curriculum evaluator knows all and realizes when to utilize each. (Zais)

Criteria

Johnson (1977) has synthesized the writings of several curriculum and evaluation specialists into a listing of composite product evaluation criteria.

   I. Need
  II. Description
     A. Technical manual
     B. Characteristics—components, appearance, time
 III. Appropriateness
     A. For Students
     B. For content
 IV. Curriculum Features
     A. Objectives
        1. General—what is to be accomplished
        2. Detailed specification
        3. Operationally stated—behavioral
        4. Consistent
        5. Value
        6. Source
        7. Compatability
     B. Content
        1. Selection basis
        2. Currency
     C. Structure
        1. Selection organization
        2. Substantive
        3. Affective
     D. General considerations
        1. Provisions for individualization
        2. Compatability with existing program
        3. Balance, scope, sequence
  V. Instructional Features
     A. Learning Theory
     B. Teaching Methods
     C. Educational Activities
     D. Learning, educational environments
     E. Evaluation Provisions

VI. Implementation
   A. Organizational factors
      1. Time
      2. Space
      3. Facilities
      4. Administrative support required
   B. Teacher capabilities
   C. Implementation strategy
VII. Empirical evaluation
   A. Formative
   B. Summative
VIII. Practical Considerations
   A. Cost-benefit
      1. initial
      2. maintenance
      3. retraining
      4. special facilities
      5. materials
      6. cost effectiveness
   B. Extended support
      1. Market
      2. Dissemination

From M. Johnson, *Intentionality in education*. Albany, N.Y.: Center for Curriculum Research and Services, 1977, pp.236–237. Reprinted by permission.

Producing the Final Report

Total curriculum evaluation is concerned with the entire curriculum, that is with the total curriculum document and its successful utilization within the educational institution. Thus, a curriculum evaluation final report deals with all of the curriculum components. Phi Delta Kappa (1971) has noted those major tasks necessary for preparing this type of report. First, attention must be given to the report's objectives. What curriculum phenomena are to be evaluated? What audience is to be considered? What decisions will be required to make the evaluation effort a success? Second, attention is given to the curriculum program itself. Here, evaluators address the conceptualization of the curriculum, its rationale and philosophical underpinning. Also, attention is on the objectives, aims, goals, content, experiences, and educational environments. Furthermore, judgment will be offered on the effectiveness of the materials used to support the curriculum. Also, the interactions of the major actors (the students and teachers) in the curriculum arena will be assessed. The report must be clear in noting just how well all students did with the program and note where special aspects of the curriculum catered to particular students with certain interests and learning styles. The evaluation report will describe the community setting. Finally, the report will identify the criteria that will be employed in judging the curriculum.

Third, consideration is given to the major results. Persons reading evaluation reports are interested primarily in what happened as a result of the program's implementation. Objectives and program discussion aside, how did the students do? What did they learn? What procedures were they able to accomplish? In addition to students' gains, were there any student losses? Furthermore, and very important to administrators and to the community are the program's costs in terms of money, time and resources. Fourth, evaluation reports deal with the relationships extant among the various components of the program. Here attention is given to congruence and contingencies. Trends that appear are addressed. Explanations regarding these relationships not only provide data that will assist in making some program adjustments, but also will present curriculum scholars with data to be utilized in continued study of curriculum as a field of disciplined inquiry.

The evaluation report should "tell it like it is." Kemmis (1977), drawing on Stake's work, made a case for just such a presentation of evaluation results. Kemmis advocated responsive evaluation as opposed to preordinate evaluation which was too often tied to a narrow set of objectives. According to Stake, evaluation qualified as responsive.

> 1) if it orients more directly to program activities than to program intents, 2) if it responds to audience requirements of information, and 3) if the different value-perspectives present are referred to in reporting the success and failure of the program. (Stake, 1974, p. 2)

This approach to evaluation is not restricted to a limited number of observation categories selected prior to the valuation. Here, evaluation has a more observational stance dealing not only with noted intentions, but also seeking instances of serendipity. Kemmis notes that the format for this type of evaluation report would be the "portrayal." In developing a portrayal the evaluator attempts to "tell the story" of the program, to inform the intended audience about the nature of the program, its features, both common and unique, what it has accomplished and not accomplished, the major issues surrounding the program, the people involved in its implementation and maintenance, and the audience intended for the program. The evaluator in writing a portrayal as the final report acts somewhat like an anthropologist describing the events of village life. The report involves people, things, places, events, activities; the evaluator in composing the report strives to synthesize the entire picture; to capture the essence of the curriculum within the educational arena. Quite likely, there will be many gray areas in such a report, but we can be successful, nevertheless, in communicating some of the program's complexity and furnish all report consumers with an appreciation of the dynamics of the curriculum in action.

The portrayal writer presents report readers with an "inside" view of the program while still addressing their concerns as outsiders. The writer strives to make the report understandable, not overly technical. This report is not a "scientific" treatise listing information generalizable to other districts' programs. It is situation specific, which as mentioned earlier in this chapter, is the common thrust of most school evaluation efforts. The report, rather than fragmenting the discussion of the curriculum program, presents it as a meaningful whole so that all consumers will know, How did the program work in our district, our institution with our students? (Kemmis, 1977)

This method is in some variance with the congruence–contingency model presented earlier. This author advocates using both models in curriculum evaluation.

EVALUATION OF THE CURRICULUM DEVELOPMENT EFFORT

The previous discussion has centered on comprehensive evaluation of the curriculum master plan—the curriculum–instruction guide—and its success within the school or educational institution. In most discussions on evaluation this technical aspect of evaluation receives prime attention. However, evaluation can be comprehensive on two other dimensions, the evaluation of the major stages of the total curriculum development effort (managerial evaluation) and the evaluation of the evaluation of these major stages (meta-evaluation).

The diagram below shows the relationships of the various levels and types of evaluation.

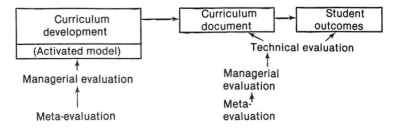

Managerial evaluation critiques the procedures activated in systematic curriculum development. Attention is given to the manner in which the curriculum philosophy and students' needs were identified and the procedures used for determining the student audience. It judges the effectiveness and accuracy of the means for translating students needs into objectives and the appropriateness of means of generating and selecting content and experiences. It assesses the procedures for conducting the technical evaluation and the quality of the technical evaluation reports. Managerial evaluation also addresses the staffing organization created and activated during the total systematic curriculum development model.

The diagram shows that technical evaluation activates the appropriateness of the curriculum document for particular student audiences. This evaluation looks at the quality of the program developed in terms of student outcomes (knowledge gained, attitudes achieved, values developed, and skills perfected). It searches for all consequences of the program. Managerial evaluation, as depicted in the diagram, assesses the quality of the processes utilized at each stage of the curriculum development model. Since technical evaluation is part of the overall curriculum model, judgment of technical evaluation is part of managerial evaluation.

Johnson (1977) notes that if it is important to evaluate planning processes (curriculum stages or activities), the resultant curriculum program guides, and the activation of programs, it also is important to assess the various evaluation approaches activated for such management evaluation. Did the managerial evaluation procedures generate the desired kinds of information and judgments? Did they clarify the nature of the conclusions wanted from the evaluation? Was the information provided by managerial evaluation used effectively by the decision makers? This evaluation of evaluation is called meta-evaluation.

> Theoretically, meta-evaluation involves the methodological assessment of the role of evaluation; practically, it is concerned with evaluation of specific evaluative performances. (Scriven, 1972, p. 84)

Johnson (1977) posits that meta-evaluation is similar to other types of evaluation, the only difference being that evaluation is the focus of the evaluative efforts. Therefore, the evaluation process can be submitted to both formative and summative meta-evaluation. In meta-evaluation, the evaluator is concerned with determining whether the managerial evaluation processes in fact were carried out and the manner of their activation.

Summative meta-evaluation gathers information so that determination can be made as to whether appropriate instruments and evaluation procedures were utilized in conducting the several phases of managerial evaluation. At this level one also critiques the quality of the evaluation reports produced that deal with managerial evaluation. The usefulness of these reports will be judged in light of the intended audiences and the types of data necessary for particular decisions.

If meta-evaluation is well done, the curriculum evaluation decision-makers will have data bases to support continuing to employ particular managerial and technical evaluation approaches and specified data gathering instruments (Johnson).

Activity 11–1   *Meta-Evaluation*

Consider the procedures that exist in your school or educational institution for evaluating the various stages of curriculum development. Establish a method for judging the effectiveness of these various evaluative approaches.

Select the evaluation process utilized for one stage of curriculum development and critique this tactic. What criteria are you employing for this evaluation of evaluation?

For example, you may assess the means employed by your school to evaluate students' successes with a new program. Or you may critique the methods employed in evaluating whether the curriculum content selection was done appropriately.

EVALUATION—CURRICULUM RESEARCH

The prime purpose of curriculum evaluation is to furnish data to aid decision-making regarding a particular curriculum. It seeks data so that judgments can be made as to whether a program worked as intended. Curriculum evaluation's major emphasis is not experimental, and the application of experimental design to evaluation problems can be judged as negating the principles that evaluation furnish data that can be employed in the continual upgrading of a program. Experimental design by its nature of keeping constant key variables prevents rather than promotes changes in the treatment. The curriculum researcher must hold treatments constant so that conclusions can be reported unequivocally. Such reporting is useful after a curriculum has been implemented and used in a school or educational institution for a year or so. But, this experimental posture makes it impossible to modify a program during its development and field testing.

Another argument against the curriculum evaluator viewing himself or herself primarily as a researcher is that the school and class environments in which curricula are developed and field tested are replete with myriad variables, some known and many unknown. It is essentially impossible to organize a sterile classroom environment in which all key variables are controlled. And, if such class environments could be created, one would find the conclusions only generalizable to environments similarly sterile. The curriculum evaluator does not aim to advance the field of curriculum knowledge with the addition of universal laws. The laboratory method is not appropriate for curriculum evaluation. But noting this does not mean that weak evaluation designs are to be employed.

Of course there are individuals who are curriculum researchers interested in and fascinated by specific interactions caused by particular curriculum components. A curriculum researcher may be striving to determine how particular students react to the mixing of film with prose material. Or the researcher may be attempting to identify what might be an optimal content sequence for particular types of learning, keeping all other major curriculum factors constant, such as instructional method, materials, environmental space, and time spent on task. The curricularists certainly should be cognizant of such research and may even participate in it. However, when he or she does, the role played is that of curriculum researcher, not curriculum evaluator. For the curriculum field, both roles are essential, but both are different.

ISSUES OF CURRICULUM EVALUATION

Currently many education scholars are writing about the nature of evaluation and its purposes within the educational arena. It is no longer being deleted from curriculum programs. Evaluation's increased prominence is due in part to educator's heightened understandings of evaluation and in part due to the mandates of state and federal offices of education that curriculum programs developed with federal funds contain an evaluation component. In many school districts and educational institutions, there is a requirement that educators conduct annual evaluations and file yearly reports of their findings.

But, many individuals writing on evaluation perceive education evaluators mired in crisis. We have a definitional problem as to the nature of evaluation. Thus, persons bring different interpretations of evaluation to the curriculum arena. Presently many of us are discovering our inadequacies in conducting curriculum evaluation. Also, we are uncovering a lack of instruments appropriate for evaluating various aspects of curriculum.

Determining the Parameters

The person who successfully evaluates curriculum not only understands the concept of curriculum, but also knows the nature of evaluation and the curriculum specifics to be evaluated. Curriculum development, taken in its entirety, is complicated requiring a legion of decisions and much data. Evaluators have the responsibility of putting boundaries on their realms of activities and gaining adequate knowledge about the decision processes extant within the evaluation system. Such understanding is prerequisite to designing and activating effective evaluation.

Curriculum evaluators who have established boundaries for curriculum evaluation are discovering a serious lack of criteria for judging programs and an absence of instruments for gathering data. But evaluation is more than collecting and recording data; it involves forming judgments about the data in terms of criteria, either implicitly understood or explicitly stated. One usually does not mention whether students learned or did not learn a particular content, but how well the students learned the content. This involves values and presently, we are weak in our determination of values. This weakness is debilitating in that evaluation is based on normative reasoning and thus requires careful delineation and processing of values. Further complicating the picture is the fact that in our pluralistic society, there are legions of values which various groups hold dear. Thus, the curriculum evaluator has to address the question, What values should guide the evaluation process? What values should guide the initial curriculum conceptualization?

Learning is multidimensional. We have planned-for learnings occurring in great numbers in response to curriculum. But, we also have unplanned-for learnings resulting from encountering particular curricula. What learnings should we address? Can we evaluate all learnings or even a majority of them to the degree necessary for stating with certainty that a particular result was because of a specified cause?

An issue confronting the field is that most curriculum evaluation is microscopic in focus rather than macroscopic. We expend energies in determining how certain students dealt with a particular curriculum aspect in a certain situation. Although such information is useful, it will not serve curriculum evaluators in other schools or educational institutions. We need instruments that will allow us to evaluate at the macrolevels of education, across school districts as well as across regions. This concern relates to the generalizability of our findings.

Curriculum evaluators have a problem with the scarcity of instruments available for gathering data. Most evaluation instruments focus on student achievement. Usually such instruments, whether standardized or teacher-made, are developed to discriminate among individuals. This is an issue relating to the evaluation standards employed, discussed earlier in this chapter. However, instruments that discriminate among programs as well as individuals are necessary. Standardized tests center on learnings common to students at a particular age rather than addressing any particular program. But, curriculum evaluators often use such information to support the continued use of their specific programs.

Evaluators are facing some testy issues in trying to deliberate success with regard to curriculum elements. Is it a binary phenomenon—one either does it or one does not? Is it a discriminating phenomenon—if only a few individuals can do it, is it of greater value and are those students achieving such performance or understanding to be ranked as more successful? Related to success is the issue of progress. What is an effective method? What is meaningful content. These questions are being raised by curriculum evaluators and researchers. A useful guideline for those engaged in curriculum evaluation is that effective means of evaluation are fluid and the knowledgeable evaluator is constantly querying himself or herself as to basic questions requiring attention.

Such questions put curriculum evaluators in the posture of inquirers rather than solely as reporters of "what happened" (Raths, 1978). Attention is given to why something worked as well as how well something worked. Postulating such questions allows one to assess the dynamics of curriculum implementation, and to critique the dynamics of the curriculum development process itself. In processing such queries, evaluators will realize that student success is varied, that not all curricula work equally well with all segments of the student population. Also, evaluators will analyze the interactions extant as a result of the new curriculum rather than centering solely on the main effects—the overall level of student achievement for instance.

A trend seems to be starting in which curriculum evaluators and curriculum researchers are working in increasing harmony to define more precisely evaluation and curriculum research and to identify variables of interest to all parties involved in curriculum activity.

Curriculum evaluation is essential to the overall process of systematic curriculum development. As we in curriculum gain greater expertise in evaluation, the efficiency of the curriculum development effort and the quality of the resulting curricula will increase.

Discussion

The chapter defined evaluation as a procedure or cluster of procedures that provides data requisite for effective decision-making regarding educational alternatives. Its major purpose is to furnish the curriculum decision maker with information not only about the end product of curriculum development—the curriculum instruction master plan, but also about the activities engaged in and curriculum elements produced at various junctures in the total curriculum development process.

Attention was given to several evaluation methodologies, essential evaluation tasks, and useful curriculum evaluation models.

The issues of internal validity and external validity were addressed. It was noted that all evaluation efforts must at least meet the criterion of internal validity. Most school evaluation efforts are concerned primarily with internal validity. That is, the curriculum evaluators wish to ascertain whether a new program is successful with the particular students in their schools or school district.

Some attention was given to the issue of standards to apply when evaluating students' achievements. Four standards were presented: the absolute maximum standard, the absolute minimum, the relative standard, and the multiple standard.

The chapter concluded with some attention to issues confronting individuals charged with evaluating curriculum programs. Evaluators still require more precise instruments and instruments that can measure student diversity. Also, workers in the evaluation field need to persevere regarding the issue of defining the field as it relates to curriculum.

Curriculum development efforts have usually given limited attention to evaluation. But the demand for accountability and the increasing necessity of and demand for being precise in our functioning are contributing to increased attention to the major milestone—curriculum evaluation.

References

Airasian, P.W. Designing summative evaluation studies. In W.J. Popham (Ed.), *Evaluation in education.* Berkeley, Calif.: McCutchan, 1974.

Brandt, R. On evaluation: an interview with Daniel Stufflebeam. *Educational Leadership,* January 1978, *35,* no. 4, 248–254.

Bross, I.D.F. *Design for decision.* New York: Free Press, 1953.

Conley, V.C. *Curriculum and instruction in nursing.* Boston: Little, Brown, 1973.

Gephart, W.J. Who will engage in curriculum evaluation? *Educational Leadership,* January 1978, *35,* no. 4, 255.

Hunt, B. Who and what are to be evaluated? *Educational Leadership,* January 1978, *35,* no. 4, 261.

Johnson, M. *Intentionality in education.* Albany, N.Y.: Center for Curriculum Research and Services, 1977.

Kemmis, S. Telling it like it is: the problem of making a portrayal of an educational program. In L. Rubin (Ed.), *Curriculum handbook, administration and theory.* Boston: Allyn & Bacon, 1977.

Phi Delta Kappa National Study Committee on Evaluation, D.L. Stufflebeam (Chair), *Educational evaluation and decision making.* Bloomington, Ind.: Phi Delta Kappa, 1971.

Raths, J.D. Encouraging trends in curriculum evaluation. *Educational Leadership,* January 1978, *35,* no. 4, 243–246 (editorial).

Scriven, M. An introduction to meta-evaluation. In P.A. Taylor & D.M. Cowley (Eds.), *Readings in curriculum evaluation.* Dubuque, Iowa: Wm. C. Brown, 1972.

Stake, R.E. The countenance of educational evaluation. *Teachers College Record,* 1967, *68,* no. 529.

Stake, R.E. Language, rationality, and assessment. In W.H. Beatty (Ed.), *Improving educational assessment and an inventory of measures of affective behavior.* Washington, D.C.: Association for Supervision and Curriculum Development, 1969.

Stake, R.E. To evaluate an arts program. In R.E. Stake (Ed.), *Evaluating arts education: a responsive approach.* Columbus, Ohio: Charles E. Merrill, 1974.

Zais, R.S. *Curriculum, principles and foundations.* New York: Thomas Y. Crowell, 1976.

Curriculum Maintenance

MANAGING THE CURRICULUM SYSTEM

In the initial stage of curriculum development, curriculum conceptualization and legitimization, those involved created a master management plan for administering the entire procedure—including the milestone event—curriculum maintenance. Curriculum maintenance encompasses the methods and means by which an implemented program is managed to assure its continued effective functioning. This major stage of curriculum activity is people-oriented; it deals with ways of fostering human functioning, both teachers' and students', with regard to the new program. Essentially, it attends to the actions of students and teachers and significant others in response to the ongoing program.

Who is answerable for this maintenance? Essentially all school personnel involved in day-to-day management of the program have this responsibility. They all have a stake in the program's continued success.

Effective curriculum maintenance results from careful planning that has occurred prior to program implementation and also from the meticulous control of curriculum variables over time. In maintaining a program, curriculum leaders strive to stabilize an organized program and to keep operational the contents, experiences, and environments. Small failures in the system are sorted out before becoming major (Lewis, 1974).

Persons responsible for program maintenance require a steady flow of accurate information in order to assess continual program performance. Essentially, this milestone activity is a type of formative evaluation. Such evaluation is required even though the program was deemed effective at the end of the major evaluation stage, for each year new students will arrive with new interests and capabilities and the same can be said of staff. Also, new materials and educational media will become available to address particular content emphases. Activities subsumed in maintaining the curriculum monitor the program's "pulse."

Curriculum maintenance is bifurcated into managing the curriculum system and managing the support systems. In these two emphases educators establish procedures for administering those activities requisite for monitoring the major curriculum components: content, experience, and environments. Educators also generate methods and means for dealing with the various person systems: students, teachers, support staff, administrative staff, and persons outside the school system.

```
┌─────────────────────────────────────┐
│     CURRICULUM MAINTENANCE          │
│          (Monitoring)               │
│                                     │
│  Managing the curriculum system     │
│  Managing the support systems       │
└─────────────────────────────────────┘
```

Throughout this textbook, the systems orientation to curriculum development has been advocated as a means by which curricula can be created, implemented and now maintained. In utilizing such an approach, curriculum leaders can better respond to the needs of individual actors, both teachers and students. Essentially, curriculum maintenance comprises the feedback and adjustment phase of the systems approach.

FIGURE 12.1   *Feedback and adjustment*

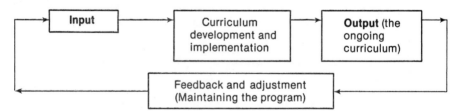

Such monitoring of performance is essential for it provides curriculum decision-makers with information as to whether planned results are in fact being achieved. This is not to be construed as a narrow assessment of education. The results intended could be divergent or autonomous student behavior. But even with such open-ended intentions, one requires data indicating whether such divergence has or is occurring in consequence of particular offerings.

Information communicated via curriculum monitoring should furnish the decision-makers with dispatches on all program phases. Such communiques can be recorded on data sheets kept in "program element-phase" folders, available to those persons charged with on-going program management. Also, data gathered in the maintaining process can come from minutes of various meetings held dealing with the program. Informal notes created by staff can be included in these "program" folders. As Bishop (1976) notes, the reason for such record keeping is not to overburden the staff members within the system, but to be systematic and facilitate decision-making and action. Also, it can provide a written record denoting the reasons that particular decisions and actions were taken. These folders can be reviewed at the end of the year and the data considered to determine whether the curriculum should be continued as is, whether minor adjustments are necessary, or whether some program aspect should be terminated or inactivated due to a modification in student population.

The monitoring function in program maintenance involves the following stages:

1. review of the total curriculum as developed and the results of the final evaluation of the program after its first year of implementation;
2. finalizing of the substages of curriculum monitoring, the setting up of tasks and listing personnel responsible for tasks and creating a calendar for specific tasks;
3. engaging of the actual monitoring, involving six stages:
   a. noting of the various effects on students' and teachers' behaviors of the curriculum elements (contents, experiences, environments and supporting materials);
   b. noting of those elements that can be maintained, continued to another quarter, another year;
   c. indicating of those portions of elements that might require major alteration or even elimination or nonactivation;
   d. observing of the various support personnel and services in relation to the on-going program;
   e. maintaining of information flow during the monitoring process;
   f. assisting of various staff, new and existing, in meeting challenges of the program in light of the changing characteristics of different student bodies and also emerging community demands.

Maintaining the program refers to its institutionalization. But, as noted in the chapter on change, an innovation must not be introduced with the notion that it can never be altered or discontinued. Monitoring furnishes one with information that will assist him or her in deciding the new program's duration and its overall character.

CURRICULUM MAINTENANCE—MONITORING THE SYSTEM

Maintaining subsumes the procedures for "overviewing" the processes and products of a particular program. It is the means by which curricularists check for order and disorder within the system. It is the "trouble shooting" requisite for assuring the success of an ongoing program. But, this activity is not solely aimed at determining whether what is achieved was actually intended. It also seeks to identify—to make evident—the unexpected in terms of needs that will require attention. Monitoring allows the curriculum person to invent and to discover the unanticipated as the curriculum functions over time. Often such "extras" when incorporated into the program become the key factors in assuring program success.

Maintaining involves intervening where appropriate, making adjustments in curriculum elements where necessary to influence positively the nature and degree of student learning, initiating activities to upgrade staff competencies to assure continuance of the program and introducing mini-programs to keep the public committed to the program.

Maintaining the program is difficult. It involves teamwork among supervisors of instruction and curriculum, as well as curriculum persons expert in the overall dynamics of curriculum activity. To achieve successful program maintenance, curriculum administrators and experts must recognize and understand the dynamic nature of the school system components and the interfaces of this system with the outside community system.

Basic Assumptions

Perhaps the major assumption about curriculum monitoring is that effective curriculum development requires follow through (Lewis, 1974). A program cannot be introduced and then forgotten. There must be a watching of the program in action so that minor modifications can be enacted. This viewing of the program in action allows for making minor change, with the result that adjustments that are made do not require great cost in terms of money, time or materials. Monitoring also allows variation suggested to be more acceptable to the staff, for they will view such modification as minor. As noted in the chapter on change, persons are most receptive to those alterations which appear to have the least change. Monitoring allows minor "tinkering" with the program. Persons tend to feel comfortable with the results of such tinkering; they can handle the minor program modifications deemed necessary.

Another major assumption essential to the monitoring aspect of program maintenance is the value of the cybernetic principle. Cybernetics relates to feedback control, the generation of information and using it to make corrections judged necessary at a particular time. Such feedback represents a type of reciprocal interaction between two or more actions in which one activity triggers a second action, which in turn has impact upon the first.

Cybernation permits rationalization of the total managerial activities related to maintaining the program. It supplies data requisite for decision-making. Cybernation frees curriculum mangers from petty distractions and enables these leaders to make decisions based on substantial data. With cybernation, curriculum decision-makers have much greater latitude in locating their facilities' efficiency, their curriculum elements' effectiveness in relation to initial intentions and current supply of resources (Michael, 1962).

Some might argue that cybernation is fine when working with machines, but inappropriate when dealing with individuals in schools. But, the components of a cybernetic system are present in most schools. As Casciano-Savignano (1978) points out, objectives are usually present; groups of individuals exist for making judgments; resources are available; processes of evaluation are noted. As stressed throughout this book, effective curriculum development creates inputs, devises systems of transforming these inputs into program, develops procedures for introducing these programs, identifies means for evaluation, and develops avenues for feeding information back into the curriculum system.

In accepting the cybernetic principle, we not only increase our effectiveness in administering the curriculum system, but we also gain insights regarding our performances within curriculum development. Most likely, we will better comprehend the various curricular elements and their interactive dynamics. We will understand that to manage curricula as a system, we require a vehicle by which to monitor and adjust the system. Lacking feedback and adjustment, our new programs, while perhaps appropriate for a particular time, are quite likely to remain static and eventually dysfunction.

A third major assumption underlying program maintenance is that those educators involved have a detailed understanding of the total curriculum development process and of their roles within it. In the curriculum game, teachers are essential team members. Therefore, they should possess competence in curriculum and decision-making in addition to expertise in instructional design and methods application. Unfortunately, many teachers shun roles in program development. Often they view themselves narrowly as only deciding what to implement in their classes. This should change. Likewise, supervisors need to be part of program monitoring and need to expand their functioning beyond that of supervising instructional behavior and student learning behavior. Supervisors are required to view the total curriculum dynamic. Administrators also should broaden their roles to encompass how individuals (staff, students and community members) are functioning within the curriculum arena. In many schools, such role adjustment is occurring, partly through enlightenment as to what curriculum is and partly in consequence to public demands that the school be more systematic and effective as a learning institution.

Another assumption basic to monitoring is that curriculum elements can be identified and means can be generated to assess their effectiveness and appropriateness. This does not mean that all variables within the curriculum arena can be or need be identified with exactitude. But, it does mean that we can identify—albeit in somewhat global terms—those dimensions of curriculum with which we are working and also obtain data from which we can deduce statements regarding the consequences of students' interactions with curricular dimensions. Implicit in this assumption is that where necessary, program adjustments will be forthcoming.

Basic Monitoring Cycle

The basic cycle for monitoring the curriculum is shown in Figure 12.2.

In effective curriculum maintenance, one would be monitoring constantly the ongoing curriculum in light of the conceptualizations of the cur-

FIGURE 12.2   *Monitoring cycle*

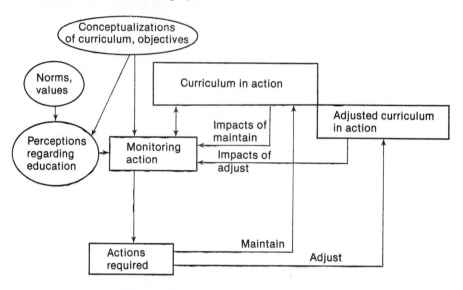

riculum and the objectives. Persons managing this monitoring are cognizant of the changing societal demands and increased knowledge about learning and the curriculum. Also impacting the monitoring action are the perceptions persons hold regarding education which are in turn influenced by the norms accepted and values held by all affected parties. Monitoring illuminates those actions required in reference to the current curriculum. One can either maintain or adjust this curriculum.

In the short run the model shows a closed system, but over an extended period of time, actions are related to the outside world via attention to norms, values, and objectives thus making the system dynamic. In light of the overall curriculum development system, persons concerned with managing the system enter this model at the monitoring action stage expending the majority of their time gathering and analyzing performance data to determine appropriate responses.

The model denotes continuous activity; one can either have operations to maintain or operations to adjust. These actions can refer to aspects of the curriculum or to the total ongoing curriculum. If persons charged with monitoring the program decide data gathered warrant maintaining the program as is, these individuals must also attend to the impacts of their decision. The impact data are fed into the monitoring action and new decisions regarding responses necessary are made. In this second round, one might again opt for maintaining the program or decide the new data warrant an adjustment in the curriculum. If the decision is to adjust, one then observes an adjusted curriculum in action and consequently attends to impacts of these modifications which are fed into ongoing monitoring. The model denotes the overriding task of monitoring, the gathering and interpreting of data regarding the ongoing program and communicating findings to involved staff. Implicit in the model is the spot checking tasks of personnel. Attention is given to particular roles and to whether such roles should be maintained or adjusted. Also implicit in the model is the establishing of procedures for accomplishing program maintenance including the organization generated for decision-making, the networks established for communicating, and the atmosphere created to encourage program maintenance.

Curriculum Elements to Monitor

Curriculum objectives: Are the objectives included in the program being addressed by the staff? Are new objectives being inserted? What effects are these new objectives having on the original program? In some cases these new objectives may be even more effective than the initial ones and should therefore be maintained.

Curriculum content: Is any of the content in the ongoing program inappropriate or unsuited for the particular students? Should the content be dropped from the program or just not used with these particular students? Is the sequence and scope of the content according to the initial program?

Curriculum experiences, instructional methods: Curricularists also address the suitability of the experiences and instructional methods. Are the students having difficulty processing information? Are the experiences providing sufficient time for the intended learning? What affective learnings are students gaining from the experiences? Are these experiences in line with program goals and objectives?

Curriculum environments: Attention to the space in which the curricular experiences occur also is monitored. Is the environment, perhaps the classroom, of sufficient size to allow the content to be processed as initially intended? Are there sufficient supplies of educational equipment for processing the content? Are there enough chairs for discussion groups? Are the spaces set aside for reflection adequate and conducive to such activity? One can also include under environment a monitoring of the lighting and ventilation. Furthermore, the curriculum materials (books, pictures, films, filmstrips, records, transparencies, audio and video tapes, recording equipment, copying equipment, etc.) can be checked regarding sufficient number, condition, appropriateness regarding student age and potential effectiveness.

Educational staff: Curricula that are maintained successfully result only from the efforts of highly qualified staff. Therefore, it is essential for the curriculum leaders and supervisors to observe the educational behaviors of the staff with regard to particular programs. Are instructional methods suggested in the curriculum master plan being employed by the staff? Are these methods continuing to be effective with the changing student populations? Are staff curriculum management roles continuing as initially planned? Are teachers introducing new educational activities and methods into the program? Are such additions having positive or negative effects on students' attainment of major program goals? Also, curriculum leaders will view in-service efforts aimed at introducing new staff to the ongoing curriculum.

School organization: Educational space is monitored so as to guarantee optimal classroom environments. One maintains classroom surroundings so that they facilitate smooth program functioning while also attending to the overall school organization. Does the school organization allow students to engage in recommended activities without disrupting other students' learning? Can students involved in activities in one part of the school move easily to another part of the school for activities scheduled next in the program sequence? Frequently, programs suggest that students experience large group instruction, then small seminar discussions, and finally individual work. Does the space available allow for such groups? Can students pass from a large group meeting to a seminar without triggering turmoil in the school? Are laboratories located near debriefing (seminar) rooms or do students waste time walking across the school campus?

School's community: Curriculum programs always are introduced into social systems, both within the school and the larger community. In maintaining a program, one monitors how the staff and lay public members are continuing to perceive the program. Is staff and community support, evident at the introduction of the program, still present? If a shift is appearing in the staff's and/or community's support, what is its nature and reasons for occurrence? Will the attitude shift and altered perceptions have a negative or positive effect upon the program?

Program's budget: During the new curriculum's evolution, the curriculum coordinator and others involved estimated the costs for its development, implementation, and maintenance. Estimates must be realistic and based on careful analysis of data and the program's scope to assure that monies allocated for all phases and maintenance of the program are adequate. Usually, staff salary is not considered a curriculum item. But teachers are the prime implementors of programs. Changes in staff salaries can have a negative effect on a program's continued existence. In some instances, an increase in staff's salaries will require the curriculum adminstrator to release auxiliary staff who are really essential to the program. If this is likely to occur, one can either negotiate for additional monies to keep such support personnel or modify the program's activities so that they can be conducted by the regular teacher.

In any curricular program there are consumable materials: paper, pencils, graph paper, notebooks, workbooks, ditto masters. One needs to monitor the use of these materials to assure that the supplies are not exhausted before the resupply period. This does not mean that someone from the curriculum office is assigned to count the number of pieces of paper teachers are using, but teachers and program support staff need to maintain some casual accounting system to assure that sufficient materials are available during the entire school year.

Methods of Monitoring

All individuals involved in the various aspects of the program—teaching, supervising, adminstering—should have responsibilities for monitoring the program to assure its maintenance as originally intended. Ideally, methods of monitoring are parsimonious in use of monies and time. Teachers responsible for instruction have limited time for doing detailed watching of the myriad aspects of the program and few periods for completing lengthy reports. Program supervisors also avoid great blocks of time recording perceptions. But someone has to devote considerable time to monitoring; the logical person is the curriculum leader. But, even this person will appreciate ways to reduce time spent in recording data and completing report forms.

The following chart may prove useful for the busy curriculum leader.

The key words of monitoring are self-correcting and fine tuning. When monitoring facilitates this, the program can be maintained, not perhaps entirely identical to its original conception, but at least in a form and format closely resembling the original design. Curricula are successfully maintained in those systems where an individual has reponsibility for such a task. This person is a system watcher, a trouble shooter, who is constantly observing the dynamics of the curriculum in action and evaluting the findings against the program's total conceptualization and its management plan.

Curriculum maintenance requires a budget over and above that allocated for staff salaries for teaching (implementing) the program. It costs money to hire a systems watcher to monitor the entire program and to administrate materials for obtaining data on the program. Of course, time available, monies allocated and the amount of detail needed are considered. If the program has been created from the ground up, then monitoring will be a major part of curriculum activity. If the program was a minor adjustment to some content area, then the degree of monitoring will be reduced correspondingly.

With regard to program maintenance, one assumes that the persons charged with making minor modificiations in the program have been officially empowered to make such decisions. It is of little value to have individuals analyze an ongoing program and then make suggestions if the staff are not required to incorporate such suggestions. The persons charged with curriculum maintenance must have official power to intervene, to require staff to modify program content, methods, and environment. Such powers are not to be interpreted as license to coerce staff into action, but it does mean that staff have to realize that the individual responsible for the total program or even a segment of it must have powers exceeding those of a classroom instructor who has to function only at one level of the program.

Although monitoring activities do not require major program alterations, the suggestions emanating from those in charge certainly have impacts on other program elements. Adjustment, however minor to a content topic covered or the elimination of only one topic, can affect the sequence of content or the appropriateness of planned experiences. Some new content or material originally recommended may have to be eliminated when data gathered via monitoring indicate that such components will eventually be dysfunctional in light of the program's major goals. Program maintenance is a longitudinal activity requiring of its director the ability to glance into the future to measure potential impacts of current suggestions on future staff actions and student learnings.

TABLE 12.1   *Curriculum monitoring form*

Curriculum Element	Monitoring Method
Content available for students	Checking to see that curriculum guides are present Getting reports, recommendations from teachers as to topics intended to be covered Using case reports to obtain data on content available
Content covered	Analysis of teachers' weekly lesson plans, comparing them to master curriculum plan Surveys, tests, evaluation reports, questionnaires Casual observations
Curriculum experiences	Classroom observation, formal and informal classroom observation schedules Student interviews, discussions with teachers Parent surveys
Observed student levels of learning	Anecdotal records, case studies Tests (standardized, teacher made—norm-referenced, criterion-referenced) Needs analyses
Students' attitudes	Reports from teachers; attitude inventories, class debriefing sessions Reports from counselors
Curriculum environments	Photographs, environment observation, audit of materials used in class Discussions with staff, students, lay advisory groups Use of video and audio tape for obtaining data on students' interactions within the environment
Educational staff functioning	Informal chats with staff Staff sharing meetings Attitude inventories Classroom observation schedules (formal and informal)

TABLE 12.1   *continued*

Curriculum Element	Monitoring Method
Follow up report on students completing program	This could be done for each class that has experienced the new program. This will provide information as to the continued usefulness of the program over time. The director of curriculum would be required to submit a period report and a final report to the assistant superintendent or superintendent.
School organization	Traffic flow patterns analysis, observations, mappings Discussions with teachers Discussions with students Recording room use as to type of activity and frequency of use Monitoring via video tape the staff-student use of the school environment
School's community	Questionnaires, information nights Bulletins, newspaper articles Dialogue with school board Radio reports Surveys Delphi techniques (see Weatherman & Swenson, 1974) on views and attitudes held Meetings with lay advisory groups Parent interviews Formal studies as to parent attitudes
Program's budget	Monthly financial reports to curriculum leader or budget director Yearly financial report dealing with expenditures, unanticipated costs

Monitoring Principles

Successfully maintained programs are ones in which curriculum leaders have given careful thought to program monitoring. The following list presents several principles that need to be kept in mind:

1. Persons engaged in monitoring must understand the total curriculum process that has occurred and the place of the maintenance function within the overall process.

2. Administrators of curriculum maintenance need to establish a firm co-operation network among all staff concerned with curriculum: teachers, administrators, supervisors, evaluators, curriculum specialists.

3. The communication network needs to identify data to be communicated in terms of behaviors (students' and teachers') and performances (on-going and final). This does not mean that only those behaviors that can be subjected to exact quantification will receive attention. In many cases, behaviors, somewhat elusive, can be described in the portrayal model. But, the description must be carefully and systematically done and focus on the kay curriculum elements so that the information culled from the observation will be of value to those individuals administering and implementing the program.

4. Established communication networks need to allow for the quick detection of program deficiencies and the rapid relay of such information to the appropriate persons or parties.

5. The total monitoring process itself needs to be observed so as to determine what procedures should be continued and what means should be adjusted or discontinued (this relates to managerial evaluation). Thus, there is a fine tuning built into the monitoring system.

6. The procedures utilized in monitoring the program should be in harmony with the overall school philosophy initially determined during curriculum conceptualization. This macro philosophical view will influence the means selected and the manner in which persons are involved in the overall monitoring function.

An Overview

Monitoring entails observing the entire program's dynamics. It addresses the atmosphere maintained, the communication networks established, the professional advice required at various junctures, the facilities furnished, the personnel supplied, and the overall master curriculum plan administrated. Program maintenance requires total staff involvement, albeit not all at the same level or with identical tasks. There will be curriculum leaders and subject specialists, educational systems experts, supervisory staff competent in observing teachers' instructional behaviors, experts in decision-making and leaders in educational management all working as a curriculum team.

Supervisors will have to be on hand to assist staff when they experience difficulties with any aspect of the program: with teaching the content, with coordinating the experiences, with organizing the environments, with coordinating the materials, with managing the evaluation procedures. Supervisors may assist in the adminstering of tests and interpreting of test data. They may counsel staff in ways to design content and in means to measure the effects of such content adjustment.

Supervisors engaged in the maintaining stage of curriculum will function both formally and informally. They may give lectures in special periods addressing particular difficulties relating to the ongoing program. They may also give demonstrations to staff in how to deal most appropriately with certain content. Supervisors also can provide input into the curriculum system, making suggestions of new strategies that might be incorporated effectively into the program.

Supervisors, curriculum leaders, curriculum specialists, systems experts, budget personnel, school psychologists, counselors, administrators, and staff all have a role and stake in maintaining the program and furnishing data that will give palpable evidence of effective program functioning over time. Much of the dialogue will be informal. The curriculum leader should establish a school atmosphere that fosters informal contact, perhaps by providing curriculum coffee hours. But, this stage of curriculum also requires a formal curriculum maintenance team, a cooperative "headship," answerable for assuring that the program's ongoing functioning is as intended.

Maintaining a curriculum also is a responsibility shared by various curriculum advisory committees, both professional committees and lay committees. These groups are supplied with up-to-date information on how every program is functioning and what minor alterations have occurred, the reasons for such modification and reports on their impact.

Educators with a systems view, approach program maintenance in light of the overall process of curriculum development. The following diagram depicts the relationship of this milestone activity to the developed program.

FIGURE 12.3   *Maintenance and curriculum development*

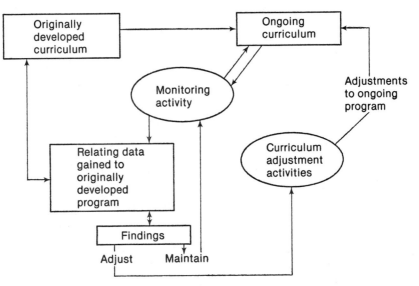

As shown in this diagram, monitoring supplies data for two major decisions, either to maintain the program or to initiate some adjustment. Figure 12.3 can be translated into a mission profile identifying milestone events and major functions to be performed.

FIGURE 12.4 *Mission profile of monitoring*

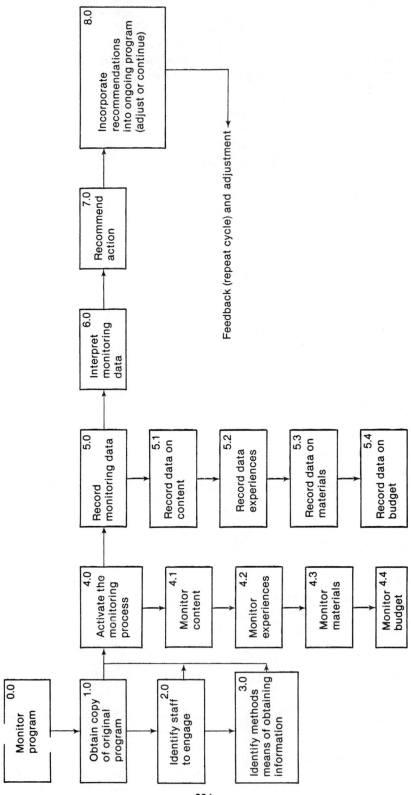

As depicted, this profile is a repeating cycle. After recommendations are incorporated, those persons accountable for monitoring observe the recommendations' impacts on the various curriculum elements. Thus one goes back to the beginning of monitoring stage 0.0.

Activity 12–1   *Monitoring*

Consider the educational institution in which you work or one to which to you have some access, and interview a curriculum leader in the central curriculum office to determine what management plan is in action for maintaining curriculum programs.

Compare the management steps followed in monitoring the program with those noted in this book. Is the program maintenance on an informal footing or is it formally organized?

Note the persons involved in the various aspects of monitoring. Should others be involved?

Attend several meetings of a group answerable for some aspect of program maintenance. Write a critique of the group's functioning with regard to whether it facilitates or retards or has no effect upon a curriculum in action.

Involvement of Central Office

Since monitoring requires viewing the entire program's dynamics, most likely the central office can best coordinate this activity. Central office staff, of course working with staff at other levels, have the perspective of the entire system and can most readily identify the impacts of various adjustments on all program elements throughout the entire educational system.

Rarely will major developments occur simultaneously in all program components. Nevertheless, it still is necessary for each to be monitored continuously to guarantee that each program's intents are achieved.

MANAGING SUPPORT SYSTEMS

Essentially, the previous discussion has centered on maintaining the curriculum program itself. However, such program continuance requires that supporting actions be established and maintained. Several support systems common in educational institutions are communication systems, in-service education, materials purchasing, special services (counseling and consultant), political lobbying. This list can be extended. The curriculum leader must ask himself or herself, What are those actions essential to allow the program to continue functioning? In some educational institutions, the only support system required will be that of communication to assure that messages pertinent to the program can be disseminated to affected staff members. Other educational institutions may concentrate on establishing an extensive in-service component to assure the continued success of a new curriculum.

Figure 12.4 noted the milestone events for monitoring a curriculum program. Paralleling this profile would be one delimiting functions for

FIGURE 12.5 *Maintaining support systems*

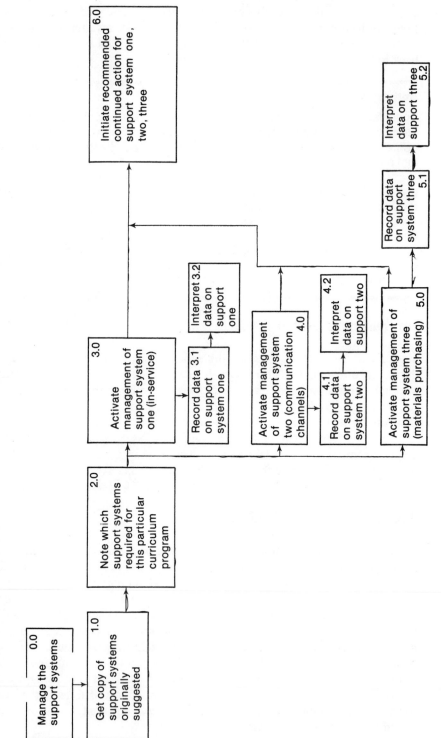

managing those systems that support the ongoing program. Ideally such support was identified at the beginning of curriculum development—specifically when curriculum leaders generated the master management plan. But, it is possible that some support systems will have to be established in response to a problem that occurs once the program has been implemented. Perhaps in the second year of the curriculum, legislation is passed that influences the student body. Legislation requiring that students have a less restrictive education environment will require that regular staff have support from staff in special education.

This profile reveals that the several support systems can be handled in parallel by different groups. The central office most likely will coordinate these support systems, but members from all staff levels will be involved.

Discussion

Curriculum maintenance refers to those procedures that allow the continued operation of a program. It involves several tactics whose prime purpose is monitoring all curriculum elements and the roles and responsibilities of persons playing support for these curriculum elements.

Curriculum maintenance is the keeping of the program's "pulse." Basic assumptions for monitoring were presented, the first being the idea that if newly created curricula are to be effective over time, there must be follow-through on the part of individuals involved with the program. The cybernetic principle plays an integral part in monitoring allowing persons to establish feedback and adjustment systems for the program.

The basic cycle of monitoring was presented in which the performances of persons involved and affected by the program are watched continually and results are analyzed bringing into play standards of performance created in the initial stages of curriculum development. If performance falls below an accepted level, then corrective action is initiated.

Essential ingredients of monitoring were discussed as well as what to monitor and methods of monitoring. A flow chart denoting the major steps necessary for observing a program in action was presented as well as one for managing support systems. The chapter concluded with mention of the roles and responsibilities of the central office.

References

Bishop, L.J. *Staff development and instructional improvement, plans and procedures.* Boston: Allyn & Bacon, 1976.

Casciano-Savignano, C.J. *Systems approach to curriculum and instructional improvement, middle school—grade 12.* Columbus, Ohio: Charles E. Merrill, 1978.

Lewis, J., Jr. *School management by objectives.* West Nyack, N.Y.: Parker, 1974.

Michael, D.M. Cybernation: the silent conquest. In M. Philipson (Ed.) *Automation, implications for the future.* New York: Vantage Books, 1962.

Weatherman, R., & Swenson, K. Delphi technique. In S. Hencley & J. Yates (Eds.), *Futurism in education.* Berkeley: McCutchan Publishing Co., 1974.

PART FOUR

Enacting the Curriculum-Instructional Plan

chapter

From Curriculum Plan
to Teaching Unit

The end product of systematic curriculum development is a curriculum master plan—a curriculum resource unit. However, this unit must be adjusted to meet the specific needs, interests, and requirements of particular student groups. A teaching unit must be drawn from the curriculum resource unit. A teaching unit resembles a resource unit. It has the same organizers, the same component parts: rationale, goals, objectives, topics, activities, materials. But the teaching unit differs in that its components are designed for a specific group of students while the resouce unit has suggestions appropriate for possible use with potential groups of students. The teaching unit's objectives, topics, activities and materials are specific recommendations for a particular class in light of certain goals.

If a teaching unit's format parallels that of a resource unit, how long is a teaching unit? There is no precise answer. A great deal depends on the number of topics included and their level of coverage. In deciding upon a teaching unit's length one attends to the scope and importance of the topics selected, the time available for topic treatment, the resources available, and the student audience. One also considers one's level of expertise in teaching the particular topic.

The unit's length (usually anywhere from two to six weeks) is not as important as its coherence. Does the teaching unit make sense in light of its overall goals and its component parts? Also, will the unit enable specific students to achieve the objectives noted? Is the unit manageable in terms of activities and materials used? Can students actually learn the intended topics by participating in the activities suggested?

It may help to distinguish resource units and teaching units by considering resource units—the outputs of systematic curriculum development—as master plans noting possible ways to involve students in their learnings. From these master plans educators select particular objectives, topics, activities, and materials to address identified needs of specific students. These needs may be determined via analysis of student, staff and/or community demands. It is important that teachers realize that their teaching unit, although written for certain students, must still reflect the overall concerns and intents of the resource units. By keeping teaching units closely aligned with the master curriculum plans, the integrity of the overall curriculum is maintained from year to year.

Most writers in the field of curriculum discuss resource units and teaching units. However, Doll (1978) introduced yet a third type, a functional unit. This functional unit contains the same components as the other two types of units. But with functional units, these components are actually constructed by the pupils working as team members. Students select the topics, the objectives, and the activities. Such units draw on the principle that the actual unit planning is of itself productive learning.

In most situations, there will be aspects of teaching units that will encourage students to select content and experiences. This author, rather than presenting readers with yet a third type of unit, prefers to keep to two levels of units, resource and teaching, acknowledging that aspects of the teaching units should allow students some involvement in final planning.

The following diagram shows the relationship of these levels of units to the final lesson plans.

FIGURE 13.1   *Relationships of resource and teaching units to final lesson plans*

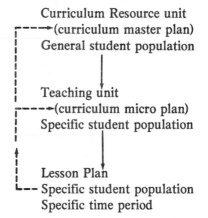

From the teaching unit, educators derive specific lesson plans which may cover one or more days. Such plans will note the topic to be covered, the specific objectives, and supporting activities and materials. The detail of lesson plans can vary tremendously from just a note as to the objective and topic for a particular day to a three or four page guide delineating how the teacher will introduce, develop and conclude the lesson.

More than just a plan. Using a unit plan is really an approach to teaching. It was introduced to the educational world around 1900 with the advance of the philosophies of Dewey and Kilpatrick. Initially, the term was used to designate all the activities and experiences designed to teach a particular topic or theme. The unit concept cut across various subject matter fields and focused on life problems. Its development resulted from the cooperative efforts of staff with the final "fine tuning" involving both teachers and their students.

The unit approach to teaching still emphasizes total patterns of learning rather than isolated segments of knowledge presented in a series of daily unrelated lessons organized in a repeating cycle of present, read, discuss, and evaluate. When properly done, this approach provides daily direction for furnishing myriad learning experiences appropriate to the interests and needs of learners.

THE TEACHING UNIT

The teaching unit furnishes the instructor with a valid framework for the conduct of his or her teaching over time. Usually, the teaching will be within the context of lessons drawn from the teaching unit. Essentially, it enables the instructor to coordinate all specific curriculum and instructional components so that they contribute to students' learnings.

As noted at the beginning of the chapter, in the teaching unit, one attends to specific objectives, contents, experiences, materials that have been systematized, edited, and modified to make them all appropriate to certain students. The purposes of the teaching unit draw from the major purposes of the resource unit; to provide the instructor with a framework, a plan of action, for guiding his or her attempts at getting students to experience the content of the unit. If a teaching unit draws heavily from a curriculum resource unit the probability is heightened that what was planned will in fact be carried out.

Jarvis and Wootton (1966) note that teaching units will be influenced by three factors: (a) the overall curriculum framework prepared by the state department of education, (b) the curriculum resource unit, and (c) the series of adopted textbooks which will determine, in large part, the subject matter of the units. In some situations, the textbook series actually is the curriculum and the teacher's editions are the teaching units. Even though this is common, it is not ideal for textbooks are not written with particular student audiences in mind. Also, teaching units should draw on multiple materials and not be locked into activities of a particular commercial series. Teaching units should allow for divergence of learning activities and varied content.

Structure of a Teaching Unit

Overview

The overview of the teaching unit describes, albeit in general terms, the topic to be covered, stressing why this content is important for the intended learners. Here, the teacher records the unit's rationale and sometimes the philosophy underpinning the unit. In this section, one will find the content outline to be covered as well as a listing of major generalizations and concepts scheduled for unit attention. Teachers are free to add to this section other materials they deem appropriate. This section links the teaching unit to the total curriculum of which the teaching unit is a part.

Objectives

The teaching unit's obectives are second-order objectives, less general than overall program objectives (first order) but still not at the behavioral level which occur in a particular lesson plan. However, teachers are free to use their judgment as to how specific the objectives will be.

The objectives in a teaching unit will relate to understandings (knowledge to be gained), problem solving skills, value and attitude development. The cognitive, affective, and psychomotor domains are addressed.

The Unit's Body

The main section of the teaching unit document can have a variety of formats. But, despite format variety, the unit's body will contain content topics and various types of learning experiences usually presented in a series of activities. These activities denote instructional methods the teacher will employ and/or particular educational experiences scheduled for students. Commonly the body of the unit is organized into opening or initiatory activities, developmental activities, and terminating or culminating activities. Materials and other educational resources necessary for these activities are noted.

Initiatory activities. These activities, suggestions for the teacher to trigger student interest in the topic and to set the stage for the unit, are most crucial. If these activities are successful, students become interested in the topic; their curiosity is piqued; they begin to relate the topic to prior learnings and to the outside world. Because of the essentialness of these activities, teachers need to contemplate ways in which the current study can be related to past experiences of the students, in which the emphases of this particular unit can be related to the overall curriculum.

Teachers can have initiatory activities that involve the display of books and pictures, the discussion of reports, the sharing of experiments, or problem presentations, the giving of demonstrations, the listening to guest speakers, or the taking of independent time at an interest center.

Teachers also can introduce units by showing and comparing pictures, presenting map and globe studies, introducing literature and poem reading, taking museum visits, coordinating class exhibits, encouraging bulletin boards, presenting documents, or giving a common assignment to raise heuristic questions.

The creative instructor looks continuously for highly motivating ways to introduce units so students will become acquainted with the unit's general scope, and major emphases, and generate key questions for investigation.

Developmental activities. Developmental activities comprise the major portion of the teaching unit. (This is also true in the resource unit.) The carrying out of these activities—covering a few days or several weeks—constitutes the assimilation or the student working period of the unit. A general guideline is that teaching units at the primary grades should not last more than 3 weeks, not more than 6 weeks at the intermediate grades, and not more than 10 weeks at the junior or senior high. But, at the secondary level, one finds that units often are geared to the common scheduling patterns—in some cases 12 weeks. At the levels of higher education, units can vary in time length from a week for a minicourse to a 16 week semester course.

It is during the developmental activities that students will encounter the content, reflect upon it, raise questions, formulate procedures for investigation, process the information, conduct experiments, act within particular environments, and use certain materials to accomplish the unit's objectives. It is in this unit section that the teacher incorporates specific notations regarding teaching strategies to employ with particular content topics. Often, since teachers are writing these units for themselves, they are rather general in noting their planned instructional methods. However, the detail should be sufficient so that the teacher can utilize the same strategy at another time, and not be left guessing as to what exactly was done initially.

Developmental activities can be divided several ways. One can have research activities in which students will read, write, interview persons, take notes, code data, use references, write reports, and conduct laboratory experiments. One also can have presentation activities involving students in announcing, describing, reporting, conducting demonstrations, engaging in pantomime, or in relating particular events. One also can have production experiences in which students draw, sketch, model, illustrate, paint, construct, write, dramatize, or role play. Here one is concerned not only with the students' end products but with the experiences through which the end products were produced.

Activities also can be clustered under appreciation, observing and listening; experimenting; organizing information; and evaluating. Each of these activities groupings would subsume other supporting activities such as raising questions, assisting fellow students, recording data, collecting, planning, outlining, summarizing, conducting meetings, and chairing debriefing sessions.

Culminating activities. Culminating activities are those planned for concluding the unit. Such activities aim at assisting students in synthesizing and summarizing all the values, attitudes, and understandings gained in the unit study. These activities provide for students sharing experiences and information, summarizing content, and relating various aspects of the learnings gained to topics studied in units. These activities also can serve as a transition from one unit to another. Also such activities can facilitate students raising further questions for examination.

These activities often serve as vehicles for evaluation, allowing students to demonstrate their understandings regarding the unit's topic. All too often culminating activities are nothing more than the administration of teacher-made tests or the completing of workbook sheets.

Evaluation activities. Evaluation activities really are not isolated in a separate section. Rather, such activities comprise an integral part of the total unit. Such activities are not solely for the purpose of obtaining evaluative data for grading students, but can also be included to educate students in procedures for assessing their own levels of learning, their own means of processing information, and to judge the quality of their own investigative products. In the teaching unit, the teacher records the ways that he or she intends to gather evidence that the objectives are being achieved as well as the means by which he or she will involve students in self assessments.

Unit Back Matter

Great variety exists in the back matter of teaching units. How detailed such a section is depends upon the degree of knowledge the teacher brings to the teaching unit and often on the amount of time available for creating the teaching unit. But, it is not uncommon to discover in this section appendices recording materials that can be used, bibliographies for both the teacher and the students, lists of films, slides, exhibits, and records that would be useful in this unit. Frequently found in a unit's back matter are lists of generalizations and scope and sequence charts for particular skills.

Principles of Organization

All instructors make teaching units, whether drawing inspiration for such units from curriculum resource units or from the spontaneity of a particular moment. The primary principle to bear in mind when constructing such a unit is that it should contain the major unit components and that these components should be organized in such a way that the probability of students achieving the unit's objectives is increased.

Another principle is that the unit's organization should "force" the teacher into behaving systematically with regard to the unit's topic. Also, the unit's arrangement should provide for balance among the types of educational experiences.

A well organized unit will allow for continuity in the intellectual development of a student. Concepts, main ideas, topics will be structured in a sequence that optimizes student learning and relates content of the unit to content of preceding and succeeding units.

A unit, carefully conceived, allows for a unified learning approach to a particular topic. The students will realize the focus of their investigations and how their functioning within the unit relates to the overall curriculum. The successful unit interrelates content, experiences, and environments to the specific unit objectives.

A final principle relating to overall unit development is that the plan should take into consideration the quality, validity, feasibility, and relevancy of the content and consider it in relation to the personalization of the content. An effective unit will not only allow the teacher to guide students in experiencing the specified content but also will furnish the instructor with means of monitoring such quality of students' experiences in light of the unit's objectives. Ragan (1977) has developed some similar ideas.

The teaching unit's content will be structured according to the curriculum design selected: separate subject design, correlated subject design, broad fields design, multidisciplinary and interdisciplinary design. These designs emphasize subject matter, but teaching units also can be developed with experience as the central unit organizer. But, as noted in earlier chapters, experience units do not exclude content.

Advantages of Employing Teaching Units

Using teaching units rests on the assumption that content so organized provides for greater clarity of learning in that students can relate content experienced to a common organizer or content topic.

Following is a list of the advantages one can derive from employing the unit procedure:

1. The unit furnishes an emphasis upon the development of understandings rather than upon the mere accumulation and memorization of isolated information. Attention is given to interrelationships among various key conceptual organizers.
2. Topics organized in a unit format allow teachers to have students expereience information and material that is current, often more so than that information provided in textbooks.
3. The unit approach assists students in realizing their studies' major foci. It furnishes opportunities in which students can relate their studies of a particular topic to other topics and to learnings gained outside the school.
4. Through the unit's variety of materials, instructional strategies, and educational activities, attention is given to the range of individual differences, interests, skills, abilities, and achievement.
5. Via a unit organization, the teacher can systematically plan for students to increase their level of responsibility for their own learning.
6. Since preparing to teach via a unit approach requires of the teacher extensive systematic planning, the teacher is better prepared to teach.
7. Units, if well done, draw on multiple sources of information with learning considered as being multisensory. Multimedia approaches to learning are enhanced by the unit organization.

8. Since a unit's content is organized according to some logic and is developed via a multitude of experiences, students' opportunities for critical thought and independent thinking are enhanced.
9. Units allow students opportunities to work independently, and thus develop initiative, self-direction and responsibility. Also units allow students to work with others both within the classroom and sometimes in the community. There are many opportunities for learning how to function within a group.
10. With the unit approach, students have opportunities to master information processing strategies commonly used in generating or ganized knowledge.
11. Units facilitate the teacher in evaluating the successes of students' learnings. This is because the activities of the unit are related clearly to unit objectives and overall goals.
12. Units allow teachers to utilize educational environments more effectively, since such environments are considered in the unit with regard to particular content intents and certain activities and objectives.

The preceding list of advantages is not an exhaustive one. Essentially, the benefits to be accrued from the employment of a teaching unit are due to the fact that the instructor in creating such a teaching unit from the curriculum masterplan is forced to consider each major curriculum component as to its function, its value and its relationship to other curriculum components. Furthermore, each curriculum component is considered in relation to the needs, interests, backgrounds of particular students. Thus, teaching becomes purposeful and systematic, not haphazard. But, this does not mean that teaching lacks spontaneity. Having a plan of action for involving students in using certain materials to investigate certain content will still allow students to discover, to follow their inclinations, to develop as individuals, both personally and academically.

Some educators argue that if an excess of planning exists, then the joy of learning is smothered and students become like products on an assembly line. This is not true. Rather, teachers who wish to encourage in their students originality, self-motivation, and independence in investigation, need to plan. They need to schedule opportunities for student reflection; they need to furnish materials and arrange interest centers that will trigger in their students questions for further investigation. Students will learn if they see reasons for their efforts. They will learn if they are cognizant of how their efforts relate to prior learnings and those scheduled for attention.

Cautions in Employing Teaching Units

In our enthusiasm for the unit approach, we should not dupe ourselves into believing that no learning can occur outside the unit approach.

1. Units are parts of the curriculum. They do not comprise the entire curriculum. There will be learning that will result from high quality

unexpected situations occurring within the classroom. Rather than neglect such learning incidences because they occur outside our plans, we should seize such moments to trigger in students particular investigations. Frequently, events occurring in the community can well be utilized to get students to investigate a particular topic. In this type of situation, one might have students develop what Doll (1978) calls a functional unit, in which students map out their approaches to an investigation. The discovery of a new book by a student may lead to significant learning.

2. The mere gathering of information between two covers does not make a unit. Nor does such accumulation, even if involving all curriculum components, guarantee that its use will be optimal within the classroom. It takes hard work on the teacher's part to translate the written teaching unit into the actual theater of the classroom. Part of the unit's success will depend upon the energy and creativity the teacher brings to the class plus the realization that there will need to be adjustments made as the unit is activated to address unplanned for discoveries. The successful teacher realizes that the unit is still a guide, not a document demanding rigid adherence.

3. There is no set length of time for a unit. Conceivably, it can be as brief as one day and as long as a semester. What determines its length is the complexity of the objectives considered and the students' academic backgrounds.

4. Units should not be used intact each year; they should undergo modification. This makes sense for teaching units are geared to particular student bodies, thus as students change from year to year, so also must the unit be adjusted. Also, there may be new materials produced that are more appropriate than materials mentioned in the original unit.

5. When teaching a unit, attention must be given to balancing the students' encounters with topics, activities, materials. This balance will be modified continually as new students experience the unit.

6. It is important for teachers to have a means of monitoring how students proceed through a unit's components. Having a plethora of activities and materials for students does not guarantee that quality learning will occur. Attention must be given to assure that activities and materials selected are indeed appropriate for the individuals in question.

7. Throughout the activation of the unit, it is essential that teachers keep the overall unit goals and objectives in mind. Monitoring of instructional strategies and educational activities should be done to determine the unit's continuing effectiveness.

Certainly, the above list could be lengthened. However, the central caution implicit in the list is that one must resist complacency after creating an effective teaching unit. One must attend to its implementation and its maintenance. Teaching, as is true of learning, is an evolutionary process. The wise instructor is cognizant of this fact and relishes the idea that such evolution holds new challenges that require attention.

Activity 13–1   *Analyzing Available Units*

Locate a teaching unit in your school or institution and compare its components with the ones noted in this chapter. Are all the key unit components included? If not, which ones are ignored? Would you be able to use this unit in
your teaching? Why?

DEVELOPING TEACHING UNITS

The general procedure by which one develops teaching units from curriculum
resource units is essentially identical to the major stages required for systematic
curriculum development: curriculum conceptualization and legitimization;
curriculum diagnosis; curriculum development—content selection; curriculum
development—experience selection; curriculum implementation; curriculum
evaluation; and curriculum maintenance. The real difference is that now one is
using the curriculum resource unit (the master macro plan) as the major source
for the teaching unit rather than going to the general body of available teachable content. Also, since the curriculum resource unit has addressed the
particular community at least in general terms, one will not have to go through
as extensive a needs analysis and curriculum diagnosis. Furthermore there will
be no major piloting prior to implementing the teaching unit. Actually the activation of the teaching unit is a type of piloting combining ongoing evaluation
and adjustment.

Steps in Creating Teaching Units

It is unlikely that the conception of curriculum determined in the master curriculum development phase will be adjusted when translating the resource unit
into a teaching unit. If one conceptualizes the curriculum content as a separate
subject or as an experience curriculum, then the teaching unit will reflect this
view.

In the first stage of translation, one considers the intended
audience. As noted before, each year the audience will change, and adjustments
will be required to assure that the teaching unit is appropriate for the new students. In essence, one is doing situational analysis in which the particular
needs, interests, backgrounds, abilities of the intended student population are
noted. From this information one selects those needs and interests that are feasible to address in light of the constraints of the school within the community as
well as with regard to the backgrounds and capabilities of the students.

The second major step—a variation of the curriculum diagnosis
stage—is establishing the teaching unit's objectives. In essence, a teaching unit
is a type of depth study dealing with only a few objectives and topics. During
this stage, objectives are checked for clarity and priority. These objectives are
critiqued against those identified and included in the curriculum resource unit
for the particular topic. The teaching unit objectives can denote the behaviors of

students but usually will not be in behavioral terms. Such behavior specificity is left to the lesson plan level. The reader is referred back to chapter seven dealing with the various levels of objectives.

The third major step is selecting and organizing (sequencing) the particular subject matter for the teaching unit. The specific organization of this subject matter is influenced in part by the conception of curriculum developed during the macro curriculum development procedures. One asks, What types of instructional foci can meet the objectives selected for the unit?

If one has organized content in a curriculum resource unit as a separate subject or a discipline, then this most likely will be used as the teaching unit organizer (e.g., a teaching unit on the *geography* of North America, *economics, geometry*). But, one might have drawn on various topics that have appeared in newspapers, or various themes that have been utilized in particular novels as content organizers. If so, then one uses these hooks upon which to hang the teaching unit content. The content selection criteria identified for selecting resource unit content also are appropriate for designating teaching unit content. (See Chapter 8 for a discussion of these criteria.) From this stage, one can generate a listing of the main ideas to be developed in the unit and then the concepts that will support these major ideas or generalizations. These concepts can be the particular foci necessary for dealing with the main ideas. An example of what might result from this stage of activity follows:

Egypt: Ancient Land in Modern Times

Central generalizations from the disciplines:

Human societies have undergone and are undergoing continual, though perhaps gradual, changes in response to various forces (History).

Guidelines for understanding thought and action in contemporary affairs can be derived from the historical backgrounds of society (History).

Places on the earth have a distinctiveness about them which differentiates them from all other places (Geography).

The art, music, architecture, food, clothing, sports, and customs of a people help to produce a national identity (Anthropology).

Specific ideas for unit attention:

Since ancient times, agriculture has been a main activity in Egypt.

The Nile River has influenced the culture of Egypt since ancient times.

The Egyptians presently are trying to bring more industrialization to their country.

Concepts upon which to focus:

Society, change, contemporary affairs, place, region, art, customs, culture.

These major generalizations and specific ideas and concepts are then incorporated into a content outline. At this point one makes the final decision as to content and also determines its particular sequences. But, one may not wish to draw content from major generalizations but rather to build the units around themes such as *America in the Twentieth Century, The Meaning of Modernity, The Place of Religion in America.*

Selecting the major foci for teaching units is much easier in districts or institutions where a master curriculum plan comprised of numerous curriculum resource units has been created. In such instances, instructors only need to draw from the topics of the curriculum resource units. However, despite the listing of major topics in resource units, educators must still select those aspects of the topics that are appropriate for specific student audiences.

In attempting to discern those resource unit topics most appropriate for selected students, educators will apply content selection criteria. Posner and Rudnitsky (1978) have suggested rating each instructional focus as 1, 2 or 3 (high to low) with regard to each criterion. The following table draws from their thinking.

TABLE 13.1   *Content selection criteria*

Total Score	Unit Focus	Significance	Interest Level (motivation)	Feasibility	Economy
6	Education	1	3	2	2
7	America in 20th Century	1	1	2	3
8	Photography	3	1	3	1
5	Futuristics	1	1	1	2

Note. See Chapter 8 for explanations of these criteria

From such a listing, one obtains a rating of various unit content foci. One can employ a similar table for noting how each subtopic in a projected teaching unit stands with regard to content selection criteria.

Posner and Rudnitsky have suggested that content can be selected and organized according to clusters of intended learning objectives: world-related objectives; concept-related objectives; inquiry-related objectives; learning-related objectives; and utilization-related objectives. The particular cluster one selects is influenced by the philosophical view one has promulgated during the first stage of curriculum conceptualization as well as what one considers to be the most manageable means of organizing content.

The world-related objectives pull from reality and can be used in those situations that deal with events, objectives, or processes that have identifiable properties. Often, world-related objectives draw on specific discipline organizations or from problems currently confronting society. Content so selected and organized focuses on the empirical relationships between events, people, and objectives as they exist within the world reality. Attention is on spatial relations, temporal relations, and physical attributes (Posner & Rudnitsky). A teaching unit on history will have its content sequenced according to the phenomenon of time (temporal relations). But, one can also have units in anthropology and sociology arranged according to time, in which events are contemplated in terms of cause and effect, antecedents and consequences. This aspect of sequence also can comprise a unit in chemistry in which the phenomena of chain reactions is the focus. In such a unit one melds the logic of the chosen content with its nature in space, all the while attending to the ways in which individuals learn.

Events in space can comprise a teaching unit in geography. Attention can be given to the nearest and the farthest region, spatial phenomena from east-to-west, from north-to-south. But one need not be limited to a unit in geography to have students attend to spatial sequences. One can develop a unit on "my neighborhood" in which students study "where I live" in relation to "where I play," "where I go to school," and "where I shop." One can even have students analyze the designs of their homes, noting the interrelations of the various rooms with regard to function (Posner & Rudnitsky).

In explaining this organizer, Posner and Rudnitsky give an example of a unit on the pond. Such a unit can focus on the dimensions of the pond, the composition of the water of the pond, the life found in the pond, and the role of ponds in the ecological scheme. One also might have a unit relating to world conflict with attention to the reasons for such conflict, the distribution of current world conflict, and the role of politics in creating and reducing such conflict.

Concept-related objectives and content reflect the organization of the conceptual world—the structure of discipline and even nondisciplined knowledge. Attention is given to those concepts that students should comprehend if they are to understand a particular subject or content area. This organizer identifies the concepts to be selected, and also suggests the logic for sequencing such concepts. Concepts can be stressed continually in various teaching units employing the spiral curriculum approach (Taba, 1962).

Also, drawing on this content organizer, one might have a unit on responsibility. Such a unit might be organized as follows:

Unit Topic—Responsibility

Grade Level: _____

Major Objective: Students will explain the concept of responsibility and through class dialogue and action within the classroom and in the community demonstrate an understanding of how responsibility applies to their lives as well as show a commitment to responsible action.

Content Topics:
Definition of responsibility;
The value of responsible action;
How responsible people act in various situations;
People acting responsibly influence the overall society.

The third unit organizer suggested by Posner and Rudnitsky (1978) is inquiry-related, drawing on the ways knowledge is created. This organizer may be somewhat difficult to use, in that one really does not divorce the processing of content from the content itself. Even if units emphasize a method or methodologies, they must be utilized with some content. One might have a unit in geography dealing with the regional method. However, in having students master the regional method, they also are apprehending the concept of geography; they are learning how to apply the method to particular geographic situations.

Content selected and organized on the basis of inquiry assumes that the subject matter will be arranged so as to duplicate the procedures a scholar would undertake in discovering generalizations and verifying knowledge. The content regarding procedures will be influenced by whether one is stressing an inductive or a deductive approach to knowledge generation. Induction would have the students studying specific situations and then relating knowledge gained from such analysis to other situations until finally, students had a sufficient number of instances to formulate a generalization. In a deductive task, one would have students consider specific situations in light of a general understanding or hypothesis to be tested.

There are a multitude of procedures available for students to employ, and each procedure advances a particular sequence of action. Thus, students experiencing such a unit would in effect follow the steps requisite for conducting the inquiry. With this emphasis, the teacher not only has the methodological content, but also the arrangement of the content through time.

The fourth way suggested by Posner and Rudnitsky (1978) for organizing learning objectives and thus content is learning related. This also is a rather nebulous organizer, for one would hope that any unit, regardless of its specific organization would be related to the learner and consider the ways in which individuals learn content, process, skills, attitudes, and values. In employing this organizer, one determines the content and experiences that contribute to a meaningful sequence of learning.

This content organizer draws primarily on our knowledge about human growth and development and the psychology of learning. Attention is given to the concept of prerequisites, those learnings that must occur if other learnings are to be triggered. Attention is given to the various types of learnings from signal learnings all the way to concept learnings (Gagne, 1970).

Thus units would be organized on the basis of presenting students with opportunities to learn information that is prerequisite to later learning. The very organization of the content is instrumental in facilitating later learning. In units in language arts, one might first have a unit organized on combining words into sentences before having a unit dealing with writing paragraphs. One would attend to paragraphs before teaching story writing.

Units that have content selected and organized drawing on our knowledge of learning also draw on what Posner and Rudnitsky (1978) call *familiarity*. Here, information is selected from that which is familiar to students and organized so that each student is gradually introduced to content less familiar. In social studies, the expanding horizons approach of organization in which one commences a study with the neighborhood or local community and gradually extends study into more distant communities exemplifies this selection and organizational principle.

Another aspect to consider in organizing units is difficulty of the material. One might organize the content in such a way that the students will experience the less difficult before proceeding to the more difficult. In language arts, one deals with simple stories before introducing novels. Many teachers have students deal with factual information before getting into concepts.

Posner and Rudnitsky (1978) note that content selected and then organized may often be done in light of the interests of the students. This draws on the general principle that students will attend to content in which they are interested with greater zest than content in which they have no interest. But, the reader should bear in mind the point made earlier in the book that students' interests may often be superficial and transitory.

Content that is selected and organized should be appropriate for students' cognitive and emotional development. Students who are at the concrete operational stage should not be presented with unit content requiring them to theorize about particular phenomena.

One should select and organize content realizing that all students bring an affective component to their learning. Instructors making teaching units should consciously attempt to specify and arrange content so that it addresses the affective aspects of students' learning and allows them to grow to higher affective levels (Posner & Rudnitsky).

The final way of organizing objectives and content suggested by Posner and Rudnitsky is utilization-related. Units employing this focus stress the application of content and process to specific situations. One might have a unit in economics on *Starting our Company.*

The units arranging content on this basis would stress those applications occurring frequently within the profession or job and the sequence of specific tasks. Certain jobs would be the unit organizers. Posner and Rudnitsky note an example of a unit in cartography. One would arrange the unit so that students would follow a procedure of analyzing a site, taking mathematical fixes, graphing phenomena observed, determining the appropriate projection to use, and then actually creating the projection. This could be a rather lengthy teaching unit, or even a series of units comprising a minicourse.

At the secondary level, one might have a unit on *Cleaning the Air.* In the various health sciences, this type of unit organizer is most useful. A unit in nursing might be *Caring for the Infant in the First Year.* The unit could stress various techniques for diagnosing infant behavior, maintaining nutritional status, providing for the safety and comfort of the infant, and promoting development of body muscles and bones (Conley, 1973).

This organizer may be more appropriate for the secondary and higher education levels where units can address the social, personal, and career goals of students. As mentioned above, this content is appropriate for teaching units in the health sciences. In the field of law, one also can have teaching unit content geared to specific aspects of the law and definite court room procedures.

Again this organizer may not be distinct, for one could argue that all units' content should have utility—a means of practical application. It may be that these organizers presented by Posner and Rudnitsky (1978) are not distinct means for organizing units, but rather are criteria that we can bring to the objectives and content we wish to address in our units. Do the objectives and content have relevance to the world? Will the objectives and the content chosen allow students to develop understandings of particular concepts? Will such objectives and the content facilitate the processing of information and encourage optimal student learning. Will the objectives and content specified be of value, utility, to students? Do the objectives and content selected draw on our knowledge of how individuals learn?

Of course, in designating teaching unit objectives and content not all of these criteria may be applied equally, but it seems to this author, that one cannot completely neglect any of them.

The fourth step in creating a teaching unit is selecting and organizing experiences that will allow students to deal with the unit's content component. (The reader should refer to Chapter 9 for a review of the criteria for selecting experiences.) In the actual development of the teaching unit, it is highly probable that one will meld selecting content (step three) with selecting and organizing experiences (step four). Also, previously discussed organizers for content will provide some guidance as to appropriate types of experiences. For example, inquiry-related objectives and content will suggest appropriate types of experiences that will furnish students with opportunities to apply specific procedures. From learning-related objectives one derives counsel as to the types of experiences that will facilitate optimal development of student understanding.

In effective teaching unit development one allows provisions for student involvement in planning some of the instructional activities. But, one keeps in mind student readiness, the type of content organizer for the unit, the level of student involvement desired and the means by which such experiences will be summarized and evaluated. The readiness will be considered in the introductory activities where the lesson focus will be related to previous lessons, where attention will be on the continuity of the curriculum and the articulation of the curriculum content and experiences with other teaching units. The unit's developmental activities comprise the major portion of the teaching unit. The experiences designed for the summary and/or concluding section of the unit will serve to provide closure to what has been learned and to relate information gained with previous information and with information anticipated in future units. But, it is the unit's developmental section which comprises the majority of the students' time. Here the instructor arranges student encounters with the unit's content utilizing various educational activities and teaching methods: sharing, experimenting, listening, discussing, reporting, constructing, planning, questioning, art experiencing and producing, debating, interviewing, evaluating, demonstrating, discussing, lecturing, and inquiring.

When considering types of experiences to incorporate into a teaching unit, one attends to the environments in which such experiences will occur. Unit experiences can occur within regular classrooms, in study halls, seminar rooms, at interest centers, in laboratories, at wet carrels, in hospital wards, in industrial laboratories, and in the community. The place of learning depends upon the overall unit objective, the students' ages and experiences, the students' objectives in relation to the unit, the facilities available, the time scheduled, the monies budgeted, as well as the instructor's expertise.

Also, in this fourth step in generating the teaching unit, one contemplates available resources and selects those which address the unit's intent and the students' specific needs. One judges the materials as to their appropriateness, their feasibility of use, their availability, their cost, and their accuracy. These materials will draw on print sources, both primary (letters, documents) and secondary (books and articles), nonprint sources (films, filmstrips, pictures, graphs, charts, audio tapes, videotapes, records, slides, slide-filmstrips packets, and computer displays). The materials will allow students to learn utilizing their visual, oral and aural ways or receiving information. The materials chosen should stimulate the right and left hemispheres of the brain as should the activities in which the materials will be employed.

The fifth step in the development of the teaching unit is that of implementation. Again, the similarity of steps in creating a teaching unit with those required in creating a resource unit is evident. But, the implementation stage of the teaching unit is really ongoing formative evaluation (piloting) in which the instructor carries out continuous action research, making those modifications deemed necessary.

With the conclusion of use of the teaching unit, the instructor analyzes formative evaluation data and does a final evaluation to assess the teaching unit's value and its effectiveness with regard to unit objectives and the overall curriculum. Major modifications in the teaching unit may result from this step.

Students and the instructor should realize that even when a teaching unit is developed and taught effectively, students have not exhausted their study of the topic. All teaching units address only aspects of content. It may be that over an extended period of time, various units comprising courses will address the major points of particular content, but even then, new vistas of investigations await students' future inquiries.

Activity 13–2   *Creating a Teaching Unit*

Follow the major steps for creating a teaching unit and prepare one for a topic you have been requested to teach or a topic which you anticipate being requested to teach. Make notes as to how you process each step in the unit development.

After completing the unit, have a colleague critique it as to its components. Make any revisions you think necessary.

Now you are ready to teach the unit. Teach it! While using the unit, be sure to monitor its effectiveness with your students noting places for modifications.

After you have taught the unit, make any alterations you believe will improve it.

You are now ready for a second utilization of the unit. Note your affective reactions to the creation and use of the unit with accompanying explanations for such feelings.

After the completion of the sixth step, the instructor is ready to return to step five, the reimplementation of the teaching unit. But the reimplementation is not just teaching the unit again, but also making necessary adjustments in objectives, content, experiences, materials and environments based on interpretation of the data gathered during the unit's first teaching. Hopefully, if the teaching unit was well conceived at the outset, there will be little need for major modifications. But, it is important to remember that there always will be some necessity for certain adjustments, if for no other reason that on the unit's second teaching, one has a different student audience.

Discussion

This chapter dealt with the creation of the teaching unit, the generating of objectives, selecting and organizing of content and related learning experiences so that the unique needs, interests and goals of particular student populations can be addressed.

The nature of the unit was discussed, indicating that it resembles in structure the macro curriculum resource unit but differs from it in that the teaching unit's components are not just suggestions for use, but actual directives to be followed with a specific student group. Advantages of employing the teaching unit approach were discussed with the accompanying note that not everything that will occur in the curriculum will be drawn from a teaching unit. Unexpected events will happen, and they should have a place in the ongoing learning of students. A list of cautions was presented lest one become too zealous in defending the teaching unit and become nonreceptive to other ways to activate curriculum with specific students.

The major steps for creating a teaching unit were presented, noting the similarity of these steps to those followed in overall systematic curriculum development. Emphasis was placed on content selection and organization with attention to five organizational bases: world-related, concept-related, inquiry-related, learning-related, and utilization-related.

The excellence of the teaching unit will depend greatly upon the quality of the curriculum master plan. Such a plan requires great expenditures of time; however, this author believes the time is well spent if students not only achieve success in their learning, but also become committed to the process of learning.

References

Conley, V.C. *Curriculum and instruction in nursing.* Boston: Little, Brown, 1973.

Doll, R.C. *Curriculum improvement, decision making and process* (4th ed.). Boston: Allyn & Boston, 1978.

Gagne, R. *Conditions of learning* (2nd ed.). New York: Holt, Rinehart & Winston, 1970.

Jarvis, O.T. & Wootton, L.R. *The transitional elementary school and its curriculum.* Dubuque, Iowa: William C. Brown, 1966.

Posner, G.J., & Rudnitsky, A.M. *Course design: a guide to curriculum development for teachers.* New York: Longmans, 1978.

Ragan, W.B., & Shepherd, G.D. *Modern elementary curriculum* (5th ed.). New York: Holt, Rinehart, Winston, 1977.

Taba, H. *Curriculum development, theory and practice.* New York: Harcourt Brace & World, 1962.

PART FIVE

Confronting the Future

chapter

Present and Future

On any given day, persons charged with making curriculum decisions confront myriad situations in which some action is required or mandate made. Frequently, the need for prompt response is such that these individuals have scant time to reflect on the nature of the situation or the demand so that the underlying issue or issues can be identified. Commonly, curriculum persons in the field are concerned with obtaining adequate funds for maintaining programs, dealing with the current demands of teacher collective bargaining units, and being in compliance with various federal guidelines regarding special programs. While these concerns are important, they do not address overall macro educational issues which signify trends likely to continue into the future.

If the total field of curriculum is to respond to immediate demands made upon it, and also to react to future demands in more precise ways, then macro issues impacting upon curriculum must be identified, interpreted, and managed. Such action requires cooperation among curricularists at all levels: universities, colleges, schools, community educational institutions, regional laboratories, and education divisions within business and industry.

NEW APPROACHES TO CURRICULUM

Decision-Making

One key issue relates to attempts to make decision-making an integral part of curricular activity. This approach to curriculum represents efforts to enable functioning within the curriculum arena to be less haphazard and based more on definite principles. Persons involved in all areas and levels of education, curriculum especially, are coming to realize that even the making of a single decision is a complex process. Phi Delta Kappa (1971) has noted that this process includes four stages: (a) becoming cognizant that a decision is required, (b) generating or denoting the decision situation, (c) making a choice as to which decision is required, and (d) making the decision and engaging in the appropriate action.

Process of Decision Making

Awareness:
Identify programmed decision situations.
Identify unmet needs and unsolved problems.
Identify opportunities which could be used.

Design:
State the decision situation in question form.
Specify authority and responsibility for making the decision
Formulate decision alternatives
Specify criteria which will be employed in assessing alternatives
Determine decision rules for use in selecting an alternative
Estimate the timing of the decision

Choice:
Obtain and assess criterion information related to each decision alternative
Apply the decision rules
Reflect on the efficacy of the indicated choice
Confirm the individual choice, or reject it and recycle

Action:
Fix responsibility for implementing the chosen alternative
Operationalize the selected alternative
Reflect on the face validity of the operationalized alternative
Execute the operationalized alternative, or recycle

From Phi Delta Kappa National Study Committee on Evaluation, D.L. Stufflebeam (Chair), *Educational evaluation and decision making.* Bloomington, Ind.: Phi Delta Kappa, 1971, p. 53. Reprinted by permission.

In essence, an individual employing the process of decision-making selects from identified alternative actions a single course which eventually will be implemented. This single action avenue must be capable of accomplishing some purpose designated as worthwhile (Bross, 1953). Throughout this textbook, this process of decision-making has been addressed both directly and indirectly when elaborating on the various procedures requisite for enacting curriculum development.

The following diagram represents the expansion of the decision-making process.

FIGURE 14.1   *Expansion of the decision-making process*

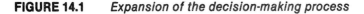
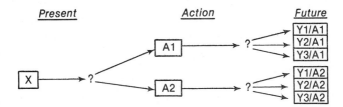

Reprinted with permission of Macmillan Publishing Co., Inc. from *Design for decision* by Irwin D.J. Bross. Copyright 1953 by Macmillan Publishing Co., Inc.

This diagram denotes particular actions possible (A1 or A2) and possible specific outcomes Y1, Y2, or Y3 in light of specific actions. The diagram is not presented as X——————▸A——————▸Y which would denote a strict causal chain. Rather it shows divergent futures which can be assigned probabilities of occurrence. The diagram above shows a probability chain.

Although information on decisions and decision theory is not a new discovery, it is rather recent to those of us in curriculum now beginning to employ decision models in our deliberations. We are coming to realize that there are means by which we can assure some consistency to our decisions and can monitor our deliberation processes.

The following diagram gives an overview of the decision-making process.

FIGURE 14.2   *Overview of the decision-making process*

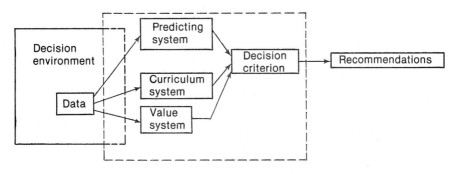

The decision environment, called a decision setting (Phi Delta Kappa, 1971) refers to the total set of environmental circumstances that will influence both analysis and choice. Data are obtained and fed into a predicting system which will generate possible outcomes and their probabilities for each action. Data fed into the curriculum system relate to information regarding the current constraints of the environment and their impact upon the various curricular components. The value system accepts data and interprets them on the basis of specified norms. From activation of this system, one obtains the desirability of "value" of possible actions and attendant outcomes. Up to this point, one has gone through the awareness and design stage of decision-making. The decision criterion is when we activate the choice stage. The recommendations refer to the final action stage of addressing the issue at hand.

As noted previously decision-making occurs within particular settings, and the nature of the settings can influence the process. The Phi Delta Kappa Study Committee on Evaluation presented a useful figure dealing with four types of decision settings or environments.

TABLE 14.1   *Decision-making settings*

High **I** **N** **F** **O** **R** **M** **A** **T** **I** **O** **N** **Low**	**Homeostasis** Activity: Restorative Purpose: Maintenance Basis: Technical standards and quality control ------------------------ **Incrementalism** Activity: Developmental Purpose: Continuous Improvement Basis: Expert judgment plus structured inquiry	**Metamorphism** Activity: Utopian Purpose: Complete Change Basis: Overarching theory ------------------------ **Neomobilism** Activity: Innovative Purpose: Inventing, testing, and diffusion solutions to significant problems Basis: Conceptualization, heuristic investigation, and structured inquiry
Small	DEGREE OF CHANGE	Large

From Phi Delta Kappa National Study Committee on Evaluation, D.L. Stufflebeam (Chair), *Educational evaluation and decision making.* Bloomington, Ind.: Phi Delta Kappa, 1971, p. 62. Reprinted by permission.

The type of activity as well as its purpose is influenced by the nature of the setting, the framefactors mentioned earlier in this textbook. The type of setting would be noted at the outset of curriculum development during situation analysis. Those readers wishing added information on this model are urged to read Phi Delta Kappa (1971).

Research and Development

Research and development activity within the educational field received a major impetus in the early 1960's when the federal government provided large grants for the establishment of Research and Development (R&D) centers. Zais (1976) drawing on the work of Chase, indicated that these R&D centers were established on the basis of five major premises: (a) such centers could perform functions either neglected or poorly performed by other educational institutions; (b) R&D centers would initiate activities that would result in specific products and processes that would enable the attainment of specific curriculum goals or solution of particular curriculum difficulties; (c) such centers would conduct research that would generate information of immediate use to the curriculum practitioner; (d) such centers would bring together cadres of individuals well qualified to work on specific problems over extended periods of time; and (e) the expenditure of public monies for such centers would be justified for they would enact evaluation procedures that would hold them accountable for their actions while allowing them flexibility in addressing educational problems.

Curricularists at universities, in schools, and in training programs for various businesses have become aware of these R&D centers and their work. Also, the literature has discussed the procedures these centers have used (Schaffarzick & Hampson, 1975). The activities of these centers plus the dialogue extant within the field regarding research and development plus the mounting demands by both government and public sectors for heightened precision and more accountability in education all have caused current curricularists to realize that the days of just drawing one's program from a commercially published textbook series or vaguely explaining educational actions are passing, if not already past.

Problems identified in the late 1960's regarding methods of education, procedures of curriculum development, approaches to curriculum organization, appropriateness of particular types of curriculum for certain student populations as well as various theoretical and philosophical issues have not been solved. But by the late 1970's, these problems and issues had become more widely recognized and directions for further research and analysis noted.

Curricularists, researchers, theoreticians, and practitioners alike, are coming to realize that the arena in which curriculum functions is highly dynamic. It is likely that there will be no single educational source or variable that will be identified, at least not in the near future, as being the prime influence upon students' learnings of content, skills, and attitudes. Some researchers are advocating that rather than looking for main effects in our research, we should attempt to seek out significant interactions extant among variables.

Increasing numbers of curricularists are realizing that curriculum activity not only means creating a program and implementing it with some type of evaluation, but also advancing the knowledge within the curriculum field. In many cases, curriculum practitioners will be teaming with curriculum theoreticians and researchers to address questions requiring responses. McNeal (1977) discusses four specific types of inquiry likely to be pursued by such curriculum teams. The first type is comprehensive curriculum inquiry, addressing five questions.

1. What major features characterize a particular curriculum?
2. What impacts on individuals in particular and societies in general result from enactment of a specific curriculum?
3. What explanations can explain the stability and change in curriculum features?

4. What explanations can furnish curricularists with insights as to how people judge the merit or worth of various curricular features?
5. What ought to characterize curricula intended for particular students in specific situations? (Walker, 1974)

The first four questions can be addressed using various empirical research methodologies, but the final question requires a response from a philosophical or normative stance.

The second major type of curriculum inquiry advanced by McNeal is synoptic activity. Most curricularists would agree that the field of curriculum is broad drawing on a multitude of widely separated fields. An issue facing us is to synthesize a common area from these myriad fields. Our future energies may not be in discovering new knowledge, but rather in melding findings of other disciplines into clusters meaningful to the realm of curriculum. This issue would have us draw knowledge relevant to curriculum from the fields of systems theory, organization theory, decision theory, planning theory, sociology, psychology, philosophy, and political sciences.

The curriculum development approach advanced in this book commenced with curriculum conceptualization and legitimization. McNeal notes that the third major type of curriculum inquiry is that of conceptualization. We require concentrated efforts to identify curricular phenomena in order to conceptualize more clearly the nature of curriculum and all those actions extant within the curriculum arena. Research in this realm will involve us in activities through which we can generate curriculum theory.

Research is not a major project that is conceived, funded, carried out, and then forgotten. Rather research, especially curriculum inquiry, should be ongoing and conducted by individuals representing all levels and fields of curriculum activity. The final major type of curriculum inquiry noted by McNeal is that of action research. Attention to action research is not of recent birth. Taba throughout her career noted the need for action research and many of the curriculum development projects in which she was involved had teachers engaged in such action. However, the thrust for action research lessened somewhat with the empirical thrust of the 1960's. The push for R & D discounted local efforts at curriculum development and research. Also, action research was reduced in importance, for university curriculum experts in the 1960's became involved in the national projects to the neglect of local curriculum efforts. Also, the R & D efforts caused many in the curriculum field to believe that solutions to the problems of educational programs only would result from research activities that would furnish generalizable conclusions. Action research was situation specific and counter to this thinking.

However, in the late 1970's a shift in the research and development posture revealed that both action research and empirical research had value at the local level. This adjustment in thinking was due in part to curricularists realizing that current curricular issues can best be solved by individuals at all levels of curriculum activity working in concert. This even includes students. Additionally, curricularists are coming to recognize individuals from the community as valuable theorists and researchers in their own right. Also, the late 1970's experienced a shift from curriculum development from colleges and laboratories to the local school arena. This has required drawing the research and development team from the local school or educational institution.

New Areas for Research

As part of the increasing research and development posture among curricularists and educators in general is a realization that investigative efforts should generate different heuristic questions and seek new areas for curricular inquiries. The following list denotes some areas to which curriculum researchers might attend:

1. The economics of curriculum activity;
2. The sociology of curriculum activity;
3. The philosophy and politics of curriculum activity;
4. The geography of curriculum activity centering on learning environments. (This relates to research focusing on environmental psychology and its impact upon curriculum activity.)

Having an inquiry posture will allow us to ask particular questions and hopefully to further our understanding of curriculum. We still have many questions unanswered or only partially answered. How can we utilize the school facility for optimizing student learning? Are there special learning environments requisite for learning concepts specific to particular knowledge realms? How much time do students require to learn certain content areas? How should certain curricula be sequenced to maximize student learning? Who should be involved in the development, implementation and teaching of various curriculum areas? What roles should teachers play, and should they play their roles alone, in concert with other professionals, and/or with persons from the lay community?

New Realms of Knowledge

Participants at all levels of curricular activity are coming to realize that the decisions demanded of them require more than just a content expertise, a general comprehension of society, and some knowledge of learning theory. In investigating the curriculum arena, we are making palpable other areas of requisite knowledge: environmental psychology, systems theory, planning theory, decision theory, organizational development, humanistic theory. Some curriculum theory is drawing on humanistic theory which garners support from existentialism and even psychoanalysis. Even with the "traditional" realms of curricular knowledge (disciplined knowledge, learning, and society), we need to contend with an explosion of knowledge.

To discuss all these new knowledge realms, even superficially, is beyond the scope of this book. However, attending to a few will allow us to realize that new realms of knowledge are indeed making some major impacts within the curriculum arena.

Systems, System/s Analysis

Systems, in general, deals with the realm of systems and their characteristics and behaviors. It influences educational and thus curricular decision-making via systems and or system analysis.

Read (1974) defines systems analysis as:

> a quantitative approach to decision making that seeks to offer the decision maker a set of alternative solutions representing a variety of costs and benefits. Its procedures include six major elements: 1) the objectives, 2) data, 3) alternative solutions, 4) costs and benefits, 5) models, and 6) the decision rule. (p. 39)

Read distinguishes between system analysis (plural) and system analysis (singular) revealing that the former analysis is complex and sophisticated utilizing mathematical models and statistical decision-making, while the latter analysis does not employ such models or procedures, at least not to the same degree.

System analysis can be considered as:

> a designing process which is used to build "from scratch" a single system for implementing one of several alternative solution strategies that meets previously established performance requirements. System analysis is an approach to problem solving that begins with a need assessment and moves systematically to define the problem and the objective, specify the requirements of a solution, identify alternative solutions and finally, design a single system for meeting the requirements of a solution. (Read, 1974, p. 36)

In reading the above definition, it becomes evident that the approach to systematic curriculum development is essentially a system (singular) analysis approach. However, there are various junctures in the approach in which systems analysis (plural) might be employed such as analyzing the cost benefits and educational benefits of alternative program solutions.

Whether one follows the system approach, the systems approach or a meld of both, knowledge of the nature of systems is requisite for curricular development. Kaufman (1972) has defined system as "the sum total of parts working independently and working together to achieve required results or outcomes, based upon needs" (p. 8).

Banathy notes that a system embodies three main features: goals, functions, and components. It exists in space or in conceptual reality for the purpose of allowing the system to achieve certain goals. The system is comprised of certain components capable of accomplishing specific functions requisite for attaining noted goals. These components are integrated to foster particular types of relationships thus creating a system that assures or increases the probability that the organization will achieve certain goals. All components of a system have a degree of interdependence. Any component that develops total independence from the other system components is no longer part of the system. If all components of a system become independent, the system ceases to exist.

All systems are units characterized by defined boundaries and an array of interrelated parts. Usually, systems are represented by various models, frequently graphic as presented in much of this book. In considering the model of a system, one addresses the entities contained within the model. One observes the space the stystem occupies; attends to the environment (or suprasystem) and its component entities; considers the system and related subsystems; indicates the location of the system's boundaries and where breaks exist in the boundaries through which inputs and outputs enter and exit the system.

Systems entities have attributes and states. One can describe systems and their component parts as open, closed, controlled, self-regulating, adaptive, random, and stable. These states suggest relationships that emerge from the interaction of such entities. The principles of interrelatedness, adjustment, dependence, interdependence, feedback relate to the nature of these relationships. These relationships also can be considered as hierarchical, centralized and equalitarian. The centralized arrangement for curriculum development is hierarchical while the "grass roots" approach to curriculum involving teachers and all parties affected by curriculum decisions is "equalitarian."

One understands the nature of a system by analyzing what the system does—its functions. Certain functions are common to all systems (general system functions) while other functions are unique to certain organizations (specific-to-the-system functions) (Banathy, 1973). Throughout this book, the general system functions of input, output, and feedback and adjustment have been discussed and presented. Another general function, discussed but not named specifically in this book, is transformation. This function is analogous to production, to the processing of the input resulting in a specific type or types of output. In essence, the total process of curriculum development is a series of transformation functions. Another general function that accompanies transformation is information transmission often discussed as communication. All systems have a general function called systemization—all those actions and energies exerted upon the organization's components to make them more related and interdependent, more system-like.

Employing systems concepts and the system (systems) approach is not limiting. This approach, while serving as the framework for directing action within the curriculum arena, allows one to introduce a variety of methods into curricular action. Case studies, surveys, questionnaires, views of myriad groups of persons affected by and interested in curriculum, and tasks forces all can be utilized in curriculum development.

Activity 14–1   *Describing One's Educational Institution as a System*

Consider the educational institution of which you are a part and describe its major components and the function of each. How would you characterize your educational institution as a system—open, closed, controlled, self-regulating, random, stable, or some combination of these? Are the relationships extant within the system hierarchical, centralized, or equalitarian?

Geographically display the system and share the model with some colleagues. Does your model need modification?

Curriculum as Theater

How can we conceptualize curricular action? What are useful metaphors to direct our thinking regarding educational matters? Grumet (1978) in the late 1970's advanced the metaphor of curriculum as theater. In her discussion she draws not only on theater but also on critical theory and phenomenology. To her view, curriculum is not the world, just as characters in a play are not the person, and the rules are not the game. What is real are the student's experiences of these forms, the student's encounters with curricular components. It is the meaning derived from such encounters that is real; this is what the student gains—his portion of reality.

In developing her metaphor, Grumet draws on psychoanalysis to explain the action that occurs in the theater. The actor suspends action for a time to gain time to investigate the concrete situation that is the content for the action. Here an individual takes the time to examine his or her response to action, to assess his or her feelings and to move through a chosen action. For the curriculum scholar and practitioner alike, the crucial point is not whether Grumet has a valid thesis, but the fact that she and others are turning to non-traditional knowledge realms in attempts to interpret curriculum more meaningfully.

Curriculum Theory

Throughout the decade of the seventies, curricularists discussed the topic of curriculum theory. Some argued that we had no curriculum theory, while others postulated its presence. Some indicated that curriculum theorizing is moribund while others placed it in a natural history stage of development (Beauchamp, 1975). Woven into this discussion of curriculum theory, which most likely will continue, is consideration of scientific theory as opposed to philosophical theory. It is not likely that the issues will be resolved, but for persons involved in the curriculum "theater," there is a need to be cognizant of and knowledgeable in the discussions.

Pinar (1975) notes that in reality curriculum theorists can be divided into two categories: the soft and the hard. These categories, while perhaps not ideal, do allow us a way by which we can classify persons in curriculum. Of course, grouping persons is risky for we rarely have sufficient data to make such classifications totally accurate. However, the soft curriculum theorists are drawing their arguments and inspiration from the humanities: history, religion, philosophy, literature, and criticism rather than from the hard sciences. Grumet is an example of a soft theorist drawing much of her inspiration from drama and philosophy. The hard curricularist are those who draw extensively on the sciences employing empirical data to justify means and possessing a consistent philosophical position for validating various ends. Curriculum persons now and in the future most likely will need full memberhship in both "hard and soft" curriculum theory camps.

The Politicization of Curriculum Process

Anyone connected, however remotely, with curriculum realizes that there are legions of pressure groups jockeying for ways to get schools to attend to this or that, to emphasize this or that, to exclude this or that. Not only must curriculum decision-makers respond, but they must, to a great degree, referee the conflicts that result when community pressure groups vie for those key positions for influencing program development.

Few curriculum persons today are unaware of the effectiveness of pressure groups. These groups engage in lobbying, bargaining, exerting economic pressure, promoting various legislation, and organizing demonstrations to make their pleasures and displeasures known to curriculum persons.

The power of various pressure groups in influencing curriculum action is made poignantly clear by Koerner (1968).

> Suppose a local board aware of the obsolescence and flaccidity of much that passes for vocation training . . . decides to reduce its program in these areas. In theory, this is one of its sovereign rights. In practice several things occur to change its mind. First, the vocational educational lobby goes to work on other members of local government and on the state legislature or state department of education to protect the extensive interests of vocational education . . . teachers. Second, the regional accrediting association comes to the aid of the status quo and makes threatening noises, suggesting and then perhaps demanding, on pain of disaccreditation . . . that the board rescind its decision. Third the NEA state affiliate "investigates" and through its considerable power "persuades" the board to a different view. (pp. 126–127)

The above quote graphically depicts the complexity of setting educational policy and making decisions that relate to particular curriculum situations. It is evident that various levels of government are involved and numerous quasi legal agencies participate. Also manifest from the above quote is that teachers are active not only in enhancing program direction within the school but also in preventing certain directions and actions from occurring. Teachers, administrators, supervisors, and curriculum persons are not passive observers. There is much struggling for those leverage points that will influence the final curriculum decision or board or department action. Also impacting upon curriculum action are the inputs of various celebrities, journalists and spokespersons for various offices of government (Kirst & Walker, 1971).

If one is dealing with curriculum in professional schools such as the health sciences and law, one also has to contend with the professional associations such as the American Medical Association and the American Bar Association in hammering out curricula that will meet the specific goals of preparing professionals for these particular fields. (Note: The reader may wish to reread chapter 5 dealing with participants involved in curriculum decision-making and action.)

Officially, government, both at the state and national level is getting into curriculum development. The federal funding of programs in bilingual and multicultural education certainly set the parameters for the resultant programs and even directed the manner in which such programs would be developed, maintained, and evaluated. In the late seventies many states had defined in law basic education, leaving local schools with only the responsibility of developing the program and maintaining it in a way that assured compliance with the curriculum model defined by the legislature.

Political action is an integral part of curriculum performance. The wise curricularist realizes that increased political activity by all members within the curriculum arena is likely to continue. Thus, parallel with curriculum development strategies will be political strategies for dealing with individuals and with groups.

Activity 14–2   *Being a Political Anthropologist*

All curricular action has political aspects to it. Focus on some program development, implementation, maintenance or evaluation activity and describe the political activities that were undertaken by all parties involved.

Generate a descriptive generalization (statement) regarding the particular politics present in your educational institution.

FUTURISTICS—GUIDE FOR CURRICULUM

> It hardly seems likely that futurism is a passing vogue. It seems more likely that the increasing concern for the future and attempts to predict it are an expression of man's increasing urge to exert some amount of control over his future, more to "proact" to it and less simply to react (Lonsdale, 1971, p. 9)

By their very nature curricular activities are future oriented representing concerted systematic efforts to prepare for some future time, however near at hand, a program that will address students' needs. The field of futuristics, a new realm of knowledge organization, holds much promise for curricularists.

A key reason for the appropriateness of this new field is that the major constant of our times is its inconstancy, its dynamics, its continual change. In such times, program planners realize a need to exercise some degree of control over the future.

Futurism, which increasingly is becoming a recognized field of scholarship, is a systematic attempt to meld creative forecasting, planning, and action. Those engaged in this new field, and curriculum leaders should be among them, are focusing their energies on the study and development of alternative futures and generating supporting scenarios elaborating on specific areas of societies or institutions. These professionals are then drawing from these projected tentative futures, significant variables likely to influence envents or persons' behaviors and then via deduction describing the kinds of educational programs that have a high probability of meeting the projected conditions. The curriculum futurist then enacts both short and long-range plans by which the data gathered in future study are translated into curricula (Lonsdale & Ohm, 1971).

Educational futurism can enable us to proact rather than to react. Hack (1971) has noted that educators most often react to events impacting upon the school and its programs: teacher militancy, federal funding, national assessment, public demands. Currently, persons charged with program development are being held responsible for assuring that the curriculum deals in some effective fashion with the public concern for ecology, various types of pollution, overpopulation, race relations, values. Often educators are presented with an untenable problem, for most do not know how to influence the future or modify public or client demands to more manageable dimensions or more in line with the accepted purposes of the educational institution.

The key question of curriculum is still, What knowledge is of most worth? But in a time of flux, or rapid and constant diversification it is most difficult to respond to such a query. Also, the query has to be modified to, What knowledge is of most worth to which groups in the population at this time? In times of instability, curriculum persons have difficulty in responding with precision. The issue of relevancy of content and experiences is paramount. What is relevant to a particular group at a certain point in time, may indeed be irrelevant or injurious to the same group at a future stage. Students making demands for relevant curriculum must be informed as to the long-term as well as short-term relevancy of the content they are requesting. To deal with relevancy requires anticipating future content appropriateness and functionality— it requires having some means of making projections of what will be needed. This necessitates a somewhat clear perception of the future or possible futures.

The curriculum person interested in futurism or futuristics realizes that this is a new field and that the study and application of this realm is quite idiosyncratic. Futures and ways of dealing with the future will be determined in large part by the perceptions individuals hold of the future and how they anticipate acting within the projected times. The future procedures available for use must be recognized as having a developmental character. Thus one should broach these methods with a posture of tentativeness realizing that modification and updating will be required.

But, curricularists who deal with futuristics must accept and apprehend the concept of alternative futures and the notion that futures can be managed in the sense that certain actions can be initiated that are likely to increase the probabilities that particular events will occur and that other actions can diminish the probability of other events arising. If the future seems to suggest that the majority of society will possess a conservative frame of reference, and curricularists and other educators consider such a posture inappropriate for a shrinking world, then there are means by which the public can be educated to accept a more liberal or perhaps more global frame of reference. If our current rates of certain resource utilization indicate resource depletion in the near future, there are actions that educators can take to get students and future adults to contemplate wise and different uses of such resources. We ought not to sit back and present curricula that reports that we will run out and then wait for the event to occur.

Curricular futurists can diminish their reliance on ruminating about the future as a linear projection of the past. The future may not be the present with its problems solved; it may be a time unrecognizable. Furthermore, the future may not be singular; it may contain myriad futures simultaneously occurring. We can have social futures, economic futures, religious futures, political futures and futures that meld these several major aspects of our existence. It is quite probable that futurists concerned with curriculum will have to learn the tactics for unlearning as well as for new learning in order to grapple with projected futures.

But futurists are confronted with a taxonomical problem of how to arrange wide-ranging predictions or composites of predictions. How shall one classify data such that one can describe the future meaningfully? Bell (1967) provides help in classifying society according to four sources of change: growth of technology, increased diffusion of goods and services, developments in the structures of society, and new relationships between the United States and the world.

Presently, the world seems to be moving in the direction of becoming increasingly empirical, worldly, secular, humanistic, pragmatic, utilitarian, contractual, epicurean or hedonistic. In a sense, the humanistic movement is one emphasizing "doing your own thing." Some persons enamoured with this movement are becoming self-centered, concerned solely with their positive self-images, their increased pleasures.

Bell also notes that we are in the process of forming bourgeois, bureaucratic, meritocratic, democratic, elites. More and more decisions are being made by clusters of highly qualified individuals. Paralleling this move is the increasing accumulation of scientific and technological knowledge that leaves many areas of decision-making beyond the scope and participation of many people.

Bell indicates that we have the institutionalization of change especially relating to research, development, innovation, and diffusion. The wise curriculum person confronted with preparing programs appropriate for the now and the future realizes that we are experiencing worldwide industrialization and modernization, increasing affluence among people, unprecedented population growth, global urbanization, diminishing of valuable agricultural lands, decreasing importance of primary and secondary occupations, the rise in world literacy and educational levels, and the increasing capability for mass destruction (Bell, 1967).

Procedures for Managing the Future

A curriculum futurist not only requires different concepts of the future, but also techniques for actually forecasting the future. Joseph (1974), in discussing futurist methods, notes that the phrase "forecasting the future" appears contradictory, for it seems to suggest that one invents future inventions prior to their conceptions by the inventors. But, despite this seeming contradiction, there have been several powerful forecasting tools created in the latter half of this century. The question is not what will happen, but rather what futures seem to have the greatest benefit for individuals and should be selected and encouraged into reality.

But, curricularists envisioning alternative futures to which curricula should respond need to realize that they cannot design and move toward a desirable educational era without contemplating the areas of society and projecting their developments. Joseph calls forecasting the window through which one can survey potential happenings. Through our glances through such windows we can get direction as to what to avoid, what to modify, and toward what we shall strive. The task is easier when we make short-range forecasts noting what the program will be next month, or at the end of this year than when we forecast for next year, or this decade or the next century. However, it has been found that our short-range forecasts seem to be too optimistic, our mid-range forecasts too pessimistic, and our long-range forecasts too inaccurate.

One can accept the concept of forecasting, but still be unclear as to how the future can be forecast. It is important to distinguish between predictions and forecasts. Predictions are statements about occurrences that are to happen in a specific future. Forecasting tells us not what *will happen,* but rather what *can* happen if certain conditions or certain events occur or continue to happen. Currently, we possess powerful techniques for making forecasts, but not for making predictions. The accuracy and inclusiveness of our forecasts depends upon the data we feed into our deliberations, the systems of logic we apply, the diversity of the techniques we utilize, and the energies we expend (Joseph).

Joseph has provided a useful overview of the major approaches to forecasting. Some of these are presented below:

Exploratory forecasting. This is a procedure for discovering possible capabilities, changes, opportunities, and problems of the future. Attention is given to identifying likely futures. Often such forecasting is an expansion of various trends that have been identified.

Normative forecasting. In such forecasting one attends to discovering various goals or norms for the future. One might actually set certain norms for the future and invent a time congruent with the norms delineated. In curriculum development, one would identify norms appropriate for future citizens and then build a program to achieve such norms.

Forecasting via modeling/simulation. In using this technique, the future is generated via activation of models of known physical, social, and environmental natural laws and how they most likely will impact on the future.

Trend forecasting. Here, individuals extrapolate trends from the analysis of the past to discover the directions and paths along which certain futures likely will evolve.

Intuitive forecasting. This procedure is something we all can do. It relates to the images, "feelings" we possess about the future. These perceptions of what is to come influence our decisions and actions which results in many of our views becoming reality. If one forecasts that it is likely that he or she will have a boat, then the resultant decision and actions (perhaps increasing one's monthly savings) actually brings the future into reality. Here we are using our intuition as a forecasting tool.

Trend extrapolation forecasting. With this procedure, one plots, using mathematics, the path of his/her discovered curves and extends them into the future. In such forecasting, one assumes that the rate of change noted in past and present happenings will continue uninterrupted into the future. This frequently is not the case, but nevertheless most forecasting commences with such trend extrapolation.

Delphi forecasting. This is, along with brainstorming, perhaps the most well-known futures procedures. It consists of a process for extracting "expert" intuitive expectations regarding the future and then after such a polling, furnishing the "experts" with the results. This process is repeated several times—three seems to be the recommended number—until the "experts" achieve consensus of opinion regarding the future.

Scenario forecasting. This procedure, also quite well known to the public, involves creating a story or description about the future. The story must draw on current happenings and likely trends. Often it notes how one can go from the present reality to some possible period. The manner of presentation is such that nonexperts can obtain a good view of the future without being inundated with technical language, mathematical models or detailed charts and graphs. In a real sense, scenario writing puts into prose form innovative, imaginative, and plausible utopias for people to contemplate.

Force analysis forecasting. In this procedure, the forces (sets of events, pressures, problems, social events) are noted, analyzed, and their probable future impact upon a particular area or event listed.

The above list does not exhaust the forecasting procedures available for the curriculum decision-maker. Those involved in forecasting future curricula can combine the conventional techniques of research and planning with the futuristic methods available.

Redefining Roles

Systematic curriculum action and related futuristic activities will require new roles of all participants in education. To meet these new roles, educators will have to possess extensive content backgrounds; educators will need to be interdisciplinarians. Presently, some studies of curriculum activity indicate that teachers are not oriented toward developing new curricula or becoming involved in futuristics. Frequently, teachers plan for their classes and conduct their lessons in a fashion that differs widely from the conceptions of the curriculum writers and developers (Kirst & Walker, 1971). Even some curriculum leaders are not oriented toward systematic curriculum development, believing that the best way to create programs is to wait for demands from the public and then respond in a "broken front" attack addressing program "bits."

Many of the points made in this book imply that educators are or can become willing and expert in assuming myriad roles, some quite different

Activity 14–3   *Forecasting the Educational Future*

Perceiving tomorrow to make ready for it and to, in fact, create it is necessary for the curricularist. Most likely systematically designed schools of the future will be strikingly different from the current educational institutions.

Engage in brainstorming either alone or with colleagues about ways in which the school and its curriculum will be different in 1985, 1995, 2005, 2015. List each way on a sheet and share it with colleagues.

The following data chart can be useful in this exercise.

Specifics in

The School	1985	1995	2005	2115
Curriculum				
content				
methods/				
experiences				
environments				
Materials				
Students				
Staff				
Schedules				
Community				
relations				
Funding				
Policy				

Drawing on data in the above chart, write a scenario of the typical school in 1995. Share this scenario with other colleagues. Is your future probable and worth assuring by current behaviors on your part? Specify what you might do to increase the likelihood of your educational future actually occurring.

from existing ones. These roles require new knowledge in areas rather novel for educators: change, futuristics, educational sociology, educational anthropology, group dynamics. Accepting such roles should allow educators to address current issues and anticipate and manage future ones.

> The future has always been and always will be the universal frontier. Futurism provides the means for probing that frontier so that we can not only prepare for what lies ahead but also try to determine the shape of things to come. (Lonsdale & Ohm, 1971)

CHALLENGES TO EDUCATION

> Educational experience is a process that takes on the world without appropriating that world, that projects the self into the world without dismembering that self, a process of synthesis and totalization in which all the participants in the dialectic simultaneously maintain their identities and surpass themselves (Pinar & Grumet, 1976).

Activity 14—4   *Life in the Post-Industrial Society—Implications for Curricularists*

The United States has been described as having passed through the industrial stage and entered a post industrial era. Currently, many futurist writers are making projections regarding the impact of events and discoveries that have just happened or are likely to come about on the education of individuals.

Acquaint yourself with some of these events/discoveries. Note what effect they will have on the programs in educational institutions and the manner in which curricularists will have to or should respond.

Event/discovery	Impact on Curriculum	Response by curricularists
1. _____	_____	_____
2. _____	_____	_____
n _____	_____	_____

A post industrial society is one in which the problems of production have been solved and the consumption of products widespread. Thus, the organizations and institutions concerned primarily with production of goods will cease to be the prime movers of the society. The key mover will be in the service industries and the intellectual institutions will supplant the business firm as the major new institution in society (Lonsdale, 1971).

The major challenge for the curriculum leader is to develop, implement, and maintain a program or series of programs that will allow individuals to take on the world and project themselves into that world for the purpose of gaining knowledge, even wisdom, while coming to a fuller understanding of themselves and triggering in themselves a continuous extension of their capabilities and individuality.

This is a continuous challenge. Creative curriculum development will cease if those of us involved in program creation believe that we have discovered the appropriate curriculum for all times. In reality, there will be the continuous grappling with the concept of curriculum extending from a narrow listing of courses to a global presentation of an existential experience.

The school's purpose will require a multitude of answers from time to time. Presently, its purpose is varied, influenced by individuals' philosophies of life and ideological views. In the late seventies there were striking differences of opinion regarding not only the school's purposes, but also what was wrong with the schools. Some persons indicated that education should be concerned now and into the foreseeable future with the furnishing of individuals with substantive information. Others exhorted educators to provide experiences that would free the spirit (Pinar & Grumet, 1976). And, as noted in the quotation beginning this section, some believed that the school should provide for both knowledge acquisition and the freeing of the spirit through greater self-understanding.

Such ideological stances fostered the creation of free and open schools as opposed to traditional schools. In the late seventies two dominant themes were woven into the educational literature: back to the basics for the foundations for effective functioning in society, and humanism for the emancipation of human spirit and heightened concern for all humanity. Along with these ideological arguments were diverse exhortations from educators and lay persons alike ranging from, "Curricula should be carefully planned," to "Curricula should arise spontaneously from the mix of persons and materials within the school environment."

Broudy and Palmer (1965) stated quite eloquently the view for some careful planning regarding curriculum.

> A technically sophisticated society simply does not dare leave the acquisition of systematic knowledge to concomitant learning, and to the by-products of projects that are themselves wholesome slices of juvenile life. Intelligence without systematized knowledge will do only for the most ordinary, everyday problems. International amity, survival in our atomic age, automation, racial integration, are not common everyday problems to which commonsense knowledge and a sense of decency are adequate. (p. 126)

Curriculum persons, regardless of whether they believe in careful planning or serendipity in education will always confront the question of how to create or encourage curricula responsive to the needs of diverse students. The issue will require deliberation regarding the distinctions between education and training. Allied with this will be the matter of whom to involve in creating such curricula. Certainly educators will have to be knowledgeable of curriculum and the means for creating it and managing it. Curricularists also will confront the dispute of whether to approach the involvement of persons in curriculum from a democratic or autocratic posture. This author would favor the democratic approach, but this means optimal involvement of persons rather than total involvement. But, successfully involving various individuals in the curriculum process requires of the curricularist knowledge of human dynamics and the various social groups from which individuals come.

Working with diverse groups both within the school and the community requires collaborating across barriers (Berman & Roderick, 1977). Curricularists and educators in general will have to work with individuals from a wide range of social and occupational backgrounds. And, we honestly will have to respect these persons and be accepting of many of their ways. As Berman and Roderick note, such collaborating will be characterized by the sharing of mutual interests, concerns, and meeting common responsibilities. The crucial task to those in curriculum is to establish the vehicles that will foster and encourage such cooperation and assure that communication is current and valid regarding all members' concerns. Collaboration should be effective if all persons involved are systematically encouraged to cooperate and if all persons realize that the school can manage diverse approaches to meeting the legions of needs expressed (Berman & Roderick).

Challenge of Knowledge

The ubiquitous knowledge explosion will continue. The question of what information is of most worth will become even more crucial as we attempt to select from the total wealth of available teachable knowledge that which will be most optimal for students in their formal schooling. Constantly, we will have to balance curricular experiences common for students with program experiences designed for the total diversity of students' interests and capabilities.

How we process this central question will be influenced by our knowledge of present society and our forecasts as to likely futures. Havighurst (1978) noted that those involved in curriculum need to analyze present and future society in order to select useful knowledge and design appropriate curricula. He notes four basic propositions for curriculum in what he and others term a post-industrial society: (a) the curriculum should emphasize the structure of knowledge rather than isolated bits of information; (b) the curriculum should be organized so that democratic cultural pluralism is supported, (c) the curriculum should be orchestrated so that students share some common knowledge useful in a post-industrial society, and (d) the curriculum must assure that students study and process civic experiences that will develop the individuals' abilities to lead a diverse number of effective lifestyles.

Not only must knowledge be selected, it must be arranged. The architectonics of knowledge will continually be part of educational dialogue. Different structures will be suggested as we learn more about the realm of knowledge and phenomenology. Curriculum persons will have to comprehend the latest in thinking regarding knowledge and also discover and document ways in which knowledge can be incorporated into curricular designs. Furthermore, curricularists will be tested to discover ways to fit curriculum programs into school building environments. Related challenges will exist with regard to selecting instructional methodologies that will optimize students' learnings. Also, we will be tested as to the means by which we will evaluate the effectiveness of our programs.

Challenges Relating to Curriculum Theory

Theory or theoretical propositions, whether drawn from scientific activities or philosophical disputation, are the underpinnings of curricular activity. In the late seventies, many in curriculum were advancing the thesis that we in curriculum had little, if any, theory. Others were disputing the value of scientific curriculum theory exhorting individuals to develop a total reliance of philosophical "theory" to support curricular actions. The task for the future, both short and long-range, is to continue to investigate the issue of curriculum theory and the search for theory, both scientific and philosophical, to provide ourselves with paradigms for better understanding curriculum development.

In the late 1970's there was a loss of faith by some in the logic of systems to solve curriculum problems. However, there were others, including this author, who believed that one could be logical, scientific, and philosophical when facing issues within the curriculum field. The challenge is not to reject logic, or systematic curriculum development, but to maintain an inquiry posture that will allow us to continue as students of curriculum as well as designers and implementors of it. We are called to furnish for our own direction and the direction of others new metaphors for conceptualizing curriculum and curricular action.

Challenge of Dealing with the Future

Proposition: If there is a commitment to planned change, the curriculum development process will become responsive to dynamic and futuristic technological and social developments. (Unruh, 1975, p. 181)

It has been proposed throughout this book that commitment to planned change will allow one to deal with the present, to understand it, and to anticipate and even manage the future so that programs generated will address the immediate and the distant needs of students not only in the practical sense of application to job situations, but in the humanistic sense of allowing persons to apprehend and appreciate their realities, and to realize their individual and group uniqueness within these realities.

Systematic curriculum development should allow us to draw on our religious, philosophical, political, economic, scientific, cultural and social orientations in allowing individuals to develop independence, autonomy, and self-reliance coupled with interdependence, collectivism and reliance (Buchen, 1974).

All of the challenges presented in this chapter are future-oriented.

All education springs from some image of the future. If the image of the future held by a society is grossly inaccurate, its education system will betray its youth. (Toffler, 1974, p. 3)

The challenges facing those involved in curriculum are not problems to be addressed by a select few. As Toffler points out, no educational institution today can address the challenges placed upon it until all its membership, including students, subject their views of the future and related challenges to critical analysis.

Accepting this caveat does not mean that we will be assured of total and constant accuracy in noting what requires our immediate and future attention. The proper orientations of our attention are most difficult for there is not just one future, but many, and these futures are not static but dynamic.

Thus to design educational systems for tomorrow (or even today) we need not images of a future frozen in amber, as it were, but something far more complicated: sets of images of successive and alternative futures, each one tentative and different from the next. (Toffler, p. 5)

All persons involved in curriculum development face hazards that can diminish the effectiveness of their actions and the resulting curricula. Our images of the future may be off center for trends perceived in the present scene may be inaccurately documented or if correct may not develop in a simple linear fashion. We deal in approximations. We approximate what the student body will be like in our plans; we estimate the likely needs of these students and the nature of available knowledge; we suggest with qualifications the inventions and discoveries that will be useful to educational designers and implementors.

Curriculum specialists involved in systematic curriculum development plus specialists in specific curriculum knowledge fields face an excess of choice. Indeed, one of our difficulties is avoiding becoming paralyzed with the plethora of knowledge choices for responding to the diversity or present and anticipated societies. Systematic curriculum development is a means by which we can process the realities of knowledge and the national and world scenes so that the curricula offered students meet, to the best degree possible, their current and future needs.

Futures Agencies

There are several organizations/associations that are concerned with the area of futures.

The RAND Corporation was charted as a semi-private, nonprofit "think tank" organization. It is concerned primarily with the systematic ongoing analysis of the future.

The World Future Society, established in 1966, deals with a global approach to the future touching on numerous areas of concern, one being education. It publishes the journal, *The Futurist.*

The Hudson Institute, Groton-on-Hudson, New York, is a private nonprofit research organization attending to public policy. It focuses primarily on the long-range planning of events related to United States national security and international relations.

The Institute for the Future was established in 1968. It deals with systematic and comprehensive studies of long-range futures. The Institute works with changes in the technological, environmental, and societal realms.

The International Society for Educational Planners, created in 1970, has the goal of strengthening the professionalism of educational planners. Additionally, it strives to advance educators' understandings of the planning process and also to facilitate cooperative actions among educational planners.

In 1967 the Office of Education established Educational Policy Research Centers at Syracuse University and the Stanford Research Institute for the purpose of generating the capabilities of thinking about the future so that current educational policies could be assessed in light of projected alternative futures.

Discussion

This chapter has presented various issues to which those of us in curriculum must attend: issues concerned with new approaches to curriculum, situations related to maintaining a research and development posture in our curricular work, problems related to new realms of knowledge and events related to the politicization of curriculum activity.

It is evident from contemplating these happenings that the field of curriculum is dynamic with legions of issues requiring our attention. However, it has been implied throughout this book, that in order to respond to current demands and to anticipate and gear up for evolving requisitions, we need to employ methods more precise than our past ways of creating curricula. The realm of futuristics was presented as one means for affording us more accuracy in our dealings. A brief treatment of what futuristics is and its value to curriculum was discussed.

This chapter concluded by centering on challenges confronting curriculum professionals. Myriad challenges exist: how to create programs that address the unique in persons as well as the common, that address the immediate requirements as well as the future requirements of individuals, that allow individuals to understand themselves more effectively and to comprehend more completely others in the human family.

Curricularists, by the very nature of their responsibilities, will have to contemplate an abundance of new knowledges and select those possessing optimal utility with regard to immediate and future times.

The realm of curriculum theory requires our continued attention. Those of us in curriculum will need to maintain an inquiry posture so that we can furnish some principles and axioms for guiding our present and future behaviors.

"It is not the crisis but the way human kind responds to crises that determines survival" (Rubin, 1975, p. 207). This speaks to the general public, but we in curriculum should remember that it applied to us. It is not the crisis, but the way we, as curriculum leaders respond to the crisis that determines our survival as professionals and more importantly determines the relevance and ultimately the survival of our programs.

References

Banathy, B.H. *Developing a systems view of education.* Belmont, Calif.: Lear Siegler/Fearon Publishers, 1973.

Beauchamp, G.A. *Curriculum theory.* Wilmette, Ill.: Kagg Press, 1975.

Bell, D. The year 2000—the trajectory of an idea. In Toward the year 2000: work in progress, *Daedalus,* summer 1967, *96,* 642–644.

Bell, D., & Deutsch, K. Baselines for the future. *Daedalus,* summer 1967, *96,* 659–661.

Berman, L.M., & Roderick, J.A. *Curriculum: teaching the what, how and why of living.* Columbus, Ohio: Charles E. Merrill, 1977.

Bross, I.D.F. *Design for decision.* New York: The Free Press, 1953.

Broudy, H.S., & Palmer, J.R. *Exemplars of teaching method.* Chicago: Rand McNally, 1965.

Buchen, I.H. Humanism and futurism: enemies or allies? In A. Toffler (Ed.) *Learning for tomorrow.* New York: Vintage Books, 1974.

Grumet, M.R. Curriculum as theater: merely players. *Curriculum Inquiry,* spring 1978, *8,* no. 1, 38.

Hack, W.G. On confronting the future. In W.G. Hack (Chrmn.) *Educational futurism 1985.* Berkeley, Calif.: McCutchan, 1971.

Havighurst, R.J. Common experience versus diversity in the curriculum. *Educational Leadership,* November 1978, *36,* no. 2, 118–121.

Joseph, E.C. An introduction to studying the future. In S.P. Hencley & J.R. Yates *Futurism in education, methodologies.* Berkeley, Calif.: McCutchan, 1974.

Kaufman, R.A. *Educational system planning.* Englewood Cliffs, N.J.: Prentice-Hall, 1972.

Kirst, M.W., & Walker, D.F. An analysis of curriculum policy making. *Review of Educational Research,* 1971, *41,* no. 5, 488.

Koerner, J.D. *Who controls American education?* Boston: Beacon Press, 1968.

Lonsdale, R.C. Futurism: its development, content and methodology. In W.G. Hack (Chrmn.) *Educational futurism 1985.* Berkeley, Calif.: McCutchan, 1971.

Lonsdale, R.C., & Ohm, R.E. Futuristic planning: an example and procedures. In W.G. Hack, (Chrmn.) *Educational futurism 1985.* Berkeley, Calif.: McCutchan, 1971.

McNeil, J.D. *Curriculum: a comprehensive introduction.* Boston: Little, Brown, 1977.

Ottinger, A.G. *Run, computer, run.* Cambridge, Mass.: Harvard University Press, 1969.

Phi Delta Kappa National Study Committee on Evaluation, D.L. Stufflebeam (Chair). *Educational evaluation and decision making.* Itasca, Ill.: F.E. Peacock Publishers, 1971.

Pinar, W.F. (Ed.) *Curriculum theorizing, the reconceptualists.* Berkeley, Calif.: McCutchan, 1975.

Pinar, W.F., & Grumet, M.R. *Toward a poor curriculum.* Dubuque, Iowa: Kendall/Hunt, 1976.

Read, E.A. Distinguishing among systems analysis, system analysis and problem analysis. *Educational Technology,* May 1974, *14,* 35–39.

Rubin, L. Observations on future schooling. In L. Rubin (Ed.) *The future of education: perspectives on tomorrow's schooling.* Boston: Allyn & Bacon, 1975.

Shaffarzick, J., & Hampson, D.H. (Eds.) *Strategies for curriculum development.* Berkeley, Calif.: McCutchan, 1975.

Toffler, A. The psychology of the future. In A. Toffler (Ed.) *Learning for tomorrow.* New York: Vintage Books, 1974.

Unruh, G.G. *Responsive curriculum development, theory and action.* Berkeley, Calif.: McCutchan, 1975.

Walker, D. What are the problems curricularists ought to study? *Curriculum Theory Network,* 1974, *4,* nos. 2–3, 217–218.

Zais, R.S. *Curriculum, principles and foundations.* New York: Thomas Y. Crowell, 1976.

Name Index

Subject Index

The Author

Francis P. Hunkins received his Ph.D. in education from Kent State University. Since 1966, he has been at the University of Washington, Seattle, where he is Professor of Education (General Curriculum).

Dr. Hunkins has authored five other books in education and has written chapters for the yearbooks of the Association for Supervision and Curriculum Development and the National Council for the Social Studies. He has authored numerous articles in professional journals and has conducted research funded by the Office of Education.

Dr. Hunkins is active in the Association for Supervision and Curriculum Development, serving on the Nominating Committee, the Resolutions Committee, and the Board of Directors. He is involved in other professional organizations and has been a consultant to various schools systems, educational institutions, and companies throughout the country. He also has spoken on curriculum matters at universities in other countries. In 1978, he was the director of a curriculum field project in Egypt funded by the Fulbright Hays Group Projects Abroad Program.

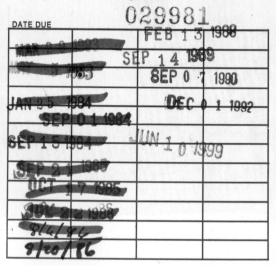